Celebrities Aga

M000316775

Celebrities Against Violence

Case Studies in Speaking Out

TRUMAN R. KEYS

McFarland & Company, Inc., Publishers
Jefferson, North Carolina

LIBRARY OF CONGRESS CATALOGUING-IN-PUBLICATION DATA

Names: Keys, Truman R., 1980– author.
Title: Celebrities against violence : case studies in speaking out / Truman R. Keys.
Description: Jefferson, North Carolina : McFarland & Company, Inc., Publishers, 2022 |
Includes bibliographical references and index.
Identifiers: LCCN 2022001660 | ISBN 9781476677552 (paperback : acid free paper)
ISBN 9781476645599 (ebook) ∞
Subjects: LCSH: Celebrities—Violence against—United States—Case studies. |
Violence—United States—Case studies. | Violence—United States—Prevention. |
Social influence. | BISAC: SOCIAL SCIENCE / Popular Culture |
SOCIAL SCIENCE / Violence in Society
Classification: LCC HV6250.4.C34 K49 2021 | DDC 362.88—dc23/eng/20220208
LC record available at https://lccn.loc.gov/2022001660

BRITISH LIBRARY CATALOGUING DATA ARE AVAILABLE

ISBN (print) 978-1-4766-7755-2
ISBN (ebook) 978-1-4766-4559-9

Front cover photograph © Shutterstock / Tiko Aramyan

Printed in the United States of America

*McFarland & Company, Inc., Publishers
Box 611, Jefferson, North Carolina 28640
www.mcfarlandpub.com*

Table of Contents

Acknowledgments

I am grateful for the continuous support of students, fellow research-ers, family, and friends. I have been working on this book for a few years, and even when life intervened, headlines and conversations brought me back to this project. I taught the subject matter in a special topics course at Western Connecticut State University. I have researched these topics and listened to students' arguments about the feasibility of celebrity messages in public health. Student presentations persuaded me of the pervasiveness, resonance, and power of celebrity narratives in popular culture—espe-cially, the ability of celebrities to "plainspeak" complex topics, including violence and violence prevention, to the public. I am convinced that this book needed to be written. Celebrities are credible vehicles for the delivery of health prevention messages. I appreciate everyone who encouraged me to continue my research on this topic.

Preface

Celebrities Against Violence: Case Studies in Speaking Out is a book about violence, and how celebrities contribute to its prevention. In 1979, violent behavior was identified by the U.S. surgeon general as a key public health priority. Violence is a significant problem in the U.S., with many communities struggling to cope with its effects. Violence prevention is a national public health priority, as incidents of invasion of privacy, home invasion, harassment, bullying, and abuse of power contribute to unwanted sexual advances, domestic violence, gun violence, police brutality, and self- and community violence. The effects of violence in America traumatize communities irrespective of local, state, and national boundaries. In the 21st century, society has been inundated with information regarding violence. Various media channels online, on TV, radio, and in print enable the public to consume the latest news story. In this context, celebrities are just like us—innocent bystanders witnessing and experiencing violence—and they are becoming public anti-violence advocates. This book focuses on the lives of celebrities, their experiences with violence and stories about their experiences in mass media, and the implications for the public healthcare system when their narratives address violence and its prevention.

Celebrities cannot entirely control how they are portrayed by the media. The media frames, shapes, and contextualizes celebrity stories to mediate the effects of those stories on public sentiment, attitudes, and behavior. To understand the extent to which violence and its prevention are impacted by these narratives, the role the narratives play in health communication must be examined. Health communication involves communication between a patient and a doctor, or between a support group and a member, or individuals who might not have sought care if it were not for seeing or hearing about a celebrity in a similar situation on TV, online, or in conversation. Perhaps in these situations, the feedback received "hits too close to home," and there is acknowledgment that something must be done to survive. Behavior, action, reaction, and inaction in these situations are communication and within the context of public health could be

1

the difference between life and death. The proliferation of messages about celebrities and violence in entertainment programming and in the news— does it play a role in public health? The goal of this book is to ascertain the inherent meaning of these messages. Should we disregard them as noise? Or do we pay attention to them? Do we alter our attitudes and our behavior? The implications are widespread, and the findings might be surprising.

In this book, I address the evolving uses of celebrity in public health and how those uses can be constructive and destructive. Each chapter provides historical context for a specific type of violence in America, analyzing pertinent theory and research while addressing celebrity involvement with the issue and the implications for the healthcare system. Each chapter facilitates the public's understanding of the role of celebrities in public health, especially in the area of violence and its prevention. The chapters also explore various perspectives regarding the effects of celebrity on violence and violence prevention and expound upon the limitations of celebrity and fame on fostering change. Applicable concepts and phenomena from a variety of disciplines, including communication studies and the social sciences (media studies, journalism, sociology, and cultural studies), as well the health professions (public health, psychology, and psychiatry) and public affairs contribute to an examination of the behavior of celebrities, the media, public health, government, and the partnership between these stakeholders. The book provides description, critical analysis, and evaluation of the meaning and significance of the prior research on violence in America and the ability of celebrities to help a nation cope with crisis and trauma.

Throughout the book, I examine a number of themes, so that readers can glean a holistic understanding of the role of celebrities in public health. Those themes include: (1) a celebrity narrative, with discussion of famous people who advocate against violence and the effects of the narrative on media coverage of violence prevention, (2) a review of the positive and negative effects of celebrity narratives on the public, (3) the implications or lack thereof for American or international healthcare systems, (4) the role of mass media and social media in framing celebrity narratives, and (5) the intersection of race, class, gender, ethnicity, or sexuality in portrayals of violence and violence prevention.

This book attempts to explain the benefits of celebrity on public health. It is geared toward anyone interested in celebrity and the role it plays in public health, including students and scholars who want to understand the effects these messages have on the public, and professionals in advertising, marketing, public relations, and public affairs who use spokespersons, pitchmen and pitchwomen, role models, and various other celebrities to "connect" with an audience.

Introduction:
Celebrity Messages Matter

Celebrity endorsements increase brand awareness. Organizations seek celebrity endorsers to increase audience exposure to and expand the reach of their brands. Because reaching an audience member and potential consumer once is insufficient, brands cannot underestimate the importance of frequency—the number of times a consumer encounters an advertisement or branded message. An audience member who has a relationship with the brand's persona, product, or service becomes a loyalist. Celebrity endorsers help maintain the relationship between brands and their loyalists. Brands develop relationships with celebrity endorsers and other influencers to retain loyalists and to attract new or prospective consumers.

Branding requires messaging that mitigates clutter and lessens over-saturation, while increasing the likelihood that ideas are engaged, a product is purchased, or a service is used. The use of celebrity endorsements should enhance the marginal value of advertisement expenditures and generate brand equity (Seitz et al., 2007). It is estimated that approximately 25 percent of all television and print advertisements in the U.S. feature celebrities (Erdogan et al., 2001; Shrimp, 2003). Moreover, research indicates that between 14 and 20 percent of all television commercials in the U.S. feature celebrities (Belch & Belch, 2013). Choi et al. (2005) found that about 9 percent of television commercials aired during prime time on the major networks in the U.S. featured a celebrity. Use of celebrities in commercials is common in the U.S. and prevalent in other countries (Money et al., 2006), such as Turkey (Yilmaz & Ersavas, 2005), New Zealand (Charbonneau & Garland, 2006), South Korea (Ferle & Choi, 2005), India (Creswell, 2008; Roy, 2006), Japan, and Taiwan (Creswell, 2008). Oftentimes, whether in television commercials or magazine advertisements, celebrity use is based on the source characteristics of popularity, likeability, physical attractiveness, and expertise (Belch & Belch, 2013). These source characteristics are increasingly salient in the contemporary era, where global society and

3

popular culture glorify fame and fortune, elevating celebrities over other sources of information.

Some research undercuts the belief that celebrity influence will increase unabated. A study of more than 2,600 advertisements found that ads with celebrity endorsements did not perform any better than non-celebrity advertisements and in some cases performed worse (Ace Metrix, 2011). Non-celebrity attributes that improved advertising performance were focused on the creative content of the advertisement—messaging, explaining the relevance of the product or service, and informing consumers about the product or service—rather than the endorser. Consumers, especially interested or engaged audience members (e.g., viewers of television commercials, listeners of radio spots, followers on social media), are more likely to respond to endorsers when certain conditions are met: "If relatively little attitude-relevant information is available in memory, attitudes are primarily based on the information provided by the celebrity endorsement, leading to stronger effects" (Knoll & Matthes, 2017, p. 69). However, endorsement effects are smaller when consumers have developed and curated their attitudes regarding a product or service. Endorsement effects are impacted by an audience's memory of attitude-relevant information. For example, when an audience becomes confused or does not understand the relationship between a celebrity and a product, service or ideology, receptivity to the advertisement can be negative. If a connection between a celebrity and a brand is established, there is always an inherent risk that a celebrity's personality or polarizing behavior will distract from the advertising campaign message, which could undercut the brand. More than a quarter of global citizens (27 percent) say they would consider stopping the purchase of a product if a celebrity endorser was reported to be engaging in misbehavior, and a similar proportion (25 percent) had already stopped buying a product for this reason (Williams, 2011). There is also an inherent risk for celebrities, whose public images could be tarnished if they are associated with a brand that endures bad publicity or a public relations crisis. These shared interests have an upside and a downside. Brand partnerships require an understanding of risk tolerance and risk management. Whatever the potential downsides, brands see celebrities as opportunities and perceive budding relationships with them as an asset.

Celebrities are given a prominent voice, and the media broadcasts their attitudes, opinions, and habits to the masses. Media reporters need good copy, and actors, athletes, and entertainers attract attention. From the standpoint of media aficionados and political activists, partnering with celebrities cuts through the cynicism and distrust that the audience, the consumer, and the voter have of anything conventional or the status quo. Celebrities have agency. They can use their narratives and the media to amplify their voices, affect purchasing decisions, consumption, and civic affairs. Phil Griffin, former MSNBC president and former *Hardball* executive producer, recognized the agency of celebrities when he "booked actress Goldie Hawn for the show after she spoke out at a press conference demanding that Congress vote on a China trade bill." Griffin's reasoning was that trade deals are boring television and using Hawn to "draw attention to a technical subject that normally did not elicit much public or press interest" enhanced the show's brand (West & Orman, 2003). The audience trusts Hawn, and other celebrities like her, who are popular, likeable, and knowledgeable about the issues, to endorse actions that shake up the establishment and inject new ideas into public discourse and policy making. With the rise of cable television, talk radio, blogs, and social media, celebrities are in demand. They are self-aware and understand their branding effect on public discourse. "The extraordinary elasticity of the celebrity image, coupled with its ability to foster strong emotional identifications, made it an ideal technology for the shaping of national consciousness" (Goldsmith, 2009, p. 33). Celebrities collaborate with commercial, governmental, nongovernmental, or philanthropic interests, with "all hands on deck" to facilitate co-branding, promote co-brand awareness, shape public perception, and influence brand effect. Public relations representatives, who seek synergy between their clients' brands, the media, and various causes that affect public perception, work to maximize their clients' influence and to leverage influence into branding omnipresence.

These public relations representatives work with various organizations' liaison officers, who read up on a celebrity's background and interests, as well as all pertinent, contemporary gossip (Brockington, 2014). These liaison officers can take longer than a year engaging in a courtship ritual of tracking and vetting celebrities before making a formal request for action or assistance. Nongovernmental organizations (NGOs), including various United Nations (UN) agencies, use liaison officers to broker celebrity commitments, persuading agents that it is in their client's interest to develop a partnership, to leverage their mutual credibility and relevance, and foster a lasting relationship. Stakeholders walk into these partnerships "with eyes wide open" and with an expectation of considerable media attention, publicity, and scrutiny. Critics are skeptical about who really benefits from these celebrity-NGO public displays of affection. Celanthropist, or a seeker of the limelight (Narapruet, 2011), is the term some media outlets use for a celebrity influencer or philanthropist. When Angelina Jolie visited refugees as a Goodwill Ambassador for the UN Human Rights Council, skeptics questioned whether her focus was on her act of selflessness or the refugee plight.

Andrew F. Cooper (2008) refers to the brand effect of celebrities in international affairs as the "Bonoisation" of diplomacy. Bono, lead singer of the band U2, and other celebrities, including George Clooney and Angelina Jolie, can access key circles of power and influence those who orchestrate governmental, nongovernmental, or philanthropic interventions. The "Bono-ization" of diplomacy forces diplomatic initiatives to operate within a broader public domain. Bono uses his mediated persona, a public image co-created by him, the media, and their accomplices, to attain public support to affect political expression (Corner, 2003). The public identifies with Bono's celebrity performance, his mediated persona, which generates more publicity and greater public scrutiny of diplomatic initiatives. The "Bono-ization" of diplomacy leverages a celebrity's mediated persona to promote humanitarianism. Jolie and Clooney use their mediated personas to bring focus to international campaigns, to affect diplomatic agendas, and to advocate for the UN's principles. There is concern that mediated personas only attract attention to international affairs and diplomacy, but "there are dangers in oversimplifying complex forms of international diplomacy and utilizing emotional responses" (Wheeler, 2011, p. 17). However, former UN Secretary-Generals Kofi Annan and Ban Ki-moon understood that the diplomacy of civil servants and celebrity diplomacy were complementary, so celebrity performance does not overshadow or devalue the UN's principles.

Personality Transfer: Branding the Public Image

A celebrity's public image can be a powerful tool. It enables a person, group, or organization to attract attention, generate interest, and persuade an audience. Many people do not admire celebrities for who they are, instead choosing admiration of their perception of celebrities and what they want celebrities to represent. An audience has the ability to transfer who they are or who they want to be onto a celebrity, and a celebrity's mission, goals, aspirations, and lived experiences can represent for an audience their best selves. This process of transference means the public image of a celebrity represents different things to different people. Audience members form an emotional connection with celebrities, which allows celebrity endorsers to humanize a brand and develop a specific identity for it (Ambroise et al., 2014). Brands want to be affiliated with certain values and symbols that celebrity endorsers accentuate in order to enhance the perceived quality of the brand (Batra & Homer, 2004). According to E-Poll Market Research (2011), the spokesperson index, a composite of awareness, appeal, and a celebrity's perceived attributes for credibility and authority, including trustworthiness, sincerity, trendiness, and influence, contributes to the rank order of the most impactful potential celebrity spokespersons. The index includes popular celebrities of different genders, generations, and racial and ethnic backgrounds, including Betty White, Tom Hanks, Sandra Bullock, Leonardo DiCaprio, Will Smith, and Jackie Chan. The index provides information that brands can use as part of their research to determine the compatibility of a potential celebrity partner. For example, the American Association of Retired Persons (AARP) knows that the attributes of Betty White—beloved *Golden Girls* actress and nonagenarian—align with the organization and its membership. In 2011, White became a spokesperson for AARP, using media coverage about her vitality to champion AARP and its mission to support the longevity of retired persons.

Celebrity accentuation in various messages, especially advertisements, contributes to the transfer of cultural meaning from an endorser's personality to a branded concept, product, or service "even when the personality assertions are not communicated verbally and explicitly" (Batra & Homer, 2004, p. 328). An organization will partner with a celebrity for a cause when the public image of the celebrity resonates with the organization's audience. Brands can use transference to change or reinforce public perception. People often have a positive view of celebrities, so when celebrities endorse a product or recommend a particular health practice, their gravitas and magnetism, their "golden glow," transfer from them to the products or practices they endorse (Howard, 2017). In the marketplace, it is important for messengers informing and persuading individual and collective decision-making to distinguish their ideas, products, services, and practices from competitors. Celebrity endorsements provide cognitive shortcuts, signaling to an audience the ideas or practices they should follow. Celebrity endorsers have an opportunity to provide a vital service to the public, creating exposure, awareness, and greater understanding in circumstances where people make complicated decisions. In an era of social media, there is increasing recognition that celebrities cultivate massive social networks, and the members of those networks are plugged into their own networks, creating a multiplier effect that dramatically increases the reach and magnitude of celebrity endorsements. All parties understand that transference can be commodified, and an idea, attitude, opinion, or action regarding a person, place, or thing can be transferred to something else, which can increase a brand's value. Commodification of celebrity endorsements is not entirely an economics issue. Celebrity narratives addressing healthcare interventions and violence prevention have intrinsic value. Fame does not inoculate celebrities against illness or violence. Their vulnerability is an asset, not a liability.

Celebrities stand for something. In his book *The Image: A Guide to Pseudo-Events in America*, historian Daniel Boorstin (1962/1992) asserted that celebrity is a function of "well-knownness." However, fame alone does not attract a brand's attention. Fame is only one of the attributes necessary for a celebrity to become a brand or for a brand to approach a celebrity with an opportunity to co-brand. The elaboration likelihood model (ELM) asserts that audience members' senses are activated by a celebrity's attributes, and depending on an attribute's perceived relevance, media users engage in elaborate or heuristic processing to determine any effect the attribute has on individual or collective decision-making (Petty & Cacioppo, 1980; Petty & Wegener, 1999). ELM posits that "…when a celebrity's selected attributes receive attention, consumers will elaborate and systematically process these attributes along the central route to persuasion" (Hung, 2014, 156). Media users who use the central route encounter messaging that elicits involvement with the celebrity endorsement, with media users choosing elaborate processing to decipher and understand the meaning embedded or coded within the message. These messages contain information, suggestions, or directives, which brands need audience members to notice in order to elicit a reaction they can observe. The goal is persistent, sustained attitude change regarding the brand. Brands desire media users to respond to as many celebrity attributes as possible along their journey on the central route, where greater involvement with the content of a celebrity endorsement intensifies media users' exposure to its persuasive communication. Research into the impact of celebrity endorsements in direct-to-consumer advertising indicates that some consumers pay attention to celebrity endorsements and view them as credible (Rollins & Bhutada, 2014). Yet the level of issue involvement was a more significant predictor of attitude and behavioral change (Bhutada et al., 2012). ELM incorporates issue and celebrity valence.

ELM and persuasive communication research explain how the central and peripheral routes aid brands in their deployment of celebrity endorsers (Hung, 2014). When focus shifts from central route to peripheral and heuristic-based processing, there is a recognition that some media users are less persuaded by celebrity attributes, so their involvement with the content of the celebrity endorsement may be more limited. According to Brown and Basil (1995) "…the concept of involvement can include a positive or negative valence (i.e., liking a celebrity or disliking a celebrity)" (p. 352), which affects "…a person's motivational state toward the celebrity created by exposure to the celebrity in the mass media" (p. 352). If the potency of the messaging in the advertisement is determined by media users to be lacking, then brands are in a less enviable position, where they must depend on celebrity attributes perceived as less salient to foster attitude change. Instead of critically analyzing information pertaining to the topic or issue front and center in the advertisement, attitude change along the peripheral route is heavily focused on responsiveness to heuristic cues, such as, celebrity attributes. Within this context, attitude change is more likely temporary, and may not withstand counterarguments.

For a celebrity to last longer than a fad, audience members need to care about her, and they learn to care about her from stories. These autobiographical stories or narratives can be told from a celebrity's perspective or involve someone else who is telling her story. The more detail-laden, intricate, and engaging the narratives, the more audiences want to read about her and similar individuals. When these narratives involve a health issue or act of violence, the public takes notice, and the issue or act becomes associated with the celebrity's public image. Public health officials should pay attention to news, social media, etc., pertaining to celebrity health narratives, and engage in a private and public dialogue with celebrities concerning the applicable health issue or act of violence to ensure their narrative conforms to evidence-based practice and mitigates misinformation regarding prevention and treatment.

Nearly everyone has been in a checkout line at a grocery store and engaged in the ritualistic behavior of reading celebrity headlines in the supermarket tabloids—picking up *People* or *USA Today* when they see celebrities' pictures on the front page. Many people tune into radio or television broadcasts or become Facebook friends or Instagram or Twitter followers in order to feel a part of celebrity fandom. When they are authentic and demonstrate how to transcend the circumstances the audience encounters, these narratives appeal to media users. Narratives about celebrities are potent, and when they involve universal themes or archetypes such as sex or violence, they are durable crowd-pleasers. The logic of branding with celebrity endorsers to motivate consumers also substantiates the use of celebrity narratives to appeal to the needs, wants, and desires of audiences. The pairing of these narratives with universal themes, including health and well-being, as well as violence and its prevention, have profound implications for global citizens.

How Celebrities Fulfill a Need to Belong

Consumers engage in an ongoing identity construction process informed by messages that emerge from celebrity narratives and endorsements. Consumers derive brand associations from their experiences and the experiences of members of their social networks. People who see affiliation with specific brands as an extension of their self-identity and group identity have a higher need to belong (NTB). High-NTB audience members are attentive to the signaling that occurs in celebrity endorsements, because the information in those messages explains how endorsed brands help individuals and groups meet affiliation needs. Audience members do not have personal relationships with celebrities; nonetheless, they form intense emotional and psychological connections with them. "In these cases, media users establish parasocial relationships with distant media figures, which creates a false sense of friendship or intimacy" (Escalas & Bettman, 2017, p. 306). For a high-NTB fan of a celebrity, the perception is that celebrity and fan are in a parasocial relationship (PSR), and they have the same trust in the celebrity that they have in a friend's advice and recommendations. Interestingly, low-NTB audience members who are not fans of a celebrity endorser still pay closer attention to the advertisement or narrative of a celebrity than to an anonymous endorser. They care more about the symbolic match between celebrity association and brand association (Escalas & Bettman, 2017). Low-NTB audience members are not pursuing PSR with the celebrity endorser; instead, there needs to be a detectable, discernable, and meaningful link between brand and celebrity.

Horton and Wohl (1956) introduced the concept of parasocial interaction (PSI) more than 60 years ago. PSI and PSR are conflated. PSI involves give-and-take between a media user (i.e., audience member) and a media personality (e.g., celebrity), who are engaged in interactions that are one-sided and limited to a given situation or mediated moment. PSI can lead to PSR. PSR conceptually expands PSI for the media user by extending the illusory relationship into what is perceived as a real-life social relationship no longer constrained to a situation or moment. "While parasocial phenomena are specific to the connections a media user makes with a media figure, transportation involves a media user's engagement with a media narrative as a whole" (Vinney & Vinney, 2017, p. 324). Regardless of the medium, media users who encounter a narrative can be transported, immersed into a distinct mental process melding attention, imagery, and feelings.

Transportation enlivens a story. When media users engage with a narrative and become enthralled in a story, their sensory experience is enhanced. During transportation, a media user's self-awareness is reduced, because she is absorbed in the narrative. Brands use celebrity endorsements and celebrity narratives to transport audiences, deflecting attention from everything else and focusing the attention of media users on the brand and celebrity. Highly transported media users respond to accentuated beliefs, values, attitudes, and symbols in a mediated narrative, which influences their awareness of and responsiveness to issues, situations, and circumstances in the story. Transportation increases a narrative's persuasiveness—it increases media users' adoption of beliefs that are in line with the narrative (Green & Brock, 2000). PSR and transportation are useful psychological and emotional processes for brands, because in a mediated environment with advertising and marketing clutter, brands need a way to attract the attention of media users and sensitize them to their content, while reducing users' awareness of competing stimuli (e.g., competitors, concerns, responsibilities, etc.).

Identification is another process that mediates the relationship of audience members with celebrity narratives. It occurs when audience members voluntarily believe they share the perspectives of a celebrity endorser, so they imitate the celebrity in order to be like and be liked by the celebrity (Kelman, 1958). Admiration of the celebrity endorser manifests into aspirations to look, behave, or even think like the celebrity. Fans become attracted to celebrity causes and are likely to take social cues from them. An audience member can have PSR with a celebrity endorser but not identify with the celebrity, and having PSR with a celebrity endorser does not guarantee the adoption of the celebrity's attitudes, values, or behavior (Wen & Cui, 2014). PSR, transportation, and identification are not mutually exclusive. As the intensity of celebrity engagement grows, the three processes may occur progressively or simultaneously.

The veracity of information exchanged between celebrities and audience members enables media users to trust celebrity endorsers, and without trust, PSR, transportation, and identification could be compromised. Celebrities' self-disclosure, their sharing of opinionated statements on various topics, matter to media users, who gain insight into celebrities' lived experiences. These narratives reveal personal and intimate information about celebrities, and many media users can relate to celebrities' honest expression of emotions. Social media is a virtual space where celebrities and media users converge, and celebrities have greater control of the narrative they share with the public. Celebrities self-disclose to media users when chronicling their day-to-day activities on blogs, uploading "selfies," sharing videos with their families, and providing communal space for fans to discuss behind-the-scenes and backstage happenings, all of which fosters perceived intimacy and bonding. The self-disclosing nature of the media, especially social media, can cultivate PSR (Chung & Cho, 2017). The effects of celebrity self-disclosure are more potent when the messenger has source credibility. Source credibility consists of two sub-dimensions, including expertise and trustworthiness. Expertise consists of an endorser's knowledge, experience, and skills pertaining to whatever is being endorsed (Hovland & Weiss, 1951), while trustworthiness is the degree of confidence a media user has that an endorser's assertions are factually accurate (Hovland et al., 1953). Self-disclosures from credible sources intensify internalization, a process that takes place when a media user "accepts an endorser's advertising claims as his or her own," and "once internalization occurs, the attitude a consumer adopts tends to be sustained…" (Chung & Cho, 2017, p. 484). The interconnectedness of self-disclosure, source credibility, PSR, transportation, identification, and internalization are addressed in the celebrity influence model and its four propositions (Wen, 2017, p. 1236):

> (1) Exposure to the mediated celebrity induces the audience's PSR with the celebrity; (2) PSR with celebrity cause the audience to identify with the celebrity; (3) identification with the celebrity then motivates the audience to align their attitudes and behavior with the celebrity; and (4) further identification with the celebrity leads to more adoption of the celebrity's beliefs and behaviors among the audience.

Underpinning the four propositions of the celebrity influence model is the concept of authenticity. To be authentic is to be genuine or accurate, to be true to self, living a life that is truly one's own. Being authentic is challenging, a source of anxiety that forces media users to seek exemplars who deal with uncertainty, who provide parables about life that help it make sense. These parables provide "a call that wrenches people's attention from everyday concerns and toward the unfamiliar," imploring media users to examine the deeper motives behind what they are doing and why they are here, "to figure out a way to relate it to what we already do know" (Janssen, 2018, p. 194). Whether the characters in these stories are fictional, alive, or deceased, these celebrities are known by the stories told about them. As a story articulates the human condition, we engage it because the characters or celebrities resemble us, and we recognize ourselves in the narrative. "When we authentically engage our stories, then truth comes into focus" (Janssen, 2018, p. 198). Celebrities occupy a peculiarly liminal space, where very few people know who they really are, which makes it challenging for fans to distinguish between celebrities' personas or caricatures and their actual selves. Liminal space can be a barrier between celebrities and the public because it complicates any effort to gather meaningful information about celebrities' lived experiences. Celebrity narratives enable celebrities to tell their tales, public stories that are more than mere information transfer, to audiences, so they can relate to celebrities' actual lived experiences instead of their personas or caricatures.

The audience gains a shared experience with story and character, which contributes to identification and PSR. Transportation into the public and personal lives of a celebrity through his or her narrative facilitates audience members not critically analyzing themselves, yet critically analyzing shared circumstances affecting a celebrity's life. Once audience members return from a celebrity's liminal space, the narrative experience can enlighten them, so that they can be their more authentic selves and engage more effectively with their public and personal selves.

Media users have a fascination with deciphering the difference between celebrities' public and personal selves. They have a desire to pierce the veil, to look behind the façade. They want to know the "real" versions of celebrities (Dilling-Nielsen, 2018). Since the turn of the century, media users have felt increasingly entitled to know more about celebrities' personal selves: "Quick media technologies hurry the sense of belonging and shift the gravity of kinship away from lineage-based to attention based" (Humphrey, 2018, p. 226). The rise of YouTube personalities as celebrity influencers has changed the celebrity-audience dynamic, leading to a demand on the part of media users for greater access to more open, honest, and vulnerable celebrities. Critical consumers do not want contrived narratives about celebrities. Instead of feeling manipulated, critical consumers yearn for different kinds of major news (e.g., coming out, divorce, illness, anxiety, etc.) in celebrities' narratives. Celebrity narratives can provide confessional moments that audience members relate to, and in these perceptually murky contexts, audience members can feel they are in a PSR with a celebrity.

Antecedents of authenticity influence whether audience members judge a celebrity during his or her confessional moments as authentic or inauthentic. Rarity and stability are two antecedents that affect a media user's assessment of a celebrity's authenticity (behavior associated with internal dispositions) in advertisements, endorsements, and narratives. Rarity is the degree to which a celebrity holds unique characteristics that may be imitated but not duplicated (Moulard et al., 2015). Subdimensions of rarity include talent, discretion, and originality. Talent is the perception that a celebrity demonstrates skill in completing a task, a regimen, or profession. Discretion involves the perception of someone being inconspicuous, shunning ubiquitous behavior, and in the case of celebrities, mitigating media oversaturation. Originality is the perception that someone thinks or acts in an independent or creative manner. Stability, the second antecedent, is the degree to which a celebrity is perceived to be firm, steadfast, and unwavering in their principles, words, and deeds (Moulard et al., 2015). Subdimensions of stability are consistency, candidness, and morality. Consistency is the perception that a celebrity's personality and attributes have not changed. Candidness is the perception that there are no inconsistences between how a celebrity feels and what a celebrity does. Morality is the perception that the celebrity is principled and exhibits strong beliefs and values. According to *What Makes a Human Brand Authentic? Identifying the Antecedents of Celebrity Authenticity* (2015), research suggests that younger people tend to value rarity, whereas older adults tend to value stability (p. 179). These antecedents demonstrate the importance of certain human brand cues in determining the behavior of audience members.

Other factors that affect the response of media users to celebrity endorsers include two key elements of the narrative rationality of celebrity narratives, the probability and fidelity of the recounting and accounting of stories we tell ourselves (Humphrey, 2018). Narrative probability addresses the rationality of the cause-and-effect sequences in a story to determine if a story hangs together and a reasonable person can comprehend the overall narrative. For narrative fidelity, audience members ponder "what are the values of the actor, are they expressed either before or during the actions taken and how consistently are those values expressed" (Humphrey, 2018, p. 227)? Observers use their experiences and competence to ascertain which stories adhere to narrative probability and fidelity. Walter R. Fisher (1984) understood that human beings need storytelling to convey who we are and to identify with one another, and that narrative rationality provides the means to examine the interplay between identity and life story. In the last 20 years, technological advancement in telecommunications and communication technology (e.g., the Internet, smartphones, quick media, etc.) forged a new creative space, where intrapersonal, interpersonal, and public communication coincide. As communication manifests, proliferates, dissipates, and reconstitutes itself faster than ever before, the effects of our stories impact intended and unattended audiences, producing foreseen and unforeseen changes in how we relate to ourselves, our kinships, and communities.

Framing Mediated Celebrity Narratives

Mediated narratives about celebrities are commonplace. Of particular importance to the public are stories about celebrity illness. Media users are receptive to celebrity self-disclosures about their medical conditions. Health communication experts recognize that the effects of these stories vary from person to person, but "an ill celebrity may become a trustworthy source in the area of health communication after disclosing his or her medical conditions" (Leung & Cheng, 2016, p. 257). The effects are magnified when ill celebrities share demographic similarities with audience members and when their narratives embody one another's lived experiences. A perceived fit between the source, the cause, and the characterization of the story will enhance the attribution of social motivations. Here is a diagnosis that audience members notice:

> Had Lance Armstrong simply been an anonymous survivor of testicular cancer, his recovery would have been compelling to very few people. The fact that Armstrong won the Tour de France, and subsequently became a celebrity, made his story a reference point for millions of people suffering from cancer or other grave diseases [Lerner, 2006, p. 1].

Lance Armstrong became a symbol for hope and a manifestation of courage. Celebrities in a similar situation use their narratives and subsequent media coverage to draw attention to illness and disease, as well as exposure to interventions (e.g., treatments and regimens) that have the potential to save lives. These celebrity narratives become compelling events that garner significant national attention and interest (Noar et al., 2014). Audience members interpret these events in terms of human action, which enables media users to assign responsibility:

> From determining what risk factors are responsible for a particular health problem, to arousing guilt in the reader for his or her own unhealthy habits, to causing a reader to blame a celebrity for poor role-modeling with substance abuse, a celebrity's actions can evoke a spectrum of reactions [Hinnant & Hendrickson, 2014, p. 5].

A celebrity health narrative is the telling of a celebrity's life story, which provides educational enrichment and entertainment. The narrative elements of their stories combine their professional profiles or public images with their well-tended private personas, with audiences craving any glimpse of their off-guard and unkempt selves (Bulck, 2017). These three aspects of celebrity health narratives make them compelling stories for public consumption. In the beginning, the celebrity health narrative is in the news, eventually escaping the confines of journalistic ethics, falling prey to people's gossip, satire, and ruminations. Somewhere along the way these narratives go viral online, become a meme, a phenomenon that dies out without active campaigning. In contemporary society, print, radio and video, the media, and social networking feed the story, and the celebrity is given an elevated platform to tell the health narrative over and over again. These collective actions keep the narrative in the public consciousness. Celebrity culture, the media, and social networks play a central role in providing media users with models to imitate and embody, encouraging a system of values and behaviors (Steele & Shores, 2015). There are various risks that celebrities encounter when telling their health narratives, including the appearance of self-importance and the valorization of inappropriate behavior, such as feigning earnestness (Markham, 2014). The risks vs. rewards of going public with a narrative is a difficult tightrope for celebrities. Elizabeth Glaser and Arthur Ashe hid their AIDS diagnoses to avoid stigmatizing their families, yet fear of their narratives being "outed" to the media led to their media disclosures. They became "moral beacons" in the movement to "go public" about their illnesses, establishing private foundations and lobbying the medical community for more funding and improved treatments (Lerner, 2006). Historians believe that Betty Ford was one of the most important First Ladies of the post–World War II period, because after her husband, President Gerald R. Ford, left office, she announced that she was an alcoholic and checked into the U.S. Naval Hospital in Long Beach, California. During her stay there, she shared a room with three other female substance abusers, and later in 1982, she co-founded the Betty Ford Center, the first treatment facility with equal numbers of beds for women and men (Stone, 2011). Non-celebrities were treated at the facility, as well as celebrities Mary Tyler Moore, Johnny Cash, and Elizabeth Taylor.

Presidents and other First Ladies admire Mrs. Ford, with President Obama acknowledging that "the Betty Ford Center will honor her legacy by giving countless Americans a new lease on life," and former First Lady Nancy Reagan calling Betty Ford an "inspiration" (Stone, 2011). "Betty Ford blurred private and public narrative boundaries and dramatically reshaped how others throughout the nation treated and interacted about serious health issues, on both personal and societal levels of discourse and action" (Beck et al., 2014, p. 245). In October 1987, Nancy Reagan self-disclosed her own health narrative: she had a mastectomy. Negative media coverage of the mastectomy, which was characterized as extreme and controversial, led to the temporary decline in the use of breast-conserving surgery. After Mrs. Reagan announced that she had a mastectomy, women were 25 percent less likely to undergo breast-conserving surgery in the fourth quarter of 1987 and the first quarter of 1988 (Nattinger et al., 1998). The celebrity health narratives of Betty Ford and Nancy Reagan are examples of the influence celebrity endorsers have over the national consciousness and a willingness to change value systems, attitudes, and behavior for individual and collective well-being.

Earvin "Magic" Johnson's announcement on November 7, 1991, that he tested positive for HIV became one of the most famous celebrity-health narratives in history. Johnson's telling and retelling of his story counteracted the dehumanization of people living with HIV/AIDS (Brown & Basil, 1995). On September 28, 1999, to the shock of those in attendance at the Senate Appropriations Subcommittee on Labor, Health and Human Services, and Education Hearing, an unmedicated Michael J. Fox displayed the effects of Parkinson's disease on his disabled body, which involved "head jerking, arms bouncing, body convulsing, voice faulting, and papers quivering" (Moe, 2012, p. 444). Fox decided he would not conceal the effects of Parkinson's disease from the politicians and bureaucrats who presided over a hearing to determine whether 75 million dollars would be awarded for Parkinson's disease research. He wanted them to view his first public appearance without being on medication, for them to accept responsibility for how their actions affected him and countless other patients living with the disease. Fox had a coming-out moment, his Parkinson's disease and disabled body no longer concealed from the public.

Fox is no different from his celebrity peers who share their health narratives at an intersection in society. One characteristic that celebrities have in common is their fame, which mediates how they interact with the public and how media users treat them. This characteristic is an aspect of who they are that affects how they encounter illness, disease, or violence, as well as how others treat them when they become aware of their predicament. Yet there are other characteristics that celebrities have in common with non-celebrities that impact their experiences with similar circumstances. Sometimes we have shared experiences with similar or like-minded individuals that enable us to understand and empathize with them. When these shared experiences are hidden, denied, or erased, societal stakeholders (e.g., public health organizations and trained healthcare professionals) pay attention to one or some of our overlapping identities, such as Michael J. Fox's fame, whiteness, cisgender maleness, and status in pop culture. But other disabled people who lack these characteristics fall through the cracks and become invisible to the people who swore an oath to provide them with care. The spectators in attendance at the congressional hearing where Fox spoke listened to him because of the characteristics that privilege him in society. Interestingly, the other characteristics that ordinarily make disabled individuals feel unwanted or invisible, such as the physical manifestations of Parkinson's disease, make Fox's narrative more compelling and credible. To many people, both disabled and able-bodied, he is an effective advocate for more funding for Parkinson's disease, because the public imbues him with their goodwill and trust. However, naysayers assert:

> Fox is in a unique position: He steps out of a metaphorical closet—one into which he can easily and voluntarily return via his medications—stands in stark contrast to other individuals who—given their visible, nonconcealable disabilities—may be in a literal closet, "attic, basement [or] backroom" or may never have the option of stepping into the metaphorical closet Fox leaves [Moe, 2012, 448].

Intersectionality is a useful tool for analyzing the presumed identity politics of Fox, a "disabled" body on display during a hearing, in a space that traditionally privileges or silences people who share overlapping identities. Intersectionality highlights the multiple avenues through which silencing and oppression are experienced and provides a way of thinking about identity and its relationship with power (Crenshaw, 2015). "The problem with identity politics is not that it fails to transcend difference, as some critics charge, but rather the opposite—that it frequently conflates or ignores intra group differences" (Crenshaw, 1991, p. 1). Fox raised millions of dollars in pursuit of new treatment options for Parkinson's disease, but will historians remember him for how he used his privilege to advocate for a cause, or will he be remembered for a shadow he cast over disabled persons and disability advocates who were not afforded a metaphorical closet to escape? Should the audience perceive his privilege as an asset to the movement for disability rights or as a detriment which invalidates him as a bona fide spokesperson for *all* disabled people? The debate regarding identity politics and intersectionality affects how celebrities tell their stories and how people react to them.

The 2000s spawned the "Katie Couric effect" (Cram et al., 2003). During the 2010s, the Angelina Jolie effect (Mapes, 2014) emerged on the pop-culture landscape. When journalist Katie Couric televised her colonoscopy on NBC's *Today Show* in 2000, colorectal cancer screening by 400 American endoscopists increased by 21 percent the next month (Cram et al., 2003). In 2005, bookings for mammograms in Australia rose by 40 percent in four Australian states after actor-singer Kylie Minogue's diagnosis of breast cancer (Chapman et al., 2005). Moreover, a month after the announcement of Minogue's breast cancer, there was a significant increase in referrals to a rapid access breast clinic in the United Kingdom (Twine et al., 2006). These celebrity effects continued into the next decade, after a 2013 *New York Times* article addressed Angelina Jolie's preventive double mastectomy (Mapes, 2014). The audience's reaction to Jolie was heightened awareness with greater communication openness to dialogues about genetic testing and the reduction of mastectomy stigma. The effects continued into the 2010s and applied to celebrities living and deceased.

American actor and comedian Robin Williams died on August 11, 2014, and his death was ruled a suicide. Suicide is an act of violence we perpetrate against ourselves, and it ends countless lives around the world. Suicide prevention is a key component of national and international violence prevention that aims to reduce mortality and boost life expectancy. On the day Williams died, the National Suicide Prevention Lifeline received 7,375 phone calls—at the time, the highest number it had ever received (Taylor, 2014). After the actor's death, there was a 20 percent increase in calls to the hotline for the National Alliance on Mental Illness (Taylor, 2014). The online and social media implications of Williams' death were profound; Google reported more than 10 million searches concerning him on the day he died (Dillman et al., 2016). Fans around the world used the Internet and social media to grieve the loss of Williams, someone they related to and loved.

When events such as Williams' death occur, non-celebrity and celebrity fans are able to grieve, post comments, critique conspiracy theories, educate one another about wellness and suicide prevention, and seek solace with like-minded individuals with minimal interference or the censorship of traditional media stakeholders. Social media has changed how media users receive and exchange news. According to the Pew Research Center (2013), one Facebook user summed up how he gets news on the massive social media platform: "I believe Facebook is a good way to find out news without actually looking for it" (p. 1). Furthermore, 64 percent of U.S. adults use Facebook, and 30 percent of U.S. adults consume news on Facebook (Pew Research, 2013). Fewer U.S. adults get their news from Twitter (16 percent use Twitter, and 8 percent consume news on Twitter), yet Twitter news consumers stand out as younger, more mobile, and more educated (Pew Research, 2013). Beyond searches for information online, social media users can characterize and curate content found on their social media networks (Brogan, 2015). They can frame information by altering narrative elements, adding, or subtracting context, and omitting foreground or background information, which affects perceptions of aggregated news about an event. In this media landscape, Internet search engines and social media platforms enable celebrities, the media, and media users to influence one another (Hoffman et al., 2017). As the media landscape continues to evolve, it is challenging to discern what is normative behavior, so it is imperative to adopt a code of conduct to enforce ethical standards.

Celebrity Advice and Its Transmission in Public Health

Celebrity endorsers and narrators use the media to convey their values and attitudes about health topics and issues, creating awareness and interest in their own stories and various products, services, causes, and campaigns. One of the three major categories with celebrity endorsements in China is medicines and nutritional supplements, and nearly half of the public service announcements (PSAs) in Hong Kong feature celebrities (Leung et al., 2018). When celebrities in Hong Kong reveal their illnesses, the public finds their personal narratives more trustworthy than related news reported by the mass media. The perception is that the media exaggerates stories reporting about a celebrity diagnosed with a serious illness (Leung & Cheng, 2016). For instance, some years ago, the famous Hong Kong female singer Sammi Cheng revealed to the public that she had major depressive disorder. "She was perceived as a brave idol to many young people in Hong Kong," posting on Twitter photographs of her health and fitness regimen, and recording for the HK Familylink Mental Health Advocacy Association a theme song to increase public awareness about mental illness and raise funds for the organization (Leung & Cheng, 2016, p. 262). The public becomes aware of celebrities because of their professional lives but gravitates toward them and develops an emotional connection the more informed it is about celebrities' personal narratives. Public health organizations should harness the goodwill bestowed upon celebrities affected by illness, disease, and violence, since their stories resonate with media users. There are 14 biological, psychological, and social mechanisms through which celebrities shape an audience's health-related behaviors (see Table 1 for the 14 mechanisms).

Table 1:
Fourteen Mechanisms Explaining Celebrity Influence

Discipline	Mechanism	Description
Economics	Signals	Celebrity endorsements act as markers that differentiate endorsed items from competitors.
	Herd Behavior	Celebrities activate people's natural tendency to make decisions based on how others have acted in similar situations.
Marketing	Meaning transfer	People consume items to acquire the endorsing celebrities' traits, which have become associated with the product.
	Source credibility	Celebrities share personal experiences and success stories associated with the endorsed item to be perceived as credible sources of health information.
	Halo effect	The specific success of celebrities is generalized to all their traits, biasing people to view them as credible medical advisors.
Neuroscience	Neural mechanisms of meaning transfer	Celebrity advertisements activate a brain region involved in forming positive associations, indicating the transfer of positive memories associated with the celebrity to the endorsed item.
	Neuropsychology of credibility	Endorsements from celebrities activate brain regions associated with trustful behavior and memory formation, thereby improving attitudes toward and recognition of the endorsed item.
Psychology	Classical conditioning	The positive responses people have toward celebrities come to be independently generated by endorsed items.
	Self-conception	People follow advice from celebrities who match how they perceive (or want to perceive) themselves.

Discipline	Mechanism	Description
	Cognitive dissonance	People unconsciously rationalize following celebrity medical advice to reduce the psychological discomfort that may otherwise result from holding incompatible views.
	Attachment	People, especially those with low self-esteem, form attachments to celebrities who make them feel independent in their actions, supported by others, and competent in their activities.
Sociology	Social networks	Celebrity advice reaches large masses by spreading through systems of people linked through personal connections.
	Commodification and social capital	People follow celebrity medical advice to gain social status and shape their social identities.
	Social constructivism	Celebrity medical advice may alter how people perceive health information and how it is produced in the first place.

Reproduced from Hoffman, S.J. & Tan, C. (2015). Biological, psychological and social processes that explain celebrities' influence on patients' health-related behaviors. Archives of Public Health, 73(3). https://doi.org/10.1186/2049-3258-73-3

Celebrities' ability to reinforce or change media users' health-related values, attitudes, and behaviors is an indication of their credibility as health advisers. Celebrity health narratives can harness public sentiment and channel empathy or outrage, which can be helpful or detrimental to public health outcomes. "Those times when patients mention the latest celebrity endorsement should be seen as meaningful opportunities to start important educational conversations rather than as annoyances" (Hoffman & Tan, 2013, p. 3). Healthcare organizations and the medical community cannot underserve the public by ignoring patient or celebrity health narratives. Instead, trained healthcare professionals need to comprehend the additive or adverse effects of narrative medicine, narrative approach, and patient and celebrity storytelling.

The focal point of narrative medicine is reading, writing, telling, and receiving stories, which aids clinicians and healthcare professionals in their development of narrative competence (Rosti, 2017). Competence within the purview of narrative medicine involves recognizing, absorbing, internalizing, interpreting, and responding to stories applicable to the health and well-being of patients. Training in narrative medicine improves communication skills, enhances empathy, self-reflection, and collaboration, while stressing the importance of adopting a patient-centered approach

(Rosti, 2017). A 2012 Institute of Medicine report estimated that $765 billion of healthcare spending was wasted in 2010, and a large portion of the waste was ascribed to ineffective or nonexistent communication (Gordon et al., 2015). A shift toward a narrative approach in public health focuses on a patient's narrative (which may rely on information obtained from a celebrity narrative) and dialogue that ensues between healthcare professionals and patients. The perspective of patients cannot be ignored, and trying to make sense of their stories, even when they seem inaccessible, is necessary to build rapport and to provide adequate services.

There is a profound and legitimate need to understand the wishes and feelings of patients, especially if the primary concern is the quality of their therapeutic experience (Sitvast, 2017). It is essential for all parties participating in or informed by the dialogue pertaining to a patient's narrative to look for common ground (i.e., healthcare professionals validating the narrative's essential message and engaging in shared decision-making in response to the message) and starting points within the narrative. "Do we hear what deeper needs and wishes the patient voices with his narrative or do we interpret his expressions too easily as symptomatic and exemplary" of the illness, disease, or problem (Sitvast, 2017, p. 3)? Patient and celebrity storytelling are as important to health communication between the public and healthcare professionals as sophisticated messaging techniques or dissemination strategies.

Storytelling relies on a communication format that connects an audience (characters) with the consequences of their choices, whereby we "ceaselessly search for echoes of our own stories in others, assessing credibility and plausibility as we go" (Neeley, 2016, p. 2). Celebrity storytelling influences patterns of care, so healthcare professionals should be aware of celebrity health narratives and try to understand why the public gravitates toward them. Healthcare professionals should determine which celebrity health narratives are more evidence-based and aligned closely with scientific recommendations (Yerramilli et al., 2018) and use these narratives to foster greater communication openness and self-disclosure between healthcare provider and healthcare recipient. Furthermore, healthcare professionals should anticipate the additive or adverse effects of media coverage of celebrity health narratives and understand the implications for public health as patients have greater access to these sources of information. The heightened level of influence of celebrity health narratives means healthcare organizations and other stakeholders in national and international public health should determine how much scrutiny celebrity health-related endorsements and narratives receive, and what restrictions are necessary to ensure they promote messages supported by research evidence.

References

Ambroise, L., Pantin-Sohier, G., Valette-Florence, P., & Albert, N. (2014). From endorsement to celebrity co-branding: Personality transfer. *Journal of Brand Management, 21,* 273–285. https://doi.org/10.1057/bm.2014.7.

Batra, R., & Homer, P.M. (2004). The situational impact of brand image beliefs. *Journal of Consumer Psychology, 14(3),* 318–330. https://doi.org/10.1207/s15327663jcp1403_12.

Beck, C.S., Aubuchon, S.M., McKenna, T.P., Ruhl, S., & Simmons, N. (2014). Blurring personal health and public priorities: An analysis of celebrity health narratives in the public sphere. *Health Communication, 29,* 244–256. https://doi.org/10.1080/10410236.2012.741668.

Belch, G.E., & Belch, M.A. (2013). A content analysis study of the use of celebrity endorsers in magazine advertising. *International Journal of Advertising, 32(3),* 369–389. https://doi.org/10.2501/IJA-32-3-369-389.

Boorstin, D. (1962/1992). *The Image: A Guide to Pseudo-Events in America.* First Vintage Books.

Brockington, D. (2014). The production and construction of celebrity advocacy in international development. *Third World Quarterly, 35(1),* 88–108. https://doi.org/10.1080/01436597.2014.8 68987.

Brogan, M.K. (2015). How twitter is changing narrative storytelling: A case study of the Boston marathon bombings. *Elon Journal of Undergraduate Research in Communications, 6(1),* 28–47. https://www.elon.edu/u/academics/communications/journal/wp-content/uploads/sit es/153/2017/06/04BroganEJSpring15.pdf.

Brown, W.J., & Basil, M.D. (1995). Media celebrities and public health: Responses to "Magic" Johnson's HIV disclosure and its impact on AIDS risk and high-risk behaviors. *Health Communication, 7(4),* 345–370. https://doi.org/10.1207/s15327027hc0704_4.

Bulck, H.V.D. (2017). "She died of a mother's broken heart": Media and audiences' framing of health narratives of heart-related celebrity deaths. *International Journal of Communication, 11,* 4965–4987. https://doi.org/10.1932-8036/20170005.

Carpentier, F.R.D., & Parrott, M.S. (2016). Young adults' information seeking following celebrity suicide: Considering involvement with the celebrity and emotional distress in health communication. *Health Communication 31(11),* 1334–1344. https://doi.org/10.1080/10410236.2015. 1056329.

Celebrity advertisements: Exposing a myth of advertising effectiveness. (2011). Ace Metrix. https://assets.b9.com.br/wp-content/uploads/2011/06/Celebrity_Ad_Exposing_A_Myth.pdf.

Chapman, S., McLeod, K., Wakefield, M., & Holding, S. (2005). Impact of news of celebrity illness on breast cancer screening: Kylie Minogue's breast cancer diagnosis. *The Medical Journal of Australia, 183(5),* 247–250. https://doi.org/10.5694/j.1326-5377.2005.tb07029.x.

Charbonneau, J., & Garland, R. (2006). The use of celebrity athletes as endorsers: Views of the New Zealand general public. *International Journal of Sports Marketing and Sponsorship, 7(4),* 31–38. https://doi.org/10.1108/IJSMS-07-04-2006-B007.

Choi, S.M., Lee, W.N., & Kim, H.J. (2005). Lessons from the rich and famous: A cross-cultural comparison of celebrity endorsement in advertising. *Journal of Advertising, 34(2),* 85–99. https://doi.org/10.1080/00913367.2005.10639190.

Chung, S., & Cho, H. (2017). Fostering parasocial relationships with celebrities on social media: Implications for celebrity endorsement. *Psychology & Marketing, 34(4),* 481–495. https://doi.org/10.1002/mar.21001.

Cooper, A.F. (2008). *Celebrity diplomacy.* Paradigm.

Corner, J. (2003). Mediated persona and political culture. In J. Corner & D. Pels (Eds.), *The media and the restyling of politics* (pp. 67–84). Sage.

Cram, P., et al. (2003). The impact of a celebrity promotional campaign on the use of colon cancer screening: The Katie Couric effect. *Archives of Internal Medicine, 163(13),* 1601–1605. https://doi.org/10.1001/archinte.163.13.1601.

Crenshaw, K.W. (1991). Mapping the margins: Intersectionality, identity politics, and violence against women of color. *Stanford Law Review, 43(6),* 1241–1299. https://doi.org/10.2307/1229039.

Crenshaw, K.W. (2015, September 24). Why intersectionality can't wait. *The Washington Post.* https://www.washingtonpost.com/news/in-theory/wp/2015/09/24/why-inter sectionality-cant-wait/.

Cresswell, J. (2008, June 22). Nothing sells like celebrity. *New York Times*. https://www.nytimes.com/2008/06/22/business/media/22celeb.html.

Dilling-Nielsen, L. (2018). "Everyone is so cynical": On authenticity in the world of Gaga. *At the Interface/Probing the Boundaries, 99*, 31–56. https://doi.org/10.1163/9789004365322_004.

Erdogan, B., Baker, M., & Tagg, S. (2001). Selecting celebrity endorsers: The practitioner's perspective. *Journal of Advertising Research, 41(3)*, 39–48. https://doi.org/10.2501/JAR-41-3-39-48.

Escalas, J.E., & Bettman, J.R. (2017). Connecting with celebrities: How consumers appropriate celebrity meanings for a sense of belonging. *Journal of Advertising, 46(2)*, 297–308. https://doi.org/10.1080/00913367.2016.1274925.

E-score celebrity special report. (2011). E-Poll Market Research. https://www.epollresearch.com/marketing/E-Score%20Celebrity%20YE%202011%202012-03-12-02-cf.pdf.

Ferle, C.L., & Choi, S.M. (2005). The importance of perceived endorser credibility in South Korean advertising. *Journal of Current Issues and Research in Advertising, 27(2)*, 67–81. https://doi.org/10.1080/10641734.2005.10505182.

Fisher, W.R. (1984). Narration as a Human Communication Paradigm: The Case of Public Moral Argument. *Communication Monographs, 51(1)*, 1–22.

Goldsmith, J.N. (2009). Celebrity and the Spectacle of Nation. In T. Mole (Ed.), *Romanticism and Celebrity Culture, 1750–1850* (pp. 21–40). Cambridge University Press. https://digitalcommons.butler.edu/facsch_papers/854.

Gordon, J.E., Deland, E., & Kelly, R.E. (2015). Let's talk about improving communication in healthcare. *Columbia Medical Review, 1(1)*, 23–27. https://doi.org/10.7916/D8RF5T5D.

Green, M.C., & Brock, T.C. (2000). The role of transportation in the persuasiveness of public narratives. *Journal of Personality and Social Psychology, 79(5)*, 701–721. https://doi.org/10.1037/0022-3514.79.5.701.

Hinnant, A., & Hendrickson, E.M. (2014). Negotiating normalcy in celebrity health behavior. A focus group analysis. *Journal of Magazine & New Media Research, 15(2)*, 1–20.

Hoffman, S.J., Natt, N., Sritharan, L., Belluz, J., Caulfield, T., Freedhoff, Y., Lavis, J.N., & Sharma, A.M. (2017). Celebrities' impact on health-related knowledge, attitudes, behaviors, and status outcomes: Protocol for a systematic review, meta-analysis, and meta-regression analysis. *Systematic Reviews, 6(1)*, 1–13. https://doi.org/10.1186/s13643-016-0395-1.

Hoffman, S.J., & Tan, C. (2013). Following celebrities' medical advice: Meta-narrative analysis. *BMJ, 347(f7151)*, 1–6. https://doi.org/10.2196/jmir.4343.

Horton, D., & Wohl, R.R. (1956). Mass communication and parasocial interaction: Observations on intimacy at a distance. *Psychiatry, 19*, 215–229. https://doi.org/10.1080/00332747.1956.11023049.

Hovland, C.I., Janis, I.L., & Kelley, H.H. (1953). Communication and persuasion: Psychological studies of opinion change. Yale University Press.

Hovland, C.I., & Weiss, W. (1951). The influence of source credibility on communication effectiveness. *Public Opinion Quarterly, 15*, 635–650. https://doi.org/10.1086/266350.

Howard, J. (2017, May 18). How celebrities' "golden glow" shines on public health. CNN. https://www.cnn.com/2017/05/18/health/celebrity-health-charlie-sheen-study/index.html.

Humphrey, M. (2018). Confession narratives and mass kinship of YouTube celebrities: A narrative rationality analysis. *Interactions Studies in Communication and Culture, 9(2)*, 225–237. https://doi.org/10.1386/iscc.9.2.225_1.

Hung, K. (2014). Why celebrity sells: A dual entertainment path model of brand endorsement. *Journal of Advertising, 43(2)*, 155–166. https://doi.org/10.1080/00913367.2013.838720.

Janssen, E.D. (2018). Did it really happen? Celebrity and authenticity. *At the Interface/Probing the Boundaries, 99*, 191–202. https://doi.org/10.1163/9789004365322_011.

Kelman, H. (1958). Compliance, identification, and internalization: Three processes of attitude change. *Journal of Conflict Resolution, 1*, 51–60. https://doi.org/10.1177/002200275800200106.

Knoll, J., & Matthes, J. (2017). The effectiveness of celebrity endorsements: A meta-analysis. *Journal of the Academy of Marketing Science, 45(1)*, 55–75. https://doi.org/10.1007/s11747-016-0503-8.

Lerner, B.H. (2006). *When illness goes public: Celebrity patients and how we look at medicine*. Johns Hopkins University Press.

Mapes, D. (2014, May 14). *The Angelina Jolie effect: One year later.* Hutch News Stories. https://www.fredhutch.org/en/news/center-news/2014/05/the-angelina-jolie-effect-one-year-later.html.

Markham, T. (2015). Celebrity advocacy and public engagement: The divergent uses of celebrity. *International Journal of Cultural Studies, 18(4),* 467–480. https://doi.org/10.1177/1367877914528542.

Moe, P.W. (2012). Revealing rather than concealing disability: The rhetoric of Parkinson's advocate Michael J. Fox. *Rhetoric Review, 31(4),* 443–460. https://doi.org/10.1080/07350198.2012.711200.

Money, R.B., Shimp, T.A., & Sakano, T. (2006). Celebrity endorsements in Japan and the United States: Is negative information all that harmful. *Journal of Advertising Research, 46(1),* 113–123. https://doi.org/10.2501/S0021849906060120.

Moulard, J.G., Garrity, C.P., & Rice, D.H. (2015). What makes a human brand authentic? Identifying the antecedents of celebrity authenticity. *Psychology and Marketing, 32(2),* 173–186. https://doi.org/10.1002/mar.20771.

Narapruet, O. (2011). Celebrity philanthropy: Reassessing fame for civil society. *Social Space,* 62–67. https://ink.library.smu.edu.sg/lien_research/88.

Nattinger, A.B., Hoffmann, R.G., Howell-Pelz, A., & Goodwin, J.S. (1998). Effect of Nancy Reagan's mastectomy on choice of surgery for breast cancer by U.S. women. *JAMA, 279(10),* 762–766. https://doi.org/10.1001/jama.279.10.762.

Neeley, L. (2016, June 13). *The value of storytelling in public health and medicine.* The Story Collider. https://docplayer.net/48033698-The-value-of-storytelling-in-public-health-and-medicine-liz-neeley-executive-director-the-story-collider.html.

Noar, S.M., Willoughby, J.F., Myrick, J.G., & Brown, J. (2014). Public figure announcements about cancer and opportunities for cancer communication. A review and research agenda. *Health Communication, 29,* 445–461. https://doi.org/10.1080/10410236.2013.764781.

Petty, R.E., & Caccioppo, J.T. (1981). Issue Involvement as a moderator of the effects on attitudes of advertising content and context. *Advances in consumer research. Association for Consumer Research (U.S.), 8(1),* 20–24. https://www.acrwebsite.org/volumes/9252/volumes/v08/NA-08.

Petty, R.E., & Wegener, D.T. (1999). The Elaboration Likelihood Model: Current Status and Controversies. In S. Chaiken & Y. Trope (Eds.), *Dual-Process Theories in Social Psychology* (pp. 37–72). Guildford Press.

The role of news on Facebook: Common yet incidental. (2013). Pew Research Center. https://www.journalism.org/2013/10/24/the-role-of-news-on-facebook/.

Rollins, B., & Bhutada, N. (2014). Impact of celebrity endorsements in disease-specific direct-to-consumer (DTC) advertisements. *International Journal of Pharmaceutical and Healthcare Marketing, 8(2),* 164–177. https://doi.org/10.1108/IJPHM-05-2013-0024.

Rosti, G. (2017). Role of narrative-based medicine in proper patient assessment. *Support Care Cancer, 25 (Suppl 1),* S3-S6. https://doi.org/10.1007/s00520-017-3637-4.

Roy, S. (2006). An exploratory study in celebrity endorsements. *Journal of Creative Communications, 1(2),* 139–153. https://doi.org/10.1177/097325860600100201.

Seitz, V.A., Razzouk, N., & Eamsobhan, S. (2007). Celebrity endorsements in U.S. and Thai magazines: A content analysis comparative assessment. *Journal of Promotion Management, 13(3–4),* 383–398. https://doi.org/10.1080/10496490802308513.

Shimp, T. (2003). *Advertising, promotion and supplemental aspects of integrated marketing communications* (6th ed.). The Dryden Press.

Sitvast, J. (2017). Importance of patient's narrative and dialogue in healthcare. *International Journal of Emergency Mental Health and Human Resilience, 19(2),* 1–3. https://doi.org/10.4172/1522-4821.1000357.

Steele, S.L., & Shores, T. (2015). Real and unreal masculinities: The celebrity image in anti-trafficking campaigns. *Journal of Gender Studies, 24(4),* 419–435. https://doi.org/10.1080/09589236.2014.959477.

Stone, A. (2011, July 9). Former first lady Betty Ford dead at 93. *USA Today.* https://usatoday30.usatoday.com/news/washington/2011-07-08-betty-ford-obit_n.htm.

Street, J. (2003). The celebrity politician: Political style and popular culture. In J. Corner & D. Pels (Eds.), *The media and the restyling of politics* (pp. 85–98). Sage.

Street, J. (2004). Celebrity politicians: Popular culture and political representation. *British Journal of Politics and International Relations, 6(4)*, 435–452. https://doi.org/10.1111/j.1467-856X.2004.00149.x

Twine, C., Barthelmes, L., & Gateley, C.A. Kylie Minogue's breast cancer. Effects on referrals to a rapid access breast clinic in the U.K. *The Breast, 15(5)*, 667–669. https://doi.org/10.1016/j.breast.2006.03.006.

Twitter news consumers: Young, mobile and educated. (2013). Pew Research Center. https://www.journalism.org/2013/11/04/twitter-news-consumers-young-mobile-and-educated/.

Vinney, C., & Vinney, L.A. (2017). That sounds familiar: The relationship between listeners' recognition of celebrity voices, perceptions of vocal pleasantness, and engagement with media. *Journal of Radio & Audio Media, 24(2)*, 320–338. https://doi.org/10.1080/19376529.2017.1346659.

Vivienne Leung, S.Y., & Cheng, K. (2016). Public's perception of celebrities with serious illness in Hong Kong and the impact of media stories of ill celebrities on health awareness and behavior. *Journal of Communication in Healthcare, 9(4)*, 256–266. https://doi.org/10.1080/17538068.2016.1247128.

Vivienne Leung, S.Y., & Cheng, K., & Tse, T. (2018). Insiders' views: The current practice of using celebrities in marketing communications in greater China. *Intercultural Communication Studies XXVII, 1*, 96–113. http://hdl.handle.net/10722/259478.

Wen, N. (2017). Celebrity influence and young people's attitudes toward cosmetic surgery in Singapore. The role of parasocial relationships and identification. *International Journal of Communication, 11*, 1234–1252. https://ijoc.org/index.php/ijoc/article/view/6146.

Wen, N., & Cui, D. (2014). Effects of celebrity involvement on young people's political and civic engagement. *Chinese Journal of Communication, 7(4)*, 409–428. https://doi.org/10.1080/17544750.2014.953964.

West, D.M., & Orman, J. (2003). *Celebrity politics*. Prentice Hall.

Wheeler, M. (2011). Celebrity diplomacy: United Nations' Goodwill Ambassadors and messengers of peace. *Celebrity Studies, 2(1)*, 6–18. https://doi.org/10.1080/19392397.2011.543267.

Williams, M. (2011, August 23). When celebrity endorsements go wrong. *Campaign Magazine*. https://www.campaignlive.co.uk/article/when-celebrity-endorsements-go-wrong/1085542.

Yerramilli, D., Charrow, A., & Caplan, A. (2018). How should clinicians respond when patients are influenced by celebrities' cancer stories? *AMA Journal of Ethics, 20(11)*, 1075–1081. https://doi.org/10.1001/amajethics.2018.1075.

Yilmaz, R.A., & Ersavas, S. (2005, May 11–13). How does the celebrity work for brand? An analysis on Turkish TV advertising. In J.K. Litterst (Moderator), *Cinema, Radio, TV* [Panel presentation] 3rd International Symposium Communication in the Millennium: A dialogue between Turkish and American Scholars, Chapel Hill, NC, United States.

1

Celebrity Suicides
and Self-Directed Forms
of Violence

The Centers for Disease Control and Prevention (CDC) identified violence as a leading public health problem as early as the 1980s (Rosenberg et al., 2006), with the World Health Assembly (WHA) concurring in 1996 (Resolution WHA49.25), leading to increasing reliance in healthcare on the World Health Organization's (WHO) expansion of what constitutes acts of violence, whether they be self-directed, interpersonal, or collective violence (Dahlberg & Krug, 2002). In the U.S., since the 1999 report from the Surgeon General, there has been a call to action regarding the threat of suicide. In the year of the report, suicide was the ninth leading cause of mortality in the U.S., responsible for nearly 31,000 deaths, which was more than 50 percent higher than the number of homicides in the U.S. in the same year. The WHO reported that every 40 seconds a person dies by suicide somewhere in the world, and more than 800,000 people die by suicide every year. During 2018, the suicides of celebrity chef, TV host, and author Anthony Bourdain (Dubin, 2018; Peele, 2018) and fashion designer Kate Spade (CBS News, 2018) shocked the public, bringing awareness to spiking suicide rates. The suicides of lead singers Chester Bennington of Linkin Park (Grow, 2017; Miller, 2017) and Chris Cornell of Soundgarden (Hunter, 2018; Vaziri, 2018) are indicative of the reality that celebrities are mortal too. During moments of despair, they are human, susceptible like everyone else to the pressures of life, which can contribute to incidents of self-harm and self-directed forms of violence. These forms of violence are insidious, since the victim and the perpetrator are the same person. Some celebrities who survive self-directed forms of violence brave public scrutiny of their personal lives to share their stories and provide insights into how to address this public health issue.

Violence against oneself includes deliberate self-harm (DSH) or

27

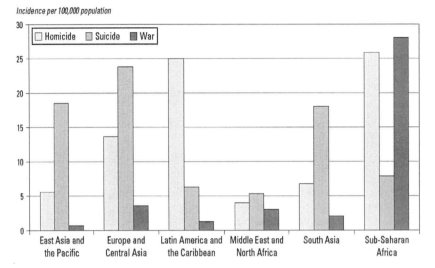

Figure 1: Homicide, Suicide, and War-Related Fatality Rates by Region, 2001
Reproduced from Lopez, A. D., Mathers, C. D., Ezzati, M., Jamison, D. T., & Murray, C.J.L. (Eds.). (2006). *Global Burden of Disease and Risk Factors.* Oxford University Press.

self-injury (SI), self-directed forms of violence, such as self-poisoning (e.g., overdoses and other poisonings) and attempted suicide, and suicide. Attempted suicide or suicidal SI involves self-harming behavior with an intent to die (Glenn et al., 2017). "Suicidality refers to the cognitions and activities of persons seeking their own death, including thoughts, actions or omissions" (Jans et al., 2012, p. 2). Oftentimes, around the world, deaths by suicide will outpace homicide and war-related mortality rates (see Figure 1).

Domestic and international healthcare organizations, both governmental and non-governmental, should identify factors impacting suicide attempt morbidity and use predictors of suicidality to mitigate a suicide-related mortality catastrophe. A variety of biological and personal history factors influence suicidal SI, including early developmental experience, demographic characteristics (e.g., age, gender, family, etc.), victim of child abuse and neglect, psychological and personality disorders, physical health and disabilities, substance abuse, history of violent behavior, and gun ownership (Krug et al., 2002). Individuals with a history of suicide attempt and non-suicidal self-injury (NSSI) are more likely to associate themselves with self-harm and death, which can trigger their self-harm-related implicit associations (i.e., outside conscious control). Research indicates that these self-harm-related implicit associations may serve as a useful behavioral marker for suicide risk, especially for individuals who are more sensitive to the recency and severity of their self-harm history (Glenn et al., 2017).

"Although, suicidal ideation does not always lead to suicide attempts, suicide attempts and deaths are commonly preceded by ideation, making suicidal ideation predictive of suicide" (Carlyle et al., 2018, p. 12). Those who engage in non-suicidal self-injury seek to harm themselves with no intent to die (Glenn et al., 2017). NSSI includes self-cutting, self-burning, and deliberate self-hitting that alters or destroys tissue. These behaviors are prevalent in adult and adolescent populations (Hoffman et al., 2010).

NSSI became an individual diagnosis in the fifth edition of the *Diagnostic and Statistical Manual of Mental Disorder*s (DSM-5; 2013) and encompasses "deliberate, non-suicidal purpose of the self-injurious act, which is not socially sanctioned" and has "happen[ed] on at least 5 days in the past year." Also, "the individual who engages in NSSI must have the aim to get to a better emotional state after the action" (Meszaros et al., 2017, p. 1–2). Many individuals who self-harm initially partake in other activities like smoking but eventually gravitate toward riskier, more compelling, and dangerous behavior, including cutting, biting, burning, and asphyxiation to achieve an emotional release (Harvey & Brown, 2012). Self-harm becomes a part of a repetitive cycle that escalates and becomes more acute. When self-harm becomes an addiction, the likelihood that cutting, scratching, carving, self-hitting, self-burning, excoriation of wounds, picking, abrading, hanging, or drowning can contribute to accidental death or suicide increases. Self-harm can be performed on any part of the body, yet most self-injurers focus on their hands, wrists, abdomen, and thighs, inflicting superficial wounds that can result in lasting disfigurement (Simeon & Hollander, 2001). Self-injury is generally not about suicide, although individuals who engage in NSSI can become suicidal. The inability to control their internal emotion regulation (e.g., reduce intense feelings of anxiety, anger, sadness, depression, guilt, shame, deadness, etc.), interpersonal motivations, or relationship dynamics can contribute to a move from low-lethality methods of self-injury (cutting, hitting, excoriation) to the high-lethality methods of suicide (firearms, hanging, overdose) and back again (Walsh, 2007).

Demographic Snapshots of Suicide and Self-Harm

Understanding the underlying risk factors that contribute to self-harm and suicide in the U.S. and international communities enables healthcare organizations to mitigate the suicide mortality rate. The CDC's 2018 nationwide study of trends in suicide rates reported about half of suicide decedents did not have a known mental health condition, and suicide and self-harm cost American citizens approximately $70 million per year in direct medical and work loss costs (Stone et al., 2018). During adolescence, antecedents of mental health conditions can emerge. Many individuals who engage in low-lethality methods of self-injury, which can be a gateway to high-level methods of suicide, begin in adolescence. Comorbidity of mental health conditions in adolescence or adulthood can increase the likelihood of partaking in riskier behaviors, which adversely affect an individual's health and well-being. International responsiveness to underlying risk factors is affected by a variety of impediments and enablers. The goal of domestic and international healthcare professionals is to overcome significant obstructions to effective intervention. There needs to be greater focus on self-harm and suicidality in adolescence, and an examination of international trends regarding these acts of violence and interrelated violence prevention.

Adolescent Turmoil in the Digital Era

Adolescents within the context of research about self-harm and suicide are individuals between the ages of 10 and 19 who engage in stigmatized behaviors triggered by the absence of autonomy, power, or control. Official figures pertaining to adolescents who self-harm represent the "tip of the iceberg" (Ystgaard et al., 2009), especially since only 10 percent of adolescents who harm themselves are admitted to a hospital after a self-harming episode (Bowen & John, 2001; Hawton et al., 2002). The official figures provide an incomplete picture, but the available data is alarming: rates of self-harm for adolescents in the U.K. are higher than in the rest of Europe, with one in five adolescents believed to have engaged in self-harming behavior (Mental Health Foundation, 2006). Diller (2018) addresses various disturbing trends in the U.S., including over the past 15 years a 166 percent increase in self-harm rates for girls aged 10 to 14, and a 62 percent increase in self-harm rates for girls aged 15 to 19. Over this time period, injury from sharp objects increased for female adolescents by 152 percent, with the bulk of the increase in cutting beginning in 2009 (Diller, 2018). Transgender youth are also experiencing a spike in self-harm and suicide rates. According to a study conducted by the Cincinnati Children's Hospital Medical Center (2016), 30 percent of transgender youth report a history of at least one suicide attempt, and nearly 42 percent report a history of self-injury. These trends are related to increases in mental health issues for adolescents, including depressive symptoms and clinical-level depression.

Many adolescents who self-harm do not share their experiences with healthcare professionals. Instead, they self-disclose to peers who also partake in self-harm or suicidal fantasies. Teen turmoil regarding self-harm and suicidal fantasies occurs in spaces marked by discourse that indicates low-lethality methods of self-injury or high-level methods of suicide are socially acceptable. Adolescents who engage in self-harm and are curious about suicide are finding spaces online, with the Internet providing a gateway to online discourse communities whose sole purpose is to help youth harm themselves. "There is a rising trend for teens to discuss cutting on the Internet and form cutting clubs at school," which is very alarming for the Canadian Mental Health Association (Brody, 2008). These online agreements to harm oneself or commit suicide together are arranged over the Internet by strangers, who share information about how to harm themselves, how to kill themselves, and learn "best practices" for accomplishing their goals of self-harm or suicide. Peers exchanging harmful or lethal information on the Internet contribute to a copy-cat or media contagion effect, where the Internet, specifically social media, forges a dangerous association between peers' self-harm and an individual's NSIS, or an individual's suicide ideation and pervasive suicide content (Carlyle et al., 2018). Online discourse communities spurred nearly 33 percent of all suicides in South Korea and an increasing frequency of suicides in other countries, including Japan and the U.S. (Luxton et al., 2012; Naito, 2007; Ozawa-de Silva, 2008). Mental health outreach should adapt to the digital era to create communal spaces online for adolescents and adults with an interest in or history with NSSI, providing web portals full of information to educate individuals about self-harm and suicide ideation. Social media can be used to tailor preventative web-based self-harm initiatives or suicide interventions to niche audiences across levels of risk.

Adolescents in these discourse communities exhibit more self-harming or suicidal tendencies because there is a higher level of communication openness in these spaces. In the digital era, discourse communities are accessible via the Internet, and smartphones are an on-ramp to the World Wide Web. By 2016, the average child in the U.S. possessed a smartphone by the age of 10 (Twenge, 2017). Smartphone use, also known as screen time, accelerated over the past decade. During that period, an increase in screen time on phones and other devices was the largest change in the lives of teenagers, a change that leaves less time for them to do things that are beneficial to their mental health, such as sleeping and seeing friends in person. Once teens are online, the "...possibility for users to remain anonymous has also been shown to increase people's willingness to communicate about problematic life circumstances," which contributes to "...conversations and disclosures regarding suicide" via social media platforms and Internet forums (Westerlund, 2013, p. 36). These online spaces enable teens to use language about self-harm and suicidal behavior or to display suicidal behavior as a language, which entails bodily and verbal expressions of suicide. There are similarities in language and linguistic repertoires—the communicative patterns and commonalities—through which adolescents represent their subjective experiences in discourse communities within domestic and international online spaces (Harvey & Brown, 2012). Suicidal behavior itself is a social act that can be interpreted as a text, and "our language about suicidal behavior comprises the social and linguistic discourse (or discourses) that determine the subject matter and boundaries of how suicide can be discussed, and related to, in a specific socio-cultural and temporal context" (Westerlund, 2013, p. 36). An analysis of messages in online discourse communities reveals key words that encapsulate the subjective experiences of adolescents accessing and using these communal spaces.

In the study *Health Communication and Psychological Distress* (2012), researchers drew upon a corpus of 1.6 million words from a U.K.-hosted adolescent health website to analyze and discern a range of keywords relating to self-harm. If parents and healthcare professionals are going to have effective outreach to adolescents, they need to pay close attention to individual accounts of self-harm and suicidality. The discourse adolescents use and the behaviors they display in their spaces are usually inaccessible to healthcare professionals. The criticism that empirical, corpus-based, medical-discourse studies lack sufficient analysis of adolescent self-harming discourse underscores a need to raise the consciousness of professionals and advance their knowledge through gaining access to the voices of the adolescents themselves (Harvey & Brown, 2012). Otherwise, tailoring support to reflect the uniqueness of the experiences of adolescents becomes extremely difficult. Research along the lines of the U.K. study is needed, where analysis of adolescents' voices yielded a categorization of keywords into salient health themes, which is a valuable linguistic resource for the identification and description of experiences, commonalities, and understandings of psychological distress traumatizing today's youth (see Tables 1 and 2).

Global Implications of Self-Harm and Suicide

Self-harm and suicidality are not confined to the industrialized, Western world, nor are Western models to understand these behaviors applicable to every country or culture. NSSI, suicide, and other self-directed forms of violence are recognized as major global health problems. The greatest burden of suicide in the present decade is in low- and middle-income countries, where annual suicide rates are 10–11 individuals per 100,000 people, with countries such as China and India leading the world in absolute number of annual deaths by suicide (Rajendra et al., 2015). DSH in India

Theme	Examples of keywords
Sexual health	sex, HIV, AIDS, STD, STI, sperm, contraception, clitoris, vagina, pregnant, period, orgasm, vulva, PMS, erection, condom, masturbate, gay, abortion, foreplay, intercourse, virgin, unprotected, lesbian, oral, pill, ovulation, herpes, thrush, chlamydia, pregnancy, tampon, testicles, genitalia, Viagra, scrotum, labia, glans, ovaries, foreskin, balls, fanny, bisexual, miscarriage
Mental health	antidepressants, cut, depressed, cuts, cutting, self-harm, scars, Prozac, angry, sad, depression, self, harm, wrists, suicide, die, overdose, addiction, addict, stress, stressed, ADHD, paranoid, mental, mad, moods, sad, unhappy, crying, personality, anxiety
Body weight/image	Eat, eating, anorexia, weight, size, overweight, fat, obese, underweight, skinny, thin, bulimia, BMI, exercise, diets, kilograms, KG, KGS, calories
Drugs/alcohol	Drugs, cannabis, cocaine, heroin, pills, alcohol, drunk, drinking, poppers, mushrooms, marijuana, crack, ecstasy, addict, stoned, LSD, cigarettes, dope
Serious conditions	cancer, HIV, AIDS, epilepsy, diabetes, anthrax, pimples,
Minor conditions	spots, acne zits, blackhead, mumps, scabies, dandruff, worms, cystitis
Medication	medicine, antidepressants, Prozac, medication, prescribed, antibiotics, tablets, pill, pills

**Table 1: Keywords by Categorization of Health Themes
in Adolescent Health E-mails**

Reproduced from Harvey, K. & Brown, B. (2012). Health communication and psychological distress: Exploring the language of self-harm. *The Canadian Modern Language Review, 68(3)*, 316–340. https://doi.org/10.3138/cmlr.1103

	Word	Frequency
1	cut	314
2	self-harm	175
3	cutting	122
4	self-harming	61
5	cuts	55
6	slit	18
7	harm	16
8	harming	12
9	self-harmer	10
10	slitting	7

**Table 2: Most Common Self-Harm-Related Keywords
in Adolescent Health Messages**

Reproduced from Harvey, K. & Brown, B. (2012). Health communication and psychological distress: Exploring the language of self-harm. *The Canadian Modern Language Review, 68(3)*, 316–340. https://doi.org/10.3138/cmlr.1103

provides a case study for the limitations of Western models of suicide prevention and medical interventions. There is international concern about applying what are perceived as Western-centric, WHO global suicide preventive policies, procedures, and interventions to halt DSH-related injuries and deaths. DSH includes intentional self-poisoning, yet the intensity with which this behavior undermines Indians, particularly in rural areas of India where pesticide suicides are prevalent, is startling (Rajendra et al., 2015). Healthcare resources in rural India are thinly spread across the countryside, so a more comprehensive and localized evidence base is needed to underpin public health strategies to mitigate DSH. These public health strategies should not exist in a vacuum, so healthcare professionals should tailor them within a national or regional cultural context. In many Western countries, attempted suicide may go against national mores, but in India, attempted suicide is a crime (Rajendra et al., 2015). In India, fear of the legal and social repercussions of reporting DSH adversely affects survivors' willingness to disclose the details of what transpired to authorities. The lack of transparency and communication openness between perpetrators of NSSI and survivors of DSH undercuts efforts to build a localized evidence base and complicates the ability of healthcare organizations to intervene. To reduce fatalities, there needs to be more information and investment to improve the quality, affordability, and accessibility of healthcare in rural and urban India.

Many middle- and low-income countries have a limited evidence base, which is derived from aggregate data compiled from clinical cases in emergency departments or inpatient units. In the study *Self-Injury in Australia: A Community Survey* (2010), researchers conducted a community-based study that consisted of a nationally representative sample of adults. At the time, the only other study that was similarly ambitious had been conducted in the U.S. The Australian cross-sectional survey involved respondents contacted via a computer-assisted telephone interview, and 12,006 Australians from randomly selected households participated, with a response rate of 38.5 percent. For this study, the four-week prevalence of SI in Australia was 1.1 percent, and the lifetime prevalence was 8.1 percent. Moreover, 51.9 percent of respondents indicated that SI occurred in the absence of suicidal thoughts, while 48.1 percent of respondents acknowledged that SI happened in tandem with suicidal thoughts. In the same study, for 73.7 percent of admitted incidents of SI, SI happened in absence of a lifetime history of suicide attempts. India and Australia are culturally distinct, yet national healthcare professionals from both countries incorporate WHO and regional models or interventions to address ever-increasing adolescent NSSI and DSH rates.

A comparative study of suicide rates among adolescents in 29 Organization for Economic Cooperation and Development (OECD) countries identified age and gender differences, as well as regional and national differences. For OECD countries (e.g., North American countries, European countries, Japan, South Korea, Australia, and New Zealand), self-organizing map (SOM) and multi-dimensional scaling (MDS) analyses "revealed that variance in the suicide gender gap is one of the significant dimensions underlying differences in the patterns of child and adolescent suicides" (Roh et al., 2018, p. 377). Many European countries had declines in male suicide rates, but female suicide rates were stable or increased. Access to firearms contributed to male suicides, so more restrictions on firearms mitigated male use of firearms for suicide. Korea and Japan exhibited increasing suicide rates for both genders, agitated by volatile economic conditions, inequality, and rapid changes in family structure. New Zealand and Finland had the first- and third-highest adolescent suicide rates, among OECD countries, with suicidality and violence being contributing factors for suicide and death among young, indigenous, Maori males in New Zealand, and more frequent use of high-lethality methods of suicide (e.g., firearms, etc.) for both male and female Finnish adolescents. Among U.S. males, access to firearms is a major risk factor for suicide ideation becoming suicide (Roh et al., 2018). In the U.S., youth who use guns to harm themselves were more than 35 times more likely to kill themselves over the next year compared to teens and young adults who used other methods of self-harm (Rapaport, 2018). Despite regional and national differences in suicide rates, suicide is a major public health issue, and its mitigation is a crucial component of national and international mental health and violence prevention.

Suicide is a leading cause of death in the U.S. According to the CDC, suicide rates increased in nearly every state from 1999 through 2016. The CDC's National Violent Death Reporting System (NVDRS) analyzed data submitted in 2015 from 27 participating states, and found that many factors contributed to suicide among those with and without known mental health conditions, including relationship problems (42 percent), crisis in the past or upcoming two weeks (29 percent), problematic substance abuse (28 percent), physical health problem (22 percent), job/financial problem (16 percent), criminal legal problem (9 percent), and loss of housing (4 percent). These factors coupled with a method for suicide, such as suicide by firearm injury, hanging, suffocation, self-poisoning via various chemicals (e.g., carbon monoxide poisoning, pesticides, etc.), illegal and legal pharmaceuticals (e.g., analgesics, psychotropic drugs, etc.), and jumping from a high place or into water contribute to death by suicide in the U.S., other Western countries, and many low- and middle-income countries (Jans et al., 2012). According to the Division of Violence Prevention of the National Center for Injury Prevention and Control (CDC, 2020), in 2013, 494,169 people were treated in emergency departments for self-inflicted injuries, while there were 41,149 suicides in 2013 in the U.S.—a rate of 12.6 per 100,000, which is equal to 113 suicides each day, or one every 13 minutes.

In 2009, U.S. students in grades 9–12 reported in the previous 12 months to have: (1) seriously considered attempting suicide (13.8 percent), (2) made a suicide plan (10.9 percent), (3) attempted suicide one or more times (6.3 percent), or (4) attempted suicide resulting in injury, poisoning, or an overdose that had to be treated by a doctor or nurse (1.9 percent). Suicide ideation is common among adolescents, and a significant portion of this population is carrying out suicide attempts (Jans et al., 2012). According to the Division of Violence Prevention of the National Center for Injury Prevention and Control (CDC, 2020), suicide was the third leading cause of death among persons aged 10–14, the second leading cause of death for persons aged 15–34, the fourth leading cause of death for persons aged 35–44, the fifth leading cause of death for persons aged 45–54, and the eighth and seventh causes of death for persons aged 55–64 and 65 years and older, respectively. The overwhelming majority of suicide decedents are white (Stone, et al., 2018). However, in 2015, the suicide rate for American Indians and Alaska Natives (AI/AN) in the 18 states participating in the NVDRS was 21.5 per 100,000, more than 3.5 times higher than rates among other racial/ethnic groups (Leavitt et al., 2018). Based on data about suicides in 16 states reporting to the NVDRS in 2010, 33.4 percent of suicide decedents tested positive for alcohol, 23.8 percent for antidepressants, and 20 percent for opiates, including heroin and prescription pain killers (Parks, Johnson, McDaniel, & Gladden, 2014).

Duality of "Werther" and "Papageno" Effects

Celebrities affect us. Adolescent and adult perpetrators of NSSI and DSH are fans of celebrities, too. Their favorite celebrities have a significant impact on their personal beliefs or have inspired them to do something. Media coverage of celebrities who partake in NSSI, DSH, or are decedents of suicide, resonates with media users. The celebrity lifestyles portrayed in the media have an influence on the attitudes of adolescent and adults toward compulsive behaviors, such as low-lethality methods of self-injury and high-lethality methods of suicide. "The traditional notion of celebrity has also changed over time, in that celebrities may be viewed as peers or competitors for emerging adults; in other words, some may view their lifestyle as attainable" (Lewallen et al., 2016, p. 254). Moreover, 10 percent or more of adults may experience celebrity worship as a carryover from their adolescence (Hyman & Sierra, 2010). The influence of celebrities and their narratives manifests during the digital era, when "…the overall consumption of the messages in new and traditional forms of celebrity media" becomes heightened due to greater exposure "…to messages about celebrity across a variety of unique channels, and it is important to consider the overall impact of these messages" (Lewallen et al., 2016, p. 266). In South Korea, where suicide rates are ranked among the highest of OECD countries, the 2008 suicide of famous Korean actress Jinsil Choi was a watershed moment, with authorities noting a drastic increase in the suicide rate after her death (Choi & Oh, 2016). Celebrities are sometimes unwilling role models for ordinary people, yet they must acknowledge this, and health-care professionals must accept that various audiences identify with celeb-rities who commit suicide. Interestingly, the significant impact of media coverage of Korean celebrity suicides on Koreans dissipates in cases of for-eign celebrity suicides. "This confirms the expectation from the literature of identity, which addressed the strong influence of an in-group celebrity sui-cide..." (Choi & Oh, 2016, p. 103). In South Korea, there are media guide-lines in place to mitigate the influence of celebrity suicide media coverage on Korean media users.

These media guidelines strongly discourage the following habits on media outlets and platforms: (1) use of the word suicide in the title of a news story, (2) news content that provides details of suicide methods, (3) news content that oversimplifies the causes or "perceived triggers" for a suicide (Choi & Oh, 2016). These media guidelines are a reaction to the "Werther effect" (see Figure 2). The "Werther effect" surmises that media users are susceptible to celebrity suicides, with some of them being at a greater risk for imitating NSSI and DSH than others, resulting in copy-cat suicides, which are most prevalent in the first few days after the dissemination of celebrity suicide news stories. Media effects are not restricted to harm-ful effects. Media coverage focusing on positive coping with adverse cir-cumstances can decrease suicide rates (Arendt et al., 2016). The potential suicide-protective effect known as the "Papageno effect" (Niederkroten-thaler, 2010) counterbalances the "Werther effect." The "Papageno effect" highlights that suicide-related traditional and new media reporting can increase or decrease suicides.

There has been much discussion about the influence of media depictions of suicidal acts on the frequency of suicide. A classic example is what happened in Germany after the publication of Goethe's popular book "The Sorrows of Young Werther" in 1774. Publication was followed by a number of suicides of young people. This was attributed to the vivid description of the young protagonist romantically killing himself after being rejected by the woman he loved. The book was subsequently banned in most of Europe.

Suicide clustering following media reporting and fictional presentation of suicide on television does occur ("Werther-effect"). According to a German naturalistic study (Schmidtke & Hafner, 1988), broadcast of a soap opera showing the railway  suicide of a 19 year-old male resulted in an increase (175%) in railway suicides among 15 to 19 year-old males. Factors associated with imitation are: time (suicides peak in the first few days after publication), amount and prominence of media coverage, similarity between victim and teenager, celebrity status of the victim, specific description of the suicide (method, time, place), romanticized and sensationalized reporting, suggestions that there is an epidemic, and simplifying the reasons for suicide (World Health Organization, 2008).

Suicide attempts and suicides among peers (Hazell & Lewin, 1993) also increase the risk. Different pathways can lead to clustering of suicides. Apart from posttraumatic stress symptoms, bereavement and assortative friendships with vulnerable peers, mere imitation is a significant factor.

Figure 2. Modeling Suicidal Behavior—The "Werther effect"

Reproduced from Jans, T., Taneli, Y., & Warnke, A. (2012). Suicide and self-harming behavior. In J.M. Rey (Ed.), *IACAPAP e-Textbook of Child and Adolescent Mental Health.* (pp. 1–35). International Association for Child and Adolescent Psychiatry and Allied Professions.

The "Papageno effect" utilizes the story of a protagonist in news coverage, which is useful and adaptable to awareness and prevention material tailored to NSSI and DSH adolescents and adults. The protagonist is portrayed as neither sensationalist nor heroic. Instead, the protagonist is a relatable boy next door, girl next door, or family next door. The protagonist encounters a crisis or the burdensome act of working through a crisis, using knowledge and intelligence to confront challenging circumstances and overcome them. "This conceptualization of the story may have influenced the quality of social comparison of participants with the protagonist" (Arendt et al., 2016, p. 723). These stories resonate with a public responsive to media entertainment use (Johnson et al., 2016). Media users find protagonists and their stories compelling because they depict harm, tragedy, profound social relationships, or conflict. These stories provide a touchstone for the audience to share individual and collective experiences, to determine what these experiences mean, and what changes, if any, need to be made to feel good about themselves. Celebrity media coverage enthralls audiences with celebrity protagonists, especially when they are foregrounded in compelling stories or engaged in fanciful or realistic circumstances, with the dual purpose of gratifying media users with entertainment and persuading them to internalize celebrity endorsements (e.g., ideas, values, products, services). A story resonates with an audience when media users see themselves and people they can relate to in it. The story should affirm media users' self-concepts, which is never an easy process. "The self-concept is central to the individual's psychological processing" (Johnson et al., 2016, p. 386), and the juxtaposition of the effects of self-affirmation and self-acceptance on media users' receptivity to the narrative components of a story explains why celebrity protagonists can be a vital asset to self-injury and suicide prevention narratives.

Self-acceptance enables our self-worth to flourish, and both affect our identity or self-concept in myriad ways. Self-affirmation is a self-defense and coping mechanism to combat threats against self-worth. Self-affirmation theory conceptualizes maintenance of self-worth as a process where individuals seek to preserve a view of themselves and their self-concepts, which they desperately want to believe are good and have integrity. During this process, people encounter threats to self-actualization in the form of ideas, beliefs, values, attitudes, opinions, and practices that seem contrary to what is normative for themselves, their group, or society. Self-affirmation uses an individual's thoughts and actions to emphasize positive qualities, to act as a buffer against threats to self, such as failures to meet social standards (Johnson et al., 2016). According to Sherman and Cohen (2006), self-affirmation diminishes the injurious effects of everyday hazards, including stress, stereotyping, or dissonance. However, self-acceptance minimizes the need to lessen self-deficits with "…an appraisal of self-deficit information as relatively benign to self-worth, thereby allowing individuals to act to improve in the area of deficit via adaptive consumption rather than to deny or avoid it via compensatory consumption" (Kim & Gal, 2014, p. 530). Adaptive consumption entails consumption of information, products, and services intended to help an individual improve in an area of deficit, whereas compensatory consumption is consumption that helps an individual deny or avoid information perceived as threatening to self-identity. Self-acceptance allows media users to recognize their flaws through the observation of others and to contemplate how all of our stories are full of flaws and mistakes. If the protagonist in the story can overcome precarious circumstances, so can everyone else, which make the mistakes and flaws less threatening. Self-acceptance paves the way for adaptive consumption and personal growth.

The implications of self-affirmation and self-acceptance for healthcare professionals interested in the incorporation of narratives of celebrity protagonists in violence prevention interventions and NSSI and DSH outreach efforts are significant. Individuals with lower levels of self-affirmation are more receptive to mediated celebrity narratives about violence prevention (e.g., NSSI, DSH, and suicide preventions), whereas individuals with higher levels of self-affirmation are less likely to need mediated narratives to sustain their self-concept. The pressures linked to self-concept maintenance are a "drag" on self-worth, so media users deploy self-affirming thoughts and actions to rebuff or diminish threats to personal or collective identities.

When our self-concept is managed and self-affirmed in a meaningful way (e.g., ego maintenance and individuality), media users are empowered to mitigate emotional or psychological stressors and rely on mediated storytelling to provide audiences a more intense and rewarding entertainment experience. Stories allow media users to transcend themselves, to alleviate the constrictions of ego maintenance and self-criticism. "In this way, entertaining narratives can play a role in the psychological well-being of the self" (Johnson et al., 2016, p. 405).

A media user who is less "wistful" may also perceive himself as stronger and less vulnerable than the protagonist in the narrative. "Wistful," within this context, means media users are more likely to commit suicide when they perceive themselves to be more like-minded or similar to celebrity protagonists who commit suicide (Arendt et al., 2016); if the celebrity protagonist could not bear to live, how can I? The media user who is "wistful" is more susceptible to the "Werther effect." The goal of healthcare professionals, especially health communication and social marketing campaign interventionists, is to lessen wistfulness, to strengthen media users' self-acceptance, to bolster their belief that if the protagonist can do it, so can they, and even if the protagonist succumbs during crisis (e.g., NSSI, DSH, suicide), they will survive. Celebrity protagonists and their narratives are popular vessels for delivering self-harm and suicide prevention messages to media users, and the media and healthcare organizations should use the "Papageno effect" to save lives.

Mediated Narratives of Celebrity Self-Harm and Suicide

Celebrities use mediums and media to self-disclose about their mental health, NSSI, or DSH, which creates intimacy between celebrities, their fans, and a curious and concerned public. Audiences pay attention to news about celebrities in general, with interest heightened whenever the news focuses on sensationalist headlines regarding a celebrity, their mental health, and self-harm or suicide. When celebrities do not want their private lives in public view, they try to restrict access and control the narrative. In cases where a family is coping with the suicide of a celebrity family member or friend, the public's right to know is eclipsed by the need to grieve and the need for privacy. Unfortunately, celebrities, their families, and friends have limited control of what is said about them in the media, especially when the entertainment value outweighs concern for privacy. To get ahead of the story, and manipulate the media coverage, celebrities are using traditional and social media to tell their own stories about mental health and self-harm. Many families or friends of celebrities who succumb to suicide act despite their grief, deciding to use public fascination and preoccupation with their dead loved ones by placing a spotlight on telltale signs that something is wrong, as well as showcasing the need for a support system and suicide prevention.

The National Institute of Mental Health (NIMH) estimates that 51.5 million American adults, or 20.6 percent of the U.S. adult population, reported a mental health disorder as of 2019 (NIMH, 2021). Many adults who live with bouts of anxiety, stress, depression, self-harm, or suicidal ideation do not seek treatment. Mental health issues are stigmatized in many communities, with some individuals suffering in silence instead of getting help from the healthcare organizations and professionals trained to assist them. The inaction of these individuals means that some of them will be counted among the tens of thousands of suicides happening in the U.S. every year (American Foundation for Suicide Prevention, n.d.). Celebrities are susceptible to issues with mental health, and if they do not seek assistance from mental health and medical professionals, they increase the likelihood that NSSI or DSH will degrade their quality of life or end their lives.

The stigmatization of mental health, NSSI, DSH, and suicide exists in rural, urban, and suburban communities, and the celebrities who live in these communities are shaped by their environment, and their environment is shaped by them. In urban communities, a popular music genre is rap or hip-hop, and when fans search for the most popular rap or hip-hop songs heard on radio stations, uploaded to social media's curated playlists, or climbing the music charts, they are unlikely to find songs about mental health, self-harm, or suicide. Hip-hop music has multigenerational appeal, with adolescents and adults clamoring for the latest content from a multicultural array of talent across the world. Many hip-hop fans were shocked when Scott Ramon Seguro Mescudi, known by his stage name, Kid Cudi, posted this on Facebook, on October 4, 2016: "Yesterday I checked myself into rehab for depression and suicidal urges. I am not at peace." He continued, "My anxiety and depression have ruled my life for as long as I can remember and I never leave the house because of it." Moreover, he wrote, "I deserve to be happy and smiling. Why not me?" Another millennial who went public about his mental health issues was *Saturday Night Live* comedian Pete Davidson (Ledbetter, 2016), who responded to Kid Cudi's announcement regarding his mental health and suicidal urges during a candid interview on *The Breakfast Club*: "Cudi's the best of all. He saved my life. I would've killed myself if I didn't have Kid Cudi." Davidson emphasized, "It's kind of comforting to know your hero goes through the same stuff you do." He continued, "I think that's why a lot of kids my age can relate to Cudi and people love him so much because he's a very emotional dude." By sharing his truth about his mental health issues in his own words, without any filter or gatekeeper, Kid Cudi inspired Davidson to persevere and tell his story about his own "depressive streak" and anxiety issues (Ledbetter, 2016). Their storytelling resonates with many men, who may feel uncomfortable discussing mental health issues.

Members of the African-American community may consider mental health issues to be stigmatized. Many fans of Will and Jada Pinkett Smith were shocked to learn their daughter, Willow Smith, engaged in self-harm. Willow released her hit single, "Whip My Hair," in 2010, when she was 10 years old, and the song went platinum. During an episode of Pinkett Smith's Facebook series, *Red Table Talk*, called "Surviving Loss," Willow disclosed that after the fame of "Whip My Hair," she was in a "dark place." Willow elaborated on her state of mind: "After all of that kind of settled down, I was listening to a lot of dark music and it was just so crazy." She mentioned that after falling into a "black hole," she began "cutting myself and doing crazy things." Pinkett Smith revealed during the episode that she was shocked and never suspected her youngest child was self-harming. Willow showed her mother scars on her inner arms, saying, "You can't even see it. There's still a little something there. Totally lost my sanity for a moment there." Fantasia Barrino, a well-known singer and *American Idol* winner, "spoke about second chances five days before being hospitalized for an overdose" (Fernandez, 2010b). During the Los Angeles recording session for *AOL Sessions*, Barrino, then 26 years old, stated, "This album I went through a lot of things. I'm happy that it took so long—because I feel like I can't do anything without a testimony. Without it being real."

For three years, Barrino had been working on her third album. As the August 24, 2010, debut of the album neared, she seemed okay to outsiders, but on August 9, she tried to end her life by taking sleeping pills and an entire bottle of Bayer aspirin (Fernandez, 2010a). The summer before her overdose "she began filming her popular VH1 reality series, *Fantasia for Real*, an attempt to share her highs and lows as she prepared her new album, continued to be the sole caretaker of her entire family, readied to tour a final time with *The Color Purple*, earned her G.E.D. and overcame her substantial financial problems" (Fernandez, 2010a). There were rumors the single mom was seeing a married man, which garnered increased scrutiny from CNN, national magazines, and local North Carolina media when the man's wife filed for divorce and blamed Barrino for the demise of their marriage (Fernandez, 2010a). Barrino's mother called her daughter to express her pain and disappointment (Fernandez, 2010a). A spokesperson for Barrino released a statement after her overdose, which emphasized that Barrino believed the man had been separated from his wife since the summer 2009, and she was heartbroken and sorry for any pain she may have caused (Fernandez & Kennedy, 2010). On August 24, 2010, Fantasia addressed a national TV audience on *Good Morning America*, opening-up to Robin Roberts (Fisher & Sher, 2010):

> I think I was just overloaded with everything, with carrying six years of so much. I always take a licking and keep on ticking … it just became heavy for me to the point that I just wanted to be away from the noise. I think everybody feels like I tried to harm myself over a man, but you know I've been in a lot of bad relationships. I think that had something to do with it because it was so heavy, it was brand new information. I was already going through so much. But I think it was just six years of everything, of me holding all that stuff on the inside and not letting it out…. I got very, very tired.

In 2014, at the age of 29, Barrino turned to social media to refute reports that she was suicidal. She used Instagram to share a screen grab of headlines claiming she struggled to cope after her break-up with the man who she was accused of cheating with in 2010 (*Daily Mail*, 2014). Her response to reports were frank: "He and I are not together. I'm not going anywhere so stop trying to make me Dead. Lmao!!! I'm just getting started" (*Daily Mail*, 2014). In 2015, she met her husband, Kendall Taylor, whom she believes was sent from

God, saying, "I asked God for someone to pray for me—someone that could cover me and my kids … and be the man of the house," and when she met her husband she exclaimed, "That's when I knew" (Rogers, 2016). Fans and detractors of Barrino and Willow should recognize that self-harming and suicidal ideation are cyclical and tied to NSSI and DSH doers' state of mind and mental health. These behaviors are habitual, and without the intervention and care of mental health and medical professionals, some individuals, whether they are celebrities or not, will not get another chance. On March 20, 2018, on the hit TV show *Dr. Phil*, singer Demi Lovato admitted to clinical psychologist Dr. Phil McGraw that she was suicidal for the first time when she was seven. She said, "I knew that if I were to take my own life, the pain would end." She added, "I turned to cutting and there was while there where my mom was afraid to wake me up in the mornings. She didn't know if she opened the door whether I would be alive or not. Every time I cut, it got deeper and deeper." Lovato has been open about her hardships with an eating disorder, mental health issues (e.g., she was diagnosed with bipolar disorder), and self-harm in interviews with various media outlets, documentaries, MTV after-specials, public service announcements, and outreach via social media (Bried, 2012; Hughes, 2012; Larkin, 2012). Lovato is a millennial, and many of her fans are teens and twentysomethings who express their admiration and support for her online.

Simon Cowell, a judge on the TV shows *American Idol* and *The X Factor,* was criticized because of remarks he made about Lovato—a fellow *X Factor* judge—during the show. "After contestant Jeff Gutt performed Mariah Carey's 'Without You,' Paulina Rubio praised the performance, but said she wanted the rocker to 'show me blood' the next time. Cowell, in turn, asked: 'You mean you want him to cut himself'" (Raftery, 2013). Shortly thereafter, Cowell followed his remark with another piece of advice for Gutt: "stab yourself." Lovato's fans took to Twitter to voice their displeasure. Fan criticism focused on making questionable or disparaging remarks about mental health or self-harm: "Of course, joking about cutting is probably never appropriate. But when you're sitting next to someone with a well-known history of self-harm—i.e., Demi Lovato—it's especially facepalm-worthy" (Parker, 2013). Despite such instances and the highs and lows she has experienced during her battle for sobriety, Lovato has not shied away from opening up to her fans about adversity in her life, and her fans' tweets confirm their intent to stand by her (Becker, 2018). During the interview on *Dr. Phil* in 2018, the doctor stressed the need for all of us to be authentic with ourselves, as well as to be our authentic selves with others. Dr. Phil thanked Demi for being authentic, recognizing her mental health issues and sharing her experiences despite the stigma associated with needing help.

Unfortunately, on the morning of July 24, 2018, Lovato, then 25 years old, was hospitalized after apparently overdosing on an unspecified drug at her Hollywood Hills home (Schmidt, 2018). Months after the incident, Lovato returned to posting on Instagram, and she posted a letter to her fans that reads, in part: "I have always been transparent about my journey with addiction"; "What I've learned is that this illness is not something that disappears or fades with time. It is something I must continue to overcome and have not done yet" (Schmidt, 2018). Lovato's mother, Dianna De La Garza, sounded optimistic when asked about Lovato's state of mind, saying, "She's happy, she's healthy, she's working on her sobriety, and she's getting the help she needs." Her mother added that she "couldn't have asked for a better team of people to save her life" and "that, in itself, encourages me about her future and the future of our family" (Reed, 2018). Lovato and Barrino both overdosed but lived to tell their stories. Despite the potential fallout from being more transparent with the public about their struggles, they continue their use of social media to disseminate their stories to fans and the public. Media users appreciate celebrity authenticity, because increased trust between celebrities and the public contributes to mutual understanding and helps build rapport between all parties. Gradually, audiences feel more closely aligned with more accessible and "regular" celebrity protagonists. For instance, media users can reply to celebrity self-harmers' Facebook posts, Instagram stories, and tweets, having an opportunity to check in with them on a regular basis. This level of intimacy was unheard of before hyperconnectivity, social media, and online discourse communities.

Celebrity self-harmers use traditional media, too, pairing real-time, on-air rebuttals of critical judgments of their missteps with grassroots campaigning. Fans and concerned members of the public use the Internet to converge online and band together to create groups of celebrity "goodwill" ambassadors, channeling fan displeasure toward anyone who lacks empathy for the plight of celebrity self-harmers. Celebrities acknowledge the support of their online devotees, careful not to stoke outrage by intervening in their ambassadors' internal affairs. Oftentimes, celebrity protagonists with a social media presence are laissez-faire in disputes between their ambassadors and the focus of their ire. These fans do online and offline outreach on behalf of their celebrity protagonists, which enables celebrities such as celebrity self-harmers to amplify their message to a broader audience. Healthcare organizations and health communication specialists should work with the media to monitor and ameliorate personal celebrity outreach, fan outreach, and sensationalistic media coverage to combat the "Werther effect" for NSSI, DSH, and suicide.

When Robin Williams committed suicide, the potential for the "Werther effect" to transpire increased. On August 11, 2014, Williams, a 63-year-old resident of unincorporated Tiburon, California, was pronounced deceased at the scene (Mejia, 2014). Williams's wife, Susan Schneider, released a statement: "This morning, I lost my husband and best friend, while the world lost one of its most beloved artists and beautiful human beings. I am utterly heartbroken"; "…we are asking for privacy during our time of profound grief" (Mejua, 2014). It is understandable for family and friends in mourning to ask for privacy, but when the decedent is a celebrity, especially a superstar like Williams, the public's fascination, and the media's inclination to fill the void or news vacuum with the most sensationalistic information about a celebrity's life and death can intrude upon a grieving family's most solemn moments. Many of the news stories during these times are meant to grab attention, and in some instances the rush to sensationalize the life and suicide of a celebrity inspires more mentally or emotionally vulnerable members of society to take their lives. Hence, "copycat" suicides occur, with media users taking information from media coverage and using it to copy the suicidal behavior of their celebrity muse.

This phenomenon is known as the "Werther's effect," and there are precautions that the media can take to mitigate copycatting and instead bolster health education about mental health and suicide prevention. A study by Carpentier and Parrott (2016) based on public responses to the aftermath of Williams's suicide identified strategies for harnessing the power of celebrity disclosures (e.g., an interview of a celebrity self-harmer or news coverage of a celebrity suicide) to improve how healthcare professionals and the media communicate with the public. Strategies from the study that have positive implications were (Carpentier & Parrot, 2016, p. 1342):

(1) First, the best placement of messages appears to be with existing material about the celebrity event. Respondents primarily sought information about Robin Williams's suicide, depression, and career. Fewer responses sought general information about mental health, suicide, or depression. Specifically, this study suggests an opportunity to educate and encourage conversation among the young adult population about depression and suicide with messages inserted within news sites and Twitter feeds reporting the event, websites about the celebrity and his or her existing works, and Facebook pages dedicated to the celebrity.

(2) Thus, the second major implication of this study is that efforts might be better placed with online and mobile outlets rather than large-scale television campaigns. Recall that the bulk of information seeking for these respondents occurred the day of the announcement and lasted no more than an hour.

(3) The third major implication of this study is that messages in places focusing on the event should acknowledge the emotional states of the media consumer. According to this study, people visiting news sites about Williams's death were likely feeling distressed by the news. Thus, a message placed within a page of information highlighting the death might be more effective if the message

responds to the emotional distress by offering empathy or solace. People visiting existing sites about celebrity's career or performances … might not be driven by emotional distress. Rather, curiosity or memory enhancement might be stronger motivators for this type of information search, rather than emotional distress. In these venues, health messages might not need to acknowledge or reflect negative emotions in the same way messages in venues focusing on the death might need to be crafted.

(4) The final implication of this study is to drive online traffic from news-oriented, social media-oriented, and celebrity focused digital media venues to educational websites about mental health.

A good example of a website with news stories about celebrity deaths is CNN.com. CNN.com covered the death of Anthony Bourdain, whose show *Anthony Bourdain: Parts Unknown* aired on CNN for five years. Bourdain, who committed suicide in June 2018, was known as the "Elvis of bad boy chefs." The Smithsonian once called him "the original rock star" of the culinary world (Stelter, 2018). Bourdain's shows won awards like the Peabody, taking him to more than 100 countries and three networks, where he showcased that through sharing a meal we can appreciate our extraordinary diversity of cultures and cuisines and how much we all have in common (Stelter, 2018). On June 8, 2018, Brian Stelter, author of the Bourdain news story, included at the end of his piece the following excerpt:

> How to get help: In the US, call the National Suicide Prevention Lifeline at 1-800-273-8255. The International Association for Suicide Prevention and Befrienders Worldwide also can provide contact information for crisis centers around the world.

The news story also included the following information about suicide and its increased prevalence throughout the U.S. (Stelter, 2018):

> Suicide is a growing problem in the United States. The US Centers for Disease Control and Prevention published a survey Thursday showing suicide rates increased by 25% across the country over nearly two decades ending in 2016. Twenty-five states experienced a rise in suicides by more than 30%, the government report finds.

This information was sandwiched between Bourdain media coverage meant to entice curious media users, including his stance regarding #MeToo, when Bourdain stood unhesitantly and unwaveringly with women, and reverence for his advocacy for marginalized populations, especially his campaign for safer working conditions for staff in the restaurant industry. News seekers who were more than curious about Bourdain's death and media users who were distressed by his death noticed information acknowledging their emotional state (Stelter, 2018):

Bourdain's death shook television viewers around the world. The most common sentiment: "I feel like I've lost a friend." The news of Bourdain's death was met by profound sadness within CNN, where "Parts Unknown" has aired for the past five years. In an email to employees, the network's President, Jeff Zucker, remembered him as an "exceptional talent."

Despite taglines such as "From 'happy dishwasher' to addiction to fame" and "The Elvis of bad boy chefs," the copy that followed these taglines gave media users insight into what the man was all about (Stelter, 2018): "I jokingly say that I learned every important lesson, all the most important lessons of my life, as a dishwasher"; "In America, the professional kitchen is the last refuge of the misfit. It's a place for people with bad pasts to find a new family"; "His good friend Michael Ruhlman said he was stunned by news of the suicide. 'The last I knew, he was in love. He was happy,'" Ruhlman told CNN's *Anderson Cooper 360*. "He said, 'Love abounds'—some of the last words he said to me."

The suicides of Bourdain and fashion designer Kate Spade stunned and saddened their millions of fans and left the public bewildered about what happened. However, the survivors of suicide used social media to share their stories, which gave individuals who had never had suicide ideation or self-harmed insight into what goes through a person's mind in these circumstances. When media users feel alone, social media provides access to heartbreak, despair, empathy, and understanding—a reflection of themselves in others, forging kinship through gestures both small and large, with the ability to save lives one tweet, post, or thread at a time (Klein, 2018). Online news stories also aided people who were more susceptible to the "Werther's effect" by including information about a suicide hotline somewhere in the coverage of the celebrity's suicide. In a Newsweek.com story by Zach Schonfeld (2017) about Chester Bennington's suicide, there was discussion among suicide experts about fear of a contagion effect, so the end of the story stated: "Please call the National Suicide Prevention Hotline if you or anyone you know is at risk: 1-800-273-8255. Suicide warning signs are listed here" (the underlined words were hyperlinks to additional information about the National Suicide Prevention Hotline and a list of suicide warning signs). Many online news stories provided similar information as the Newsweek.com story, which contributed a 14 percent spike in calls to the National Suicide Prevention Hotline the day after news of Bennington's suicide (Grow, 2017). Suicide hotline calls were up 25 percent following the deaths of Bourdain and Spade. The Crisis Text Line, an organization that allows people to text 741-741 or send messages through its Facebook page in order communicate with a crisis counselor, noted that contacts increased 115 percent from the week before the suicides of Bourdain and Spade (Golgowski, 2018). "The top two emotions texters discussed were scared and pained," Liz Eddy, Crisis Text Line's director of communications, told HuffPost (Golgowski, 2018). Two months after Robin Williams' death, suicide hotlines were still experiencing a spike in calls (Schonfeld, 2014).

Rise in Self-Harm and Suicide Challenge Status Quo

Researchers who worked on the study *Trends in Emergency for Non-fatal Self-Inflicted Injuries Among Youth Aged 10 to 24 Years in the United States, 2001–2015* analyzed emergency department visit rates for self-infliction for patients 10 to 24 years old (Mercado et al., 2017). Findings indicated there was a steady rate of incidences from 2001 to 2007, but mid-way through 2008 there was a boom in nonfatal self-inflicted injuries. These findings are applicable to trends in NSSI and DSH in other countries. In 2016, British cabinet member and former Health Secretary Jeremy Hunt severely criticized the National Health Service's care of troubled young people. "Child and adolescent mental health services (CAMHS) were the 'biggest single area of weakness in NHS provision,' and beset by 'big problems,' including failure to intervene early enough when problems such as eating disorders emerged, which meant that 'too many tragedies' were occurring," he said (Campbell, 2016). Moreover, in 2016, Sarah Brennan, then chief executive of YoungMinds, identified inadequate assistance and lack of specialist support for youth, where it is apparent they have psychological problems. She echoed the sentiments of the American study: "It's extremely worrying that the number of young people needing hospital treatment for self-harm has risen sharply. There needs to be far more investment in early intervention, so that problems are dealt with when they first emerge" (Campbell, 2016). DSH can lead to loss of life, and the healthcare system seems unprepared or too inflexible to adapt to rising rates in self-harm and suicide.

Dr. Kelly Posner helped develop the Columbia-Suicide Severity Rating Scale, and her research focuses on the identification of people with suicidal leanings and ensuring help is available. Dr. Posner pointed out that more policemen die of suicide than die on the job; more soldiers die of suicide than in combat; and more firefighters die of suicide than die in fires (Solomon, 2018). She champions prevention as a crucial step in saving the lives of adolescents, media users, soldiers, and first responders, who are engaged in behavior that harms their body and increases their mortality. Dr. Posner maintains: "If we don't ask and monitor, we have a lost opportunity for prevention. There's a dangerous myth, if you ask people about suicidal feelings, it causes people to become suicidal; in fact they are relieved.

Aggressive screening could be transformative" (Solomon, 2018). According to the WHO's 2014 global report on preventing suicide, the number of countries with an established surveillance system for suicide attempts is limited. The WHO's *Practical Manual for Establishing and Maintaining Surveillance Systems for Suicide Attempts and Self-Harm* is a tool that general hospitals in various countries can use to establish surveillance systems for suicide attempts and self-harm, based on medical records. Medical records play a vital role in these systems, because they catalogue suicide attempts presented to healthcare facilities (usually hospitals), and these records help healthcare professionals identifying and addressing "...knowledge gaps and improving service provision for individuals presenting to hospitals following attempted suicide and self-harm" (WHO, 2016, p. 8). These medical records enable a hospital-focused surveillance system to examine cases of NSSI and DSH and determine varying levels of self-harm and suicidal intent, and varying underlying motives, beyond only suicide attempts characterized by high levels of suicidal intent.

In most low- and middle-income countries (e.g., India, Jamaica, etc.) hospital-focused surveillance systems do not exist, so these countries must build upon local registries of suicide attempts at a patchwork of local and regional hospitals and coalesce these registries into dedicated hospital-based surveillance systems of self-harm and suicide attempts. Even in countries with hospital-focused surveillance systems such as Ireland to subnational registries in Ireland's neighbors the U.K. and Northern Ireland, "comparison between established systems is often hindered by difference between systems" (WHO, 2016, p. 5). Many national systems for suicide prevention surveillance include data coded using the *International Classification of Diseases* (ICD). The ICD is maintained by the WHO, and it provides an international standard for the classification of diseases and medical conditions. Over the decades, the ICD has been revised, with the U.S. using Tenth Revision (ICD-10) for classification of deaths, and the clinical modification of the Tenth Revision (ICD-10-CM) for classification of nonfatal events requiring medical care (e.g., hospitalizations or emergency department visits). The power of ICD-10-CM is "if an event is recorded a particular way it may influence how the event is described in medical documentation. If the medial record does not provide sufficient supporting documentation," which the clinician should provide, "an ICD-10-CM code for intentional self-harm might not be assigned" (Hedegaard et al., 2018, p. 4).

For example, an adolescent patient who has attempted suicide should be assessed by a clinician. The clinician conducts an interview with the patient, parents, relatives, and other influential individuals in the patient's life. These individuals and any evidence collected pertaining to the attempted suicide contribute to a clinician's fact-finding investigation and risk assessment. A piece of evidence that would elaborate on the circumstances that contributed to the suicide attempt would be a handwritten suicide note. The handwritten suicide note should impart knowledge regarding the patient's state of mind and condition, so the clinician can put this information in the patient's medical documentation and use it to assign an ICD-10-CM code for intentional self-harm. Yet, if there is no handwritten suicide note, and family members were unaware there was a problem, the clinician might not attribute the adolescent patient's behavior to self-harm. The clinician could justify not assigning the ICD-10-CM code for self-harm for this patient's emergency department visit. In this scenario, the patient will be harmed because the care provided will be different than if the patient was correctly diagnosed as a self-harmer or suicidal, and the data will be inaccurate, because the case was not properly coded. The hospital-focused surveillance system is only as good as its data.

With different national standards, comparing data sets and coding across countries is difficult. Moreover, the level of complexity within a country can be daunting. A lack of a federal requirement in the U.S. has further complicated the coding process, where some states allow voluntary reporting, other states have mandates, and healthcare systems or facilities may have policies requiring external cause coding, all of which undermine the completeness and quality of ICD coding (Hedegaard et al., 2018). Until these factors are addressed in a comprehensive manner, variations from to state to state and facility to facility will adversely affect the accuracy of external cause coding. Healthcare professionals worked with the federal government to address this issue in Healthy People 2020, shifting focus to "…increasing the percentage of states (and the District of Columbia) with statewide hospital discharge data systems that routinely collect external cause of injury codes for 90% or more of injury-related discharges" (Hedegaard et al., 2018, p, 4).

Knowledge is power, and within the context of self-harm and suicide, it may be the difference between life and death. Interventions can be a useful and effective means of delivering persuasive information to clinicians, patients, self-harmers and their families, friends, and community members. For example, an intervention could educate clinicians that the handwritten suicide note is becoming a thing of the past. Social media is pervasive for everyone, not only adolescents, so emergency physicians need to search for e-suicide notes. Review of a patient's text messages and social networking accounts should be used by healthcare providers to confirm a patient's identity and history (Chhabra & Bryant, 2016). Applications such as Snapchat have been used to identify, provide context, and affect treatment in instances of DSH. Furthermore, self-harmers and their loved ones, especially those coping with mental health histories which make them susceptible to NSSI or DSH, could use interventions that educate them about clinical considerations for the patient and family, including counseling regarding the disinhibiting effects of drugs or alcohol, securing or removing firearms and lethal medications and substances, ensuring a supportive person is at home, and scheduling follow-up appointments (Jans et al., 2012, p. 22).

Professional association interventions for healthcare providers should emphasize that during an emergency department visit, before treatment ends and before discharging the patient, it is important for emergency department staff and any primary care providers or referrals consulted during the patient's hospitalization to have "...prepared a plan to deal with the crisis, making sure that supporting contact (e.g., telephone) is available 24 hours a day" (Jans et al., 2012, p. 21–22). Healthcare providers, patients, and their families could benefit from interventions that delineate between inpatient and outpatient services. In some instances, inpatient treatment or hospitalization is required to address suicidality and recurring events. However, outpatient treatment is possible when healthcare providers and a family agree it is the best course of action for the patient. Daniel and Goldston (2009) identify other useful measures ranging from interventions to foster help-seeking behaviors and improve follow-up to organizing support for the suicidal youth to strategies to improve parent-child relationships.

References

American Foundation for Suicide Prevention (n.d.). *Suicide statistics.* https://afsp.org/suicide-statistics.

American Psychiatry Association. (2013). *Diagnostic and Statistical Manual of Mental Disorders (5th ed.)—DSM-5.* American Psychiatry Association.

Arendt, F., Till, B., & Niederkrotenthaler, T. (2016). Effects of suicide awareness material on implicit suicide cognition: A laboratory experiment. *Health Communication, 31(6)*, 718–726. http://dx.doi.org/10.1080/10410236.2014.993495.

Becker, H.A. (2018, March 16). *Tweets about Demi Lovato's sobriety are so emotional & fans are so supportive.* Elite Daily. https://www.elitedaily.com/p/tweets-about-demi-lovatos-sobriety-are-so-emotional-fans-are-so-supportive-8520906.

Bowen, A., & John, A. (2001). Gender differences in presentation and conceptualization of adolescent self-injurious behavior: Implications for therapeutic practice. *Counselling Psychology Quarterly, 14(4)*, 357–379. http://dx.doi.org/10.1080/09515070110100956.

Bried, E. (2012, August 17). Demi Lovato opens up. *Self Magazine.* https://www.self.com/gallery/demi-lovato-opens-up-slideshow.

Brody, J.E. (2008, May 6). The growing wave of teenage self-injury. *New York Times.* https://www.nytimes.com/2008/05/06/health/06brod.html.

Campbell, D. (2016, October 31). NHS figures show "shocking" rise in self-harm among young. *The Guardian.* https://www.theguardian.com/society/2016/oct/23/nhs-figures-show-shocking-rise-self-harm-young-people.

Carlyle, K.E., Guidry, J.P.D., Williams, K., Tabaac, A., & Perrin, P.B. (2018). Suicide conversations on Instagram™: Contagion or caring? *Journal of Communication in Healthcare, 11(1)*, 12–18. https://doi.org/10.1080/17538068.2018.1436500.

CBS News. (2018, June 11). *Kate Spade, renowned fashion designer, dead in apparent suicide.* https://www.cbsnews.com/news/kate-spade-fashion-designer-dead-in-suicide-police-say-2018-06-05/.

Centers for Disease Control and Prevention. (2018, June 7). *Suicide rising across the US: More than a mental health concern.* National Center for Injury Prevention and Control. https://www.cdc.gov/vitalsigns/suicide/index.html.

Centers for Disease Control and Prevention. (2020, July 1). *Web-based Injury Statistics Query and Reporting System (WISQARS).* National Center for Injury Prevention and Control. https://www.cdc.gov/injury/wisqars/fatal.html.

Chhabra, N., & Bryant, S.M. (2016). Snapchat toxicology: Social media and suicide. *Annals of Emergency Medicine, 68(4),* 527. https://doi.org/10.1016/j.annemergmed.2016.05.031.

Choi, Y.J., & Oh, Hyungna (2016). Does media coverage of a celebrity suicide trigger copycat suicides? Evidence from Korean cases. *Journal of Media Economics, 29(2),* 92–105. http://dx.doi.org/10.1080/08997764.2016.1170020.

Cincinnati Children's Hospital Medical Center. (2016, August 31). High rates of suicide and self-harm among transgender youth. *ScienceDaily.* www.sciencedaily.com/releases/2016/08/160831110833.htm.

Cohen, G.L., & Sherman, D.K. (2014). The psychology of change: Self-affirmation and social psychological intervention. *Annual Review of Psychology, 65,* 333–371. https://doi.org/10.1146/annurev-psych-010213-115137.

Cudi, K. (n.d.) Home [Facebook page]. Facebook. Retrieved January 24, 2021, from https://www.facebook.com/kidcudi/posts/its-been-difficult-for-me-to-find-the-words-to-what-im-about-to-share-with-you-b/10154706102758586/.

Dahlberg, L.L., & Krug, E.G. (2002). Violence: A global public health problem. In E.G. Krug, L.L. Dahlberg, J.A. Mercy, A.B. Zwi, & R. Lozano (Eds.), *World Report on Violence and Health* (pp. 1–21). WHO Press.

Daily Mail Reporter. (2014, January 2). *"Stop trying to make me dead!" Fantasia Barrino turns to social media to slam reports that she's suicidal.* https://www.dailymail.co.uk/tvshowbiz/article-2533029/Fantasia-Barrino-turns-social-media-slam-reports-shes-suicidal.html.

Daniel, S., & Goldston, D. (2009). Interventions for suicidal youth: A review of the literature and developmental considerations. *Suicide & Life Threatening Behavior, 39(3),* 252–268. https://doi.org/10.1521/suli.2009.39.3.252.

Diller, L. (2018, February 28). Why are so many of my teen patients cutting themselves? We need to fix this now. *USA Today.* https://www.usatoday.com/story/opinion/2018/02/28/social-media-one-reason-my-teen-patients-cutting-themselves-lawrence-diller-column/376741002/.

Dillman Capentier, F.R., & Parrott, M.S. (2016). Young adults' information seeking following celebrity suicide: Considering involvement with celebrity and emotional distress in health communication strategies. *Health Communication, 31(11),* 1334–1344. http://dx.doi.org/10.1080/10410236.2015.10563293.

Dubin, A. (2018, November 30). *Eric Ripert speaks out for the first time since discovering friend Anthony Bourdain dead by suicide.* Bravo TV. https://www.bravotv.com/top-chef/the-feast/eric-ripert-speaks-out-for-first-time-since-anthony-bourdain-suicide-in-france.

Fernandez, M.E. (2010a, August 27). Fantasia Barrino opens up about her dark days and her painful healing process. *Los Angeles Times.* https://www.latimes.com/archives/la-xpm-2010-aug-27-la-et-fantasia-barrino-opens-up-0827-story.html.

Fernandez, M.E. (2010b, August 11). Days before her hospitalization, Fantasia Barrino vowed to get "back to herself." *Los Angeles Times.* https://latimesblogs.latimes.com/music_blog/2010/08/fantasia-barrino-vowed-to-get-back-to-herself-before-overdose.html.

Fernandez, M.E., & Kennedy, G.D. (2010, August 10). American Idol, Fantasia Barrino hospitalized after overdose but is in stable condition. *Los Angeles Times.* https://latimesblogs.latimes.com/showtracker/2010/08/american-idol-fantasia-barrino-hospitalized-after-overdose.html.

Fisher, L., & Sher, L. (2010, August 24). *Fantasia Barrino on Suicide Attempt: "I Just Wanted to Be Away from the Noise."* ABC News. https://abcnews.go.com/Entertainment/fantasia-barrino-suicide-attempt-abc-news-exclusive/story?id=11466950.

Forty-Ninth World Health Assembly. (1996, May 20–25). *Resolution WHA49.25—Prevention of violence: A public health priority.* World Health Assembly. https://www.who.int/violence_injury_prevention/resources/publications/en/WHA4925_e ng.pdf.

Glenn, J.J., Werntz, A.J., Katerina Slama, S.J., Steinman, S.A., Teachman, B.A., & Nock, M.K. (2017). Suicide and self-injury-related implicit cognition: A large-scale examination and replication. *Journal of Abnormal Psychology, 126(2)*, 199–211. http://dx.doi.org/10.1037/abn 0000230.

Golgowski, N. (2018, June 11). *Calls to suicide hotlines rise sharply after celebrity deaths.* Huff-Post. https://www.huffpost.com/entry/calls-to-suicide-hotlines-rise-sharply-after-celebrity-deaths_n_5b1e89dbe4b0bbb7a0dfb768.

Grow, K. (2017, August 4). Chester Bennington's last days. Linkin Park singer's mix of hope, heaviness. *Rolling Stone.* https://www.rollingstone.com/music/music-news/chester-benningtons-last-days-linkin-park-singers-mix-of-hope-heaviness-124862/.

Harvey, K., & Brown, B. (2012). Health communication and psychological distress: Exploring the language of self-harm. *The Canadian Modern Language Review, 68(3)*, 316–340. https://doi.org/10.3138/cmlr.1103.

Hawton, K., Rodham, K., Evans, E., & Weatherall, R. (2002). Deliberate self harm in adolescents: Self report survey in schools in England. *British Medical Journal, 325(7374)*, 1207–1211. http://dx.doi.org/10.1136/bmj.325.7374.1207.

Hedegaard, H., Schoenbaum, M., Claassen, C., Crosby, A., Holland, K.M., & Proescholdbell, S. (2018). Issues in developing a surveillance case definition for nonfatal suicide attempt and intentional self-harm using International Classification of Diseases, Tenth Revision, Clinical Modification (ICD-10-CM) coded data. *National Health Statistics Reports, 108*, 1–19. https://www.cdc.gov/nchs/data/nhsr/nhsr108.pdf.

Hoffman, R., Hinkle, M.G., & Kress, V.W. (2010). Letter writing as an intervention in family therapy with adolescents who engage in nonsuicidal self-injury. *The Family Journal: Counseling and Therapy for Couples and Families, 18(1)*, 24–30. https://doi.org/10.1177/1066480709355039.

Hughes, S.A. (2012, March 7). Demi Lovato talks about ongoing battle with eating disorder, self-harm on special "Stay Strong" (video). *The Washington Post.* https://www.washingtonpost.com/blogs/celebritology/post/demi-lovato-talks-about-ongoing-battle-with-eating-disorder-self-harm-on-special-stay-strong-video/2012/03/07/gIQAzAFJxR_blog.html.

Hunter, G. (2018, May 21). Chris Cornell widow rips probe year after Detroit death. *The Detroit News.* https://www.detroitnews.com/story/entertainment/people/2018/05/15/chris-cornell-widow-rips-probe-detroit-death/34918321/.

Jans, T., Taneli, Y., & Warnke, A. (2012). Suicide and self-harming behavior. In J.M. Rey (Ed.), *IACAPAP e-Textbook of Child and Adolescent Mental Health* (pp. 1–35). International Association for Child and Adolescent Psychiatry and Allied Professions.

Johnson, B.K., Slater, M.D., Silver, N.A., & Ewoldsen, D.R. (2016). Entertainment and expanding boundaries of the self: Relief from the constraints of the everyday. *Journal of Communication, 66(3)*, 386–408. https://doi.org/10.1111/jcom.12228.

Kim, S., & Gal, D. (2014). From compensatory consumption to adaptive consumption: The role of self-acceptance in resolving self-deficits. *Journal of Consumer Research, 41(2)*, 526–542. https://doi.org/10.1086/676681.

Klein, A. (2018, June 11). After Anthony Bourdain and Kate Spade suicides, social media lit up with survivors' stories. *The Washington Post.* https://www.washingtonpost.com/news/inspired-life/wp/2018/06/11/after-anthony-bourdain-and-kate-spade-suicides-social-media-lights-up-with-survivors-stories-of-how-they-made-it-through/.

Krug, E.G., Dahlberg, L.L., Mercy, J.A., Zwi, A.B., & Lozano, R. (Eds.). (2002). *World report on violence and health.* WHO Press. https://www.who.int/violence_injury_prevention/violence/world_report/en/full_en.pdf?u a=1.

Leavitt, R.A., Ertl, A., Sheats, K, Petrosky, E., Ivey-Stepohnson, A., & Fowler, K.A. (2018). Suicides among American Indian/Alaska Natives—National violent death reporting system, 18 states, 2003–2014. *Morbidity and Mortality Weekly Report, 67(8)*, 237–242. https://doi.org/15585/mmwr.mm6708a1.

Ledbetter, C. (2016, October 26). *Pete Davidson of "Saturday Night Live" says Kid Cudi "Saved My Life."* Huff Post. https://www.huffpost.com/entry/saturday-night-live-pete-davidson-kid-cudi_n_5810ad2ce4b02b1d9e63dbc1.

Lewallen, J., Miller, B., & Behm-Morawitz, E. (2016). Lifestyles of the rich and famous: Celebrity media diet and the cultivation of emerging adults' materialism. *Mass Communication and Society, 19(3)*, 253–274. https://doi.org/10.1080/15205436.2015.1096945.

Lopez, A.D., Mathers, C.D., Ezzati, M., Jamison, D.T., & Murray, C.J.L. (Eds.). (2006). *Global Burden of Disease and Risk Factors.* Oxford University Press.

Luxton, D.D., June, J.D., & Fairall, J.M. (2012). Social media and suicide: A public health perspective. *American Journal of Public Health, 102(S2)*, S195-S200. https://doi.org/10.2105/AJPH.2011.300608.

Martin, G., Swannell, S.V., Hazell, P.L., Harrison, J.E., & Taylor, A.W. (2010). Self-injury in Australia: A community survey. *The Medical Journal of Australia, 193(9)*, 506–510. https://doi.org/10.5694/j.1326-5377.2010.tb04033.x.

Mazziotta, J. (2018, June 11). Suicide hotline calls jumped 25 percent following deaths of Anthony Bourdain and Kate Spade. *People Magazine.* https://people.com/health/suicide-hotline-calls-up-25-percent-anthony-bourdain-kate-spade-deaths/.

McGraw, P. [Dr. Phil Show]. (2018, March 20). *Demi Lovato on contemplating suicide at 7: "I had this fascination with death"* [Video]. YouTube. https://www.youtube.com/watch?v=XCBZHnZw6rI.

Meijia, P. (2014, August 11). Robin Williams found dead in California home. *Newsweek.* https://www.newsweek.com/robin-williams-found-dead-california-home-264021#:~:text=Actor%20and%20comedian%20Robin%20Williams,been%20a%20suici de%20by%20asphyxiation.

Mental Health Foundation. (2006). *Truth hurts—Report of the national inquiry into self-harm among young people.* Mental Health Foundation. https://www.mentalhealth.org.uk/sites/default/files/truth_hurts.pdf.

Mercado, M.C., Holland, K., Leemis, R.W., Stone, D.M., & Wang, J. (2017). Trends in emergency department visits for nonfatal self-inflicted injuries among youth aged 10 to 24 years in the United States, 2001–2015. *JAMA, 318(19)*, 1931–1933. https://doi.org/10.1001/jama.2017.13317.

Messzaros, G., Horvath, L.O., & Balazs, J. (2017). Self-injury and externalizing pathology: A systematic literature review. *BMC Psychiatry, 17(1)*, 160–180. https://doi.org/10.1186/s12888-017-1326-y.

Miller, K. (2017, September 15). Chester Bennington's son appears in 2 moving suicide prevention videos. *Self Magazine.* https://www.self.com/story/chester-benningtons-son-appears-in-moving-suicide-prevention-videos.

Naito, A. (2007). Internet suicide in Japan: Implications for child and adolescent mental health. *Clinical Child Psychology and Psychiatry, 12(4)*, 583–597. https://doi.org/10.1177/1359104507080990.

National Institute of Mental Health. (2021, January 5). *Mental illness.* https://www.nimh.nih.gov/health/statistics/mental-illness.shtml.

Niederkrotenthaler, T., Voracek, M., Herberth, A., Till, B., Strauss, M., Etzersdorfer, E., Eisenwort, B., & Sonneck, G. (2010). Role of media reports in completed and prevented suicide: Werther v. Papageno effects. *The British Journal of Psychiatry, 197(3)*, 234–243. https://doi.org/10.1192/bjp.bp.109.074633.

Ozawa-de Silva, C. (2008). Too lonely to die alone: Internet suicide pacts and existential suffering in Japan. *Culture, Medicine, and Psychiatry, 32(4)*, 516–551. https://doi.org/10.1007/s11013-008-9108-0.

Parker, L. (2013, December 4). *Simon Cowell jokes about cutting ... in front of Demi Lovato.* Yahoo. https://www.yahoo.com/entertainment/blogs/tv-news/simon-cowell-jokes-cutting-front-demi-lovato-033356768.html?_devicefull.

Parks, S.E., Johnson L.L., McDaniel, D.D., & Gladden, M. (2014). Surveillance for Violent Deaths—National Violent Death Reporting System, 16 states, 2010. *Morbidity and Mortality Weekly Report, 63(ss01)*, 1–33. http://www.cdc.gov/mmwr/preview/mmwrhtml/ss6301a1.htm.

Peele, S. (2018, October 7). What killed Anthony Bourdain. *Psychology Today.* https://www.psychologytoday.com/us/blog/addiction-in-society/201810/what-killed-anthony-bourdain.

Raftery, L. (2013, December 5). Simon Cowell jokes about cutting, enrages Demi Lovato fans. *TV Guide.* https://www.tvguide.com/news/simon-cowell-x-factor-cutting-demi-lovato-1074262/.

Rajendra, R., Krishna, M., Majgi, S., Heggere, N., Robinson, C., & Poole, R. (2015). A feasibility study to establish a deliberate self-harm register in a state hospital in southern India. *British Journal of Medical Practitioners, 8(1),* 43–48.

Rapaport, L. (2018, March 20). *Guns tied to high suicide risk for teens with self-harm history.*

Red Table Talk—Surviving Loss (n.d.). Home [Facebook page]. Facebook. Retrieved January 24, 2021, from https://www.facebook.com/redtabletalk/videos/surviving-loss/564337 010632445/.

Reed, A. (2018, September 19). Demi Lovato's mom recounts singer's overdose: I didn't know "if she was going to make it." *USA Today.* https://www.usatoday.com/story/life/people/2018/09/19/demi-lovatos-mom-opens-up-singers-overdose-didnt-know-if-she-going-make-not/1355453002/.

Reuters. https://www.reuters.com/article/us-health-teens-suicide-risks/guns-tied-to-high-suicide-risk-for-teens-with-self-harm-history-idUSKBN1GW2Z0.

Rogers, R. (2016, July 21). Fantasia opens up about her suicide attempt: "I was a broken woman." *Billboard Magazine.* https://sports.yahoo.com/news/fantasia-opens-her-suicide-attempt-broken-woman-215734297.html.

Roh, B., Jung, E.H., & Hong, H.J. (2018). A comparative study of suicide rates among 10–19-year-olds in 29 OECD countries. *Psychiatry Investigation, 15(4),* 376–383. https://doi.org/10.30773/pi.2017.08.02.

Rosenberg, M.L., et al. (2006). Chapter 40: Interpersonal violence. In D.T. Jamison et al. (Eds.), *Disease control priorities in developing countries* (2nd ed.; pp. 755–770). The International Bank for Reconstruction and Development/The World Bank.

Schmidt, S. (2018, August 6). Demi Lovato breaks silence after apparent drug overdose: "I will keep fighting." *The Washington Post.* https://www.washingtonpost.com/news/morning-mix/wp/2018/08/06/demi-lovato-breaks-silence-after-apparent-drug-overdose-i-will-keep-fighting/.

Schonfeld, Z. (2014, October 12). Two months after Robin Williams' death, suicide hotlines still see a spike in calls. *Newsweek.* https://www.newsweek.com/two-months-after-robin-williams-death-suicide-hotlines-still-see-spike-276813.

Schonfeld, Z. (2017, July 20). After Chester Bennington's death, suicide experts fear a contagion effect. *Newsweek.* https://www.newsweek.com/chester-bennington-suicide-linkin-park-chris-cornell-639940.

Simeon, D., & Hollander, E. (Eds.). (2001). *Self-injurious behaviors, assessment and treatment.* American Psychiatric Publishing.

Solomon, A. (2018, June 8). Anthony Bourdain, Kate Spade, and the preventable tragedies of suicide. *The New Yorker.* https://www.newyorker.com/news/daily-comment/preventable-tragedies.

Stelter, B. (2018). *CNN's Anthony Bourdain dead at 61.* CNN. https://www.cnn.com/2018/06/08/us/anthony-bourdain-obit/index.html.

Stone, D.M., Simon, T.R., Fowler, K.A., Kegler, S.R., Yuan, K., Holland, K.M., Ivy-Stephenson, A.Z., & Crosby, A.E. (2018). Vital signs: Trends in state suicide rates—United States, 1999–2016 and circumstances contributing to suicide—27 states, 2015. *Morbidity and Mortality Weekly Report, 67(22),* 617–624. https://www.cdc.gov/mmwr/volumes/67/wr/mm6722a1.htm.

Twenge, J.M. (2017, November 21). 5 reasons why self-harm and depression have tripled in girls. *Psychology Today.* https://www.psychologytoday.com/us/blog/our-changing-culture/201711/5-reasons-why-self-harm-and-depression-have-tripled-in-girls.

United States Public Health Service. (1999). *The Surgeon General's call to action to prevent suicide.* Department of Health and Human Services, U.S. Public Health Service. https://www.sprc.org/resources-programs/surgeon-generals-call-action-prevent-suicide.

Vaziri, A. (2017, May 18). *Chris Cornell: The startling suicide of an eclectic talent.* SF Gate. https://www.sfgate.com/music/article/Soundgarden-frontman-Chris-Cornell-dead-at-52-11156288.php.

Walsh, B. (2007). Clinical assessment of self-injury: A practical guide. *Journal of Clinical Psychology: In session, 63(11),* 1057–1068. https://doi.org/10.1002/jclp.20413.

Westerlund, M. (2013). Talking suicide: Online conversations about a taboo subject. *Nordicom Review, 34(2),* 35–46. https://doi.org/10.2478/nor-2013-0052.

World Health Organization. (2014). *Preventing suicide: A global imperative*. WHO Press. https://www.who.int/mental_health/suicide-prevention/exe_summary_english.pdf?ua=1.

World Health Organization. (2016). *Practice manual for establishing and maintaining surveillance systems for suicide attempts and self-harm*. WHO Press. https://apps.who.int/iris/bitstream/handle/10665/208895/9789241549578_eng.pdf?sequence=1&isAllowed=y.

Ystgaard, M., Arensman, E., Hawton, K., Madge, N., van Heeringen, K., Hewitt, A., Jan de Wilde, E., De Leo, D., & Fekete, S. (2009). Deliberate self-harm in adolescents: Comparison between those who receive help following self-harm and those who do not. *Journal of Adolescence, 32(4)*, 875–891. http://dx.doi.org/10.1016/j.adolescence.2008.10.010. Medline:19028399gg.

2

Rihanna Survives
Intimate Partner Violence

Domestic violence has existed for thousands of years. However, before the 1970s, no terms existed to describe the problem. Couples, families, communities, and countries emphasized the private nature of domestic disputes: "the problem hovered behind the closed curtains of private family life" (Ashcraft, 2019, p. 3). On this issue, the cultural norms of the "common man" and well-to-do were in accord, as there was uniform agreement that society was never to intrude upon the "domestic forum." Leave it to individual parties to resolve disagreements—do not undercut the mirage of domestic tranquility, where violence plays no part in family life (Dobash & Dobash, 1979; Wardell et al., 1983). The battered women's movement was in response to a society that pretended battered women did not exist, or that if they did exist, they should contend with the problem in private. Gradually, women challenged the status quo, "not only to increase awareness of and assistance for the plight of the abused woman but also to gain public acceptance of a reinterpretation of the nature of domestic violence" (Ashcraft, 2019, p. 4). In 2003, the CDC defined domestic violence as physical, sexual, or psychological harm by a current or former partner that can occur among heterosexual or same-sex couples and does not require sexual intimacy. According to UNICEF (2000), domestic violence is any gender-based violence contributing to the harm or suffering of female victims and survivors, including threats of violence, coercion, or arbitrary deprivation of liberty, occurring in public or private places and spaces (e.g., in a place built of brick and mortar, an online community, etc.). Each year, an estimated 5.3 million incidents of domestic violence occur within the U.S., which results in approximately 2 million injuries and 1,300 deaths (CDC, 2003).

Since the 1970s, domestic violence public policy and research have continued to evolve, with new terminology, such as battering, intimate partner violence (IPV), and spouse abuse emerging from a society more willing to accept that violence can be committed by a spouse, ex-spouse, or current or former boyfriend or girlfriend. IPV is often a repeated offense, men and women are its victims, and offenders and their victims can be of any sexual orientation (National Center for Injury Prevention and Control, 2003). Nearly one-third of female homicide victims reported in police records are killed by an intimate partner (Federal Bureau of Investigation, 2001). Abused women live with more physical health problems, have a higher occurrence of depression, and are more susceptible to drug and alcohol abuse and suicide attempts (Golding, 1996; Kaslow et al., 1998). IPV is a serious women's health problem, with adverse effects on physical, mental, social, psychological, and reproductive health (Pico-Alfonso et al., 2006; Rahman, 2015). Females are usually the victims of gender-based violence, which involves unequal power relationships between men and women (*Violence Prevention: The Evidence*, 2009). In the February 2016 report produced by Test Kitchen, written by Melissa Jeltsen and published by the Huffington Post, titled *This Is Not a Love Story: America's Deadly Domestic Violence Problem*, it determined in January 2016, 112 people were killed in IPV homicides, including children and bystanders. Men were the alleged perpetrators of these fatal attacks 89 percent of the time, and 77 percent of the victims were women. Within the report, Daniel Saunders, a professor at the University of Michigan's School of Social Work, mentioned that men and women engaged in IPV have different motives for killing, with women usually trying to protect themselves or their children, and men killing usually not because they are afraid but are motivated by extreme jealousy and possessiveness.

Every year, incidents in IPV entail economic costs to the healthcare system and employers, ranging from expenses related to services provided to perpetrators, victims, and survivors, to lost productivity for individuals directly and indirectly affected by IPV, including friends and family. IPV impacts the most vulnerable members of a family and community: one in four children in the U.S. witnesses parental IPV during their lifetime, and approximately one out of every 15 children witnesses episodes on an annual basis (Hamby et al., 2011). Many IPV victims do not seek out assistance until they are emotional or physically overwhelmed or in fear for their lives (Petersen et al., 2004), presenting a challenge for the domestic violence programs in the U.S. and its territories, who serve at least 60,000 survivors in a 24-hour-time period (National Network to End Domestic Violence, 2009). Domestic violence programs work with healthcare professionals and law enforcement to address incidents resulting in bruises, broken bones, head injuries, lacerations, internal bleeding, and other acute effects of IPV that require medical attention and hospitalization.

Acute effects are oftentimes accompanied by chronic health conditions, including arthritis, irritable bowel syndrome, chronic pain, pelvic pain, ulcers, and migraines (Shahzadi et al., 2012). Pregnant victims are at a heightened risk of miscarriage, pre-term labor, and injury to or death of the fetus. Oftentimes, victims "…are made to feel guilty for 'provoking' the abuse and are frequently subjected to intense criticism," triggering copious amounts of stress, fear, anxiety, and depression (Shahzadi et al., 2012, p. 2). Abuse and isolation for IPV victims is terrifying, and with little or no money of their own, victims experience anguish when contemplating leaving their perpetrator (Shahzadi et al., 2012). IPV includes physical, psychological, and financial violence, and experts consider it one of the most insidious and pervasive forms of violence in society (Wray et al., 2004).

It is difficult for domestic and international organizations to ascertain the severity of IPV because of the covert nature of the behavior. Nonetheless, IPV has been documented in every race, religion, class, and level of education (Straus & Gelles, 1986). During the period when battering transitioned from being a private, family issue to an issue involving public policy and law enforcement, greater awareness of IPV and its societal implications changed the national and international narratives for gender-based violence. In the 1990s, it became apparent that there was another shift taking hold, and the problem of domestic violence shifted from the legal to the public health domain (Cole & Flanagin, 1998, 1999). The shift empowered national and international health agencies, including the American Medical Association, the American College of Physicians, the CDC, and the WHO, among others (American College of Physicians, 1998; Foege et al., 1995; Marwick, 1998; World Health Assembly, 1996). In the aftermath of the shift, successful IPV interventions address social norms, beliefs, and practices related to domestic violence for perpetrators, victims, survivors, family members, friends, or bystanders living around and interacting with anyone directly involved in abuse (Wray et al., 2004). The interventions are tailored to various communities and niche audiences.

Cultural Implications of IPV Interventions

One survey estimated that 16 percent of African American women have experienced IPV by a husband or partner within a five-year period (Falik & Collins, 1996). Alarmingly, some research indicates that black women were victims in more than 53 percent of the violent deaths occurring in the homes of female victims (Bailey et al., 1997). Health communicators working with other experts in health promotion and education need to understand the limitations of general campaign interventions on domestic violence being targeted at racial or ethnic communities. They can make better use of planning and resources to develop a series of media campaigns and community-mobilization efforts to persuade community members to change their attitudes from tolerance of domestic abuse to condemnation (Wray et al., 2004). Media segmentation and media planning enable health communicators to accurately reach with frequency niche audiences or subgroups in domestic media markets. Interventions and practices that are evidence-based have some effectiveness in being transplanted from specific domestic media markets to other markets. Interventions are studied, tailored, and retailored to accommodate social norms of target audiences, adapting whenever possible to the sensibilities of communities.

The 2012 nationwide Haiti Demographic and Health Survey revealed that IPV impacts 15–19-year-old girls, with as many as 43 percent of them being victims. The IPV incidence rate for this demographic in Haiti is almost one-and-a-half times the global average (Cayemittes et al., 2013). Adolescents and young adults experiencing IPV in Haiti and other countries are at higher risk for substance abuse, suicidal behavior, suicide attempts, unsafe sex, non-use of contraception, unintended pregnancy, abortion, depression, sexually transmitted infections, and AIDS (Exner-Cortens et al., 2013; Foshee et al., 2013; Holmes & Sher, 2013). More IPV interventions need to focus on young people and low-income communities and teach healthy relationship skills, which is a crucial step in IPV prevention and a public health imperative (Gage et al., 2016). International organizations such as Amnesty International, with its Stop Violence Against Women media campaign, have synthesized visual and textual elements in local campaigns created by local artists in order to appeal to natives in culturally specific ways (Goehring et al., 2017). One of the localized media campaigns was tailored to Hungary, a country that has faced national and international criticism for IPV (Human Rights Watch, 2013), which has been described as an "insurmountable problem" for Hungarian women (*Hungary: Cries Unheard*, 2007). Unfortunately, focus on local communities is not enough—the campaigns need to be effective. Amnesty International consultants analyzed the completed 2010 media campaign in Hungary and found it lacked focus, resulting in fragmented research and campaigning, diluting a unified voice against domestic violence, which did little to reduce violence or raise funds to combat IPV (Wallace & Smith, 2010). As health communicators work with partners in health promotion and health education in various countries, regions, and other localized communities, it is necessary for them to engage with community stakeholders to develop a comprehensive and holistic campaign and outreach efforts.

Health communicators have tried a variety of approaches to engage natives. In Lebanon, narrative exemplars and a celebrity spokesperson were used in anti-domestic violence advertisements (El-Khourby & Shafer,

2016). Works of fiction, like Afghan diasporic writer Atiq Rahimi's *The Patience Stone*, effectively increased awareness of female experiences with IPV during the reign of the Taliban (Bezhan, 2008; Zabihzadeh et al., 2015). These narratives are works of activism meant to curb domestic violence, shifting the views and perspectives of women and young adults about the violence they endure. Greater awareness engenders an environment more conducive to introspection. For countries that are more patriarchal or where religious definitions for basic rights focus more on men than women, health campaigns combating IPV should have extensive formative research into natives. In Pakistan, an Islamic country where male power is pervasive throughout every aspect of society, women encounter abuse on a regular basis. Studies in Pakistan have garnered national and international attention: (1) an estimated 99 percent of housewives and 77 percent of working women are beaten by their husbands (Watts & Zimmerman, 2002), (2) other sources, including a 2005 Domestic Violence in Asian Communities Fact Sheet, state that 32.8 percent of male respondents admitted to having slapped their wives, and 77.10 percent admitted to engaging in non-consensual sex with their wives (Ali, 2007); and (3) beyond physical abuse, in one study husbands admitted to shouting or yelling at their wives, even when they were pregnant (Shaikh, 2000). Sometimes, anger toward Pakistani women manifests in physical abuse, including burning women with kerosene or gasoline and acid throwing, with intimate partners and in-laws found to be involved in this act (Goodman et al., 1993).

When Pakistani wives point out behavior that is counterproductive to their husbands and their household, including husbands being addicted to alcohol, or other substance abuse, they are met with violence. Pakistani men justify their violent behavior toward women with the assertion "...that the religion gives them such a liberty, which is a totally falsified belief as quoted by Qura'an" (Ali, 2007, p. 31). Recommendations and strategies for Pakistani natives affected by IPV need to address the cultural realties prevalent in Pakistani society, aiding men and women in their introspection regarding IPV in their daily lived experiences. According to *Strategies and Recommendations for Prevention and Control of Domestic Violence Against Women in Pakistan* (Ali, 2007), there is a need for the Pakistani government to emphasize the importance of IPV through public initiatives, especially awareness programs for both men and women, with information disseminated by nurses, doctors, and psychologists working with governmental organizations and NGOs. Furthermore, there need to be religious definitions of the basic rights of women within the parameters set by Islamic teaching and literature. Another Asian country addressing the prevalence of IPV is China. Since the late 1980s, activist groups and NGOs have battled violence against women in China, with some government cooperation with these efforts (Chew, 2011). The segment of the Chinese population most responsive to reports of IPV being a serious social problem are those who are urban, educated, and mobilized on social media, and with easy Internet access in China's urban areas, anti-domestic violence forums, websites, and web-savvy promotional material are making an impact (Chew, 2011). IPV impacts men and women, yet women are more adversely affected by it—a finding that is the same across continents throughout the world. Regional and national boundaries and the cultural norms of a specific place or space mediate whether recommendations and strategies are perceived by natives as more persuasive and compelling.

IPV Messaging in the Media

The media is an influencer in IPV dialogue occurring within and between communities, including healthcare practitioners, policy makers, law enforcement, perpetrators, victims, survivors, and national and international audiences. Media portrayals shape public perception about IPV, impacting beliefs about "the causes of IPV, attributions of responsibility, and emotional responses to IPV" (Bullock, 2007; Carll, 2003; Jasinski, 2001). The content, wording, and presentation of IPV-related information influence media users' interpretation of a news or entertainment story (Carlyle et al., 2014). Media portrayals of IPV are framed to serve certain objectives. In the agenda-setting of media conglomerates and media outlets, IPV victims and survivors are usually less of a priority than sensationalism, profit motives, and maintaining instead of contesting normative behavior in societies. Media framing involves media producers, content purveyors, editors, journalists, advertisers, PR officers, executives, elected officials, and bureaucrats in the governmental, for-profit, and non-profit sectors existing within local, state, regional, national, and international borders. These individuals highlight particular elements of a story, selecting and organizing information around a central theme, while minimizing or omitting other information for the purpose of creating a coherent storyline. This process increases the salience of aspects of the story preferred by the media (Carlyle et al., 2014). These salient media perspectives promote specific interpretive conclusions for media users (De Vreese, 2005; Gross & D'Ambrosio, 2004).

Carlyle and colleagues (2008) identify news media coverage engaged in framing, specifically episodic framing, where social issues such as IPV are depicted "as limited to events only and not placed in a broader interpretation or context" (De Vreese, 2005, p. 56). Healthcare practitioners prefer thematic frames to episodic frames for news media coverage, because they are broader in context, situating acts of violence in a social context audiences infer requires societal level solutions (Carlyle et al., 2008). Healthcare practitioners want to focus attention on IPV trends instead of an individual IPV incident. Focus on IPV trends should be encouraged in the media, which has the power to emphasize contextual factors related to the incidence and severity of IPV, increasing public support and responsiveness (e.g., appraisals of risk and severity, as well as emotional reactions including empathy and distress) and spurring the accountability of public officials responsible for the existence and alleviation of IPV (Carlyle et al., 2014). Unfortunately, media coverage often relies on episodic frames that misrepresent the causes of violence (Easteal et al., 2015), engaging in victim-blaming, and ignoring or erasing intersecting problematic social norms about violence, race, and gender (Carlyle, 2017).

When IPV is covered, there are concerns about the media portrayals. Newspapers overreport incidents of IPV involving homicide, especially the murder of the victim. This finding is not shocking, since homicide is the most "newsworthy" form of IPV. Nonetheless, media coverage of homicide is disproportionate, with its "relative contribution" as an overall cause of death (Frost et al., 1997). Media overrepresentation of homicide and other severe forms of IPV may intimidate victims of other forms of IPV and keep them from leaving violent relationships, because they are fearful that the chances of being killed will be greatest when they try to leave (Carlyle et al., 2008). Moreover, when the media only covers the physical dimension of IPV, "...the effects of other forms of victimization go unacknowledged despite the severity of their effects" (Carlyle et al., 2008, p. 182). A recent example of news media coverage regarding IPV that demonstrates the divergent paths media outlets and decision makers can take to address the issue involves coverage of domestic violence incidents in the National Football League (NFL). In 2014, Ray Rice, then a running back with the Baltimore Ravens, did something more common in the NFL than anyone wants to admit, as displayed in a surveillance video from an Atlantic City hotel, where he is shown knocking his then-fiancée, Janay Palmer, unconscious with a blow to the face, then dragging her off of an elevator (Gentzler & Romano, 2016). The ensuing media coverage focused on the physical dimension of the altercation. Other NFL-related IPV media events that were speculated about around the same time were the Oakland Raiders drafting accused rapist Gareon Conley, the Cincinnati Bengals selecting Joe Mixon, who was caught on a video knocking a woman unconscious, and the Cleveland Browns' draft pick Caleb Brantley, whose behavior was similar to Mixon's (Carter, 2017). There are more IPV incidents involving NFL players.

Media coverage of these incidents focused on the physical manifestations of violence, contributing to the perception of the NFL in the zeitgeist of the early twenty-first century as a league with a serious domestic violence problem, in an era when over two-thirds of those surveyed, both fans and non-fans, believe the league has a problem (Carter, 2017). Oftentimes, the psychological, emotional, and financial harm female victims suffer is missing from the discussion of IPV incidents involving NFL players. The media glare is on the more sensational characteristics of the story, leading to perpetrator-bashing or victim-bashing, with limited or no focus on the physical, psychological, and emotional factors impacting player behavior. Unacknowledged in most media coverage is the extent to which a player's lived experiences, and the lived experiences of his partner, their identities, and backgrounds, affect their behavior during IPV incidents.

There is concern that the media decentralizes personal responsibility in some of its storytelling or overemphasizes personal choices within domestic violence narratives without examining the intersectional aspects of class and ethnicity. Outside of the U.S., in other large democracies, such as Brazil, incidents of gender violence are "often set up as either tragedies or common events" in the media, even concealing aggressors' responsibility under the rhetoric of a "crime of passion" (Souza-Leal et al., 2018, p. 21). In the U.S., another challenge originated in the 1970s, with the coverage of domestic violence in news sections spanning from "human interest" to the "crime beat." Historically, the 1970s marked the use of a rhetorical blueprint in the media that involved the deployment of episodic framing, with attention on the discrete acts of one person against another, decontextualizing any representations other than those dependent on male violence, where a male batterer is acting on his own, ironically with little mention of the role the patriarchy plays in national cultures where men are allowed and encouraged to control women (Enck-Wanzer, 2009). Somehow, the tried-and-true approach of focusing on exceptional physical violence for sensationalism occurs without thoroughly examining how society, especially the media, does not hold men accountable for its framing of narratives about male batterers or hold media stakeholders accountable for their negligence and lack of willpower or interest to provide gender-equitable storytelling about "…cycles of power and control perpetuated by deep financial inequities, psychological torture, and legal disparities" that contribute to domestic violence (Enck-Wanzer, 2009, p. 12).

Research about press coverage of same-sex IPV incidents in Spain uncovered heterosexist bias sustained by episodic frames akin to the news coverage of violence against women during earlier years (Carratalá, 2016). In *Press Coverage of Same-Sex Domestic Violence Cases in Spain* (2016), there is an assertion that there is an inaccurate contextualization of women in the media coverage of same-sex violence (p. 61):

…images of the victim, lack of contextualization (with an informative approach that is limited to describe the fact, as a singular case and not as an expression of a wider phenomenon of violence), prevalence of police sources and intimate surroundings (without incorporating public authorities or experts), absence of information about support resources or services, and use of expressions that associate the attack with an emotional/passionate manifestation and present the aggressor with certain attributes that may diminish his responsibility for the crime.

Critics of the status quo are discouraged that these episodic frames persist, yet, in recent years, some local media outlets throughout the U.S. and in other countries are taking steps to confront the troubling history associated with traditional media coverage of IPV. They get ahead of the story, to control the narrative and gauge audience receptivity to initiatives meant to counteract the adverse effects of IPV. WRAL-WRAZ Raleigh-Durham was among the broadcasters that introduced local TV initiatives in response to troubling NFL domestic violence headlines (Malone, 2014). WRAL staffers and law enforcement officials worked the phones during a telethon to galvanize community efforts to combat domestic violence. Other initiatives included eNOughNC campaign radio and TV public service announcements lasting 60 and 90 seconds, which were also aired during live sporting events and shown on the big screen at Durham Bulls baseball games (Malone, 2014).

Narration and Social Merchandising

Most of the interventions for IPV were offered to small groups, with fewer than 50 participants, which mainly consisted of community-based group interventions for female victims (Constantino et al., 2015). In response to the severity of IPV as a domestic and international problem, interventions need greater reach than many community-based group interventions, so healthcare stakeholders who can rely on media outlets as reliable partners should co-create mediated interventions that appeal to savvy media users. Healthcare practitioners building working relationships with the media have to forge an agenda, test informative and persuasive messages, and determine the best means of delivering these messages to audiences. During an era when media users seem increasingly aware of the ills associated with IPV and its effects on a variety of constituencies, including women and same-sex partners, IPV media campaigns should play an important educational role, prioritizing issues, approaches, conceptualizations, and terminology to shape the common collective imagination (Berenguer & García-Gordillo, 2017). Two overarching strategies—narration and social merchandising—aid healthcare and media partners in ramping-up their informative and entertainment capacities in their IPV outreach to media users. Use of narration and social merchandising are not a panacea; both strategies have been used to undermine and bolster IPV outreach.

Domestic Violence in Men's and Women's Magazines: Women Are Guilty of Choosing the Wrong Men, Men Are Not Guilty of Hitting Women (2011) is a study that used qualitative narrative analysis on 10 leading magazine titles over 10 years. The study revealed that men's magazines tolerated and celebrated domestic violence, while women's magazines conveyed that women bear responsibility for both genders. The narratives, frames, and storytelling in these magazines did nothing to address the patriarchal cultural structures that enable violence against women (VAW). Unfortunately, none of the narratives in these magazines included men taking responsibility for having been or for being violent, and no narratives of women overcoming the fear in their lives and learning to feel secure (Nettleton, 2011). "There are no narratives about how men and women might come to terms" with a culture and society "where violence is venerated" (Nettleton, 2011, p. 154). Furthermore, men's magazines contribute to the problem of male-sanctioned violence when they have no advice for men on how to deal with anger and violence, omitting suggestions or recommendations for how men can help other men express themselves without being abusive. Men's magazines hide the ramifications of IPV, using episodic framing in storytelling omitting "stories of the fear and injuries women sustain" (Nettleton, 2011, p. 155). Another study by Pamela Hill Nettleton (2018) analyzed domestic violence discourse in 72 issues of *Maxim* magazine, a widely circulated men's magazine. The study revealed that the magazine's stories situate men as the definers of women's value and worth: "messages signal troubling assumptions and ideology: women exist to please men, and have little other value or redeeming qualities" (p. 11).

U.S. Tabloid Magazine Coverage of a Celebrity Dating Abuse Incident: Rihanna and Chris Brown (2012) is a study that examines how the media frames dating abuse. Researchers analyzed characteristics of media coverage in *People, In Touch Weekly, Us Weekly, Star Magazine, National Enquirer, OK!,* and *Life & Style Weekly* between February 16, 2009, and April 6, 2009. The target audience for these magazines is predominantly female, with their representation ranging from 67 percent to 85 percent of the readership. The vast majority of IPV articles (83 percent) pertaining to abuse incidents, including circumstances of abuse in Rihanna and Chris Brown's relationship, discuss abuse as problematic, yet the dominant frame for the majority of the IPV articles (53 percent) was that abuse is romantic, erotic, normal, or the victim's fault (Rothman et al., 2012). Most news frames communicated mixed messages about dating abuse: "it's wrong, but also sexy, potentially deserved, and often a component of supposedly loving relationships" (Rothman et al., 2012, p. 741). Perhaps celebrity victims of IPV can wrestle the narrative, framing, and storytelling from the tabloids and use their advocacy to improve future tabloid framing of dating abuse incidents.

The misgivings critics have of episodic frames in magazines are applicable to newspaper coverage of IPV. In her study of Utah newspapers, Cathy Ferrand Bullock (2007) made similar observations as Rothman and colleagues (2012), agreeing that the majority of news media coverage, whether in magazines or newspapers, is patriarchal, which influences individual and public views about IPV.

> Utah newspapers' coverage of domestic violence fatalities can be divided into three categories. In the first and largest, coverage (or lack of coverage) obscured domestic violence in general; ignored domestic violence's roots in socially accepted, gender-based power imbalances; and tended to portray solutions as resting with male-dominated institutions such as the law enforcement and legal systems. This coverage represented views consistent with the strong patriarchal culture in which the newspapers were embedded [p. 51].

If celebrity victims, be they Rihanna or other high-profile tabloid targets, are able to seize the narrative, they will have greater control over the story that is told, as well as more leverage in negotiating framing in media coverage. Media outlets want greater celebrity access, so they may acquiesce to pressure for less sensationalism and more thematic framing in exchange for greater celebrity exposure. The outcome of this arrangement could be enhanced insight into the lived experiences of media users' favorite celebrities. Celebrity narratives could give victims and survivors of VAW a platform to set the agenda for the discussion of IPV, specifically domestic violence plaguing female victims (who may be teenagers) and children living in abusive circumstances.

Media users are responsive to various narrative forms, whether they are stories told by celebrities about themselves, stories about celebrities framed by an independent party, such as a journalist, paparazzi, blogger, or another entity, or crowd-pleasing fictional accounts that attract interest and buzz. Empirical evidence supports the notion that even fictional stories affect real-world attitudes and opinions about social issues (Dill-Shackleford et al., 2015). Both fictional and nonfictional stories are mechanisms for change, because they "reduce the feeling that persuasion is being attempted, and the audience therefore experiences less psychological reactance" (Dill-Shackleford et al., 2015, p. 970). Narration is useful for transporting the audience to a safe space where they feel less averse toward social issues depicted in the story, which should enable media users to identify with the character in the narrative (Moyer-Gusé & Nabi, 2010). News media coverage reliant on celebrity narration is appealing to media users, yet the potential of celebrity narration is limited by the tabloidization of news and entertainment content, which might explain why celebrity narration has not been elevated in many IPV public health campaigns. These campaigns could be co-created and co-branded by celebrities working with healthcare stakeholders, including local municipalities, regional and national governments, NGOs, and commercial enterprises.

Commercial enterprises that rely on narration, such as telenovelas and other entertainment-education programming, and social merchandising are disguised as a public service. Social merchandising uses commercial strategies to sell prosocial messages pertinent to social issues. Some health communicators are weary of social merchandising, since it champions commercial enterprises cross-promoting issues varying from female empowerment to gender equality to IPV to audiences, while in the same pitch selling commodities, whether it be lipstick, a telenovela, a brand, or the ideology of a socially responsible network, with the emphasis being on making a profit. Supposedly, socially responsible commercial enterprises use narration and social merchandising to benefit the enterprise more than media users. There is a potential for a bait-and-switch, where media users feel scammed by enterprises pretending to care about their well-being. "There is a fine line between presenting audiences with a social merchandising insertion about domestic violence and turning domestic violence into something satirical, justifiable, and at times, erotic" (Joyce & Martinez, 2017, p. 224). These commercial enterprises could do more harm than good.

The NFL has a domestic violence problem. It is a commercial enterprise that has attempted social merchandising with two well-known brands: football, the profitable sport and national pastime, and the music of Rihanna, IPV victim and international superstar. In September 2014, when the NFL was dealing with the Ray Rice domestic violence controversy, "the network decided that beginning the game with a song by Rihanna—a victim of domestic violence at the hands of her ex-boyfriend Chris Brown in 2009—and a comedic segment also slated for the pre-game would be distasteful" (Dockterman, 2014, p. 2). Instead, the network focused exclusively on the Ray Rice controversy. Rihanna took to Twitter to express her outrage regarding how her music was mishandled by the NFL; her song "Run This Town" was dropped because of potentially controversial lyrics: "Feel it comin' in the air. Hear the screams from everywhere. I'm addicted to the thrill. It's a dangerous love affair." Rihanna had 37.2 million followers at the time. Her fans and supporters were not happy that it seemed like the NFL and CBS were punishing a domestic violence victim by not using her music, in response to a perpetrator of VAW. It did not take long for the NFL and CBS to decide they wanted to bring back Rihanna's music for the segment, but Rihanna was having none of it. CBS decided to drop "Run This Town" from the *Thursday Night Football* opening. These commercial enterprises, the NFL and CBS, confused their consumers with mixed messaging and failed social merchandising, missing an opportunity to partner with Rihanna, a known victim of IPV, a survivor of IPV, and an advocate for female empowerment. Could the NFL and CBS have co-created an IPV prevention campaign with Rihanna and used her celebrity and social media platform to educate their consumers, promote awareness, and stimulate change on this very important social issue and problem in the NFL?

Rihanna Speaks, We Listen

Fans and supporters of Rihanna believe she is genuinely herself. She lives her life unapologetically, and the public sees her scars and flaws. They support her—they appreciate the bond they forged with someone they perceive as authentic (Robinson, 2015). Perhaps the most public scars and flaws of Rihanna involve the trials and tribulations she experienced in her dysfunctional relationship with former boyfriend Chris Brown. In 2009, the international pop star, musician, and businesswoman had a growing roster of endorsements, fashion spreads, and millions in the bank (Martz & Sher, 2009). Robyn Rihanna Fenty and Chris Brown had been friends since 2005 and went public with their romantic relationship in 2008 (Goldberg, 2013). Before the IPV that occurred during February 2009, Brown was known for being a young, popular singer with a large fan base of teenage girls (Enck & McDaniel, 2012). Brown had a "squeaky-clean" image, but this image changed after news media coverage of his assault of Rihanna, with reports that he was acting "shockingly out of character" (Hoffman, 2009; Leonard, 2009). Why? On February 8, 2009, the former couple were involved in an argument and assault in his parked car in the Hancock Park area of Los Angeles around 12:30 a.m. (Fisher & Zhou, 2009). On August 31, 2009, while on CNN's *Larry King Live*, Brown admitted his guilt and apologized for assaulting Rihanna, but claimed he did not remember hitting her. Many fans of both young celebrities have engrained in their memory the picture of Rihanna's face, swollen, bloody, and beaten, that TMZ released shortly after the incident (Gay, 2014). For some media users, the picture was too graphic, yet it provided the public with a glimpse into a reality many women experience in abusive relationships.

IPV occurs among adults, specifically young adults, for a variety of reasons. According to the study *Courtship Violence Among College Students* (1981), college students reported experiencing courtship violence, including threats, being pushed, slapped, punched, struck with an object, assaulted with a weapon, choked, and other types of violence. The study identified some of the causes of IPV: (1) jealousy, (2) disagreement over drinking, (3) anger over sexual denial. The study also found that a residence (e.g., home, a dormitory, or an apartment) was a likely place for IPV occurrence (51.3 percent) and revealed a high incidenct rate of IPV in vehicles (21.6 percent). During these IPV incidents, individuals "…were more likely to report themselves to have been the victim, with 71% of study respondents asserting they were the victim, when asked, 'Would you consider yourself the victim or aggressor in the incident?,' with only 28.9% of respondents perceiving themselves as the aggressor" (Makepeace, 1981). In regard to the Rihanna IPV incident, the following facts underscore why no one should doubt she was the victim (Duke & Rowlands, 2009):

> It was not Rihanna who called police but someone who heard her screams for help, according to a sworn statement by Los Angeles Police Detective DeShon Andrews. Andrews said the incident began when Rihanna, who was riding in the sports car driven by Brown, found a text message on his cell phone from a woman… "who Brown had a previous sexual relationship with." "A verbal argument ensued," followed by the physical attack, the statement said. It went on to describe the assault in great detail, saying Brown punched her numerous times and put her in a head lock, restricting her breathing and causing her to start to lose consciousness. He threatened to "beat the s—t out of you" and kill her, according to the statement, and also bit her ear and her fingers.

Rihanna was taken to Cedars-Sinai Medical Center for treatment, and Brown turned himself into the Los Angeles Police Department (Goldstein, 2009). An investigation commenced and Rihanna was issued a Domestic Violence Emergency Protective Order (Duke & Rowlands, 2009).

In November 2009, Rihanna sat down for an in-depth interview with Diane Sawyer. She told Sawyer that during the night Brown beat her, he had "no soul in his eyes" (Martz & Sher, 2009). She continued, "It wasn't the same person that says I love you. It was not those … eyes" (Martz & Sher, 2009). Nonetheless, to the shock of many fans and the media, Rihanna and Brown reunited after the assault, which, she told Sawyer, was a mistake. Rihanna explained that she was blinded by love and had convinced herself that she needed to protect Brown from scrutiny. She pondered aloud, if "he just, he lost me, I just need to let him know; don't do anything stupid … this is what I was thinking about" (Martz & Sher, 2009). Rihanna was not making excuses for her behavior; she was trying to explain her state of mind and the factors that affected her decision-making. She told Sawyer, "I'm a human being and people put me on a very unrealistic pedestal.

And all these expectations, I'm not perfect" (Martz & Sher, 2009). Brown responded to the interview in a statement to MTV News: "While I respect Rihanna's right to discuss the specific events of February 8, I maintain my position that all of the details should remain a private matter between us" (Rodriguez, 2009).

Rihanna and Brown relied upon different approaches for public engagement regarding IPV, which is not shocking, since there are gendered differences in reporting threats of violence, and "...almost always a difference between the man's self-report and woman's report, with the woman most often reporting higher frequencies" of threats and violent behavior when a particular threat of violence or act of violence was reported to authorities (Edleson & Brygger, 1986, p. 381). In addition to the perceptions aggressors and victims have of themselves and their culpability in IPV incidents, the public's perceptions matter. According to a Boston Public Health Commission survey of Rihanna and Brown's peers, teenagers (who were counted amongst their fans) found that 51 percent blamed Brown, while 46 percent thought Rihanna was responsible for the altercation (Forman, 2009). Beyond public opinion, there were the legal implications for Brown, who was charged with a crime. Brown reached a plea deal for the assault case. He was sentenced to five years of probation, required to serve 180 days in jail, or about 1,400 hours in "labor-oriented service," with a directive from the judge to undergo a year-long domestic violence class that was coupled with a "stay away" order for Rihanna until he completed the class (Duke & Rowlands, 2009). Rihanna left the courtroom before the judge sentenced Brown. She emerged from the public relations ruckus as an ascendant figure with a bully pulpit to galvanize the public, especially younger women, in their pursuit of female empowerment, and she became the manifestation of female angst about VAW.

Rihanna has expressed her reservations in regard to being a role model. In 2010, the year after the altercation with Brown, she released a controversial song and music video with rap/hip-hop artist Eminem. "Love the Way You Lie" and its video featured actors Dominic Monaghan and Megan Fox, who depict a couple enthralled in shoving and kissing alongside cheating, theft, and bar fights. The video culminates in a burning house, with the couple being consumed in digitally rendered flames (Enck & McDaniel, 2012). Eminem wrote the song with Rihanna in mind, alluding to her troubled relationship history in the lyrics: Next time I'm pissed, I'll aim my fist at the drywall/Next time? There will be no next time—I apologize" (*Billboard*, 2010). Rihanna talked with *Access Hollywood* about her decision to collaborate with Eminem. "It's something that, you know, [Eminem and I have] both experienced on different sides, different ends of the table," she said (Dinh, 2010). She continued:

It just was authentic. It was real. It was believable for us to do a record like that, but it was also something that needed to be done and the way he did it was so clever. He pretty much just broke down the cycle of domestic violence and it's something that a lot people don't have a lot of insight on, so this song is a really, really powerful song and it touches a lot of people (Dinh, 2010).

The public response was mixed. Some media users appreciated the complexities of domestic violence depicted in the song and video, while critics lamented the "irresponsible glorification" of VAW that exploited victims (Enck & McDaniel, 2012). Some news media coverage framed the song and video as "…highlighting the dangers of an abusive relationship and, indirectly, deliver[ing] the message that it's better to walk out before its's too late" (Concepcion, 2010).

Media users were also split in response to the rekindling of Rihanna and Brown's romantic relationship. On August 20, 2012, Rihanna was featured on *Oprah's Next Chapter*, where she referred to the night of her altercation with Brown as the night she lost her best friend and went on to explain how, despite her anger, she felt protective of Brown. Brown also addressed the state of their relationship in late 2012, "…speaking out, letting his fans know that even he doesn't have the perfect answer" (Glinow, 2012). In 2013, Rihanna addressed the failed attempt to rekindle the relationship: "I decided it was more important for me to be happy … and I wasn't going to let anybody's opinion get in the way of that. Even if it's a mistake, it's my mistake" (Gay, 2014). Rihanna and Brown experienced the cycle of abuse described by antiviolence activists, including honeymoon, explosion, remorse, and reconciliation, which can be a perilous loop that repeats again and again (Enck & McDaniel, 2012). According to the *Vanity Fair* article, "Rihanna in Cuba: The Cover Story" (2015), Rihanna would later assert:

I was very protective of him. I felt that people didn't understand. Even after…. But you know, you realize after a while that in that situation you're the enemy. You want the best from them, but if you remind them of their failures, or if you remind them of bad moments in their life, or even if you say I'm willing to put up with something, they think less of you—because they know you don't deserve what they're going to give. And if you put up with it, maybe you are agreeing that you [deserve] this, and that's when I finally had to say, "Uh-oh, I was stupid thinking I was built for this." Sometimes you just have to walk away.

Throughout the tumultuous years after her assault, Rihanna never forgot the platform she had and how her messages of female empowerment resonated with young women. In 2013, a fan reached out to her on Twitter for relationship advice. The fan inquired, "Hey Rih, I hope it's not a bad time to message. Just been down lately and wondering if you had any words of encouragement. Trust issues with men" (Tate, 2013). According to *Rihanna Gives Fan Relationship Advice* (2013), Rihanna quickly responded:

> Anytime I have trust issues, I often assume that it has a lot to do with myself. Most of the time it's difficult to differentiate. Intuition and insecurities! But no one ever wants to wait to figure it out. Whatever we do, we don't want to feel stupid! So we tend to jump the gun with no evidence to back it up. That's the biggest mistake anyone could ever make. My advice, which is exactly what I've done, is s--- isn't making sense to me, I'm out. I mean cold turkey! I always need to step out of it to see it for what it is cuz I refuse to let a man play me. If he has no respect, he just doesn't. But you don't have to allow it or be bound by it [*sic*].

In 2014, Rihanna used her platform to stand up for victims of domestic violence, condemning the NFL and CBS for penalizing her, a survivor of IPV, by cutting her pre-recorded performance of *Run This Town*, which was meant to air before *Thursday Night Football*. CBS decided to use its airtime to focus on the Ray Rice domestic violence incident, concerned that using Rihanna as part of the embedded news and entertainment coverage for the *Thursday Night Football* programming would set an inappropriate tone (Gay, 2014).

Rihanna disagreed, expressing her disappointment to media users via social media. She is one of many women who survived a male batterer, and many of her fans felt she was being punished by male-dominated commercial enterprises (i.e., the NFL and CBS) for the misdeeds of a male batterer (i.e., Ray Rice). Rihanna contributed to a counter-narrative that rebuffed the corporate "talking points," and she regained control of the narrative. When CBS approached her about reinstating the use of her song, which it had temporarily stopped using, she refused. In response, CBS dropped the pre-recorded performance for that season of *Thursday Night Football*. In this moment, the public's perception of Rihanna changed, with her fight for self-determination shifting her public identity from victim to survivor to advocate. Her narrative transformation came to fruition—she became a fighter and advocate against VAW.

Domestic violence advocates are interested in aiding victims in crisis. Domestic violence victims seek advocates who are willing to listen attentively and provide victims with emotional and informational resources (Babin et al., 2012). Many victims of VAW do not realize they have options, so advocates facilitate access to support services and assistance, including legal, medical, and counseling services. Advocates also staff crisis hotlines, work in emergency shelters, and sponsor or motivate social advocacy (Bennet et al., 2004; Peled & Edleson, 1994). Rihanna participates in and sponsors social advocacy for victims and survivors of VAW. Research shows that "participants exposed to the celebrity spokesperson conditions elicited more positive attitudes" (El-Khoury & Shafer, 2016, p.

942), which promotes positive processing of the message and "may also support increased attention to the message" (El-Khoury & Shafer, 2016, p. 942). Rihanna and other celebrity spokespeople for victims of VAW and IPV have an elevated platform and bully pulpit to engender more positive attitudes toward social change, specifically, social support for victims and survivors of VAW and IPV. "That is, it may be that across all the opportunities one individual may have to act and across all the individuals who have more positive norms and beliefs about acting would be more likely to act, on average, than those who do not" (Nabi, Southwell, & Hornik, 2002, p. 446). Health communication scholars, healthcare practitioners, educators, advocates, and survivors of VAW and IPV are increasingly aware of the role social media can play in strategically connecting VAW and IPV victims to individuals with relevant and pertinent information for their survival and well-being (Weathers, Sanderson, Neal, & Gramlich, 2016). "Social media has quickly evolved into a space where the individual's voice has the potential to be heard, and it should not be ignored, especially in dealing with powerful issues such as domestic violence" (Weathers et al., 2016, p. 66).

Rihanna is a well-known social media user, and she has large followings on Twitter, Instagram, and Snapchat. She has used these social media platforms to address domestic violence issues. In 2018, she criticized Los Angeles–based Snap Inc., owner of Snapchat, when it ran an ad that asked users "to decide whether they wanted to slap her or punch Chris Brown" (Bloomberg, 2018). The ad for the "Would You Rather" trivia game used an image of Rihanna next to an option to "Slap Rihanna," and an image of Brown next to an option to "Punch Chris Brown." Rihanna felt the ad made a mockery of her altercation and IPV incident with Brown (Perez, 2018). Snapchat removed the ad, which the public learned had been placed by a mobile-gaming company. Snap Inc. apologized and took responsibility for its mistake. Despite the removal, screenshots of the ad circulated online and received criticism from activist Brittany Packnett and Chelsea Clinton (Perez, 2018). Snapchat users complained about the ad (Hartmans, 2018). The company released a statement that read, in part, "The advert was reviewed and approved in error, as it violates our advertising guidelines" (France, 2018).

The company's response failed to counteract Rihanna's posted statement on her Instagram story (Hartmans, 2018):

> Now SNAPCHAT I know you already know you ain't my fav app out there! But I'm just trying to figure out what the point was with this mess! I'd love to call it ignorance but I know you ain't that dumb! You spent money to animate something that would intentionally bring shame to DV victims and made a joke of it!!! This is not about my personal feelings, cause I don't have much of them … but all the women, children and men that have been victims of DV in the past

and especially the ones who haven't made it out yet ... you let us down! Shame on you. Throw the who app-oligy away.

Rihanna posted her Instagram story around 11:00 a.m. eastern standard time, and Snap Inc.'s stock value dropped 4 percent. The drop triggered another company apology a few hours later, with the company calling the ad "disgusting" (Hartmans, 2018). Snap's apologies did not prevent Rihanna's call-out post on Instagram from costing the company approximately $800 million—a reaction to Rihanna's fans and socially conscious media users, who decided to delete the platform from their smartphones (Stefansky, 2018). Some of those fans were celebrities. Chrissy Teigen took to Twitter to announce that the Rihanna Snapchat scandal was a contributing factor in her decision to stop using Snapchat (Pasquini, 2018). Rihanna rallied celebrities and non-celebrities, men and women to support domestic violence and IPV victims and survivors. Rihanna did something amazing. Her actions contributed to a social mobilization campaign that moved social norms and intentions to act in a positive direction—it manifested in some positive aggregate effects for individuals, families, and a society at large affected by domestic violence and IPV.

Healthcare Reacts to Domestic Violence and IPV

Domestic violence and IPV are interrelated health issues. They impact millions of people around the world. They necessitate medical care, with emergency room visits higher than other acts of violence (WHO, 2005). Battered persons suffer from physical and mental pain, and a variety of social problems, which result in injuries and long-term health impacts (El-Khoury & Shafer, 2016). The National Network to End Domestic Violence (NNEDV) strongly encourages battered persons attempting to leave an abusive relationship to create a safety plan, reach out to their local domestic violence coalition, and seek assistance with planning and resources (Jeltsen, 2016). Research indicates that without early prevention that promotes healthy, respectful relationships in families, there is a greater likelihood that unhealthy parent-child relationships will develop, which mitigate positive family dynamics built on respect, trust, and positive interactions and non-violent communication and conflict resolution (The National Intimate Partner and Sexual Violence Survey Summary Report, 2010). In 2011, the Institute of Medicine operationalized language in the Affordable Care Act—the 2010 legislation that focused the U.S. healthcare system on disease prevention and health promotion through screening and early intervention (U.S. Centers of Medicare and Medicaid

Services, 2013)—with the identification of eight evidence-based, clinical services central to women's health and well-being, including IPV screening and intervention (Gee et al., 2011). The U.S. Preventive Services Task Force (USPSTF) issued a B- recommendation (meaning there is high certainty that the net benefit is moderate or there is moderate certainty that the net benefit is moderate to substantial) for IPV screening of women 14 to 46 years in age, who should be screened by a healthcare clinician, and in the event of a positive screen, be referred to or provided intervention services (Moyer, 2013).

The USPSTF released updated recommendations for screening in 2012, reiterating that screening can identify IPV victims, and screening has minimal adverse effects (Nelson et al., 2012). Unfortunately, according to a 2011 systematic review, not all clinicians comply with the recommendations, with 9 to 40 percent of clinicians routinely screening for IPV (Todahl & Walters, 2011). Barriers to IPV screening for clinicians include personal discomfort with IPV, inadequate resources, lack of time, inadequate training, privacy issues pertaining to an IPV screening, perceptions that it is not the clinician's role to conduct a IPV screening, fear of offending patients, or not knowing how to respond to woman disclosing IPV (Sprague et al., 2012). Barriers coupled with a sometimes-daunting process of identifying individuals who have experienced IPV, which can vary with each patient, is complicated by legal, safety, and privacy considerations, as well as victim-batterer, victim-healthcare provider, and setting-specific dynamics (Miller et al., 2015). Another factor impacting IPV screening and interventions is the identification of best tools and practices for ongoing staff education and training (Hamberger et al., 2015). The process should also involve an integration of healthcare in clinical settings and community-based service providers, which enables more efficient and effective referrals that are crucial for victims and survivors to successfully access services (Ghandour et al., 2015).

Healthcare clinicians see more than just victims of IPV; they see the perpetrators of IPV too. According to prior studies, 13 to 23 percent of male patients self-report being batterers (Burge et al., 2005; Ernst et al., 2012; Jaeger et al., 2008; Oriel & Fleming, 1998; Singh et al., 2014), and 2 out of 3 male batterers report seeing a regular doctor for routine care (Singh et al., 2014). Men do not disclose that they are batterers during medical encounters, but healthcare clinicians may become aware that their male patients are IPV perpetrators in other ways, such as disclosures by victims, documentation in medical records, and behavior directly disclosed or witnessed (Ganley, 1998; Penti et al., 2017). The American Academy of Family Physicians (2014) recognizes the role family physicians play in recognizing the perpetration of IPV, but little research has been done regarding best practices in these circumstances, so many physicians feel unprepared to interact with male batterers (Penti et al, 2017).

There has been some progress in interventions in the health sector regarding the intersection between IPV and improved national and international mental health awareness and responsiveness. Policies have been introduced in several countries and international NGOs regarding implementing routine inquiry about IPV in mental health settings (Davis, 2014; NICE, 2014; Stewart & Chandra, 2016; WHO, 2013). There is still much work to be done. In the study *Improving Mental Health Service Responses to Domestic Violence and Abuse* (2016), findings indicated many mental health professionals do not ask about IPV and that service users do not readily disclose IPV in the absence of direct inquiry. This finding, coupled with IPV being under-documented and, when recorded, often lacking detail, jeopardizes IPV victims' lives and leaves their children or other dependents in harm's way. In the *Journal of Poverty Law and Policy* (2003), Markham addresses a lack of understanding on the part of mental health service providers regarding abusers' control of victims' insurance and their use of that power to control treatment, which endangers the IPV victims. These victims find it hard to trust domestic violence advocates, which can compromise their ability to seek assistance and to cooperate with those trying to help them. The unwillingness of victims to self-disclose pertinent information relevant to their mental health history or other important details could be intentional or accidental. They may withhold information about their abuse, their state of mind, and their medical history because of lack of trust or their inability to remember (Markham, 2003). In response to these circumstances, the healthcare system must build better rapport with victims and survivors by being all-encompassing in its pro–IPV victim and survivor scope and services, fostering greater synchronicity between counselors, physicians, nurses, attorneys, social workers, and law enforcement.

To keep IPV victims and their loved ones safe from recurring violence, an important part of any response to sexual violence, stalking, and IPV is to hold these assailants (any perpetrators, batterers, and their accomplices) accountable for their behavior. If victims believe law enforcement will not hold assailants accountable for their aggression or VAW, reluctance to leave the circumstances that jeopardize their well-being may supersede their instincts to survive. Survivors may already be reticent about the disclosure of their victimization, due to shame, embarrassment, or fear of retribution from perpetrators (The National Intimate Partner and Sexual Violence Survey Summary Report, 2010). There is a need for enhanced training efforts within the healthcare and criminal justice systems to better engage and support IPV victims and work with them, their families, and local communities to prevent IPV, and once it occurs, to hold assailants accountable.

Advocates play a vital role. Rihanna and many men and women like her understand: "It is equally important to continue addressing the beliefs, attitudes and messages that are deeply embedded in our social structures and that create a climate that condones sexual violence, stalking, and intimate partner violence" (The National Intimate Partner and Sexual Violence Survey Summary Report, 2010, p. 4). These advocates are part of a solution—a solution that is multifaceted and complex and requires various stakeholders within and outside of healthcare to adequately address VAW, domestic violence, and IPV.

References

Ali, T.S., Khan, N. (2007). Strategies and recommendations for prevention and control of domestic violence against women in Pakistan. *Journal of Pakistan Medical Association, 57*(1), 27–32. https://ecommons.aku.edu/pakistan_fhs_son/171.

American Academy of Family Physicians. (2014). *Violence (Position Paper).* https://www.aafp.org/about/policies/all/violence-position-paper.html.

Amnesty International. (2007). *Hungary: Cries unheard: The failure to protect women from rape and sexual violence in the home.* https://www.amnesty.org/en/documents/eur27/002/2007/en/.

Ashcraft, C. (2000). Naming knowledge: A language for reconstructing domestic violence and systemic gender inequity. *Women and Language, 23*(1), 3–10.

Babin, E.A., Palazzolo, K.E., & Rivera, K.D. (2012). Communication skills, social support, and burnout among advocates in a domestic violence agency. *Journal of Applied Communication Research, 40*(2), 147–166. http://dx.doi.org/10.1080/00909882.2012.670257.

Bailey, J.E., Kellerman, A.L., Somes, G.W., Banton, J.G., Rivara, F.P., & Rushforth, N.P. (1997). Risk factors for violent death of women in the home. *Archives of Internal Medicine, 157*(7), 777–782. https://doi.org/10.1001/archinte.1997.00440280101009.

Bennet, L., Riger, S., Schewe, P., Howard, A., & Wasco, S. (2004). Effectiveness of hotline, advocacy, counseling, and shelter services for victims of domestic violence: A statewide evaluation. *Journal of Interpersonal Violence, 19*(7), 815–829. https://doi.org/10.1177/0886260504265687.

Bezhan, F. (2008). Obedient and Resistant: Afghanistani Women in Maryam Mahboob's Short Stories. *Women's Studies International Forum, 31*(5), 373–382.

Billboard Staff. (2010, July 23). Eminem feat. Rihanna, "Love the way you lie." https://www.billboard.com/articles/review/1068964/eminem-feat-rihanna-love-the-way-you-lie.

Black, M.C., Basile, K.C., Breiding, M.J., Smith, S.G., Walters, M.L., Merrick, M.T., Chen, J., & Stevens, M.R. (2011). *The National Intimate Partner and Sexual Violence Survey (NISVS): 2010 Summary Report.* National Center for Injury Prevention and Control, Centers for Disease Control and Prevention. https://www.cdc.gov/violenceprevention/pdf/nisvs_report2010-a.pdf.

Bloomberg. (2018, March 15). *Rihanna is telling fans to delete Snapchat over its domestic abuse ad. Now the company's stock is plunging.* https://fortune.com/2018/03/15/rihanna-snapchat-dv-ad-stock/.

Bullock, C.F. (2007). Framing domestic violence fatalities: Coverage by Utah newspapers. *Women's Studies in Communication, 30*(1), 34–63. https://doi.org/10.1080/07491409.2007.10162504.

Burge, S.K., Schneider, F.D., & Ivy, L., & Catala, S. (2005). Patients' advice to physicians about intervening in family conflict. *Annals of Family Medicine, 3*(3), 248–254. https://doi.org/10.1370/afm.287.

Carll, E.K. (2003). News portrayal of violence and women: Implications for public policy. *American Behavioral Scientist, 46*(12), 1601–1610. https://doi.org/10.1177/0002764203254616.

Carlyle, K.E. (2017). The role of social media in promoting understanding of violence as a public health issue. *Journal of Communication in Healthcare, 10*(3), 162–164. https://doi.org/10.1080/17538068.2017.1373907.

Carlyle, K.E., Orr, C., Savage, M.W., & Babin, E. (2014). News coverage of intimate partner violence: Impact on prosocial responses. *Media Psychology, 17(4)*, 451–471. https://doi.org/10.10 80/15213269.2014.931812.

Carlyle, K.E., Slater, M.D., & Chakroff, J.L. (2008). Newspaper coverage of intimate partner violence: skewing representations of risk. *The Journal of Communication, 58(1)*, 168–186. https://doi.org/10.1111/j.1460-2466.2007.00379.x.

Carratalá, A. (2016): Press coverage of same-sex domestic violence cases in Spain. *Revista Latina de Comunicación Social, 71*, 40–65. http://dx.doi.org/10.4185/RLCS-2016-1083en.

Carter, S.L. (2017, May 2). The NFL has a serious violence problem. *Chicago Tribune.* https://www.chicagotribune.com/opinion/commentary/ct-nfl-sexual-assault-violence-20170502-story.html.

Cayemittes M, Busangu MF, Bizimana JD, Barrère B, Sévère B, Cayemittes V, Charles E. (2013). *Enquête Mortalité, Morbidité et Utilisation des Services, Haïti, 2012* [Mortality, morbidity and services utilization survey], Haïti, 2012. MSPP, IHE, and ICF.

Centers for Disease Control and Prevention. (2003). *Costs of intimate partner violence against women in the United States.* National Center for Injury Prevention and Control. https://www.cdc.gov/violenceprevention/pdf/IPVBook-a.pdf.

Chew, M.M. (2011). Analysis of an anti-domestic violence internet forum in China: Mutual help, open communication, and social activism. *China Media Research, 7(1)*, 65–73.

Concepcion, M. (2010, August 5). Eminem tackles abuse in "love the way you lie" clip. *Billboard.* https://www.billboard.com/articles/columns/viral-videos/957009/eminem-tackles-abuse-in-love-the-way-you-lie-clip.

Constantino, R.E., Braxter, B., Ren, D., Burroughs, J.D., Doswell, W.M., Wu, L., Hwang, J.G., Klem, M.L., Joshi, J.B.D., & Greene, W.B. (2015). Comparing online with face-to-face HELPP intervention in women experiencing intimate partner violence. *Issues in Mental Health Nursing, 36(6)*, 430–438. https://doi.org/10.3109/01612840.2014.991049.

Davis, S. (2014). *Annual report of the Chief Medical Officer 2013: Public mental health priorities-investing in the evidence.* United Kingdom Department of Health. https://mrc.ukri.org/documents/pdf/chief-medical-officer-annual-report-2013/.

de Vreese, C.H., Boomgaarden, H.G., & Semetko, H.A. (2011). (In)direct framing effects: The effects of news media framing on public support for Turkish membership in the European Union. *Communication Research, 38(2)*, 179–205. https://doi.org/10.1177/0093650210384934.

Dill-Shackleford, K.E., Green, M.C., Scharrer, E., Wetterer, C., & Schackleford, L.E. (2015). Setting the stage for social change: Using live theater to dispel myths about intimate partner violence. *Journal of Health Communication, 20(8)*, 969–976. https://doi.org/10.1080/10810730.2015.1018622.

Dinh, J. (2010, July 27). *Rihanna says Eminem Collabo was "something that needed to be done."* MTV. http://www.mtv.com/news/1644486/rihanna-says-eminem-collabo-was-something-that-needed-to-be-done/.

Dockterman, E. (2014, September 16). Rihanna dropped from Thursday night football after she slams NFL and CBS. *Time.* https://time.com/3386650/rihanna-nfl-ray-rice/.

Duke, A., & Rowlands, T. (2009, June 22). *Chris Brown pleads guilty in Rihanna assault case.* CNN. https://www.cnn.com/2009/SHOWBIZ/Music/06/22/chris.brown.hearing/.

Edleson, J.L., & Brygger, M.P. (1986). Gender differences in reporting of battering incidences. *Family Relations: An Interdisciplinary Journal of Applied Family Studies, 35(3)*, 377–382. https://doi.org/10.2307/584364.

Eisenberg, N., & Miller, P.A. (1987). The relation of empathy to prosocial and related behaviors. *Psychological Bulletin, 101(1)*, 91–119. https://doi.org/10.1037/0033-2909.101.1.91.

El-Khoury, J.R., & Shafer, A. (2016). Narrative exemplars and the celebrity spokesperson in Lebanese anti-domestic violence public service announcements. *Journal of Health Communication, 21(8)*, 935–943. https://doi.org/10.1080/10810730.2016.1177146.

Enck, S.M., & McDaniel, B.A. (2012). Playing with fire: Cycles of domestic violence in Eminem and Rihanna's "Love the way you lie." *Communication, Culture & Critique, 5(4)*, 618–644. https://doi.org/10.1111/j.1753-9137.2012.01147.x.

Enck-Wanzer, S.M. (2009). All's fair in love and sport: Black masculinity and domestic violence in the news. *Communication and Critical/Cultural Studies, 6(1)*, 1–18. https://doi.org/10.1080/14791420802632087.

Ernst, A., Weiss, S.J., Morgan-Edwards, S., Rihani, T., Coffman, B., Clark, R., Lucero, M., Jansen, L., Brokmeyer, J., Kaul, E., Hegyi, M., Ramone B., & Valdez, M. (2012). Derivation and validation of a short emergency department screening tool for perpetrators of intimate partner violence: The Perpetrator Rapid Scale (PERPS). *Journal of Emergency Medicine, 42*, 206–217. https://doi.org/10.1016/j.jemermed.2011.01.032.

Exner-Cortens, D., Eckenrode, J., & Rothman, E. (2013). Longitudinal associations between teen dating violence victimization and adverse health outcomes. *Pediatrics, 131(1)*, 71–78. https://doi.org/10.1542/peds.2012-1029.

Falik, M.M., & Collins, K.S. (Eds.). (1996). *Women's health: The Commonwealth Fund Survey.* Johns Hopkins University Press.

Federal Bureau of Investigation. (2001). *Crime in the United States 2000—Uniform Crime Reports.* U.S. Department of Justice. https://ucr.fbi.gov/crime-in-the-u.s/2000.

Fisher, L., & Zhou, M. (2009, June 22). *Rihanna and Chris Brown come face to face in court.* ABC News. https://abcnews.go.com/Entertainment/story?id=7892781&page=1.

Forman, E. (2009, March 14). Teens split on blame in assault case. *The Salem News.* https://www.salemnews.com/archives/teens-split-on-blame-in-assault-case/article_2ad95d2c-f143-5d73-812e-8da6ab92b886.html.

Foshee, V.A., Reyes, H.L., Gottfredson, N.C., Chang, L.Y., & Ennett, S.T. (2013). A longitudinal examination of psychological, behavioral, academic, and relationship consequences of dating abuse victimization among a primarily rural sample of adolescents. *Journal of Adolescent Health, 53(6)*, 723–729. https://doi.org/10.1016/j.jadohealth.2013.06.016.

France, L.R. (2018, March 16). *Rihanna criticizes Snapchat for ad referencing domestic violence.* CNN. https://www.cnn.com/2018/03/15/entertainment/rihanna-snapchat/index.html.

Frost, K., Frank, E., & Maibach, E. (1997). Relative risk in the news media: A quantification of misrepresentation. *American Journal of Public Health, 87(5)*, 842–845. https://doi.org/10.2105/ajph.87.5.842.

Gage, A.J., Honore, J.G., & Deleon, J. (2016). Short-term effects of a violence-prevention curriculum on knowledge of dating violence among high school students in Port-au-Prince, Haiti. *Journal of Communication in Healthcare, 9(3)*, 178–189. https://doi.org/10.1080/17538068.2016.1205300.

Ganley, A. (1998). Health care responses to perpetrators of domestic violence. In A. Ganley & C. Warshaw (Eds.), *Improving the health care response to violence: A resource manual for health care providers* (pp. 89–106). Family Violence Prevention Fund.

Gay, R. (2014, September 16). *Rihanna's suffered domestic violence—& no one will let her forget it.* Refinery 29. https://www.refinery29.com/en-us/2014/09/74527/rihanna-song-cut-cbs-nfl-domestic-violence.

Gee, R.E., Brindis, C.D., Diaz, A., Garcia, F., Gregory, K., Peck, M.G., & Reece, E.A. (2011). *Current Opinion in Obstetrics and Gynecology, 23(6)*, 471–480. https://doi.org/10.1097/GCO.0b013e32834cdcc6.

Gentzler, D., & Romano, C. (2016, October 17). *After "worst decision of my life," Ray Rice speaks out about domestic violence.* NBC Washington. https://www.nbcwashington.com/news/local/after-worst-decision-of-my-life-ray-rice-speaks-out-about-domestic-violence/57695/.

Ghandour, R.M., Campbell, J.C., & Lloyd, J. (2015). Screening and counseling for intimate partner violence: A vision for the future. *Journal of Women's Health, 24(1)*, https://doi.org/10.1089/jwh.2014.4885.

Glinow, K.V. (2012, October 5). *Chris Brown, Rihanna's rekindled relationship explained in "real" video.* HuffPost. https://www.huffpost.com/entry/chris-brown-rihanna-video-back-together_n_1942066.

Goehring, C., Renegar, V., & Puhl, L. (2017). "Abusive furniture": Visual metonymy and the Hungarian stop violence against women campaign. *Women's Studies in Communication, 40(4)*, 440–457. https://doi.org/10.1080/07491409.2017.1368760.

Goldberg, S. (2013, May 6). *Rihanna and Chris Brown's relationship through the years.* CNN. https://www.cnn.com/2013/02/08/showbiz/celebrity-news-gossip/rihanna-chris-brown-through-the-years/index.html.

Golding, J.M. (1996). Sexual assault history and limitations in physical functioning in two general population samples. *Research in Nursing and Health, 19(1)*, 33–44. https://doi. org/10.1002/(SICI)1098-240X(199602)19:1%3C33::AID-NUR4%3E3.0.CO;2-M.

Goldstein, M. (2009, February 12). *Chris Brown and Rihanna: The whole story.* Spin. https:// www.spin.com/2009/02/chris-brown-and-rihanna-whole-story/.

Goodman, L.A., Koss, M.P., & Russo, N.F. (1993). Violence against women: Physical and mental effects. Part I: Research findings. *Applied and Preventive Psychology, 2(2)*, 79–89. https://doi. org/10.1016/S0962-1849(05)80114-3.

Gross, K., & D'Ambrosio, L. (2004). Framing emotional response. *Political Psychology, 25*, 1–29. https://doi.org/10.1111/j.1467-9221.2004.00354.x.

Hamberger, L.K., Rhodes, K., & Brown, J. (2015). Screening and intervention for intimate partner violence in healthcare settings: Creating sustainable system-level programs. *Journal of Women's Health, 24(1)*, 91–96. https://doi.org/10.1089/jwh.2014.4861.

Hamby, S., Finkelhor, D., Turner, H., & Ormond, R. (2011). *Children's exposure to intimate partner violence and other family violence.* National Survey of Children's Exposure to Violence— Juvenile Justice Bulletin. https://www.ncjrs.gov/pdffiles1/ojjdp/232272.pdf.

Hartmans, A. (2018, March 15). *Rihanna responds to the Snapchat ad making light of Chris Brown's brutal attack on her. "Shame on you."* Business Insider. https://www.businessinsider. com/rihanna-chris-brown-snapchat-ad-response-2018-3.

Hoffman, J. (2009, March 19). Teenage girls stand by their man. *New York Times.* https://www. nytimes.com/2009/03/19/fashion/19brown.html.

Holmes, K., & Sher, L. (2013). Dating violence and suicidal behavior in adolescents. *International Journal of Adolescent Medicine and Health, 25(3)*, 257–261. https://doi.org/10.1515/ ijamh-2013-0059 International. https://www.mspp.gouv.ht/site/downloads/EMMUS%20V %20web.pdf.

Huggins, A. (2009, August 31). *Chris Brown says he still loves Rihanna.* CNN. https://www.cnn. com/2009/SHOWBIZ/Music/08/31/chris.brown.interview/.

Human Rights Watch. (2013). *Hungary: Chronic domestic violence—Stronger police action, more shelters needed.* https://www.hrw.org/news/2013/11/06/hungary-chronic-domestic-violence.

Jaeger, J.R., Spielman, D., Cronholm, P., Applebaum, S., Holmes, W.C. (2008). Screening male primary care patients for intimate partner violence perpetration. *Journal of General Internal Medicine, 23(8)*, 1152–1156. https://doi.org/10.1007/s11606-008-0634-9.

Jasinski, J.L. (2001). Theoretical explanations for violence against women. In C. Renzetti, J. Edleson, & R. Bergen (Eds.), *Sourcebook on violence against women* (pp. 5–21). Sage.

Jeltsen, M. (2016, February 1). *This is not a love story.* Huff Post. https://testkitchen.huffing tonpost.com/this-is-not-a-love-story/#.

Joyce, S.N., & Martinez, M. (2017). From social merchandizing to social spectacle: Portrayals of domestic violence in TV Globo's prime-time telenovelas. *International Journal of Communication, 11*, 220–236. https://ijoc.org/index.php/ijoc/article/view/5905/1894.

Kaslow, N.J., Thompson, M.P., Meadows, L.A., Jacobs, D., Chance, S., Gibb, B., Bornstein, H., Hollins, L., Rashid, A., & Phillips, K. (1998). Factors that mediate and moderate the link between partner abuse and suicidal behavior in African American women. *Journal of Consulting and Clinical Psychology, 66(3)*, 533–40. https://doi.org/10.1037//0022-006x.66.3.533.

Kimberg, L.S. (2008). Addressing intimate partner violence with male patients: A review and introduction of pilot guidelines. *Journal of General Internal Medicine, 23(12)*, 2071–2078. https://doi.org/10.1007/s11606-008-0755-1.

Leonard, E. (2009, September 14). Chris Brown: "I'm very ashamed." *People*, 80–82.

Makepeace, J.M. (1981). Courtship violence among college students. *Family Relations Family Relations: An Interdisciplinary Journal of Applied Family Studies, 30(1)*, 97–102. https://doi. org/10.2307/584242.

Malone, M. (2014, September 29). *NFL domestic violence spate sparks local TV initiatives.* Broadcasting & Cable. https://www.nexttv.com/news/nfl-domestic-violence-spate-sparks-local-tv-initiatives-134372.

Markham, D.W. (2003). Mental illness and domestic violence: Implications for family law litigation. *Journal of Poverty Law and Policy, 37*, 23–35. https://safehavensonline.org/media/com_ library/resources/66-mental-illness-and-dv.pdf.

Martz, G., & Sher, L. (2009, November 6). *Rihanna exclusive: "He had no soul in his eyes."* ABC

News. https://abcnews.go.com/2020/rihanna-exclusive-good-morning-america/story? id=9005078.

Miller, E., McCaw, B., Humphreys, B.L., & Mitchell, C. (2015). Integrating intimate partner violence assessment and intervention into healthcare in the United States: A systems approach. *Journal of Women's Health, 24(1),* 92–99. https://doi.org/10.1089/jwh.2014.4870.

Moyer, V.A. (2013). Screening for intimate partner violence and abuse of elderly and vulnerable adults: U.S. preventive services task force recommendation statement. *Annals of Internal Medicine, 158(6),* 478–486. https://doi.org/10.7326/0003-4819-158-6-20130319000588.

Moyer-Gusé, E., & Nabi, R.L. (2010). Explaining the effects of narrative in an entertainment television program: Overcoming resistance to persuasion. *Human Communication Research, 36(1),* 26–52. https://doi.org/10.1111/j.1468-2958.2009.01367.x.

Nabi, R.L., Southwell, B., & Hornik, R. (2002). Predicting intentions versus predicting behaviors: Domestic violence prevention from a theory of reasoned action perspective. *Health Communication, 14(4),* 429–449. https://doi.org/10.1207/S15327027HC1404_2.

National Network to End Domestic Violence (NNEDV) Report. (2009). *Domestic Violence counts 2008: A 24-hour census of domestic violence shelter and services across the United States.* NNEDV. https://nnedv.org/content/domestic-violence-counts-2008-census-report/.

Nelson, H.D., Bougatsos, C., & Blazina, I. (2012). Screening women for intimate partner violence: A systematic review to update the 2004 U.S. Preventive Services Task Force recommendation. *Annals of Internal Medicine, 156(11),* 796–808. https://doi.org/10.7326/ 0003-4819-156-11-201206050-00447.

Nettleton, P.H. (2011). Domestic violence in men's and women's magazines: Women are guilty of shooting the wrong men, men are not guilty of hitting women. *Women's Studies in Communication, 34(2),* 139–160. https://doi.org/10.1080/07491409.2011.618240.

Nettleton, P.H. (2018). *Maxim* is a bully: Making women the victim for male pleasure. *The Journal of Magazine Media, 18(2),* 1–18. https://aejmcmagazine.arizona.edu/Journal/Spring2018/ Nettleton.pdf.

NICE. (2014). *PH50: Domestic violence and abuse: Multi-agency working.* United Kingdom National Institute for Health and Care Excellence. https://www.nice.org.uk/guidance/ph50/ resources/domestic-violence-and-abuse-multiagency-working-pdf-1996411687621.

Oriel, K.A., Fleming, M.F. (1998). Screening men for partner violence in a primary care setting. A new strategy for detecting domestic violence. *Journal of Family Practice, 46(6),* 493–498.

Pasquini, M. (2018, March 24). Chrissy Teigen says she stopped using Snapchat after Rihanna scandal. *People Magazine.* https://people.com/celebrity/chrissy-teigen-stopped-using-snapchat-rihanna/.

Peled, E., & Edleson, E. (1994). Advocacy for battered women: A national survey. *Journal of Family Violence, 9(3),* 285–296. https://doi.org/10.1007/BF01531952.

Penti, B., Timmons, J., & Adams, D. (2018). The role of the physician when a patient discloses intimate partner violence perpetration: A literature review. *Journal of the American Board of Family Medicine, 31(4),* 635–644. https://doi.org/10.3122/jabfm.2018.04.170440. PMID: 29986990.

Penti, B., Tran, H., Timmons, J., Rothman, E.F., & Wilkinson, J. (2017). Physicians' experiences with male patients who perpetrate intimate partner violence. *The Journal of the American Board of Family Medicine, 30(2),* 239–247. https://doi.org/10.3122/jabfm.2017.02.160258.

Perez, L. (2018, March 15). Snapchat apologizes for "disgusting" Chris Brown-Rihanna domestic violence ad. *The Hollywood Reporter.* https://www.hollywoodreporter.com/ news/rihanna-calls-snapchat-chris-brown-domestic-violence-ad-1094732.

Petersen, R., Moracco, K.E., Goldstein, K.M., & Clark, K.A. (2004). Moving beyond disclosure: Women's perspectives on barriers and motivators to seeking assistance for intimate partner violence. *Women & Health, 40(3),* 63–76. https://doi.org/0.1300/j013v40n03_05.

Pico-Alfonso, M.A., Garcia-Linares, M.I., Celda-Navarro, N., Blasco-Ros, C., Echeburua, E., & Martinez, M. (2006). The impact of physical, psychological, and sexual intimate male partner violence on women's mental health: Depressive symptoms, posttraumatic stress disorder, state anxiety, and suicide. *Journal of Women's Health, 15(5),* 599–611. https://doi.org/10.1089/ jwh.2006.15.599.

Rahman, M. (2015). Intimate partner violence and termination of pregnancy: A cross-sectional

study of married Bangladeshi women. *Reproductive Health, 12,* 102–109. https://doi.org/
10.1186/s12978-015-0095-7.

Robinson, L. (2015, October 6). Rihanna in Cuba: The cover story. *Vanity Fair.* https://www.
vanityfair.com/hollywood/2015/10/rihanna-cover-cuba-annie-leibovitz.

Rodriguez, J. (2009, November 6). *Chris Brown responds to Rihanna interview.* MTV. http://
www.mtv.com/news/1625767/chris-brown-responds-to-rihanna-interview/.

Rothman, E.F., Nagaswaran, A., Johnson, R.M., Adams, K.M., Scrivens, J., & Baughman, A.
(2012). U.S. tabloid magazine coverage of a celebrity dating abuse incident: Rihanna and
Chris Brown. *Journal of Health Communication, 17(6),* 733–744. https://doi.org/10.1080/108
10730.2011.635778.

Shahzadi, N. K., Qureshi, M.B.H., & Islam, M. (2012). Effect of domestic violence on women
psychology in Pakistan. *Language in India, 12(10),* 293–311.

Shaikh, M.A. (2000). Domestic violence against women—perspective from Pakistan. *Journal of
Pakistan Medical Association, 50(9),* 312–314.

Singh, V., Tolman, R., Walton, R., Chermack, S., & Cunningham, R. (2014). Characteristics of
men who perpetrate intimate partner violence. *The Journal of the American Board of Family
Medicine, 27(5),* 661–668. https://doi.org/10.3122/jabfm.2014.05.130247.

Souza-Leal, B., de-Carvalho, Carlos-Alberto, & Antunes, E. (2018). Violence against Brazilian
women in public and mediatic spheres. *Media Education Research Journal, 26(55),* 19–27.
https://doi.org/10.3916/C55-2018-02.

Sprague, S., Madden, K., Simunovic, N., Godin, K., Pham, N.K., Bhandari, M., & Goslings, J.C.
(2012). Barriers to screening for intimate partner violence. *Women Health, 52(6),* 587–605.
https://doi.org/10.1080/03630242.2012.690840.

Stefansky, E. (2018, March 17). Snapchat lost $800 million after Rihanna criticized its offensive
ad. *Vanity Fair.* https://www.vanityfair.com/style/2018/03/rihanna-chris-brown-snapchat-
ad#:~:text=Snapchat%20Lost.

Stewart, D.E., & Chandra, P. (2016). *The World Psychiatric Association (WPA) International
Competency-Based Curriculum for Mental Health Care Providers on Intimate Partner Violence
and Sexual Violence against Women.* WPA. https://3ba346de-fde6-473f-b1da-536498661f9c.
filesusr.com/ugd/e172f3_c4cf4b0c0df34141ab9d439ea715176a.pdf.

Tate, A. (2013, December 16). *Rihanna gives fan relationship advice: "I refuse to let a man
play me."* International Business Times. https://www.ibtimes.com/rihanna-gives-fan-
relationship-advice-i-refuse-let-man-play-me-1510456.

Todahl, J., & Walters, E. (2011). Universal screening for intimate partner violence: A systematic review. *Journal of Marital and Family Therapy, 37(3),* 355–369. https://doi.org/
10.1111/j.1752-0606.2009.00179.x.

Trevillion, K., Corker, E., Capron, L., & Oram, S. (2016). Improving mental health services
responses to domestic violence and abuse. *International Review of Psychiatry, 28(5),* 423–432.
http://dx.doi.org/10.1080/09540261.2016.1201053.

UNICEF. (2000). *Domestic Violence against Women and Girls.* Innocenti Research Center.
https://www.unicef-irc.org/publications/pdf/digest6e.pdf.

United States Centers of Medicare and Medicaid Services. (2013). *Fact Sheet: Women's preventive services coverage, non-profit religious organizations, and closely-held for-profit entities.* Department of Health and Human Services. https://www.cms.gov/CCIIO/Resources/
Fact-Sheets-and-FAQs/womens-preven-02012013.

Wallace, T., & Smith, H.B. (2010). *A synthesis of the learning from the Stop Violence Against
Women campaign, 2004–2010.* Amnesty International. https://www.amnesty.org/en/
documents/act77/008/2010/en/.

Watts, C., & Zimmerman, C. (2002). Violence against women: Global scope and magnitude.
Lancet, 359(9313), 1232–1237. https://doi.org/10.1016/S0140-6736(02)08221-1.

Weathers, M.R., Sanderson, J., Neal, A., & Gramlich, K. (2016). From silence to #WhyISayed:
Locating our stories and finding our voices. *Qualitative Research Reports in Communication,
17(1),* 60–67. https://doi.org/10.1080/17459435.2016.1143385.

Winfrey, O. [Oprah Winfrey Network]. (2012, August 20). *Oprah's Next Chapter: Rihanna opens
up about Chris Brown* [Video]. YouTube. https://www.youtube.com/watch?v=NU_fl6cnqgQ.

World Health Organization. (2005). *Multi-country study on women's health and domestic violence against women: Summary report of initial results on prevalence, health outcomes and women's responses.* WHO Press. https://www.who.int/reproductivehealth/publications/violence/24159358X/en/.

World Health Organization. (2009). *Promoting gender equality to prevent violence against women.* WHO Press. https://apps.who.int/iris/handle/10665/44098.

World Health Organization. (2013). *Responding to intimate partner violence and sexual violence against women: WHO clinical and policy guidelines.* WHO Press. https://apps.who.int/iris/bitstream/handle/10665/85240/9789241548595_eng.pdf.

Wray, R.J., Hornik, R.M., Gandy, O.H., Stryker, J., Ghez, M., Mitchell-Clark, K. (2004). Preventing domestic violence in the African American community: Assessing the impact of a dramatic radio serial. *Journal of Health Communication, 9(1),* 31–52. https://doi.org/10.1080/10810730490271656.

Zabihzadeh, S., Hashim, R.S., & Chua Chen Wei, G.C. (2015). Domestic violence against women in Atiq Rahimi's *The Patience Stone. Journal of Language Studies, 15(3),* 51–66.

Zurbano Berenguer, B., & Garcia-Gordillo, M. (2017). Methodological proposal for the evaluation of the ethical quality of news about violence against women. *Communication & Society, 30(1),* 73–85. https://doi.org/10.15581/003.30.1.73-85.

3

Overcoming the Trauma
of Family Violence

Celebrity Encounters with Abusive Fathers

In a letter written on December 20, 2012, to members of the National Task Force on Children Exposed to Violence, then–Attorney General Eric H. Holder, Jr., stated:

> First, thank you for your extraordinary work on the report on children exposed to violence that you presented to me on December 12, 2012. It details not only the shocking, national scope of this phenomenon, but also lays out 56 concrete recommendations for responding. Your findings are the result of countless hearings, listening sessions, and meetings with experts, community members, advocates, and survivors over the past year. They make clear that, of the 76 million children in the United States, an estimated 46 million are exposed to violence, crime, and abuse on an annual basis. And they indicate, this is much more than a public health crisis which imposes a cost burden on our health care system amounting to hundreds of billions of dollars each year. It is also a significant public safety and criminal justice problem—with growing financial and human costs.

Holder was gratified that the task force had been created by his 2010 landmark Defending Childhood Initiative and proud of its work. Violence is a public health problem, and among its most vulnerable targets are children (Margolin & Gordis, 2004).

The idealization of the family and behavior deemed normative for families in various societies obfuscate family violence including domestic violence and child maltreatment. There should be a differentiation between acceptable and unacceptable family behavior, particularly when there are disagreements or strife, and abuse or battery. Family members argue and display inappropriate behaviors, such as lashing out verbally, raising their voices, and saying hurtful things. These behaviors can take an emotional, psychological, and physical toll on family members. According to Gael

Surgenor (2009), in New Zealand, half of all murders are committed by a family member. Each year, the police deal with approximately 70,000 calls about family violence, which authorities believe is a fraction of the total number of family violence incidents (Surgenor, 2009). Many of incidents of family violence go unreported. An international study pertaining to the prevalence of child sexual abuse in 21 countries worldwide found that between 7 percent and 36 percent of women and between 3 percent and 29 percent of men report childhood sexual victimization (Finkelhor, 1994). Prevalent studies of child abuse indicate that childhood maltreatment is 10 times greater than reported (Creighton, 2002). According to Widom (1989), one in six maltreated boys and girls goes on to become a violent offender, while one in eight sexually abused boys goes on to become a sexual offender (Salter et al., 2003).

Abusive behaviors do not exist in a vacuum. A family's environment can provide conditions that turn normal family discord into something more dysfunctional. Power differentials between partners or between parents and children oftentimes make women and children more likely to be victimized in families prone to violence. The first place many individuals turn when they want to preserve their wellness and well-being is their family, but if the family is the problem, and individuals are legally compelled to stay with them or to work problems out, then the idealization of the family in society subverts autonomy and undermines safety. "Because families are made up of interconnected subsystems (e.g., marital, parent-child), violence in one family subsystem can spill over into other family subsystems" (Margolin & Gordis, 2004, p. 154). More than 50 percent of female victims of domestic violence live in a household with children under the age of 12 years old (U.S. Department of Justice—*Violence by Intimates*, 1998). Children who observe aggression between their parents, who are also victimized, in various circumstances, may perceive aggression and conflict as an acute threat, complicating internal efforts to regulate their own emotions and hypervigilance to cues of interpersonal conflict (Margolin & Gordis, 2004). The safety of these children is at an increased risk because of severe disruptions in parent-child relations. The National Center on Child Abuse and Neglect estimated that approximately 23 per 1,000 children are victims of maltreatment—the manifestation of their physical abuse, sexual abuse, and neglect (Sedlack & Broadhurst, 1996). Some national studies have estimates as high as 49 per 1,000 children experiencing maltreatment (Straus et al., 1998). The focus of this chapter is family violence, especially child maltreatment perpetrated by fathers or father figures.

Various countries differentiate between domestic violence and family violence in order to explicate and examine the effects of violence on family members who are not in an intimate relationship. The Australian Government's National Plan to Reduce Violence Against Women and Their Children (COAG, 2009) distinguishes between domestic or IPV and family violence by defining family violence more broadly as violence between family members, as well as violence between intimate partners. Children in households and families throughout the world are victims too. "Children may be silenced by fear for their mothers, fear of getting hurt themselves, and/or fear of undesired changes in their lives as a result of the violence or their mothers' responses to it" (Chetty & Agee, 2009, p. 37). Children are traumatized in households and families prone to violence, yet not all children are affected or react to exposure to family violence the same way (Geffner et al., 2003). Holden (2003) emphasizes describing children's experiences with family violence with the term "exposed" rather than "witnessed" or "observed" because it is more inclusive of the ways children may experience family violence. Holden (2003) focuses on aspects of children's exposure including prenatal events, being victimized, participating, intervening, being an eyewitness, overhearing, observing the initial effects, experiencing the aftermath, hearing about the violence or being oblivious to it. Despite exposure to family violence, children are resilient when dealing with familial adversity. The introduction of adequate support systems and coping skills can help adults and children mitigate the adverse effects of family violence, as well as mediate risk factors associated with family violence or buffer their exposure (Huang et al., 2015; O'Brien et al., 2013; Stark, 2009). Research indicates a variety of support systems and coping skills that work, such as positive parenting (Levendosky et al., 2003), positive self-esteem (Bolger & Patterson, 2001), positive relationship with at least one caring and non-abusive adult (Lynskey & Ferguson, 1997), parents and peers who disapprove of antisocial behavior (Herrenkohl et al., 2005), involvement in a religious community, and easy child temperament and cognitive ability (Buckner et al., 2003).

Sometimes support systems and coping skills are not enough. A variety of factors mediate children's responsiveness to the risk factors of family violence and maltreatment. Some of these factors interact with one another including contextual, familial, and environmental factors, and produce positive and negative effects on children (Fosco et al., 2007; Hester et al., 2000). Other factors that affect children's resiliency are the magnitude and frequency of violence (Sternberg et al., 1993), maternal mental health problems (Huang et al., 2010; Levendosky et al., 2006), stressful life events (Levendosky et al., 2003), and parental substance abuse (Onyskiw, 2003). Minority status paired with a low-income level can exacerbate violence in households and among families already struggling with intermittent or steady poverty, neighborhood disadvantage, and community violence. One or more of these factors, when commingled with the personal characteristics of a child, influences his or her perceptions and interpretations of abuse (Grych & Fincham, 1990; Herrenkohl et al., 2008; Onyskiw, 2003). Culture, gender, and family socialization are factors that influence individual and societal perception of behavior characterized or uncharacterized as family violence (Chetty & Agee, 2009).

Race is another salient factor for in family violence. Whether the focus is on Black children in countries such as the U.S., or Indian children in countries such as New Zealand, these children's homes oftentimes are their only refuge from racism, so when violence invades their safe space, it intensifies their insecurity and vulnerability (Hester et. Al., 2000; Wali, 2001). Men from immigrant communities encounter anger, disrespect, oppression, and discrimination in their dealings with members within and outside of their communities. Sometimes the pressures thrust upon them are personalized and internalized, and they act out. "Social structural inequalities based on race/ethnicity, social class and legal status create numerous disadvantages for working class Latino immigrants in their adaptation to the new culture" (Hancock & Siu, 2009, p. 129). These disadvantages trigger some boyfriends, husbands, and fathers to redirect toward family members the pain and anguish they experience in their host culture, developing coping mechanisms such as excessive drinking or womanizing to defend against their own disempowerment (Flores-Ortiz, 2000; Hancock & Siu, 2009; Morash et al., 2000). The Bureau of Justice Statistics (2002) indicates that while there are similar rates of domestic violence across Hispanic, white, Black, and American Indian populations, there are still differences, such as racial or ethnic minorities not seeking services for domestic violence as often as their white counterparts, cultural and language barriers, and prior experiences of racism. Minority children may experience more risk factors, including poverty, living in households lacking services, racism, prejudice, and discrimination, which reduce their chances of resiliency and mitigate their likelihood for positive outcomes in abusive environments (Arrington & Wilson, 2000; Gewirtz & Edleson, 2007).

According to Widom and White's (1997) longitudinal study, rates of arrest for violent crimes by age 29 for Black and white youth who were abused or neglected were higher than the rates for youth who were not maltreated. These youth witness violence at home and emulate it. Prior history of abuse in a youth's family is a risk marker in forming subsequent abusive relationships. "For this reason, the study of domestic violence is an imperative for family communication scholars, who are well prepared to examine relational nuances that may subtly reinforce and contribute to the maintenance of violence" (Stamp & Sabourin, 1995, p. 284). Furthermore, young people's vulnerability to violence in relationships is heightened by strong peer norms, inexperience, age differences in relationships, and lack of access to services (Flood & Fergus, 2008). Family violence affects young people in childhood and adulthood. It weakens bonds between family members, harms bystanders, and facilitates abuse in future relationships (e.g., parent-child relationships and romantic relationships). The only way to ensure family violence does not foment and spread is to prevent it.

The UN Convention on the Rights of the Child declared the freedom of children from all forms of violence to be a universal right (UN, 1989, Article 19), which would be expanded to include an obligation of nations, especially its national signatories, to "…take all appropriate legislative, administrative, social and educational measures to protect the child from all forms of physical or mental violence, injury or abuse, neglect or negligent treatment, maltreatment or exploitation, including sexual abuse, while in the care of parent(s), legal guardian(s) or any other person who has the care of the child." (UN, 2011, p. 3). Countries around the world recognize the ruinous effect family violence has on society. UNICEF (2019) reported that more countries have ratified the Convention on the Rights of the Child as of November 2005 than any other human rights treaty in history—a total of 192 countries.

Negligence and Maltreatment Impair Childhood and Adult Development

In a 1962 issue of the *Journal of the American Medical Association*, physician C. Henry Kempe and his colleagues published "The Battered-Child Syndrome," an article that shaped scientists' and the public's perception of the problem of child abuse (Nelson, 1984). Violence toward women, especially what was referred to as wife abuse, garnered attention in the 1970s (Gelles, 1985). The evolution of the coverage of child abuse and wife abuse led to greater scrutiny of family violence. Silence that traditionally stifled discussion of family violence was attributable to three factors: (1) lack of awareness, (2) general acceptance, and (3) denial (Star, 1980). Overtime, these factors lessened in their potency, as society became more sensitive to the effects of violence on adults and children. In the U.S. and other countries, the public is increasingly aware of the toll violence takes on individuals and their families in various facets of society. Media outlets and their audiences are no longer in denial, being more likely to frame family violence as another form of criminal violent behavior. Now violence in the home is perceived as a family issue, a violence issue, a criminological issue, and a social problem.

Despite the shift in perceptions about family violence, there is still dissension about whether family violence is a public issue or a private matter. However, when family violence involves negligence—when neglect is a precursor to interpersonal violence within a family—the matter is no longer a private one. Instead, it becomes a criminological issue and social problem. Neglect is the most common type of child maltreatment. "Unlike physical or sexual abuse, where something is actually *done*, neglect is *failure to do* something. Types of neglect include not providing food, clothing or medical attention. It can include failure to supervise, provide a safe environment or provide proper education" (Kendall-Tackett, 2001, p. 3). A neglectful parent can also provide food and clothing but be emotionally absent. Neglectful parents live in urban, suburban, and rural areas, in poverty-stricken, middle-class, and wealthy neighborhoods. Child maltreatment occurs in families across the demographic spectrum. In violent families, both fathers and mothers can be the perpetrators of violence against one another and their children. Yet violence that is part of a broader pattern of relational control oftentimes involves male partners and fathers (Graham-Kevan & Archer, 2003; Johnson, 2005). Female partners and mothers influenced by their partners' relational control use ways of separating violence and the men who enact it from "the real him." "This justification defined the men they loved as good people who sometimes 'weren't themselves' or were affected by things beyond their control and thus should not be held accountable for abusive actions" (Wood, 2000, p. 5). Many men and women believe an individual's pathology, psychology, and behavior are more important risk factors for family violence than social gender norms (Worden & Carlson, 2005), which underscores why many women experiencing their partners' relational control have a tendency to blame themselves. They believe they did something to enrage their partners. They have low self-worth and feel they do not deserve better treatment. Instead of blaming the norms of a patriarchal society and the structural elements of IPV, they use "…symbolic, cognitive strategies that women employ in their efforts to make sense of and justify their partners' violence" (Wood, 2000, p. 2).

Children in households with fathers exerting relational control and IPV are in danger. The implications for children in abusive families outlive adolescence and continue into adulthood. Children anticipate violence at home, expect it in their relationships, and learn that it is a primary means of conflict resolution (Fein, 1993). Children model their parents. Conflict resolution may begin with verbal negotiation, but in abusive families, disagreements and conflicts escalate quickly along a continuum from verbal negotiation to verbal abuse, physical violence, and physical abuse. Violent behaviors include pushing, shoving, grabbing, slapping, kicking, biting, hitting with a hard object, hitting with a fist, beating, and using a knife or gun (Straus, 1979). Another implication of children in abusive families is the manifestation of emotional abuse. Verbal aggressiveness adversely affects children, especially when they encounter name-calling, mocking, and hateful and shaming speech. Moreover, children can become emotionally scarred when parents abandon or threaten to abandon them. Children take these experiences into adulthood. Their trauma becomes the source of many negative internal messages that they replay in their minds (Kendall-Tackett, 2001). This cycle of violence with its origin in childhood predisposes the survivor to violence in later years (Dolon & Hendricks, 1991). Neglected or abused children have an increased likelihood of arrest as both juveniles and adults for committing violent crimes (Widom, 1992). Many male batterers were beaten as children or witnessed family violence. Exposure to these circumstances may cause female victims to regard abuse or neglect as normative behavior (Hancock & Siu, 2009). "Some adult survivors recount how their mothers or fathers made them feel responsible for the abuse that was inflicted upon them. These children often end up in abusive relationships as adults" (Kendall-Tackett, 2001, p. 4). Unfortunately, the abusers may repeat what happened to them in childhood, blaming their victims for the abuse.

Women affected by family violence in childhood often have an impaired sense of self. They may perceive their own feelings as unreliable and use the reactions of others to gauge which feelings are appropriate in various situations. Their childhood experiences can make them more easily manipulated, which can increase their risk of revictimization (Nam & Lincoln, 2017). A survey of 5,908 French women in stable relationships reported that one in seven women with a childhood history of maltreatment reported serious abuse by her spouse (Jaspard et al., 2003), while a British survey of 1,207 women attending primary care services identified a significant co-occurrence of sexual and physical abuse in both childhood and adulthood (Cold et al., 2001). When confronted by adversity, these women might have difficulty asking others for help, participating in support networks, and taking advantage of available services (Kendall-Tackett, 2001).

Theoretical Considerations for Understanding Exposure to Childhood Abuse

According to developmental psychopathology violence is jointly determined by the nature of the violence exposure and the developmental capacities of the child. There is a focus on understanding childhood stressors, which contributes to an explanatory framework for healthcare professionals and social scientists and aids in their understanding of how violence exposure disrupts the developmental tasks of youth. Moreover, examination of subtle and common processes in youth development can reveal underlying behavioral, cognitive, affective, and physiological stressors that trigger counterproductive and adverse behavior (Cicchetti & Toth, 1995). Figure 3 provides a model of developmental progression for antisocial behavior, which is based on growing up in a violent family. Developmentally, the model depicts several negative consequences for a child in an abusive familial environment, including becoming socially unresponsive, emotionally blunted, passive, apathetic,and inattentive (Browne & Herbert, 1997; Patterson et al., 1989). Another perspective is trauma theory, which recognizes that personal loss and feeling threatened manifest in highly stressful environments for youth exposed to family violence (De Bellis, 2001). These environments can lead to altered psychological, biological, neurological, and cognitive functioning. These symptoms are pathways to other developmental difficulties, such as compromised academic functioning, substance abuse, dating violence, and personality disorders (Margolin, 2005). When confronted with stressful events, whether witnessing abuse, being neglected, or verbally or physically harmed, children release hormones and activate brain circuits to cope. When these events occur regularly, children stop shutting off their stress responses. The result is toxic stress, which is the strong, frequent, or prolonged activation of the body's stress management system. This outcome can produce neurochemical changes and adaptations in children that are detrimental to a child's well-being (Cohen et al., 2009).

Another perspective is the family systems theory. According to this theory, the family is the primary source of protection and violence for children. When the family fluctuates between safe haven and danger zone, children become confused, and their perception of their parents may alternate between friend and foe (Margolin, 1998). From this perspective, there is concern for the erosion of the family system, which overwhelms children, disconnects parents, and depletes everyone's emotional and physical resources, the result being a violation of a child's sense of well-being and safety (Margolin et al., 2001). In these circumstances, vulnerability and resilience influence the course of violence-related problems over time. Vulnerability factors explain how and why a child is susceptible to the effects of violence. Specific child characteristics, such as feeling responsible for the parents' aggression, can render some children more vulnerable than others, while salient family characteristics, including the parents' withdrawal and emotional unavailability, increase the likelihood of childhood problems (Rutter, 1994). Despite these challenges, children are resilient, able to adapt, cope, and overcome adversities associated with family violence (Masten

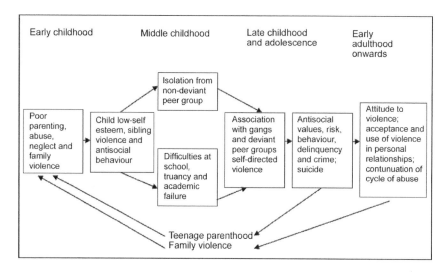

Figure 3: The Developmental Progression from Childhood Maltreatment to Antisocial and Violent Behavior

& Coatsworth, 1998; McGloin & Widom, 2001; O'Brien et al., 1995). It is necessary to understand vulnerability versus resilience to understand the effects of exposure to problem behaviors and family violence.

Previous perspectives focus on a micro-level of analysis, examining frameworks and factors that affect interpersonal relations between family members. A more macro-level of analysis shifts the focus to societal explanations for greater violence in households. The economic or social-structural model explains family violence arising from socially structured stress, which is unevenly distributed to lower-income, unemployed, and more illness-prone families (Coser, 1967; Gelles, 1974). The sociocultural explanation for family violence relies on explicating the roles of attitudes and norms in societies, cultures, and subcultures that promote the use of violence and linking these phenomena to higher rates of IPV and abusiveness in households (Straus et al., 1980). Individuals who have experienced abuse or neglect are more susceptible to the effects of violence in the media (Browne & Hamilton-Giachritsis, 2005). In advertising and video games, women are usually contextualized as sexual objects and victims instead of empowered protagonists (Stankiewicz & Rosselli, 2008). Some social scientists attribute youth violence to the media and attribute the social tolerance of violence to watching media violence (C.A. Anderson et al., 2003). A form of social learning, in which audiences consuming media learn violence through observation, occurs. A White Ribbon Foundation report titled *An Assault on Our Future* (2008) documents that among children and young people in Australia, there is already some degree of tolerance for violence against girls and women. Media portrayals in the news also inform audiences about social learning, and news is never "…produced or 'read' in isolation from surrounding texts and instead affirms news as discursively and culturally intersected and invested in a range of narratives" (Little, 2015, p. 607). Narratives of family members who have witnessed abuse or survived it are impactful, perhaps generating greater media effects when embedded in news and entertainment content than depictions of women and youth that contribute to social tolerance of violence. When these narratives are a component of strategies and interventions, they promote community awareness about family violence and educate audiences on core concepts of vulnerability and resilience.

Celebrity Narratives Recount Overcoming Abusive Fathers

According to the Report of the American Psychological Association Presidential Task Force on Violence and the Family (1996), a child exposed to a father committing domestic violence is at the strongest risk for transmitting violent behavior from one generation to the next. Furthermore, past abuse influences every area of neglected and abused children's lives, from adolescence to adulthood. It often takes time for partners, fathers, and mothers who have witnessed or experienced abuse to realize that the "get-over-it" strategy is temporary, and that they need to process their experiences, get support, set some boundaries, and visualize their capacity for wellness (Kendall-Tackett, 2001). Some celebrities grew up in abusive families, and the trauma derived from these experiences affects their personal and public lives. The searing glare of the media makes it difficult for celebrities to shield themselves from scrutiny, so some of them use the attention to create awareness about family violence. These celebrities use their personal stories to educate the public about how families and communities are vulnerable to neglect and abuse. Their narratives resonate with the public, because they embody cogent themes of vulnerability, resilience, recovery, and rebirth.

Many country music fans might be shocked to learn that country music star, Shania Twain lived in an abusive household when she was young. Twain is better known for having the bestselling album by a female artist in the U.S. (Hattenstone, 2018). In her 2011 memoir, *From This Moment On*, Twain disclosed to the public that there have been times when she wanted to die. "The book was part confessional, part warning, part self-help manual for people going through similar crises" (Hattenstone, 2018). Twain used the memoir to promote self-awareness and uplift people in need.

She grew up in Ontario, Canada, and never knew her biological father, and her stepfather, Jerry, was an Ojibwa Native American, much discriminated against, alcoholic, violent and mentally ill. Unfortunately, it was not uncommon for Twain's relatives to die prematurely from neglect and alcohol abuse. In her memoir, Twain discusses an incident where Jerry beat her mother, Sharon, until she was unconscious, then plunged her head in the toilet. Twain, who was 11 years old at the time of the incident, smashed a chair across Jerry's back. He responded by punching her in the jaw. Twain remembers punching him back. She details the abuse she encountered in her family, especially her ordeal with her father, whom she claims abused her psychologically and physically. In order to cope, she learned to block it all out.

According to Simon Hattenstone (2018), Twain does not address her sexual abuse in her memoir, but when asked about it, she stated, "Uh huh, uh huh. I'm not going to go into details about it. I don't mind saying it, because I do think it's important that people understand you can survive these things." Twain survived, but by the age of 8, she was singing in bars to help her family pay the bills. She endured family violence beginning at the age of 10. She graduated from school in 1983 and moved to Nashville, but in 1987, while on the verge of a country music breakthrough, she learned that her parents had been killed in a car crash. She made the decision to go back home to Ontario to become a surrogate mother to her four siblings. Twain supported them by performing at a local resort. Years, later, after divorcing her philandering husband, she felt more empowered in her relationships. She told Hattenstone (2018) about a romantic partner, Frédéric Thiébaud: "Freddy pays the price, because I'm like: If I'm ever getting married again, this is me. I don't think Mutt [Lange; her producer and, later, husband] ever knew me. That's the difference." When asked by Hattenstone (2018) if she would choose what she has now if she could live her life over again, she offered this surprising response: "I would never choose for my son's family to be broken." She continued, "Look at my situation. My parents could have killed each other. Maybe we would have been better off in foster homes, but I decided not to turn my family in, many times. There is something in me that says a family should stay together."

Twain could have turned her parents in to the authorities, but she decided it was better to keep her family together. Was her decision a healthy choice for herself, or did she sacrifice her own well-being for her younger siblings to have their parents? Would her siblings have had better lives with a foster family? Is it surprising that an empowered Twain, post-split from a husband who had cheated on her with her former best friend, asserted, "I would be one of those people who would keep my marriage together for my child.... I tried to keep Mutt." Some fans may find Shania Twain's complexity perplexing. Perhaps the public should accept that people like Twain, who were neglected or abused as children, carry the scars of family violence throughout their lifetimes. Furthermore, Twain's fans and people who have had similar childhood experiences probably can relate to her. She is a successful celebrity, but she has demons and scars like everyone else.

South African model and Academy Award–winning Charlize Theron is known for many bold and daring roles, including her performance as serial killer Aileen Wuornos in the film *Monster*. In 2004, on Primetime Thursday, Theron told Diane Sawyer a story that she had never told on television. On the night of June 21, 1991, Theron's father—a big, tall man—got into an altercation with his family. Theron told Sawyer, "He could be very serious but loved to laugh as well, and enjoyed life. He also had a disease. He was an alcoholic" (ABC News, 2004). She continued, "He was a verbal abuser." Earlier in the day on June 21, a 15-year-old Theron had returned home from boarding school, and her aunt called to warn of her father's agitation. He and his brother would be returning home after a bout of drinking. "Nature gives you instinct. And I knew something bad was going to happen," said Theron.

When her father returned home, he began shooting, first at the locked gate to the home, then through the kitchen door, according the testimony of Theron's mother. Her mother also testified that he began banging on Theron's bedroom door, saying, "Tonight I'm going to kill you both with the shotgun." After the threat, Theron's father fired his gun again, this time shooting into her room. Then her mother grabbed her own handgun and shot the two men, killing her husband and wounding his brother. According to Theron's police statement, she asked her mom: "What happened?" The answer: "Charlize, I shot them.... I shot them." Theron told Sawyer, "I know what happened," she said. "And I know that if my daughter was in the same situation, I would do the same thing." The attorney general ruled that her mother had acted to defend herself and her daughter. Theron believes she "bears the scar of that night on her heart, like a tattoo." She told Sawyer: "It's a part of me, but it doesn't rule my life." Theron believes she has an incredible life, and she wants the public to know that she does not go through life suffering. She will always remember the tragic circumstances that unfolded in 1991, but the incident does not define her.

Tatum O'Neal also had a "crazy life," including good and bad times. At the age of 10, she won an Academy Award for her performance in the film *Paper Moon*. In 2004, during an interview on *Dateline NBC*, reporter Stone Phillips addressed her beatings, hunger, neglect, sexual molestation, underage drinking, underage driving, car crashes, suicide attempts, and drug use. The heights of O'Neal's stardom included being the youngest Academy Award winner in the history of the competition, but her drug addiction led to the loss of the custody of her children. During the interview with Phillips, O'Neal mused about her life as depicted in her book, *A Paper Life*, "…a story of survival, about a gutsy little girl forced to rely on wits and determination when adults let her down—much like the orphan she played in the movie that made her famous." O'Neal self-disclosed that her mother stayed drunk for years. O'Neal was molested as a child. O'Neal asserted, "Yeah. When parents are off getting drunk or getting high or taking pills in another room, and leaving little children with, you know, people who don't watch their kids, this is what happens." She would eventually live with her father, Ryan O'Neal, who was a major star. She competed for his attention, as he entertained female celebrities including Ursula Andress, Angelica Huston, and Diana Ross. Real friction bubbled up to the surface when she won the Academy Award and garnered more attention than her famous dad. Phillips addressed a passage from her book, where she wrote, "People tell me that when I got the Oscar nomination, Ryan slugged me." She has no memory of the incident. When reflecting on her father's temper, she discussed his "abusive streak a mile wide." "I mean, there was always a slugging thing. Or a backhand, or throwing out of the car or whatever. It was a rough, just rough around the house." She was perplexed by her father's behavior. The abusiveness was intermixed with stints on the mid–1970s Hollywood party circuit. "Doesn't every dad bring their daughter to the Playboy Mansion? No, I guess not. Ok, I was there. I don't know what I was doing there. I was being raised by Ryan." Despite the tumultuous childhood Tatum O'Neal experienced, and the adverse effects it had on her in adulthood, she went on *Megyn Kelly Today* in March 2018, to share a special message for her estranged father: "I don't want to hold on to anger and resentments. I want to have a free, happy and guilt-free life." She continued, "My dad did a lot of good for me and I have to just respect his life and his process. Maybe someday he and I will have a moment where we reconcile."

Hopefully, adults who grow up with abusive fathers can forgive themselves, perhaps reconcile with their families regarding the abuse, and move forward. O'Neal suggests forgiveness as a part of her own journey of self-love and healing. The relationship between celebrity father and celebrity daughter portrayed in O'Neal's narrative provided the public with a bird's-eye view of their lived experiences and demonstrated that dysfunctional family communication affects everyone. Aside from the trips to the Playboy Mansion and the intense verbal, physical, and emotional altercations, Ryan, and Tatum O'Neal were more like their fans than many people realized at the height of their fame. Halle Berry understands that fans relate to her because they have gone through similar experiences, and she has shared personal insights about domestic violence. Her mother was abused by her father when Berry was a child, and Berry would later endure domestic violence herself (Gennis, 2015). During the 2015 Creative Conscience Award gala, Berry was honored for her volunteer work at the Jenesse Center, a Los Angeles–based domestic violence intervention program. During her speech at the gala, Berry said, "I wasn't married to a man who beat me up, but my mother was" (Gennis, 2015). She recalled watching her mother being "kicked down stairs" and hit in the head with a wine bottle. "She stayed for too long and her children, my sister and I, saw far too much and I've suffered the damage of being a child of domestic violence," Berry said. Berry's outreach provides services to children who have witnessed family violence. She has empathy for little girls, who, like her, witnessed their mothers enduring domestic violence. Berry shared this thought about her mother: "Knowing that she wanted nothing more then for her little girls to see her be empowered and be a woman of strength, but having no way to make that happen was heartbreaking for me." In adulthood, Berry is empowered, using her agency to uplift and support women and children in violent families. Before leaving the stage at the gala, Berry reflected on her 15 years of work with the Jenesse Center: "The reason I say this organization is my heart and soul is because I understand the good that it does and the lives that it changes and the impact it has on women and children in our community."

Tyler Perry is another celebrity who uses his platform, both in the media spotlight and behind the scenes, to support women and children who endure family violence. Perry is a survivor of childhood abuse. In a 2010 appearance on *The Oprah Winfrey Show*, Perry disclosed that he experienced severe emotional and physical abuse at the hands of his father (Freeman, 2010). He told Oprah, "It was a living hell." He exclaimed, "I think that everyone who's been abused, there is a string to the puppet master, and they're holding you hostage to your behaviors and what you do." He continued, "At some point, you have to be responsible for them. What I started to do is untie the strings and chase them down to where they came from. And I was able to free myself and understand that even though these things happened to me, it was not me."

Perry counts Winfrey as a mentor and friend, and she has something in common with many of the members of his dedicated fanbase: Black women have played a significant role in Perry's success. Black women see themselves or someone they know in Perry's depictions of Black women and Black family life. He understands them. He has reverence for his Black mother, who protected him from his abusive father's violence (Freeman, 2010): "She would take me everywhere to protect me, so I went to hair salons, and I went to Lane Bryant, and I would listen to all these women— you know, a little boy, listening. I soaked up everything." Perry is known for producing, writing, directing, and starring in many of his ownfilms, but as his work shifted away from comedy in a more serious direction, he saw promise in championing the movie *Precious*. Lee Daniels, who directed and co-produced the film, once responded to a question pertaining to the challenge of attracting funding for *Precious* with the reply, "Who wants to finance a movie about a 300-pound black girl?" One answer: Tyler Perry.

After seeing a rough cut of *Precious*, Perry signed up as an executive producer. Why? He identified with the main character, later stating that in his childhood, "I was in a house like the one in *Precious*." Perry recognized that the world needed to know the story of Precious, a disadvantaged girl in urban America, and he persuaded Winfrey to sign on as executive producer to aid Daniels and himself in funding the film. Before the movie opened, Winfrey stated (Freeman, 2010):

> How many times have I seen and not seen the Preciouses of the world? How many times have I seen that girl on the street? How many times have I seen her on the corner of Michigan Avenue in Chicago, waiting on a bus? How many times have I seen that girl coming out of Walgreens? How many times have I seen her and not seen her?

Girls like Precious are easy to ignore and perhaps despise, but the outreach of Daniel, Perry, and Winfrey through the film ensured that girls, women, boys, and men like Precious are seen and understood. The film *Precious* chronicles the struggles of a girl who is fighting to be seen and understood, and she can only do it with the support of others, including a teacher and social worker. Daniels endured his own struggle to get *Precious*—his adaptation of Sapphire's best-selling 1996 novel, *Push*—created, and the film was made possible because of the support he received from victims of family violence, specifically, Perry and Winfrey. Befittingly, Perry's outreach manifested into a story of survival, and through the main character in *Precious*, he was able to share with a global audience his message to "understand that even though these things happened to me, it was not me."

Considerations for Interventionists in Family Violence

Traditionally, Child Protective Services (CPS) focuses on legal and policy considerations related to child victims, whereas the primary goal of domestic violence advocacy is the safety and the best interest of adult victims (Summers, 2006). This chapter primarily focuses on the welfare of children who are exposed to family violence, yet it also addresses domestic violence, which usually involves an entanglement of adult and child victims. Children who experience family violence oftentimes are exposed to domestic violence, and these types of violence are regulated and penalized according to a variety of state laws and child protection responses. Where the violence takes place can be as important as the type of violence a child and his or her mother or guardian endures. What constitutes family and domestic violence? Is it only physical abuse? What about psychological abuse, or verbal abuse? Every jurisdiction, municipal, state, federal or international, determines what constitutes family violence, and how those harmed should be made whole, which contributes to a lack of consensus about how to best respond procedurally and practically in family violence cases.

From a law-enforcement perspective, historically, husbands and fathers were legally permitted to use force in their families. According to Summers (2006), police usually did not intervene in family and domestic violence situations, because men in the family could use physical force against wives and children. These social and legal mores changed with the activism of domestic violence advocacy organizations and the passage of the Violence Against Women Act. Now many police officers participate in specialized domestic violence training. Furthermore, governmental organizations and funding organizations support these efforts. For instance, the Office for Victims of Crime of the U.S. Department of Justice provides funding for state police training academies to help with the response to family violence. Some police departments have created specialized domestic violence units. Ultimately, the goal of law enforcement is to work with prosecutors to enforce the law, keep intimate partners and children safe, and hold perpetrators accountable. However, too often, children—the most vulnerable witnesses of family violence—fall through the cracks. Summers (2006) addressed this reality in the breakdown of American Bar Association (ABA) and the Association of Governments data, which was collected through surveys of multiple police departments. The results indicated the following: 38 percent did not investigate to determine if children were exposed to domestic violence each time they responded to a domestic violence call; 24 percent did not have a law or policy requiring officers to report if children were exposed to domestic violence; 44 percent of officers did not call CPS when they learned that children had been exposed to domestic violence; 39 percent of officers follow up to see if families followed through with a suggested referral; and 85 percent of departments did not receive any special funding to respond to children exposed to domestic violence.

Funding is necessary to design effective responses for children exposed to violence. These responses should be created collaboratively between agencies and organizations that understand a variety of complex needs, and the network of child and family research and program evaluations must reflect this diversity of needs. Despite a need for child-focused interventions, many children exposed to family violence do not receive services to address the consequences (National Institute of Child Health and Human Development, 2002). Many programs and services have not been tested outside of ideal, tightly controlled conditions, and their effectiveness in community settings is limited (Cohen et al., 2004; Snell-Johns et al., 2004; Lieberman et al., 2005). For example, a shelter departure intervention designed for domestic violence victims and their children when they leave the shelter must consider how the family will live in the community, but most research contributing to these interventions does not examine partner-child aggression before and after a family's stay at a domestic violence shelter (McDonald et al., 2011). If a perpetrator is abusive toward his partner and children before they enter the emergency shelter, then there is a greater likelihood he will be violent toward the children after the family leaves the emergency shelter. Any comprehensive intervention should take this factor into consideration. When interventions do not adequately encompass community settings into their formative and summative research, the effectiveness of the intervention is undercut. "Underlying this finding may be a tendency for families who decline services to terminate contact with a service agency" (Cross et al., 2013, p. 752). Practitioners and researchers should take special care to attend to children, parents, and guardians who decline services. One approach to mitigate attrition rates for these services is to more effectively tailor services to families. These families need to be retained in preliminary program evaluations and other types of summative research if these interventions are going to be effective.

The intervention of the Safe Start Demonstration Project sites achieved optimal outcomes for children and families, with emphasis on the early detection and identification of the symptoms of exposure to violence; the education of community partners and practitioners; the establishment of protocols, policies, procedures, and supervision that detail responses to child exposure to violence; the institution of mandated reporting to CPS and other referrals to applicable agencies and organizations; and coordinated messaging in interventions that connects everyone providing care to children and families (Cohen et al., 2009). A preliminary program evaluation of a 10-session group intervention designed to address children exposed to domestic violence took the lessons of Safe Start into consideration, yet stressed the need to balance the intervention's planning, coordination and assessment with a framework for engaging children (Lee et al., 2012). Refinement of these interventions aids future interventions. Refinement requires funding, practitioners, research participants, and agency and organizational support, as well as the utilization of community settings to engage families who need services and referral partners in order to coordinate the access and use of services.

Additional funding is needed to improve the instruments and screening processes for neglect and child abuse. Some agencies and organizations have been working on instruments to screen parents for child abuse, but the effectiveness of these instruments to predict child abuse or neglect is limited. Screening for child abuse in primary care settings involves a variety of techniques, such as physical examinations and screening questionnaires (U.S. Preventive Services Task Force, 2004). Screening for domestic violence in families can help identify family violence affecting children, yet "… evidence suggests that these instruments had fairly high sensitivity but low specificity for identifying future child maltreatment when administered…" (U.S. Preventive Services Task Force, 2004, p. 158). Funding has produced results for interventionists in health education and health promotion. New Zealand provides interventionists with insight into the benefits of a multipronged campaign to build awareness and understanding among various target groups (Surgenor, 2009). Interventionists in New Zealand used qualitative research consisting of interviews and focus groups with the public and found that New Zealanders did not have a clear understanding of the nature and scope of family violence. Many New Zealanders perceived family violence as only physical violence.

In 2005, the New Zealand government established the multiagency Taskforce for Action on Violence Within Families to address the issue. The taskforce rolled out an ambitious messaging campaign called "It's Not OK," which was initially funded through 2010 (Surgenor, 2009). Formative research was conducted before the campaign commenced, and tracking surveys were conducted at regular intervals after its launch. Through the interrelated elements of community action, communication/mass media, and research and evaluation, the campaign achieved its goals and objectives, which were to increase awareness of family violence, increase understanding of family violence and its many effects, and increase acknowledgment that we can all help do something about family violence. An independent research company did summative research to determine the effectiveness of the campaign. The summative research found that campaign awareness registered 95 percent, that approximately one in four individuals (24 percent) had changed views about family violence, that 22 percent of the public took action in response to the campaign, and that two-thirds of the public felt the campaign helped them better understand behaviors they should not tolerate (Surgenor, 2009). Like New Zealand's "It's Not OK" campaign, celebrities used the media to promote education about family violence, and the messages embedded in their narratives promoted awareness and understanding about abuse, survival, and redemption. The celebrity encounters with family violence discussed in this chapter involve celebrities sharing their narratives with the public, which increased national and international consciousness about family violence.

REFERENCES

ABC News. (2004, January 8). *Charlize Theron's family tragedy.* ABC. https://abcnews.go.com/Primetime/story?id=132413&page=1#.

American Psychological Association Presidential Task Force on Violence and the Family (1996). *Violence and the family: Report of the APA Presidential Task Force.* American Psychological Association.

Anderson, C.A., Berkowitz, L., Domerstein, E., Huesmann, L.R., Johnson, J.D., Linz, D., Malamuth, N.M., & Wartella, E. (2003). The influences of media violence on youth. *Psychological Science in the Public Interest, 4(3)*, 81–110. https://doi.org/10.1111/j.1529-1006.2003.pspi_1433.x.

Arrington, E.G., & Wilson, M.N. (2000). A re-examination of risk and resilience during adolescence: Incorporating culture and diversity. *Journal of Child and Family Studies, 9(2)*, 221–230. https://doi.org/10.1023/A:1009423106045.

Bolger, K.E., & Patterson, C.J. (2001). Pathways from child maltreatment to internalizing problems: Perceptions of control as mediators and moderators. *Development and Psychopathology, 13(4)*, 913–940. https://doi.org/10.1017/S0954579401004096.

Bradley, R.H., & Corwyn, R.F. (2002). Socioeconomic status and child development. *Annual Review of Psychology, 53*, 371–399. https://doi.org/10.1146/annurev.psych.53.100901.135233.

Briere, J., & Elliott, D.M. (2003). Prevalence and psychological sequelae of self-reported childhood physical and sexual abuse in a general population sample of men and women. *Child Abuse & Neglect, 27(10)*, 1205–1222. https://doi.org/10.1016/j.chiabu.2003.09.008.

Browne, K., & Herbert, M. (1997). *Preventing family violence.* Wiley.

Browne, K.D., & Hamilton-Giachritsis, C.E. (2005). The influence of violent media on children and adolescents: A public-health approach. *Lancet, 365(9460)*, 702–710. https://doi.org/10.1016/S0140-6736(05)17952-5.

Buckner, J.C., Mezzacappa, E., & Beardslee, W. (2003). Characteristics of resilient children living in poverty: The role of self-regulatory processes. *Development and Psychopathology, 15(1)*, 139–162. https://doi.org/10.1017/s0954579403000087.

Bureau of Justice Statistics. (2002). *Hispanic victims of violent crime, 1993–2000.* United States Department of Justice. https://www.bjs.gov/content/pub/pdf/hvvc00.pdf.

Burman, E., & Chantler, K. (2005). Domestic violence and minoritisation: Legal and policy barriers facing minoritized women leaving violent relationships. *International Journal of Law and Psychiatry, 28*, 59–74. https://doi.org/10.1016/j.ijlp.2004.12.004.

Chetty, M., & Agee, M. (2009). Childhood exposure to domestic violence: Reflections of young immigrants of Indian origin. *New Zealand Journal of Counseling, 29(1)*, 36–53. https://www.nzac.org.nz/assets/Uploads/Journals/4.-Childhood-Exposure-to-Domestic-Violence.pdf.

Cicchetti, D., & Toth, S.L. (1995). A developmental psychopathology perspective on child abuse and neglect. *Journal of the American Academy of Child and Adolescent Psychiatry, 34(5)*, 541–565. https://doi.org/10.1097/00004583-199505000-00008.

Cohen, E., Groves, B.M., & Kracke, K. (2009). *Issue Brief #1: Understanding children's exposure to violence.* The Safe Start Center. https://ojjdp.ojp.gov/sites/g/files/xyckuh176/files/programs/safestart/IB1_UnderstandingChildrensExposuretoViolence.pdf.

Cohen, J.A., Deblinger, E., Mannarino, A.P., & Steer, R. (2004). A multisite, randomized controlled trial for children with abuse-related PTSD symptoms. *Journal of the American Academy of Child & Adolescent Psychiatry, 43(4)*, 393–402. https://doi.org/10.1097/00004583-200404000-00005.

Coid, J., Petruckevitch, A., Feder, G., Chung, W., Richardson, J., & Moorey, S. (2001). Relation between childhood sexual and physical abuse and risk of revictimization in women: A cross-sectional survey. *Lancet, 358(9280)*, 450–454. https://doi.org/10.1016/s0140-6736(01)05622-7.

Coser, L.A. (1967). *Continuities in the study of social conflict.* Free Press.

Council of Australian Governments. (2009). *National plan to reduce violence against women and their children.* Commonwealth of Australia. https://www.dss.gov.au/sites/default/files/documents/05_2012/a_snapshot.pdf.

Creighton, S.J. (2002). Recognizing changes in incidence and prevalence. In K.D. Browne, H. Cross, A.B., Jaycox, L.H., Hickman, L.J., Schultz, D., Barnes-Proby, D., Kofner, A., & Serodji, C. (2013). Predictors of study retention from a multisite study of interventions for children and families exposed to violence. *Journal of Community Psychology, 41(6),* 743–757. https://doi.org/10.1002/jcop.21568.

De Bellis, M.D. (2001). Developmental traumatology: The psychobiological development of maltreated children and its implications for research, treatment, and policy. *Development and Psychopathology, 13(3),* 539–564. https://doi.org/10.1017/s0954579401003078.

Dolon, R., & Hendricks, J. (1991). Breaking the cycle of family violence: Services for children in shelters for battered women. *Free Inquiry in Creative Sociology, 19,* 31–35.

Fein, M.L. (1993). *Integrated anger management: A common sense guide to coping with anger.* Praeger.

Finkelhor D. (1994). The international epidemiology of child sexual abuse. *Child Abuse & Neglect, 18(5),* 409–418. https://doi.org/10.1016/0145-2134(94)90026-4.

Flood, M., & Fergus, L. (2008). *An Assault on Our Future: The Impact of Violence on Young People and Their Relationships.* White Ribbon Foundation. https://eprints.qut.edu.au/103828/1/__qut.edu.au_Documents_StaffHome_staffgroupB%24_bozzetto_Documents_2017001017.pdf.

Flores-Ortiz, Y.G. (2000). Theorizing justice in Chicano families. Occasional Paper No. 43. Julian Samora Research Institute. https://jsri.msu.edu/upload/publications/occasional-papers/oc43v2.pdf.

Fosco, G.M., DeBoard, R.L., & Grych, J.H. (2007). Making sense of family violence: Implications of children's appraisals of interparental aggression for their short- and Longterm functioning. *European Psychologist, 12(1),* 6–16. https://doi.org/10.1027/1016-9040.12.1.6.

Freeman, D.W. (2010, October 22). *Tyler Perry, Oprah talk sexual abuse: Who victimized little Tyler.* CBS News. https://www.cbsnews.com/news/tyler-perry-oprah-talk-sexual-abuse-who-victimized-little-tyler/.

Geffner, R., Igelman, R.S., & Zellner, J. (2003). Introduction. Children exposed to interparental violence: A need for additional research and validated treatment programs. In R. Geffner, R.S. Igelman, & J. Zellner (Eds.), *The effects of intimate partner violence on children* (pp. 1–10). Haworth Maltreatment & Trauma Press.

Gelles, R.J. (1974). *The Violent Home: A study of physical aggression between husbands and wives.* Sage.

Gelles, R.J. (1985). Family violence. *Annual Review of Sociology, 11,* 347–367. https://doi.org/10.1146/annurev.so.11.080185.002023.

Gennis, S. (2015). Halle Berry opens up about childhood experience with domestic violence. *TV Guide.* https://www.tvguide.com/news/halle-berry-childhood-domestic-violence/.

Gewirtz, A., & Edleson, J.E. (2007). Young children's exposure to adult domestic violence: Toward a developmental risk and resilience framework for research and intervention. *Journal of Family Violence, 22(3),* 151–163. https://doi.org/10.1007/s10896-007-9065-3.

Graham-Kevan, N., & Archer, J. (2003). Intimate terrorism and common couple violence: A test of Johnson's predictions in four British samples. *Journal of Interpersonal Violence, 18(11),* 1247–1270. https://doi.org/10.1177/0886260503256656.

Greenfield, L.A., Rand, M.R., Craven, D., Klaus, P.A., Perkins, C.A., Ringel, C., Warchol, G., Maston, C., & Fox, J.A. (1998). *Violence by Intimates: Analysis of data on crimes by current or former spouses, boyfriends, and girlfriends.* United States Department of Justice [NCJ-167237]. https://www.bjs.gov/content/pub/pdf/vi.pdf.

Grych, J.H., & Fincham, F.D. (1990). Marital conflict and children's adjustment: A cognitive contextual framework. *Psychological Bulletin, 108*(2), 267–290. https://doi.org/10.1037/0033-2909.108.2.267.

Hancock, T.U., & Siu, K (2009). A culturally sensitive intervention with domestically violent Latino immigrant men. *Journal of Family Violence, 24,* 123–132. https://doi.org/10.1007/s10896-008-9217-0.

Hanks, P. Stratton, & C. Hamilton (Eds.), *Early prediction and prevention of child abuse: A handbook* (5–22). Wiley.

Hattenstone, S. (2018, April 22). Shania Twain on abuse, betrayal and finding her voice: "I wanted a break—but not for 15 years." *The Guardian*. https://www.theguardian.com/music/2018/apr/22/shania-twain-unexpected-return-freak-illness-country-pop-star.

Herrenkohl, T.I., Sousa, C., Tajima, E.A., Herrenkohl, R.C., & Moylan, C.A. (2008). Intersection of child abuse and children's exposure to domestic violence. *Trauma, Violence, and Abuse: A Review Journal, 9(2)*, 84–99. https://doi.org/10.1177/1524838008314797.

Herrenkohl, T.I., Tajima, E.A., Whitney, S.D., & Huang, B. (2005). Protection against antisocial behavior in children exposed to physically abusive discipline. *Journal of Adolescent Health, 36(6)*, 457–465. https://doi.org/10.1016/j.jadohealth.2003.09.025.

Hester, M., Pearson, C., & Harwin, N. (2000). *Making an impact: Children and domestic violence.* Jessica Kingsley.

Holden, G.W. (2003). Children exposed to domestic violence and child abuse: Terminology and taxonomy. *Clinical Child & Family Psychology Review, 6(3)*, 151–160. https://doi.org/10.1023/a:1024906315255.

Holder, Jr., E.H., Leary, M.L., & Hanes, M. (2012). *Report of the Attorney General's National Task Force on Children Exposed to Violence.* United States Department of Justice. https://www.justice.gov/defendingchildhood/cev-rpt-full.pdf.

Huang, C.-C., Son, E., & Wang, L.-R. (2010). Prevalence and factors of domestic violence among unmarried mothers with a young child. *Families in Society, 91(2)*, 171–177. https://doi.org/10.1606/1044-3894.3978.

Huang, C., Vikse, J.H., Lu, S., & Yi, S. (2015). Children's exposure to intimate partner violence and early delinquency. *Journal of Family Violence, 30(8)*, 953–965. https://doi.org/10.1007/s10896-015-9727-5.

Jaspard, M. (2003). *Les violences envers les femmes en France: Une enquête nationale* [Violence against women in France: A national survey]. La Documentation Française. https://journals.openedition.org/plc/860?lang=en.

Johnson, M.P. (2005). Domestic violence: It's not about gender—or is it? *Journal of Marriage and Family, 67(5)*, 1126–1130. https://doi.org/10.1111/j.1741-3737.2005.00204.x.

Kelly, M. [Megyn Kelly TODAY]. (2018, March 27). *Tatum O'Neal shares a message with her father: "Forgiveness is the best policy"* [Video]. YouTube. https://www.youtube.com/watch?v=96FF7IqZzg0.

Kempe, C.H., Silverman, F.N., Steele, B.F., Droegemueller, W., & Silver, H.K. (1962). The battered child syndrome. *Journal of the American Medical Association*, 181(1), 107–112. https://doi.org/10.1001/jama.1962.03050270019004.

Kendall-Tackett, K. (2001). *The hidden feelings of motherhood: Coping with mothering stress, depression and burnout.* New Harbinger.

Lee, J., Kolomer, S., & Thomsen, D. (2012). Evaluating the effectiveness of an intervention for children exposed to domestic violence: A preliminary program evaluation. *Child Adolescent Social Work Journal, 29(5)*, 357–372. https://doi.org/10.1007/s10560-012-0265-1.

Levendosky, A.A., Huth-Bocks, A., Shapiro, D., & Semel, M. (2003). The impact of domestic violence on the maternal child relationship and preschool-age children's functioning. *Journal of Family Psychology, 17(3)*, 275–287. https://doi.org/10.1037/0893-3200.17.3.275.

Levendosky, A.A., Leahy, K., Bogat, G.A., Davidson, W.S., & von Eye, A. (2006). Domestic violence, maternal parenting, maternal mental health, and infant externalizing behavior. *Journal of Family Psychology, 20(4)*, 544–552. https://doi.org/10.1037/0893-3200.20.4.544.

Lieberman, A.F., Van Horn, P., & Ghosh Ippen, C. (2005). Toward evidence-based treatment: Child-Parent Psychotherapy with preschoolers exposed to marital violence. *Journal of the American Academy of Child and Adolescent Psychiatry, 44(12)*, 1241–1248. https://doi.org/10.1097/01.chi.0000181047.59702.58.

Little, J. (2015). "Family violence happens to everybody": Gender, mental health and violence in Australian media representations of filicide 2010-2014. *Continuum: Journal of Media & Cultural Studies, 29(4)*, 605–616. https://doi.org/10.1080/10304312.2015.1025366.

Lynskey, M.T., & Fergusson, D.M. (1997). Factors protecting against the development of adjustment difficulties in young adults exposed to childhood sexual abuse. *Child Abuse and Neglect, 21(12),* 1177–1190. https://doi.org/10.1016/s0145-2134(97)00093-8.

Margolin, G. (1998). Effects of domestic violence on children. In P.K. Trickett & C.J. Schellengach (Eds.), *Violence against children in the family and community* (pp. 57–102). American Psychological Association.

Margolin, G. (2005). Children's exposure to violence: Exploring developmental pathways to diverse outcomes. *Journal of Interpersonal Violence, 20(1),* 72–81. https://doi.org/10.1177/0886260504268371.

Margolin, G., & Gordis, E.B. (2004). Children's exposure to violence in the family and community. *Current Directions in Psychological Science, 13(4),* 152–155. https://doi.org/10.1111/j.0963-7214.2004.00296.x.

Margolin, G., Oliver, P.H., & Medina, A.M. (2001). Conceptual issues in understanding the relation between interparental conflict and child adjustment: Integrating developmental psychopathology and risk/resilience perspectives. In J.H. Grych & F.D. Fincham (Eds.), *Interparental conflict and child development: Theory, research, and applications* (pp. 9–38). Cambridge University Press.

Masten, A.S., & Coatsworth, J.D. (1998). The development of competence in favorable and unfavorable environments: Lessons learned from research on successful children. *American Psychologist, 53(2),* 205–220. https://doi.org/10.1037//0003-066x.53.2.205.

McDonald, R., Jouriles, E.N., Rosenfield, D., Corbitt-Shindler, D. (2011). Predictors of domestically violent men's aggression toward children: A prospective study. *Journal of Family Psychology, 25(1),* 11–18. https://doi.org/10.1037/a0022449.

McGloin, J.M., & Widom, C.S. (2001). Resilience among abused and neglected children grown up. *Development and Psychopathology, 13(4),* 1021–1038. https://doi.org/10.1017/s095457940100414x.

Morash, M., Bui, H.N., & Santiago, A.M. (2000). Cultural-specific gender ideology and wife abuse in Mexican-descent families. *International Review of Victimology, 7(1–3),* 67–91. https://doi.org/10.1177/026975800000700305.

Nam, S.I., & Lincoln, K.D. (2017). Lifetime family violence and depression: The case of older women in South Korea. *Journal of Family Violence, 32,* 269–278. https://doi.org/10.1007/s10896-016-9844-9.

National Institute of Child Health and Human Development. (2002). *Children exposed to violence: Current status, gaps, and research priorities. Workshop summary.* National Institutions of Health. www.nichd.nih.gov/publications/pubs/upload/children_violence. pdf.

Nelson, B.J. (1984). *Making an issue of child abuse: Political agenda setting for social problems.* University of Chicago Press.

O'Brien, K.L., Cohen, L., Pooley, J.A., & Taylor, M.F. (2013). Lifting the domestic violence cloak of silence: Resilient Australian women's reflected memories of their childhood experiences of witnessing domestic violence. *Journal of Family Violence, 28(1),* 95–108. https://doi.org/10.1007/s10896-012-9484-7.

O'Brien, M., Margolin, G., & John, R.S. (1995). Relation among marital conflict, child coping, and child adjustment. *Journal of Clinical Child Psychology, 24(3),* 346–361. https://doi.org/10.1207/s15374424jccp2403_12.

Onyskiw, J.E. (2003). Adjustment in children exposed to intimate partner violence: Clinical research. In R. Geffner, R.S. Igelman, & J. Zellner (Eds.), *The effects of intimate partner violence on children* (pp. 11–45). Haworth Maltreatment & Trauma Press.

Patterson, G.R., DeBaryshe, B.D., & Ramsey, E.A. (1989). Developmental perspective on antisocial behavior. *American Psychologist, 44(2),* 329–335. https://doi.org/10.1037/0003-066X.44.2.329.

Phillips, S. (2004, October 15). *Tatum O'Neal shares survival story.* Dateline—NBC News. https://www.nbcnews.com/id/wbna6254330.

Rutter, M. (1994). Family discord and conduct disorder: Cause, consequence, or correlate? *Journal of Family Psychology, 8(2),* 170–186. https://doi.org/10.1037/0893-3200.8.2.170.

Salter, D., McMillan, D., Richards, M., Talbot, T., Hodges, J., Bentovim, A., Hastings, R., Stevenson, J., & Skuse, D. (2003). Development of sexually abusive behavior in sexually victimized males: A longitudinal study. *Lancet, 361(9356),* 471–476. https://doi.org/10.1016/S0140-6736(03)12466-X.

Sedlack, A.J., & Broadhurst, D.D. (1996). *Third National Incidence Study of Child Abuse and Neglect*. National Center of Child Abuse and Neglect, U.S. Department of Health and Human Services. https://library.childwelfare.gov/cwig/ws/library/docs/gateway/Blob/13635.pdf?r=1&rpp=-10&upp=0&w=+NATIVE%28%27IPDET+PH+IS+%27%27nis-3%27%27%27%27%29&m=6&order=+NATIVE%28%27year%2Fdescend%27%29.

Snell-Johns, J., Mendez, J.L., & Smith, B.H. (2004). Evidence-based solutions for overcoming access barriers, decreasing attrition, and promoting change with underserved families. *Journal of Family Psychology, 18(1)*, 19–35. https://doi.org/10.1037/0893-3200.18.1.19.

Stamp, G.H., & Sabourin, T.C. (1995). Accounting for violence: An analysis of male spousal abuse narratives. *Journal of Applied Communication Research, 23(4)*, 284–307. https://doi.org/10.1080/00909889509365432.

Stankiewicz, J.M., & Rosselli, F. (2008). Women as sex objects and victims in print advertisements. *Sex Roles: A Journal of Research*, 58(7–8), 579–589. https://doi.org/10.1007/s11199-007-9359-1.

Star, B. (1980). Patterns of family violence. *Social Casework: The Journal of Contemporary Social Work, 61(6)*, 339–346. https://doi.org/10.1177/104438948006100603.

Sternberg, K.J., Lamb, M.E., Greenbaum, C., Cicchetti, D., Dawund, S., Cortes, R.M., Krispin, O., & Lorey, F. (1993). Effects of domestic violence on children's behavioral problems and depression. *Developmental Psychology, 29(1)*, 44–52. https://doi.org/10.1037/0012-1649.29.1.44.

Straus, M. (1979). Measuring intrafamily conflict and violence: The conflict tactics (CT) scale. *Journal of Marriage and the Family, 41(1)*, 75–88. https://doi.org/10.2307/351733.

Straus, M.A., Gelles, R.J., & Steinmetz, S.K. (1980). *Behind closed doors: Violence in the American family*. Anchor/Doubleday.

Straus, M.A., Hamby, S.L., Finkelhor, D., Moore, D.W., & Runyan, D. (1998). Identification of child maltreatment with the Parent-Child Conflict Tactics Scales: Development and psychometric data for a national sample of American parents. *Child Abuse and Neglect, 22(4)*, 249–270. https://doi.org/10.1016/s0145-2134(97)00174-9.

Summers, A. (2006). *Children's exposure to domestic violence: A guide to research and resources*. National Council of Juvenile and Family Court Judges. https://ncsc.contentdm.oclc.org/digital/collection/famct/id/172/.

Surgenor, G. (2009). "It's not ok" shines a light on family violence. *Communication World, November–December*, 42–43. https://www.iabc.com/wp-content/uploads/2014/10/Case-In-Point15.pdf.

Ulaby, N. (2009, September 28). *Oprah, Tyler Perry and a painful, "precious" life*. NPR. https://www.npr.org/templates/story/story.php?storyId=113213188.

UNICEF (2019). *Convention on the Rights of the Child: Frequently asked questions*. https://www.unicef.org/child-rights-convention/frequently-asked-questions.

United Nations. (1989). *The Convention on the Rights of the Child*. United Nations. https://ec.europa.eu/anti-trafficking/sites/default/files/un_convention_on_the_rights_of_the_child_1.pdf.

United Nations. (2011). *General Comment 13: The Right of the Child to Freedom of all Forms of Violence. Committee on the rights of the child: Convention on the Rights of the Child*. The United Nations Committee on the Rights of the Child. https://www.refworld.org/docid/4e6da4922.html.

United States Preventive Services Task Force. (2004). Screening for family and intimate partner violence: Recommendation statement. *The Annals of Family Medicine, 2(2)*, 156–160. https://doi.org/10.1370/afm.128.

Wali, R. (2001). Working therapeutically with Indian families within a New Zealand context. *Australia and New Zealand Journal of Family Therapy, 22(1)*, 10–17. https://doi.org/10.1002/j.1467-8438.2001.tb01295.x.

Widom, C.S. (1989). The cycle of violence. *Science, 244(4901)*, 160–166.https://doi.org/10.1126/science.2704995.

Widom, C.S. (1992). *The cycle of violence*. National Institute of Justice, United States Department of Justice. https://digitalcommons.law.ggu.edu/cgi/viewcontent.cgi?article=1033&context=nij-rib.

Widom, C.S., & White, H. (1997). Problem behaviors in abused and neglected children grown up: Prevalence and co-occurrence of substance abuse, crime, and violence. *Criminal Behavior and Health, 7(4)*, 287–310. https://doi.org/10.1002/cbm.191.

Wood, J.T. (2000). "That wasn't the real him": Women's dissociation of violence from the men who enact it. *Qualitative Research in Review, 1*, 1–7.

Worden, A.P., & Carlson, B.E. (2005). Attitudes and beliefs about domestic violence: Results of a public opinion survey: II. Beliefs about causes. *Journal of Interpersonal Violence, 20(10)*, 1219–1243. https://doi.org/10.1177/0886260505278531.

4

Bullied Disney Channel Alumnae Selena Gomez, Demi Lovato, and Zendaya Fight Back

Bullying and victimization are worldwide problems. These violent behaviors affect people of varying ages, genders, races, ethnicities, religions, occupations, and socioeconomic statuses. Global citizens are all very different, but one experience many individuals share is being subjected to bullying or victimization. This chapter focuses on school and university students who bully or are themselves bullied. The chapter also examines the implications of celebrity narratives about bullying and victimization for violence prevention, especially the use of celebrity storytelling to mitigate the adverse effects of bullying on millennial and Generation Z media consumers in the United States and abroad. Pioneering work about the causes and effects of bullying originate in Norway (Olweus, 1973). Unfortunately, it took the 1982 suicides of three victims of bullying to jolt the Norwegian public into recognizing that bullying is a social justice issue (Olweus, 1993).

In the 1980s, other countries also began to discuss bullying in a national discourse. Japan identified it as a serious social problem between 1994 and 1995, when 16 students committed suicide under circumstances suspected as victimization (Morita et al., 1999). This incident stimulated research into bullying as a social problem for pupils in Japan. In the United Kingdom, the decade also saw the publication of the first book about bullying and victimization (Tattum & Lane, 1988). After the book was published, research into the social problem became an independent area of social and scholarly inquiry (Tattum & Herbert, 1993). The U.K. was not unique in Europe at the time. The 1980s were a period of reckoning for the continent, where many countries started to realize that they were not adequately addressing bullying and victimization. In 2014, the Irish Health Behavior in School-Aged Children survey of children between the ages of

8½ and 10½ reported that 36 percent of children had been bullied at school once in the past few months (Gavin et al., 2015), little changed from 37 percent reported in 2006 (Gabhainn et al., 2007) and 2010 (Kelly et al., 2012). Interestingly, unlike with older school children, no significant gender or social class differences were observed for the younger children (Gavin et al., 2015).

In the U.S., the 1999 Columbine High School shooting in Littleton, Colorado, began a movement in the legislative arena for legislation addressing bullying or "peer abuse." There were no laws passed until Columbine occurred, and in the three-year period after it, 15 laws were passed (Olweus & Limber, 2010). Within 10 years of the attack, 41 states had passed laws that address bullying (Olweus & Limber, 2010). By 2015, every state, in addition to the District of Columbia and some territories, had passed bullying laws (Temkin, 2015). Efforts to pass a federal law that specifically addresses bullying and victimization have stalled, but all 50 states have some type of antibullying legislation on the books, and 40 of those states have additional detailed policies in place for bullying (Olweus & Limber, 2010).

The Centers for Disease Control and Prevention (CDC) published a consensus statement in 2014 with the following definition for bullying: "any unwanted aggressive behavior by another youth or group of youths who are not siblings or current dating partners that involves an observed or perceived power imbalance and is repeated multiple times or is highly likely to be repeated" (Gladden et al., 2014). The definition for bullying evolves depending on who is providing the definition. For children, the focus is on the victim's experience instead of the bully's intent (Guerin & Hennessy, 2002; Madsen, 1996). Oftentimes, adolescents focus on the victim's feelings to decide whether a behavior is classified as bullying (Hellström et al., 2015). The association between distress and peer victimization may justify the inclusion of the negative effect on the victim as a criterion for bullying (Goldsmid & Howie, 2014). The effect on the victim is judged subjectively, which is why incidents that may be irrelevant for some bullies or bystanders may be of importance for the exposed child (Mishna et al., 2006). In a study by Smith and Levan (1995), six- and seven-year-olds endorsed a much wider definition of bullying than researchers. Children perceived actions ranging from "fighting with someone" to "shouts at you because they are cross" as bullying. This more expansive definition would encompass the research of Hoover et al. (1992), which found that high school students' perceptions and interpretations of bullying included non-responsive events. Moreover, Madsen's (1996) research is also applicable, considering the finding that only 5 percent of young adult pupils mentioned the intention of the bully as a defining factor.

Bullying and School Climate

Bullying increases with less structure and supervision. As students get older, adult supervision decreases. According to the American Association of University Women Educational Foundation (2001), some areas of learning environments where those victimized by bullying are most vulnerable include playgrounds, lunchrooms, and hallways. These more unsupervised spaces contribute to students feeling unsafe and afraid in and around schools (Astor et al., 2001). In these spaces, aggressive youths affiliate with other aggressive youths (Cairns & Cairns, 1994), and peer group members tend to have similar involvement in bullying behaviors (Espelage et al., 2007). For school children, vulnerable spaces and aggressive peers create a combustible and dangerous environment. During the 2010-2011 school year, 27.8 percent of students ages 12 to 18 reported being bullied at school (Office of Juvenile Justice and Delinquency Prevention, 2013). Some additional insights gleaned from the 2010-2011 school year: almost 18 percent reported having been made fun of, called names, or insulted; eight percent reported being pushed, shoved, tripped, or spit on; 5 percent reported being threatened with harm; over 3 percent reported being forced to do things they did not want to do; almost 3 percent reported that they had property destroyed; and 9 percent of students reported being cyberbullied.

Verbal harassment plays an important role in traditional and online bullying, especially for children, adolescents, and adult youth. The types of verbal harassment that school and university students encounter include slurs and jokes. Students describe a broad range of sociocultural and physical attributes that are the subject of degrading language, including facial features, body parts and size, clothing, academic ability, peer groups, socioeconomic status, and athletic ability (Wessler & De Andrade, 2006). In addition, most students participating in programs at the Center for the Prevention of Hate Violence reported being targeted for their race, gender, sexual orientation, and religion (Wessler & De Andrade, 2006). Examples of degrading language include the following:

Racist language: (1) What do an apple and a Black person have in common? They both hang from trees. (2) What do you do if you see a Black limping? Stop laughing and reload. (3) How do you get a Mexican out of your back yard? Hang one in the front yard.

Sexually degrading language: (1) I was in the hall talking to my friends and this guy comes up and looks me in the eye then says, "You're just a slut! You should get away from 'my' school you little whore." I was terrified. The boy walked away. (2) I hear other girls in my school calling me a "skanky whore" and "ho" behind my back.

Homophobic language: (1) Then during lunch, a group of guys walked by and asked him for a blow job and told him "Don't drop the soap" in gym class.

Getting off the bus, instead of people saying his name, they yelled "cock-sucker" or "Queer!" (2) While walking in school one day, I heard people talking and pointing at me, "That fucking dyke. Yeah, she's a freak."

Anti-Religious language: (1) My father also died in a concentration camp. He fell out of the guard tower. (2) What's the difference between a Jew and a pizza. A pizza doesn't scream when you put it in the oven. (3) When I was walking down the hall someone I know made a comment toward a [Muslim] girl saying, "Gimme my sheets back, bitch," then she stepped on the back of her dress so she fell.

Girls and boys are both bullied. Boys reported higher rates for damage to property and being pushed, shoved, tripped, or spit on, while girls reported higher rates of being ridiculed, being the subject of rumors, and being purposely excluded from activities (Office of Juvenile Justice and Delinquency Prevention, 2013). Figure 4 provides a list of behaviors that manifest into a plethora of direct and indirect exemplars of bullying.

Bullying occurs throughout schooling, peaking during the middle school years. According to the Office of Juvenile Justice and Delinquency Prevention (2013), in 2010-2011, sixth graders reported bullying 37 percent of the time, which was more than eighth graders (31 percent of the time), who reported it more than tenth and twelfth graders (28 percent and 22 percent respectively). This trend does not continue online, with cyberbullying peaking in high school instead of middle school (Office of Juvenile Justice and Delinquency Prevention, 2013). For cyberbullying, "the intent is to inflict online social cruelty on victims by threatening, harming, humiliating,

	Direct Bullying	Indirect Bullying
Verbal Bullying Using verbal threats to intentionally inflict social cruelty on someone	Threats, insults, teasing, taunting, name calling, snickering, laughing at someone out of cruelty	Rumors
Physical Bullying* Using physical force to intentionally inflict pain on another person	Hitting, kicking, pushing, stealing, sexual misconduct, killing someone	Physically moving away from someone as means to be hurtful
Material Bullying Taking away belongings to intentionally cause another person duress	Damage to belongings, extortion of money	Hiding belongings or pawning and playing "keep away"
Relational Bullying* Participating in behavior that intentionally positions the victim as the scapegoat	Back-stabbing, setting someone up to take blame, blackmail	Social exclusion, breaking confidences, manipulating friendships, micro-aggressions, looks and stare-downs, slander

Figure 4. The Manifestations of Direct and Indirect Bullying through Verbal, Physical, Material and Relational Behavior.

Reproduced from Miller, S. (2012). Speaking My Mind: Mythology of the Norm: Disrupting the Culture of Bullying in Schools. *The English Journal*, 101 (6), pp. 107–109.

Flaming	Online fight
Harassment	Repetitive, offensive messages sent to a target
Outing and trickery	Discovering personal information about someone and then electronically sharing that information without the individual's permission
Exclusion	Blocking an individual from buddy lists or other electronic communications
Impersonation	Pretending to be the victim and electronically communicating negatively or inappropriately with others as if the information is coming from the victim
Cyberstalking	Using electronic communication to stalk someone by sending repeated threatening messages
Sexting	Sending nude/inappropriate photos of another person without that individual's consent

Figure 5. Types of Cyberbullying

Reproduced from Kowalski, R. M., Giumetti, G. W., Schroeder, A. N., & Lattanner, M.R. (2014). Bullying in the digital age: A critical review and meta-analysis of cyberbullying research among youth. *Psychological Bulletin*, 140 (4), 1073–1137. https://doi.org/10.1037/a0035618

and engendering fear and helplessness in the victim" via "text messages, emails, social networking sites, mobile phones, chat rooms, blogs, IM, pictures, video clips, forwarding confidential emails or messages" (Miller, 2012). There are various types of cyberbullying (see Figure 5).

Bullying evolves with electronic forms of communication, whether it's cyberbullying on Facebook or Twitter, or victimization experienced during texting or online gaming (Moreno & Vaillancourt, 2017). Environments for cyberbullying are treacherous, because technologically savvy bullies can remain anonymous and untraceable when posting messages, videos, photos, and fake profiles for wide distribution (Hornor, 2018). Unfortunately, once a post, tweet, text or video is distributed, it can be recorded by someone else, even if deleted, making circulation inevitable. Students in middle and high school recognize the perils associated with communication technology and the need for social networking safety, but they are less likely to take steps to protect themselves from cyberbullying when using social media access points, such as, social networking sites, cell phones, and personal email (Roberto et al., 2014). Interventions addressing education and behavioral modification should begin as early as middle school, in order to help students feel positive about taking proactive steps to ensure their safety. Self-awareness and self-efficacy are necessary components of any antibullying, anticyberbullying, and anti-cyberbullying victimization (CBV) outreach.

Based on 20,793 interviews for the Ipsos Cyberbullying Global Advisor Survey (2018) conducted between March 23 and April 6, 2018, among adults aged 18 to 64 in the U.S. and Canada, and adults aged 16 to 64 in 26 other countries (Argentina, Australia, Belgium, Brazil, Chile, China, France, Germany, Great Britain, Hungary, India, Italy, Japan, Malaysia, Mexico, Peru, Poland, Romania, Russia, Saudi Arabia, Serbia, South Africa, South Korea, Spain, Sweden, and Turkey), there are key findings pertaining to opinions and perspectives about bullying and cyberbullying: (1) majorities in every country feel existing antibullying measures are insufficient, (2) global awareness of cyberbullying is increasing, but 25 percent of the people surveyed have never heard of it, (3) globally, one in three parents reports that a child in the community has experienced cyberbullying, and (4) cyberbullying done by classmates is most prevalent in Great Britain, followed by Canada and South Africa. Comparative cross-cultural analysis of cyberbullying and CBV affirms the body of knowledge on the prevalence of cyberbullying, specifically as a problem affecting all cultures and regions (Gómez et al., 2018).

Causality and Disparities in Bullying

Causality refers to a cause-and-effect relationship, and within the context of bullying it helps determine who is the cause of the bullying, the bully or the bullied. Internal causality refers to individuals who attribute responsibility to oneself and self-blame, while external causality focuses blame for the bullying on others (Danielson & Emmers-Sommer, 2016). Youths affected by internal causation blame themselves for being bullied, which can lead to internalizing problems (Perren et al., 2013). Self-blame takes two forms, including behavioral self-blame and characterological self-blame. Behavioral self-blame occurs when an outcome, such as bullying, cyberbullying, or CBV, is associated with one's modifiable behaviors which can be controlled or changed, whereas characterological self-blame happens when an outcome is blamed one one's nonmodifiable behaviors, which cannot be controlled or changed (Janoff-Bulman, 1979). Both variations of self-blame are detrimental, but characterological self-blame is more likely to trigger depression, prolonged victimization, and maladjustment (Shelley & Craig, 2010).

Both bullies and victims are at risk for short-term and long-term adjustment challenges including academic problems (Fonagy et al., 2005), psychological difficulties (Swearer et al., 2001), and social relationship problems (Goldbaum et al., 2003; Graham et al., 2003; Ladd, 2003). The implications for victims of bullying do not cease once they transition from childhood and adolescence into adulthood. Adults who were bullied in their youth must deal with lingering issues of causality, self-blame, and short-term and long-term adjustment challenges. These adults have an increased frequency of anxiety, depression, and suicidality (Arseneault, 2017). Bullying is a pediatric health problem for school children that when left untreated can manifest into psychiatric disorders and emotional distress in adulthood.

Epidemiological evidence pertaining to bullying, cyberbullying, and CBV addresses the implications of causality and self-blame on victims' well-being. The prevalence of bullying victimization based on sexual orientation (e.g., sexual attraction, sexual behavior, and sexual identity) and gender identity is high—gay males and transgender youth experience bullying and harassment more than other youth (Rivara & Le Menestrel, 2016). Students with disabilities are 1.5 times more likely to be bullied than youth without disabilities (Blake et al., 2012). Some research indicates that students with specific learning disabilities were almost six times more likely to perpetrate bullying than their peers (Twyman et al., 2010). Weight status (being overweight or obese) can be a factor in bullying among school-aged children and youth (Puhl & Latner, 2007). Among 5,749 children, aged 11 to 16, girls with higher body mass index (BMI) were more likely to be the targets of bullying behavior than their average-weight peers (Janssen et al., 2004). Moreover, as girls' BMI increased, the likelihood of them being the targets of verbal, physical, and relational bullying behavior rose. Victimization of children who are overweight or obese oftentimes adversely react to bullying behavior and become less active, which in turn leads to increased weight gain and greater scrutiny from peers (Gray, et al., 2009). Other disparities that have been identified and are important in any discussion of bullying behavior yet are less consistent in epidemiological evidence are the association between socioeconomic status, immigration status, minority religious affiliations, and youth with intersectional identities. For instance, most studies examine an identity group in isolation instead of acknowledging that multiple intersecting identities can exacerbate or attenuate health outcomes for bullies and their victims (Bowleg, 2008; McCall, 2005). More research is needed on a variety of identity groups in isolation and where they intersect with other identities.

Understanding the Interpersonal, Spatial, and Macrosystem Considerations

Bullies and victims have identifiable roles within a school's social system. The roles ascribed to them are based on their predictable behavior. The roles include bully, victim, bully-victim, and bystander. These roles inter-act and contribute to the cycle of aggressive behavior (Barboza, et al., 2009; Bradshaw et al., 2008). Bullies are dominant, quick-tempered, impulsive, and easily frustrated, which adversely affects victims, who can be socially isolated, insecure, anxious, and cautious (Espelage & Swearer, 2003). Par-ents of bullies tolerate their children's aggressiveness, sometimes inflict-ing their children with maltreatment, whether it be physical punishment or emotional outbursts (Olweus, 1993). Perhaps bullies mirror their par-ents, and victims are the unfortunate recipients of bullies' anger and angst. Some victims' households have an overbearing parent who fosters a con-trolling family structure (Espelage & Swearer, 2003). Some victims of bul-lying become bullies themselves. Barboza and associates (2009) identified a pattern where victims become bullies in later years in school. For example, the United States Secret Service found that 71 percent of 41 school shooters who orchestrated attacks in 37 different schools reported that their peers bullied, threatened, or harassed them (Vossekuil, Fein, Reddy, Borum, & Modzeleski, 2004). The roles of bully, victim, and bully-victim are inter-connected in the school's social system, and their interaction perpetuates a cycle of bullying that sustains prevalence rates. The fourth role in the social system involves bystanders, who allow bullying to occur without inter-vening or encourage the bullying to continue (Wiens & Dempsey, 2009). The school's social system and its environment are a determining factor in children's and youth's capacities for social engagement and explorations of power and power imbalances (Swearer & Hymel, 2015).

Understanding how communication and relationship dynamics enable or diffuse aggressive behavior is essential to decreasing prevalence rates. Supportive communication embedded within interpersonal com-munication, self- and mediated awareness, and health education and pro-motion should help children and youth resolve their problems without resorting to bullying involvement. Supportive communication within mul-tiple settings (i.e., home, neighborhood, school, and community) entails sending and receiving emotional support, which are messages that convey affection, concern, or empathy for a peer or counterpart (Matsunaga, 2010; Xu & Burleson, 2001). Bullied individuals lacking social support usually have higher levels of suicidal ideation. (Rigby & Slee, 1999). These victims experience negative emotional and psychological consequences (e.g., dis-tress, suicidal tendency, loneliness, and low self-esteem) when they lacked adequate social support (Kaltiala-Heino et al., 1999). Supportive commu-nication is imbued with the four dimensions of social support: the affec-tion, concern, and empathy of emotional support; the restoration of a peer's or counterpart's self-esteem, which is known as esteem support; network support, which builds linkages and relationships between someone who needs assistance, and someone qualified to give it; and informational support, which focuses on sharing advice and suggestions (Matsunaga, 2011). Social support reminds bullies, victims, victim-bullies, and bystanders that awareness, educational, and coping resources are available, and that the utilization of these resources can lead to a reevaluation of the conditions associated with bullying involvement and other troubling events (Matsunaga, 2011). For instance, social support can provide victims with an outlet for verbalizing their thoughts and assessing the role they play in bullying involvement. Supportive communication can assuage the distress of victims and neutralize their suffering (Hunter & Borg, 2006; Smith, 2000, 2004).

The 2014 evaluation of a bullying and cyberbullying presentation called the Arizona Attorney General's Social Networking Safety Promotion and Cyberbullying Prevention Program determined that outreach targeting school children was an effective intervention, because it relied on supportive communication. The evaluation was the first of its kind—a school- and community-based field experiment that collected data in a "real-world" setting using appropriate procedures (Roberto, et al. 2014). Three key goals of the intervention were to change students' attitudes, intentions, and behaviors, while persuading them that they were personally vulnerable to the real and credible threats of bullying and cyberbullying, and educating students about things they can do (i.e., recommendations) to reduce the threats. The 45-minute presentation focused on social networking safety promotion and cyberbullying prevention. Key components of the presentation were defining cyberbullying, sharing anecdotal narratives and news stories of behaviors that constituted cyberbullying, and reviewing Arizona's cyberbullying prevention laws. Interventionists rely on supportive communication in this program and others to decrease prevalence rates. Furthermore, the Arizona Attorney General's Social Networking Safety Promotion and Cyberbullying Prevention Program, Media Heroes (Wölfer et al., 2014), and Cyberbullying: A Prevention Curriculum (Limber et al., 2008) consistently recommend four responses to victims: (1) do not retaliate, (2) seek social support, (3) save evidence, and (4) notify authorities. Various websites dedicated to antibullying, including stopbullying.gov, stopcyberbullying.org, wiredsafety.org, and safeteens.com agree with these recommendations (Savage et al., 2017).

Focus on communication and relationship dynamics is important. However, there are other factors that impact bullying that may receive less attention. Lefebvre's (1991) theory of the production of space is applicable to the role that school-built environments play in intensifying bullying. Spatialization entails building layout, green space layout, placement of things in these layouts, and recognition that how people navigate these spaces can reproduce dominant-subordinate social relations in society. Efforts to implement antibullying interventions in children- and youth-centered spaces mean the environment must have antibullying spaces to foster new social relations between potential bullies, bullies, victims, victim-bullies, and bystanders. These spaces can be added to, underutilized, repurposed, or new spaces. Some spaces can aggravate bullying behaviors, especially when the designers of these spaces fail to factor in safety from bullying and harassment. Glover and Murphy's (2003) concept of school safety is helpful to interventionists who need guidance in understanding how to maneuver a school's ecosystem, both its physical environment and evolving social-emotional climate.

Outside of the school environment, there is a macrosystem. It consists of societal beliefs, values, and norms, which are personified in our ideologies and laws (Rivara & Le Menestrel, 2016). The macrosystem is as important a contextual factor impacting bullying and victimization as peers, parents, and schools. Macrosystem-level of analysis aids interventionists who are interested in understanding how school children and youths are socialized by dominant cultural beliefs. The macrosystem trains children and youths to join favored and unfavored groups in a society through socialization. The process of socialization or learning can spread negative stereotypes about peers and contribute to them being labeled as different or an outsider. Through socialization, the separation of individuals into favored and unfavored groups occurs in environments outside of school, even indirectly or directly in a school environment. Interventionists who want to combat bullying and victimization use their understanding of a macrosystem to comprehend students who initiate bias-based bullying that labels people as the other, denigrates them, and marginalizes and socially isolates students who are different, whether they are LGBT, overweight or obese, disabled, a person of lower economic status, an immigrant, a member of a religious minority, or have an intersectional identity.

Interventionists are also concerned that the macrosystem contributes to stigmatization, specifically "attacks motivated by a victim's actual or perceived membership in a legally protected class" (Greene, 2006, p. 69). Russell and colleagues (2012) attest that interventionists are concerned about general forms of bullying and bias-based bullying and harassment, which explains their focus on initiatives and outreach at various levels of society. Interventionists recognize that they can mitigate adverse outcomes on students, including substance abuse, mental health challenges, and problems with grades and truancy, when they embark on research that clarifies the relationship between both general forms of bullying and bias-based bullying and negative outcomes. A recent meta-analysis (Ttofi et al., 2008; sponsored by The Swedish National Council for Crime Prevention) conducted a systematic review of 59 reports describing evaluations of 30 international school-based bullying prevention and intervention programs. These studies were conducted in Australia, Austria, Belgium, Canada, Czechoslovakia, Cyprus, Denmark, England and Wales, Finland, Germany, Greece, Iceland, Ireland, Israel, Italy, Luxembourg, Japan, Malta, New Zealand, Northern Ireland, Norway, Portugal, Scotland, Spain, Sweden, Switzerland, the Netherlands, and the U.S. Ttofi and colleagues (2008) concluded that 12 anti-bullying programs (e.g., Andreou et al., 2007; Ertesvag & Vaaland, 2007; Evers et al., 2007; Melton et al., 1998; Raskauskas, 2007; Salmivalli et al., 2005) were effective in reducing bullying and victimization.

The most important components of these prevention and intervention programs were parent training, improved playground supervision, disciplinary methods, school conferences, information for parents, classroom rules, classroom management, and multimodal videos (i.e., synthesis of audio and visual mediums via communication technology). Cooperative group work and videos were useful in efforts to decrease victimization. The evolution of communication technology allows interventionists to create preventions and interventions that incorporate both multimodal outreach and cooperation between peers, parents, and schools (Noar et al., 2009). Mediated outreach offers researchers, interventionists, schools, and traditional and social media platforms and their users an opportunity to encounter and engage bullying behavior in a more immersive, participatory, and continuous environment. An increasing reliance on multimodal video and online preventative and interventionist content in outreach to bullies, victims, bully-victims, and bystanders, as well as their parents and communities, reinforces the centrality of communication in any efforts to address prevalence rates. Both interpersonal and mediated communication are needed to combat all variations of bullying.

Bandura's (2008) social cognitive theory (SCT) helps researchers and interventionists understand how anyone affected by bullying gains knowledge about it and how to react to bullying involvement through by observing the interactions of otherst in social settings or in the media. When applied to persuasive message development through storytelling and narratives, the theory fosters attitude and behavioral change via peer modeling (Hinyard & Kreuter, 2007; Noar et al., 2015). SCT explains how individuals respond to an actor or someone perceived as a peer or friend, performing a shared behavior in a narrative. As the story unravels, the reader, viewer, or listener identifies with the protagonist or antagonist. A recent study addressing a cyberbullying intervention illustrated one outcome of the study: "In this study, SCT was used to design an intervention message that aimed to encourage certain anti-bullying strategies by illustrating how one can successfully navigate an instance of being cyber-bullied by adopting the recommended responses" (Savage et al., 2017, p. 125). Celebrity narratives that adhere to the tenets of SCT might be useful for prevention and interventions when celebrity storytelling is applicable to bullies, victims, bully-victims, or bystanders. Celebrity storytelling can build narrative accounts incorporating past events, which are relatable to parents and their children. These stories help the parties involved to reorganize their experiences, perhaps furthering their understanding of the perspectives of others (Danielson & Emmers-Sommer, 2016; Weick, 1993). In our current media age, celebrity narratives that are suitable for sharing via traditional, new, and social media have the potential to reduce the prevalence rates of general forms of bullying, bias-based bullying, victimization and CBV.

Disney Channel Celebrity Alumni Take a Stand Against Bullying

For decades, the Disney Channel has been a powerhouse in youth entertainment. Tweens and teens from *The Mickey Mouse Club* to TV shows airing today were taken from obscurity and launched into superstardom. From Mouseketeers Britney Spears, Justin Timberlake, and Christina Aguilera to recent Disney Channel alumni Selena Gomez, Demi Lovato, and Zendaya, all owe a debt of gratitude to the media giant for introducing them to a massive audience. Yet, for some of these celebrities, fame came with bullying. Gomez, Lovato, and Zendaya became celebrities during the era of social media, and they use all media to take a stand against bullying. They share personal stories about being bullied in school and online, and they use their experiences to empower their fans and repudiate violence. Lovato has been a part of interventions against bullying since participating in the 2009 and 2010 one-minute public service announcements (PSAs) for PACER's National Bullying Prevention Center (teensagainstbullying.org). She followed these PSAs with a 31-second PSA for the antibullying media campaign STOMP Out Bullying: Change the Culture. STOMP Out Bullying is the leading national antibullying and cyberbullying organization for children and young adults in the U.S. The organization is dedicated to changing the culture. Lovato partnered with STOMP Out Bullying because of its educational and preventive messages about homophobia, LGBTQ discrimination, racism, and hatred, and because the organization hones in on violence deterrence in schools, online, and in communities across the country. Lovato can relate to kids who get bullied. She has addressed her experiences on various occasions over the past 20 years, telling *People Magazine*, "I had a really tough time when I was in middle school" (Hogan, 2012). In an interview published on October 4, 2014, on YouTube titled *Demi Lovato*

Goes into Detail about Her Bullying Experiences, she shared one of her experiences with being bullied:

> I was changing my clothes in the locker room and all of the other girls came in and one girl um um said I had taken her clothes or hidden them or something. And I said, look, no I really didn't. Um, I don't know where your clothes went, but I didn't touch them. And, um, it hasn't just her and her friends huddling around me t became a lot of the girls, especially, um the bully type girls in school, who were bigger than I was, who were taller, who were ready to fight; I ran out of the locker room and I went upstairs, and I just remember huddling in one of the bathroom stalls, and like hearing the other girls running up and down the hall looking for me.
>
> Lovato was traumatized by the experience. She continued with her recollection of her victimization: If someone had done something, and said, hey are you okay, or um, is there anyway I can help or stood up for me in that moment where I was in the locker room and everyone was ganging-up on me. I think that I wouldn't have been affected as hard as I was with the bullying had someone done that.

Lovato continued, "It's important for every bystander to know they have a purpose. Because they have the potential that maybe possibly even save someone's life." In her discussion with *People Magazine* (2012), Lovato emphasized how dire her interactions with bullies had become:

> People would write "hate petitions" [about me] and send them around to be signed. They'd have CD-bashing parties of my demos. They'd come to my house, stand across the street and yell things. It was a very emotional time for me, and all I wanted to do was get away.

Lovato's painful experiences affected her perception of herself, but as she matured, she was able to use storytelling in her role as an ambassador for Secret's "Mean Stinks" campaign. The campaign encouraged girls to "gang up for good" and end bullying in school (Hogan, 2012). In this instance and others, Lovato chose to interact with the campaign's target audience. In her role as an ambassador, she visited New York City's Young Women's Leadership School to talk about the "Mean Stinks" campaign. Her goal was to get young women to buy-in and demonstrate their commitment to the campaign. She wanted the audience to know, "It's a conversation starter: 'Hey, why is your pinky blue?' 'This is a pinky promise that I'm not going to bully people, that me and my friends are ganging up for good.'" By making a pinky swear, symbolized by wearing blue nail polish on their pinky fingers, they pledged to have a "Drama-Free School Year." To increase the appeal of the campaign, Secret announced it would donate one dollar from the purchase of every Mean Stinks clinical-strength deodorant to the cause. Years later, when Lovato became a major recording artist and celebrity, she instilled the self-esteem–boosting messages found in her antibullying campaigns into her music. When she dropped her hit single "Sorry Not Sorry," many listeners believed the song was about getting revenge on an ex-lover, but according to Demi, "...it's actually [directed] towards them [the bullies]," and she wanted them to know, "I'm in a really good place in my life today, and I'm not sorry about it" (Dzhanova, 2017). When Lovato was sitting with Yahoo Music at a private Spotify showcase for her diehard fans in Los Angeles, she revealed that the lyrics from the song, such as "payback is a bad bitch" and "now I'm out here looking like revenge, feelin' like a 10" are meant for school bullies who made her life hell when she was 12 years old. When she performed the song at the 2017 American Music Awards, Lovato literally rose above the pervasive negativity of bullying. When the performance began, hateful social media messages about her weight, appearance, and talent scrawled across the screen, as she rose from the audience like a phoenix and used her lyrics to combat bullies (Lipshutz, 2017). The song reached the top 20 in the U.S. and countries from around the world (Dzhanova, 2017). Despite the empowering tone of "Sorry Not Sorry," the bullying took a toll on Lovato, who has been outspoken about her mental health struggles. She has mentioned that being open and telling her story, helps: "I get messages all the time, on Instagram and Twitter and fan letters, that say that I've helped them. They've struggled with mental illness as well, and they've been able to get treatment they've needed because of me or I've inspired them to get help" (Parker, 2017). Another Disney alumna, Zendaya, was 18 years old when she was bullied on live television by a woman twice her age.

Zendaya is more than just another rising star in Hollywood. She is a young woman who has demonstrated poise, wit, guile, and guts in the face of public bullying. On the red carpet at the 2015 Academy Awards, Fashion Police host Giuliana Rancic noticed that the *K.C. Undercover* actress had dreadlocks and said on live television that Zendaya must have smelled of "patchouli" and "weed" (Steiner, 2015). Zendaya reflected on the experience on Instagram, without naming Rancic: "There is a fine line between what is funny and disrespectful." She continued, "Someone said something about my hair at the Oscars that left me in awe. Not because I was relishing in rave outfit reviews, but because I was hit with ignorant slurs and pure disrespect." As media users read Zendaya's Instagram post, it became apparent that the post was a PSA against bias-based bullying:

> To say that an 18 year old young woman with locs must smell of patchouli oil or weed is not only a large stereotype but outrageously offensive. I don't usually feel the need to respond to negative things but certain remarks cannot go unchecked. I'll have you know my father, brother, best childhood friend and little cousins all have have locs. Do you want to know what Ava DuVernay (director of the Oscar nominated film Selma), Ledisi (9 time Grammy nominated

singer/songwriter and actress), Terry McMillan (author), Vincent Brown (Professor of African and African American studies at Harvard University), Heather Andrea Williams (Historian who also possesses a JD from Harvard University, and an MA and PhD from Yale University) as well as many other men woman and children of all races have in common? Locs. None of which smell of marijuana. There is already harsh criticism of African American hair in society without the help of ignorant people who choose to judge others based on the curl of their hair.

Later, Rancic apologized for her comments on Twitter. The day after the incident, she issued an on-camera apology.

Later that same year, Zendaya had to contend with a tweet of a photo of her with her parents, Claire Stoermer and Kazembe Ajamu Coleman (Rayne, 2015). The Twitter user captioned the photo with these words: "they made a gorgeous ass child lol." Other tweets called her parents "ugly," with Twitter users claiming they "would cry" if their parents looked like hers (Rayne, 2015). Zendaya's tweet to shut down the haters read:

> First, I'm gonna pray for you. While you're so concerned about what my parents look like, please know that these are two of the most selfless people in the world. They have chosen to spend their entire life, not worried about trivial things such as look and insulting people's parents on Twitter, but instead became educators who have dedicate their lives to teaching, cultivating and filling young shallow minds. (One of the most important yet underpaid jobs we have) So please, log out, go to school, hug a teacher and read a textbook … and while you're at it, go look in the mirror and know that you too are beautiful, because such hateful things only stem from internal struggles. Bless you.

A couple years after the incidents with Rancic and mean-spirited Twitter users, Zendaya came across a deleted tweet that body-shamed a young woman. According to the Huffington Post Canada, in the original tweet, user Eskimo Jay wrote, "never trust a top half posting ass female lmfao," which insulted the size of a woman's body (Patel, 2017). In response, Zendaya tweeted: "[*sic* throughout] Stumbling across this is stupid shit, she is fine as hell head to toe and garunteed doesn't know you exist my man. As for her, slay on queen." She added, "Can we find her @…. I'd love for her to be a @dayabyzendaya model." Zendaya's fashion line, Daya by Zendaya, is curated by the actress and her stylist, Law Roach, and the brand is designed for all ages, shapes, and nationalities (Patel, 2017). Shortly thereafter, social media users were able to identify the woman as Twitter user @_illestCee. She replied to Zendaya's Twitter offer: "I'm really speechless right now because becoming a plus-size model has been my number-one goal."

Zendaya has developed an online presence associated with supporting young women and promoting antibullying, so it was not surprising when she paired-up with Verizon as part of its #weneedmore campaign. The campaign strives to provide underprivileged youth and underserved areas with exposure to hands-on science and technology. When asked about the campaign and its target audience, Zendaya said, "I really just want them to know that they can use their voice for good, that they have a voice, they exist and, again, using technology and my platform for things that are important" (Ironson, 2017). When asked for advice on dealing with some of the downfalls of the Internet, like cyberbullies, she provided good advice for victims of CBV (Ironson, 2017):

> My biggest advice for dealing with cyberbullying is quite simple, just turn it off. That's the luxury of it. It's one thing to be dealing with bullying in your face, but it's another to have it online. It's different if they go to your school, but it's usually a random person. That happens to me all the time. Trust me, I deal with a gazillion haters all day every day, I don't know who they are. My biggest advice for dealing with cyber bullying is quite simple, just turn it off. Somebody said something that was really powerful … they were saying that allowing someone on the internet to affect you is literally like allowing a stranger to jump in your care at a red light, scream all these heinous, terrible things at you and then get out. In real life, how would you react? You'd be like, "What the hell? Who are you and why are you in my car?" It's literally a stranger who doesn't know you … and in real life, you'd laugh it off.

In 2018, STOMP Out Bullying teamed up with Zendaya and her *Spider-Man: Homecoming* costar Tom Holland to create a PSA for the organization's antibullying awareness campaign. In the PSA, Zendaya and Holland discuss being the targets of bullies and how—with the power of inclusion, diversity, and kindness—young people can end bullying and change the culture. The PSA was introduced by their *Spider-Man: Homecoming* co-stars Laura Harrier and Jacob Batalon at a surprise visit to a neighborhood high school. Selena Gomez, another movie star, musician, and Disney alumna, also supports kids and young adults who are in school or college, especially young women. She champions inclusivity and kindness and refuses to cower to bullies. In 2014, Gomez addressed a commenter, who reportedly wrote, "Please kill yourself and burn in hell with cancer because your fans are ugly retarded sluts!" on one of her pictures (Sitzer, 2014). Gomez wrote on one of the bully's pictures, "The comment you left about cancer was absurd." Her poised but stern Instagram response continued:

> How distasteful of a young woman. I have gone through that battle with fans and family members. You can dislike someone but to wish something that could happen to you or your family is uncalled for sweetheart. You won't be winning "anyone's" heart that way. Trust me. Educate yourself a tad more. God bless love. Be an amazing woman. You're beautiful.

This commenter's behavior is indicative of the CBV that Gomez and her fans experience. After one of her fans disclosed online that she wanted to kill herself, others encouraged her to go through with it, even exclaiming, "Cut, cut, cut" (Sitzer, 2014). Gomez's Instagram response sums up her discontent with the situation: "My fans don't do this to others. That's not what I stand for so you can gladly stop being a fan of me. I only encourage love, confidence, kindness." In 2015, when TMZ posted a picture of her in a bikini on a Mexican beach and wrote, "things are getting thick down in Mexico" (Yahr, 2015), Gomez used Instagram to respond. Unfortunately, she had to respond to more body-shaming in 2018, again taking to Instagram to respond (Jackson, 2018):

> The beauty myth—an obsession with physical perfection that traps modern woman in an endless cycle of hopelessness, self-consciousness, and self-hatred as she tries to fulfill society's impossible definition of flawless beauty. I chose to take care of myself because I want to, not to prove anything to anyone. Wind in her sails.

Later in 2018, Gomez had to deal with the controversy associated with remarks made about her by Stefano Gabbana of Dolce & Gabbana. Posted on the Italian celebrity fashion account @thecatwalkitalia, Gabbana commented on a picture of Gomez, and his comments translated to "She's so ugly!!!" The reaction in defense of Gomez was swift and resolute, as exemplified by the response of Tommy Dorfman, star of the Netflix suicide and bullying drama, *13 Reasons Why*. Dorfman wrote, "You're tired and over, your homophobic, misogynistic, body-shaming existence will not thrive in 2018. It is no longer tolerable or chic. Please take many seats" (Wallace, 2018). Gabbana seemed unfazed by the backlash. Instead of apologizing, he defiantly exclaimed, "Say sorry to me" (Matera, 2018). The back-and-forth between Gabbana and Gomez's supporters underscores that reacting to cyberbullies is not always effective. David Cook, a cybercrime lawyer, recognized that while many people admire the response of Gomez and her fans to cyberbullying, they are sending the wrong message to her young and impressionable fans (Bird, 2014). Gomez can afford bodyguards and public relations experts to help her negotiate an online attack, should she provoke one, but her fans likely do not have the same kind of support. He asserts, "You shouldn't engage in any kind of banter or insults back, because things can escalate quickly" (Bird, 2014). Yet others believe it is appropriate to respond to CBV. "We need celebrities to change the culture," said Marjorie Nolan Cohn, national spokesperson for the Academy of Nutrition and Dietetics (Yahr, 2015). She continued, "It's sad but true—this is who we look up to as a society. If they're not saying anything, [sending] a positive message is going to be a much harder and longer road."

If celebrities such as Gomez, Lovato, and Zendaya can be criticized and demeaned for their appearance, media users might feel they do not stand a chance under this heightened level of scrutiny. Perhaps celebrity narratives addressing the various types of bullying are more than infotainment—their stories are our stories, and together these stories give us purpose and meaning. In response to body-shaming, Gomez posted a picture of herself in a bathing suit on Instagram with the caption (Yahr, 2015): "I love being happy with me y'all" and "#theresmoretolove."

Prevention Saves Lives

All variations of bullying are a manifestation of violence. Bullying adversely impacts the health of various groups, including bullies, victims, peers, family members, schools, and communities. Across their lifespans, as these groups react to bullying behavior, there are health and safety hazards linked to bullying, victimization, cyberbullying, and CBV. These variations of bullying exist in societies across the world. Some communities have invested in antibullying awareness and prevention, whereas others are in the early stages of confronting bullying involvement. All societies need to develop health policies for bullying prevention (Srabstein & Leventhal, 2010). *Intervening in Primary Care Against Childhood Bullying: An Increasingly Pressing Public Health Need* (2014), a study published in the *Journal of the Royal Society of Medicine*, states: "The effectiveness of different approaches to identification of bullied children in schools, general practice, school nursing, emergency departments, pediatric clinics, children and adolescent mental health services (CAMHS) and other services where children present needs to be investigated" (p. 221). In the United Kingdom, policies addressing bullying target actions taken at the school level, including staff being provided with support to design and implement antibullying initiatives (U. K. Department of Education, 2013). These policies and initiatives have had limited effect and produced modest results (Samara & Smith, 2008). In certain circumstances, antibullying interventions led to the further victimization of the bullied child (Merrell et al., 2008). A course correction occurred, and to increase recognition of bullying as a community problem, some UK charities threw their support behind a "community trigger" that allows members of communities "to request a review in situations where there have been several complaints about bullying" (Dale et al., 2014, p. 220). In the U.S., interventionists argue that a course correction is needed, and that best practices in the macrosystem need to be identified and replicated nationwide. These practices can be grouped together into four categories, including learning environment, healthcare, social media, and law enforcement.

There are a variety of learning environments where children congregate with their peers, including daycare facilities, school buildings, spaces and venues for after-school activities, the homes of family and friends, and mediated and virtual realities created with communication technology. Many of these environments have tangible and concrete surroundings that provide a physical dimension or loci for bullying to occur (Fram & Dickmann, 2012). Some learning environments are on smart devices (phones, tablets, laptops, etc.) and online. Texting, gaming, and social media play an outsize role in peer relations for Generation Alpha (ages younger than 10), Generation Z (children born in the mid- to late 1990s), and millennials (adults in their 20s and 30s). Because the landscape for outreach, interventions, and prevention is varied, many efforts have had limited success. The groundbreaking work of Dan Olweus, a researcher and professor in Norway, provided the foundation for the Olweus Bullying Prevention Program, which has received international recognition (Hoover & Stenhjem, 2003). This program, as well as others like it, emphasizes the following components: (1) student engagement (informal discussions, focus groups, and surveys) to ascertain their attitudes and opinions regarding bullying, (2) at the classroom level, rules against all variations of bullying are introduced, explained, and enforced (e.g., classroom discussions, meetings are held with parents, etc.), (3) schoolwide rules against bullying are adopted, reviewed, and revised regularly (e.g., a system of supervision is developed), and (4) at the individual level, interventions are implemented with bullies, victims, bully-victims, and bystanders, and parents are included in resolution strategies (Schoen & Schoen, 2010). These components integrate the antibullying message into the ongoing operations and curriculum of the school.

Another program, Second Step, emphasizes helping students develop social skills and emotion management in order to foster problem-solving and cooperation. Edwards and colleagues (2005) examined the effectiveness of Second Step on 455 fourth- and fifth-grade students, and findings indicated significant gains in anger management, impulse control, empathy, and prosocial behavior. Teachers play an important role in antibullying interventions like Olweus Bullying Prevention Program and Second Step, because they are key agents in the creation and maintenance of safe environments for school children. They intervene at both the classroom and individual levels. "Teachers' efforts might be further described as 'talking the talk' and 'walking the talk'" (Hirschstein et al., 2007, p. 4). They have to implement policies and initiatives, which entails embedding components of an intervention into classroom lesson plans, and if a lesson plan contributes to students believing there are inconsistencies between their thoughts, beliefs, or attitudes and what is being advocated in the intervention, instructors and administrators will need to provide impromptu or "on the fly" guidance or coaching for students involved in bully-victim problems. Teachers play an integral role in antibullying interventions such as Olweus' research, which was the touchstone for another program, the Stop Bullying Now! campaign. This campaign was developed by Stan Davis, and it offers schools and communities many options (Schoen & Schoen, 2010, p. 70):

> The resources include, but are not limited to, videos, DVDs, guidebooks, kits, and ideas for organizing events and working with the local media. Materials are accessible to parents, administrators, educators, health care providers, and safety professionals. The Stop Bullying Now! website is a hub of information and materials to combat this formidable problem.

Healthcare providers (HCPs), including physicians, psychologists, social workers, and nurses in the U.S. and abroad, are too often on the periphery of efforts to prevent, educate, and address bullying, cyberbullying, and CBV. HCP's need to establish themselves as important stakeholders in antibullying prevention and interventions. Sometimes policymakers underestimate the role of HCPs. HCPs need to screen patients and clients in high-risk groups for variations of bullying and victimization, such as children with special needs, children who are under- or overweight, and youth who identify as lesbian, gay, bisexual, transgender, or queer/questioning (McClowry et al., 2017). When HCPs speak with victims, they are in a unique position to reinforce that bullying is not the child's fault, and that children should never ignore bullying (U.S. Department of Health and Human Services, 2020). Parents respect HCPs and are likely to adhere to their directives. HCPs' advice for parents should entail avoiding blaming the child, talking about bullying directly, and making it clear that bullying is being taken seriously. HCPs should also advise parents to refrain from contacting the other parents involved and to instead contact school personnel or other officials to act as mediators (U.S. Department of Health and Human Services, 2020).

When HCPs interact with victims during screenings in clinical settings, paper or online intake forms are important (Scott et al., 2016). "These screening forms may be useful in the case of bullying, as studies suggest it may be better to ask youth about their exposure to bullying and cyberbullying using a questionnaire rather than asking them directly" (Moreno & Vaillancourt, 2017, p. 365). The most common screening form used in the U.S. is called the Guidelines for Adolescent Preventive Services (GAPS) form, which addresses bullying and a variety of health behaviors and experiences (Elster & Kuznets, 1994). Oftentimes, during a consultation with an HPC, children do not want their parents to be present when they discuss their experiences with bullying (Neinstein, 2016). HCPs should have individual time with children to discuss topics that are more private or stigmatizing. During these discussions, Lam and colleagues (2009) suggest HCPs pose four questions: (1) how often do you get bullied (or bully others)? (2) how long have you been bullied (or bullied others)? (3) where are you bullied (or bullying others)? and (4) how are you bullied (or how do you bully others)? These questions are applicable to children who encounter cyberbullying, since many victims who experience it endure traditional bullying.

Cyberbullying and CBV are a problem for children and young adults. Despite the efforts of major social media platforms, including Facebook, Twitter, Snapchat, YouTube, and Instagram, which have established a minimum age for users, 61 percent of young people had their first social media account before they had reached the minimum age (Safety Net, 2018). Youth are on social media for longer periods of time and use multiple profiles, and some of them experience cyberbullying, which can have adverse effects on their health and well-being. "There is an appetite among young people for greater interventions to disrupt cyberbullying, with 83% of young people saying that social media companies should do more to tackle cyberbullying on their platforms" (Safety Net, 2018). Standard procedure for many social media platforms to address "bad behavior" online is for company moderators to review flagged behavior and to determine if it should be removed (Milosevic, 2016). More advanced policies are emerging where companies provide children and caregivers with the tools to address cyberbullying or refer them to NGOs.

These policies coalesce human moderators and community self-moderation (i.e., greater participation and responsibility of users in reporting cases of bulling involvement) to work together in the collection of evidence to establish that a case constitutes cyberbullying. These advanced policies reflect the realignment of companies' perspectives regarding empowering "…children through provision and participation rights guaranteed to children by the United Nations Convention on the Rights of the Child" (Milosevic, 2016, p. 5175). The shift toward better e-safety with more community self-regulation is warranted but is incomplete due to "… an independent assessment of the effectiveness of the current policies and enforcement mechanisms from children's perspective, which currently does not exist" (Milosevic, 2016, p. 5176). To improve their efforts, social media companies should continue working with the Federal Partners in Bullying Prevention Steering Committee, which is an interagency effort co-led by the Department of Education and the Department of Health and Human Services. If these companies do not fully realign to address cyberbullying and CBV, they will not be able to avert regulation.

The law enforcement issues for both bullying and cyberbullying are ever-changing. Bullying behaviors can be considered illegal behavior, such as assault, extortion, child pornography, criminal harassment, sexual harassment, or violation of civil rights (Cornell & Limber, 2015; UNICEF, 2012). Within a learning environment for children, graduated consequences for bullying behavior that are dependent on the context and severity of the behavior and the characteristics of the students involved should be established (Kowalski et al., 2012; Swearer et al., 2009; U.S. Department of Education, Office for Civil Rights, 2010). In the absence of a federal law against bullying and cyberbullying, individual states are addressing the matter, oftentimes in reaction to an event that gains statewide or nationwide media coverage. For instance, in New Jersey, events involving sexting and cyberbullying garnered national media coverage and intensive statewide media coverage in 2011. "In January 2011, New Jersey Assemblywoman Pam Lampitt introduced a bill designed to divert first-time sexting offenders who might otherwise face child porn charges into a 'diversionary' education program" (Albury & Crawford, 2012, p. 471). In September 2011, greater attention and media scrutiny was paid to how New Jersey legislatively responded to the case of Tyler Clementi, who committed suicide after his roommate allegedly shot a video of Clementi with a man and posted it online. The outcome was the enforcement of tougher harassment, intimidation, and bullying protocols in conjunction with the state's Anti-Bullying Bill of Rights (McClowry et al., 2017; Temkin, 2015). Interventionists including researchers, HCPs, antibullying awareness campaign and prevention specialists, policymakers, law enforcement officials, and children and their caregivers want persuasive messages about the ills associated with all variations of bullying to compel bullies, victims, bully-victims, and bystanders to have empathy for one another and to think before they act.

REFERENCES

Albury, K., & Crawford, K. (2012). Sexting, consent and young people's ethics: Beyond *Megan's Story*. *Continuum: Journal of Media & Cultural Studies, 26(3)*, 463–473. https://doi.org/10.10 80/10304312.2012.665840.

Andreou, E., Didaskalou, E., & Vlachou, A. (2007) Evaluating the effectiveness of a curriculum-based anti-bullying intervention program in Greek primary schools. *Educational Psychology, 27(5)*, 693–711. https://doi.org/10.1080/01443410601159993.

Arseneault L. (2017). The long-term impact of bullying victimization on mental health. *World Psychiatry, 16(1)*, 27–28. https://doi.org/10.1002/wps.20399.

Astor, R.A., Meyer, H.M., & Pitner, R.O. (2001). Elementary and middle school students' perceptions of violence-prone school subcon texts. *Elementary School Journal, 101(5)*, 511–528. http://www.jstor.org/stable/1002121.

Bandura, A. (2008). Social cognitive theory of mass communication. In J. Bryant & M.B. Oliver (Eds.), *Media effects: Advances in theory and research* (3rd ed., pp. 121–153). Routledge.

Barboza, G.E., Schiamberg, L.B., Oehmke, J., Korzeniewski, S.J., Post, L.A., & Heraux, C.G. (2009). Individual characteristics and the multiple contexts of adolescent bullying: An ecological perspective. *Journal of Youth and Adolescence, 38(1)*, 101–121. https://doi.org/ 10.1007/s10964-008-9271-1.

Bird, N. (2014, July 15). *Was Selena Gomez wrong to slam her Instagram bully publicly?* Yahoo Lifestyle. https://uk.style.yahoo.com/was-selena-gomez-wrong-to-slam-her-instagram-bully-publically-172608315.html.

Blake, J.J., Lund, E.M., Zhou, Q., Kwok, O.-M., & Benz, M.R. (2012). National prevalence rates of bully victimization among students with disabilities in the United States. *School Psychology Quarterly, 27(4)*, 210–222. https://doi.org/10.1037/spq0000008.

Bowleg, L. (2008). When Black+ lesbian+ woman ≠ Black lesbian woman: The methodological challenges of qualitative and quantitative intersectionality research. *Sex Roles, 59(5–6)*, 312–325. https://doi.org/10.1007/S11199-008-9400-Z.

Bradshaw, C.P., O'Brennan, L.M., & Sawyer, A.L. (2008). Examining variation in attitudes toward aggressive retaliation and perceptions of safety among bullies, victims, and bully/victims. *Professional School Counseling, 12(1)*, 10–21. https://doi.org/10.1177/2156759X0801200102.

Cairns, R.B., & Cairns, B.D. (1994). *Lifelines and risks: Pathways of youth in our time.* Cambridge University Press.

The Children's Society and Young Minds (2018). *Safety net: Cyberbullying's impact on young people's mental health.* Children's Society. https://www.basw.co.uk/system/files/resources/basw_53023-8.pdf.

Cornell, D., & Limber, S.P. (2015). Law and policy on the concept of bullying at school. *The American psychologist, 70(4)*, 333–343. https://doi.org/10.1037/a0038558.

Dale, J., Russell, R., & Wolke, D. (2014). Intervening in primary care against childhood bullying: An increasingly pressing public health need. *Journal of the Royal Society of Medicine, 107(6)*, 219–223. https://doi.org/10.1177/0141076814525071.

Danielson, C.M., & Emmers-Sommer, T.M. (2016). "It was my fault": Bullied students' causal and controllable attributions in bullying blogs. *Journal of Health Communication, 21(4)*, 408–414. https://doi.org/10.1080/10810730.2015.1095817.

Daniixcx. (2014, October 4). *Demi Lovato goes into detail about her bullying experience* [Video]. https://www.youtube.com/watch?v=Q7KFV-iJQkw.

Development Services Group, Inc. (2013). *"Bullying." Literature review.* Office of Juvenile Justice and Delinquency Prevention. https://www.ojjdp.gov/mpg/litreviews/Bullying.pdf.

Dzhanova, Y. (2017, September 24). *Demi Lovato's latest hit song is dedicated to her childhood bullies.* NBC News. https://www.nbcnews.com/news/us-news/demi-lovato-s-latest-hit-song-dedicated-her-childhood-bullies-n804341.

Edwards, D., Hunt, M.H., Meyers, J., Grogg, K.R., & Jarrett, O. (2005). Acceptability and student outcomes of a violence prevention curriculum. *The Journal of Primary Prevention, 26(5)*, 401–418. https://doi.org/10.1007/s10935-005-0002-z.

Elster, A.B., & Kuznets, N.J. (1994). American Medical Association Guidelines for Adolescent Preventive Services (GAPS): Recommendations and rationale. Williams and Wilkins. https://somepomed.org/articulos/contents/mobipreview.htm?9/15/9456.

Ertesvåg, S.K., & Vaaland, G.S. (2007). Prevention and reduction of behavioral problems in school: An evaluation of the Respect program. *Educational Psychology, 27(6)*, 713–736. https://doi.org/10.1080/01443410701309258.

Espelage, D.L., Green, Jr., H.D., & Wasserman, S. (2007). Statistical analysis of friendship patterns and bullying behaviors among youth. *New Directions for Child and Adolescent Development* (118), 61–75. https://doi.org/10.1002/cd.201.

Espelage, D.L., & Swearer, S.W. (2003). Research on school bullying and victimization: What have we learned and where do we go from here? *School Psychology Review, 32(3)*, 365–383. https://doi.org/10.1080/02796015.2003.12086206.

Evers, K.E., Prochaska, J.O., Van Marter, D.F., Johnson, J.L., & Prochaska, J.M. (2007). Trans-theoretical-based bullying prevention effectiveness trials in middle schools and high schools. *Educational Research, 49(4)*, 397–414. https://doi.org/10.1080/00131880701717271.

Fonagy, P., Twemlow, S.W., Vernberg, E., Sacco, F.C., & Little, T.D. (2005). Creating a peaceful school learning environment: The impact of an antibullying program on educational attainment in elementary schools. *Medical Science Monitor, 11(7)*, CR317-CR325.

Fram, S.M., & Dickmann, E.M. (2012). How the school built environment exacerbates bullying and peer harassment. *Children, Youth and Environments, 22(1)*, 227–249. https://doi.org/10.7721/chilyoutenvi.22.1.0227.

Gavin, A., Keane, E., Callaghan, M., Molcho, M., Kelly, C., Nic Gabhainn, S. (2015). *The Irish health behavior in school-aged children (HBSC) study 2014*. Department of Health, Ireland. http://www.nuigalway.ie/media/nuigalwayie/content/images/aboutus/newsandevents/2014-HBSC-Nat-Rep.pdf.

Gladden, R.M., Vivolo-Kantor, A.M., Hamburger, M.E., & Lumpkin, C.D. (2014). *Bullying surveillance among youths: Uniform definitions for public health and recommended data elements*. National Center for Injury Prevention and Control, Centers for Disease Control and Prevention and United States Department of Education. http://www.cdc.gov/violenceprevention/pdf/bullying-definitions-final-a.pdf.

Glover, R.L., & Murphy, H.R. (2003). *School safety management: Practical approaches, current theories, and standards* (2nd ed.). Civic Research Institute.

Goldbaum, S., Craig, W.M., Pepler, D., & Connolly, J. (2007). Developmental Trajectories of Victimization: Identifying Risk and Protective Factors. In J.E. Zins, M.J. Elias, & C.A. Maher (Eds.), *Bullying, victimization, and peer harassment: A handbook of prevention and intervention* (p. 143–160). Haworth Press.

Goldsmid S, & Howie P. (2014). Bullying by definition: An examination of definitional components of bullying. *Emotional Behavioral Difficulties, 19(2)*, 210–25. https://doi.org/10.1080/13632752.2013.844414.

Graham, S., Bellmore, A., & Juvonen, J. (2003). Peer Victimization in middle school: When self- and peer views diverge. *Journal of Applied School Psychology*, 19(2), 117–137. https://doi.org/10.1300/J008v19n02_08.

Gray, W.N., Kahhan, N.A., and Janicke, D.M. (2009). Peer victimization and pediatric obesity: A review of the literature. *Psychology in the Schools, 46(8)*, 720–727. https://doi.org/10.1002/pits.20410.

Greene, M.B. (2006). Bullying in schools: A plea for measure of human rights. *Journal of Social Issues, 62*(1), 63–79. https://doi.org/10.1111/j.1540-4560.2006.00439.x.

Guerin, S., & Hennessy, E. (2002). Pupils' definitions of bullying. *European Journal of Psychology of Education, 17(3)*, 249–261. https://doi.org/10.1007/BF03173535.

Hellström, L., Persson, L., & Hagquist, C. (2015). Understanding and defining bullying—adolescents' own views. *Archives of Public Health, 73(1)*, 4. https://doi.org/10.1186/2049-3258-73-4.

Hinyard, L.J., & Kreuter, M.W. (2007). Using narrative communication as a tool for health behavior change: A conceptual, theoretical, and empirical overview. *Health Education & Behavior, 34(5)*, 777–792. https://doi.org/10.1177/1090198106291963.

Hirschstein, M.K., Van Schoiack Edstrom, L., Frey, K.S., Snell, J.L., & MacKenzie, E.P. (2007). Walking the talk in bullying prevention: Teacher implementation variables related to initial impact of the Steps to Respect program. *School Psychology Review, 36(1)*, 3–21. https://doi.org/10.1080/02796015.2007.12087949.

Hogan, K. (2012, September 20). Demi Lovato is ambassador for new anti-bullying campaign. *People Magazine*. https://people.com/celebrity/demi-lovato-reveals-bullying-story-program/.

Hoover, J.H., Oliver, R., & Hazler, R.J. (1992). Bullying: Perceptions of adolescent victims in the midwestern USA. *School Psychology International, 13(1)*, 5–16. https://doi.org/10.1177/0143034392131001.

Hoover, J.H., & Stenhjem, P. (2003). Bullying and teasing of youth with disabilities: Creating positive school environments for effective inclusion. *Examining Current Challenges in Secondary Education and Transition, 2(3)*, 1–7. http://www.ncset.org/publications/issue/ncsetissuebrief_2.3.pdf.

Hornor, G. (2018). Bullying: What the PNP needs to know. *Journal of Pediatric Healthcare, 32(4)*, 399–408. https://doi.org/10.1016/j.pedhc.2018.02.001.

Hunter, S.C., & Borg, M.G. (2006). The influence of emotional reaction on help seeking by victims of school bullying. *Educational Psychology, 26(6)*, 813–826. https://doi.org/10.1080/01443410600941946.

Ironson, S. (2017, April 5). *Zendaya gives advice for fighting off cyberbullies*. Elite Daily. https://www.elitedaily.com/entertainment/celebrity/zendaya-advice-cyber-bullying/1850643.

Jackson, D. (2018, March 20). Selena Gomez slams body-shaming comments about bikini pictures. *Newsweek*. https://www.newsweek.com/selena-gomez-instagram-selena-gomez-body-shammers-francia-raisa-selena-gomez-853451.

Janoff-Bulman, R. (1979). Characterological and behavioral self-blame: Inquiries into depression and rape. *Journal of Personality and Social Psychology, 37(10)*, 1798–1809. https://doi.org/10.1037/0022-3514.37.10.1798.

Janssen, I., Craig, W.M., Boyce, W.F., and Pickett, W. (2004). Associations between overweight and obesity with bullying behaviors in school-aged children. *Pediatrics, 113(5)*, 1187–1194. https://doi.org/10.1542/peds.113.5.1187.

Kaltiala-Heino, R., Rimpelä, M., Marttunen, M., Rimpelä, A., & Rantanen, P. (1999). Bullying, depression, and suicidal ideation in Finnish adolescents: School survey. *British Medical Journal, 319(7206)*, 348–351. https://doi.org/10.1136/bmj.319.7206.348.

Kelly, C., Gavin, A., Molcho, M., & Nic Gabhainn, S. (2012). *The Irish health behavior in school-aged children (HBSC) study 2010*. Department of Health, Ireland.

Kowalski, R., Limber, S., & Agatston, P. (2012). *Cyberbullying: Bullying in the digital age* (2nd ed.). Wiley-Blackwell. https://www.drugsandalcohol.ie/17360/1/nat_rep_hbsc_2010.pdf.

Ladd, G.W. (2003). Probing the adaptive significance of children's behavior and relationships in the school context: A child by environment perspective. In R.V. Kail (Ed.), *Advances in child development and behavior* (pp. 43–104). Academic Press.

Lamb, J., Pepler, D.J., & Craig, W. (2009). Approach to bullying and victimization. *Canadian Family Physician, 55(4)*, 356–360.

Lefebvre, H. (1991). *The production of space*. Blackwell.

Limber, S. (2002). *Addressing youth bullying behaviors*. Proceedings of the Educational Forum on Adolescent Health—Youth Bullying, American Medical Association. http://www.ncdsv.org/images/AMA_EdForumAdolescentHealthYouthBullying_5-3-2002.pdf.

Limber, S.P., Kowalski, R.M., & Agatston, P.W. (2008). Cyber bullying: A prevention curriculum for grades 6–12. Hazelden.

Lipshutz, J. (2017, November 19). Demi Lovato discusses anti-bullying AMAs performance, her "courageous" guest Danica Roem. *Billboard*. https://assets.billboard.com/articles/news/amas/8039505/demi-lovato-interview-amas-sorry-not-danica-roem.

Lipson, J. (Ed.). (2001). *Hostile hallways: Bullying, teasing, and sexual harassment in school*. American Association of University Women Educational Foundation. https://files.eric.ed.gov/fulltext/ED454132.pdf.

Madsen, K.C. (1996). Differing perceptions of bullying and their practical implications. *Education and Child Psychology, 13(2)*, 14–22.

Matera, A. (2018, June 15). Stefano Gabbana responds to Selena Gomez cyberbullying comments. *Teen Vogue*. https://www.teenvogue.com/story/stefano-gabbana-selena-gomez-cyberbullying-response.

Matsunaga, M. (2010). Testing of a mediational model of bullied victims' evaluation of received support and post-bullying adaptation: A Japan-U.S. cross-cultural comparison. *Communication Monographs, 77(3)*, 312–340. https://doi.org/10.1080/03637751003758235.

Matsunaga, M. (2011). Underlying circuits of social support for bullied victims: An appraisal-based perspective on supportive communication and postbullying adjustment. *Human Communication Research, 37(2)*, 174–206. https://doi.org/10.1111/j.1468-2958.2010.01398.x

McCall, L. (2005). The complexity of intersectionality. *Signs: Journal of Women in Culture and Society. 30(3)*, 1771–1800. https://doi.org/10.1086/426800.

McClowry, R.J., Miller, M.N., & Mills, G.D. (2017). What family physicians can do to combat bullying. *The Journal of Family Practice, 66(2)*, 82–89.

Melton, G.B., Limber, S.P., Flerx, V., Nation, M., Osgood, W., Chambers, J., Henggeler, S., Cunningham, P., & Olweus, D. (1998). *Violence among rural youth*. Final report to the Office of Juvenile Justice and Delinquency Prevention.

Merrell, K.W., Gueldner, B.A., Ross, S.W., & Isava, D.M. (2008). How effective are school bullying intervention programs? A meta-analysis of intervention research. *School Psychology Quarterly, 23(1)*, 26–42. https://doi.org/10.1037/1045-3830.23.1.26.

Miller, S.J. (2012). Speaking my mind: Mythology of the norm—Disrupting the culture of bullying in schools. *The English Journal, 101(6)*, 107–109.

Milosevic, T. (2016). Social Media Companies' Cyberbullying Policies. *International Journal of Communication, 10*, 5164–5185. https://ijoc.org/index.php/ijoc/article/viewFile/5320/1818.

Mishna, F., Pepler, D., & Wiener, J. (2006). Factors associated with perceptions and responses to bullying situations by children, parents, teachers, and principals. *Victims Offenders, 1(3)*, 255–88. https://doi.org/10.1080/13632752.2013.844414.

Moreno, M.A., & Vaillancourt, T. (2017). The Role of Health Care Providers in Cyberbullying. *The Canadian Journal of Psychiatry, 62(6)*, 364–367. https://doi.org/10.1177/0706743716684792.

Morita, Y., Soeda, H., Soeda, K., & Taki, M. (1999). Bullying in Japan. In P.K. Smith, Y. Morita, J. Junger-Tas, D. Olweus, R. Catalano, & P. Slee (Eds.), *The nature of school bullying: A cross-national perspective* (pp. 309–323). Routledge.

National Academies of Sciences, Engineering, and Medicine (2016). *Preventing bullying through science, policy, and practice*. The National Academies Press. https://doi.org/10.17226/23482.

Neinstein, L.S. (2016). *Adolescent health care and young adult healthcare* (6th revised ed.). Wolters Kluwer.

Newall, M. (2018). *Cyberbullying: A global advisor survey*. Ipsos Public Affairs. https://www.ipsos.com/sites/default/files/ct/news/documents/2018-06/cyberbullying_june2018.pdf.

Nic Gabhainn, S., Kelly, C., & Molcho, M. (2007). *The Irish health behavior in school-aged children (HBSC) study 2006*. Department of Health, Ireland. http://www.nuigalway.ie/hbsc/documents/hbsc_2006_english_version.pdf.

Noar, S.M., Black, H.G., & Pierce, L.B. (2009). Efficacy of computer technology-based HIV prevention interventions: A meta-analysis. *AIDS, 23(1)*, 107–115. https://doi.org/10.1097/QAD.0b013e32831c5500.

Noar, S.M., Myrick, J.G., Zeitany, A., Kelley, D., Morales-Pico, B., & Thomas, N.E. (2015). Testing a social cognitive theory-based model of indoor tanning: Implications for skin cancer prevention messages. *Health Communication, 30(2)*, 164–174.

Olweus, D. (1973). *Hackkycklingar och översittare: Forskning om skolmobbning* [Whipping boys and bullies: Research on bullying at school]. Almqvist & Wicksell. https://doi.org/10.1080/10410236.2014.974125.

Olweus, D. (1993). *Bullying at school: What we know and what we can do*. Blackwell.

Olweus, D., & Limber, S.P. (2010). Bullying in school: Evaluation and dissemination of the Olweus Bullying Prevention Program. *The American journal of orthopsychiatry, 80(1)*, 124–134. https://doi.org/10.1111/j.1939-0025.2010.01015.x.

Pacer's National Bullying Prevention Center. (2009, Spetember 25). *Demi Lovato stands up against bullying* [Video]. Youtube. https://www.youtube.com/watch?v=ZtCC1N8AJws.

Pacer's National Bullying Prevention Center. (2010, October 4). *Demi Lovato PSA Facebook campaign* [Video]. Youtube. https://www.youtube.com/watch?v=BrKfehh7lgk.

Parker, L. (2017, September 17). *Demi Lovato talks childhood bullying, Raya dating, mental health awareness: "I have an awesome life today."* Yahoo. https://www.yahoo.com/lifestyle/demi-lovato-talks-childhood-bullying-raya-dating-mental-health-awareness-awesome-life-today-201814869.html.

Patel, A. (2017, January 30). *Zendaya offers modelling job to woman body-shamed online*. HuffPost Canada. https://www.huffingtonpost.ca/2017/01/30/zendaya-bullied-girl_n_14496280.html.

Perren, S., Ettekal, I., & Ladd, G. (2013). The impact of peer victimization on later maladjustment: Mediating and moderating effects of hostile and self-blaming attributions. *Journal of Child Psychology and Psychiatry, 54(1)*, 46–55. https://doi.org/10.1111/j.1469-7610.2012.02618.x.

Puhl, R.M., and Latner, J.D. (2007). Stigma, obesity, and the health of the nation's children. *Psychological Bulletin, 133(4)*, 557. https://doi.org/10.1037/0033-2909.133.4.557.

Raskauskas, J. (2007). *Evaluation of the Kia Kaha anti-bullying program for students in years 5–8*. New Zealand Police. https://www.police.govt.nz/resources/2007/kia-kaha-anti-bullying/evaluation-of-the-kia-kaha-anti-bullying-programme-for-students-in-years-5-8.pdf.

Rayne, N. (2015, August 28). Zendaya shuts down cyber bullies who called her parents ugly. *People Magazine*. https://people.com/tv/zendaya-shuts-down-cyber-bullies-who-called-her-parents-ugly/.

Rigby, K., & Slee, P. (1999). Suicidal ideation among adolescent school children, involvement in bully-victim problems, and perceived social support. *Suicide and Life-Threatening Behavior, 29(2)*, 119–130. https://doi.org/10.1111/j.1943-278X.1999.tb01050.x.

Rivara, F., & Le Menestrel, S. (Eds.). (2016). *Preventing bullying through science, policy, and practice*. The National Academies Press. https://www.ncbi.nlm.nih.gov/books/NBK390413/.

Roberto, A.J., Eden, J., Savage, M.W., Ramos-Salazar, L., & Deiss, D.M. (2014). Outcome evaluation results of school-based cybersafety promotion and cyberbullying prevention intervention for middle school students. *Health communication, 29(10)*, 1029–1042. https://doi.org/10.1080/10410236.2013.831684.

Russell, S.T., Sinclair, K.O., Poteat, V.P., and Koenig, B. (2012). Adolescent health and harassment based on discriminatory bias. *American Journal of Public Health, 102(3)*, 493–495. https://doi.org/10.2105/AJPH.2011.300430.

Salmivalli, C., Kaukiainen, A., & Voeten, M. (2005). Anti-bullying intervention: Implementation and outcome. *The British Journal of Educational Psychology, 75(Pt. 3)*, 465–487. https://doi.org/10.1348/000709905X26011.

Samara, M., & Smith, P.K. (2008). How schools tackle bullying, and the use of whole school policies: Changes over the last decade. *Educational Psychology, 28(16)*, 663–676. https://doi.org/10.1080/01443410802191910.

Savage, M.W., Deiss, D.M., Jr., Roberto, A.J., & Aboujaoude, E. (2017). Theory-Based Formative Research on an Anti-Cyberbullying Victimization Intervention Message. *Journal of Health Communication, 22(2)*, 124–134. https://doi.org/10.1080/10810730.2016.1252818.

Schoen, S., & Schoen, A. (2010). Bullying and harassment in the United States. *The Clearing House: Journal of Educational Strategies, Issues and Ideas, 83(2)*, 68–72. https://doi.org/10.1080/00098650903386444.

Scott, E., Dale, J., Russell, R., & Wolke, D. (2016). Young people who are being bullied—do they want general practice support? *BMC Family Practice, 17(116)*, 1–9. https://doi.org/10.1186/s12875-016-0517-9.

Shelley, D., & Craig, W.M. (2010). Attributions and coping styles in reducing victimization. *Canadian Journal of School Psychology, 25(1)*, 84–100. https://doi.org/10.1177/0829573509357067.

Sitzer, C. (2014, July 14). "I have seen too much to not say anything": Selena Gomez slams Instagram bully—who wished cancer on the starlet. *In Touch Weekly*. https://www.intouchweekly.com/posts/selena-gomez-slams-instagram-bully-who-wished-cancer-on-the-starlet-40442/.

Smith, P.K. (2000). *Bullying: Don't suffer in silence* (2nd ed.). HMSO.

Smith, P.K. (2004). Bullying: Recent developments. *Child & Adolescent Mental Health, 9(3)*, 98–103. https://doi.org/10.1111/j.1475-3588.2004.00089.x.

Smith, P.K., & Levan, S. (1995). Perceptions and experiences of bullying in younger pupils. *The British Journal of Educational Psychology, 65(Pt. 4)*, 489–500. https://doi.org/10.1111/j.2044-8279.1995.tb01168.x.

Sony Pictures Entertainment. (2017, September 26). *Spider-man: Homecoming—Stomp Out Bullying PSA* [Video]. Youtube. https://www.youtube.com/watch?v=5cNSdIb6XUg.

Steiner, A.M. (2015, February 24). Giuliana Rancic clarifies apology to Zendaya after Oscar night comments about her dreadlocks. *People Magazine*. https://people.com/tv/zendaya-blasts-giuliana-rancic-for-criticizing-her-oscars-dreadlocks/.

STOMP Out Bullying. (n.d.). *Demi Lovato 31 second PSA*. https://www.stompoutbullying.org/demi-lovato-speaks-out-against-bullying.

STOMP Out Bullying. (n.d.). *Spider-Man: Homecoming stars and STOMP Out Bullying surprise high school students to raise anti-bullying awareness*. https://www.stompoutbullying.org/spider-man-homecoming-stars-and-stomp-out-bullying-surprise-high-school-students-raise-anti-bullying-awareness.

Swearer, S.M., & Hymel, S. (2015). Understanding the psychology of bullying: Moving toward a social-ecological diathesis-stress model. *The American Psychologist, 70(4)*, 344–353. https://doi.org/10.1037/a0038929.

Swearer, S.M., Limber, S.P., & Alley, R. (2009). Developing and implementing an effective anti-bullying policy. In S. Swearer, D.L. Espelage, & S.A. Napolitano (Eds.), *Bullying prevention and intervention: Realistic strategies for schools* (pp. 39–52). Guilford Press.

Swearer, S.M., Song, S.Y., Cary, P.T., Eagle, J.W., & Mickelson, W.T. (2001). Psychosocial correlates in bullying and victimization: The relationship between depression, anxiety, and bully/victim status. In R.A. Geffner, M. Loring, & C. Young (Eds.), *Bullying behavior: Current issues, research, and interventions* (p. 95–121). Haworth Maltreatment and Trauma Press/The Haworth Press.

Tattum, D., & Herbert, G. (Eds.) (1993). *Countering Bullying: Initiatives by schools and local authorities*. Trentham Books.

Tattum, D., & Lane, D. (Eds.) (1988). *Bullying in Schools.* Trentham Books.

Temkin, D. (2015, April 27). *All 50 states now have a bullying law. Now what?* HuffPost. https://www.huffpost.com/entry/all-50-states-now-have-a_b_7153114.

Ttofi, M.M., Farrington, D.P., & Baldry, A.C. (2008). *Effectiveness of programs to reduce school bullying: A systematic review.* The Swedish National Council for Crime Prevention. https://www.bra.se/download/18.cba82f7130f475a2f1800023387/1371914733490/2008_ programs_reduce_school_bullying.pdf.

Twyman, K.A., Saylor, C.F., Saia, D., Macias, M.M., Taylor, L.A., & Spratt, E. (2010). Bullying and ostracism experiences in children with special health care needs. *Journal of Developmental & Behavioral Pediatrics, 31(1)*, 1–8. https://doi.org/10.1097/DBP.0b013e3181c828c8.

UNICEF Canada. (2012). *Bullying and cyberbullying: Two sides of the same coin.* https://www.unicef.ca/sites/default/files/imce_uploads/TAKE%20ACTION/ADVOCATE/DOCS/cyberbulling_submission_to_senate_committee.pdf.

United Kingdom Department for Education. (2013). *Preventing bullying: Guidance for schools on preventing and responding to bullying.* http://www.education.gov.uk/schools/pupilsupport/behaviour/bullying.

United States Department of Education, Office for Civil Rights. (2010). *Dear colleague letter: Harassment and bullying.* https://www2.ed.gov/about/offices/list/ocr/letters/colleague-201010.pdf.

United States Department of Health and Human Services. (2021). Stopbullying.gov.

Vossekuil, B., Fein, R.A., Reddy, M., Borum, R., & Modzeleski, W. (2004). *The final report and findings of the Safe School Initiative: Implications for the prevention of school attacks in the United States.* U.S. Secret Service and U.S. Department of Education. www2.ed.gov/admins/lead/safety/preventing attackreport.

Wallace, F. (2018, June 14). This is why Selena Gomez's fans have gone after Stefano Gabbana. *Vogue.* https://www.vogue.com.au/celebrity/news/this-is-why-selena-gomezs-fans-have-gone-after-stefano-gabbana/news-story/0de7712c61e5f633b11f427084c86c76.

Weick, K.E. (1993). The collapse of sensemaking in organizations: The Mann Gulch disaster. *Administrative Science Quarterly, 38(4)*, 628–652. https://doi.org/10.2307/2393339.

Wessler, S.L., & De Andrade, L.L. (2006). Slurs, Stereotypes, and Student Interventions: Examining the Dynamics, Impact, and Prevention of Harassment in Middle and High School. *Journal of Social Issues, 62(3)*, 511–532. https://doi.org/10.1111/j.1540-4560.2006.00471.x.

Wiens, B.A., & Dempsey, A. (2009). Bystander involvement in peer victimization: The value of looking beyond aggressors and victims. *Journal of School Violence, 8(3)*, 206–215. https://doi.org/10.1080/15388220902910599.

Willard, N. (2010). *Sexting & youth: Achieving a rational response.* Centre for Safe and Responsible Internet Use. https://core.ac.uk/download/pdf/25816704.pdf.

Wölfer, R., Schultze-Krumbholz, A., Zagorscak, P., Jäkel, A., Göbel, K., & Scheithauer, H. (2014). Prevention 2.0: Targeting cyberbullying @ school. *Prevention Science, 15(6)*, 879–887. https://doi.org/10.1007/s11121-013-0438-y.

Yahr, E. (2015, April 23). The dangerous psychology of celebrity fat-shaming—and how stars can fight back. *Washington Post.* https://www.washingtonpost.com/news/arts-and-entertainment/wp/2015/04/23/the-dangerous-psychology-of-celebrity-fat-shaming-and-how-stars-can-fight-back/.

Yudes-Gómez, C., Baridon-Chauvie, D., & González-Cabrera, J. (2018). Cyberbullying and problematic internet use in Colombia, Uruguay and Spain: Cross-cultural study. *Media Education Research Journal, 26(56)*, 49–58. https://doi.org/10.3916/C56-2018-05.

Zendaya [@Zendaya]. (2015, August 22). *First, I'm gonna pray for you. While you're so concerned about what my parents look like, please know* [Tweet]. Twitter. https://twitter.com/Zendaya/status/635230949047857153?ref_src=twsrc%5Etfw.

5

Jennifer Hudson
and Gun Violence

During the 1985 Surgeon General's Conference, the working group on homicide stated the following position (Cron, 1986):

> Violence in the United States has become so pervasive that it can no longer be usefully viewed as only a problem of disparate acts by individual offenders. Violence is a public health problem because of the toll it enacts in injuries and deaths, especially among younger people. Too many victims are victimized again and again.... Public health has continually redefined its role so as to address more effectively the changing needs of a changing nation. It is for public health to accept the challenge presented to our country by violence and its consequences.

Between 1985 and 1995, 49.7 percent of scholarly journal articles identified the most frequently cited cause of violence as access to firearms (Winett, 1998). Access to firearms implies there is widespread availability of guns. Issues relevant to firearm access include firearm education, gun safety, and sufficient regulatory oversight of guns and ammunition, manufacturing, marketing, sales, importation, storage, possession, and use. Six hundred fifty million (nearly 75 percent) of the world's small arms are owned by civilians, with 270 million owned by U.S. citizens (Small Arms Survey, 2007). Some of these weapons contribute to gunshot incidents, accidents, and injury. Injuries to the extremities often result in fractures that may lead to hemorrhages, infections, amputations, or permanent trauma due to joint or bone deformities. Brain and spinal cord injuries pose complex challenges, leaving irreversible damage such as paralysis, sexual dysfunction, limited movement, seizure disorders, bowel problems, incontinence, and severe facial disfigurations (Buchanan, 2011, p. 53).

Societal memory of the role guns played in homes and communities shifted away from emphasis on guns as recreational equipment to a Second Amendment–protected tool necessary for self-defense. The Second Amendment of the U.S. Constitution emphasizes a citizen's right to bear arms, as it reads: "A well regulated Militia, being necessary to the security of a free State, the right of the people to keep and bear Arms, shall not be infringed." Various socio-political actors worked to shape public and political perception about society's changing mores regarding the role guns should play in households and communities across the country. An incident emblematic of this cultural shift took place in 1977. That year, Harlon Carter assumed control of the National Rifle Association of America (NRA), and the sign outside of the NRA headquarters that read "Firearms Safety Education, Marksmanship Training, Shooting and Recreation" was altered to proclaim: "The Right of the People to Keep and Bear Arms Shall Not Be Infringed" (Winkler, 2011, p. 65, 68). The NRA's individual-rights theory of the Second Amendment has grown in the decades since the sign outside of the NRA headquarters changed (Collins, 2014). Many Americans wonder if access to guns has become more pervasive as mores have changed. Gun advocates, NRA critics, politicians, and law enforcement have varying reactions to the proliferation of guns in the country as mores change. During the cultural shift on guns, laws, regulations, policy, law enforcement, public health, and research evolved too.

Some guns end up in the wrong hands through illegal means. In the U. S., the Bureau of Alcohol, Tobacco, Firearms, and Explosives (ATF) regulates and investigate gun trafficking. As the mores of society changed, the regulatory and enforcement powers of the ATF and other government entities have been constrained. For example, in 1986, the Firearm Owners' Protection Act placed limits on the ATF's inspections of dealers and its ability to keep records regarding suspicious dealer purchasing patterns (Cook, 2013). Various efforts in Congress, state legislatures, and litigation since 1986 to regulate guns met resistance in 2005, when Congress intervened on behalf of the gun industry: the industry was immunized from lawsuits in which the damages were due to misuse of a gun (the Protection of Lawful Commerce in Arms Act, PL 109–92). Then the courts stepped in (Cook, 2013, p. 27):

> With the *District of Columbia v. Heller* decision in 2008, the US Supreme Court for the first time discovered in the Second Amendment a personal right to keep a handgun in the home for self-protection, with the suggestion that this personal right might also bar other sorts of regulations. Two years later in *McDonald v. City of Chicago*, the Court indicated that the constitutional restriction also applied to states and local governments.

These U.S. Supreme Court rulings are perceived as giving Americans a personal right to "keep and bear arms" and they are interpreted as a limit to gun regulation in the federal, state, and local arena. As these court rulings occurred, the Tea Party emerged on the political scene.

Boser and Lake (2014) identified one key characteristic of Tea Party rhetoric: its pro-gun agenda. This agenda was exemplified by former Alaska governor Sarah Palin. During the run up to the 2010 midterm elections, Palin remarked on Twitter, "Commonsense Conservatives & lovers of America": "Don't Retreat, Instead—RELOAD!" During and after this period, firearms research funding has been extraordinarily difficult to attain, with funding drying up because Congress enacted the Dickey Amendment (Galea et al., 2018). The amendment is understood as a ban on funding for gun-related research, and it has adversely impacted a variety of federally funded scientific agencies. The dearth of exhaustive research about firearms has implications for many facets of American life. There is a concern that serious gaps exist in society's understanding of the negative consequences of firearms, and lack of awareness regarding actions that can mitigate these consequences makes families and communities less safe. A deep divide exists between pro-gun and anti-gun advocates, and in an era of more frequent school shootings and gun-related attacks that range from small to large, public support for each side seems unpredictable. Perhaps neither pro-gun nor anti-gun advocates fully comprehend the effects of gun violence (Buchanan, 2011, p. 51):

> Gun violence does not just affect the individual shot or threatened. Secondary victimization also includes relatives, colleagues, and other people close to the person(s) directly injured, as well as caregivers and perpetrators. Secondary survivors are frequently overlooked but can experience multiple health, social, and economic outcomes. Little is understood about the timing dimensions and manifestations of trauma and anxiety secondary survivors may experience with serious consequences: loss of confidence, employment, well-being, family connections.

The tug-of-war between pro-gun and anti-gun advocates is the backdrop for trends in enforcement, legislation, legal proceedings, and research that contribute to an environment where more guns are in circulation in the U.S. and around the world. Of the 18,361 criminal homicides in 2009, 68 percent were by gunshot, and 50 percent of all suicides are committed with firearms (Cook, 2013). Public health professionals are troubled by these trends. Researchers and healthcare experts uncovered another trend: gun violence contributes to racial and ethnic disparities in mortality. For black males aged 15 to 34, homicide victimization rates in 2009 (consistent with earlier years) were 16 times higher than rates among non–Hispanic white males in the same age group (Cook, 2013). Moreover, for black males aged 15 to 34, homicide is the leading cause of death. It is the second leading cause of death for Hispanic males (Cook, 2013). Gun violence degrades the quality of life of all communities, specifically among males aged 15 to 34, with 84 percent of homicides for this demographic occurring because of gun violence (Cook, 2013). As social mores evolve, pro-gun and anti-gun advocates are on the frontlines, exerting influence on politicians, regulators, courts, and communities.

Communities can no longer ignore the debate in an era when gun violence impacts various facets of families' lives, with children enduring school and university shootings (e.g., Columbine High School massacre, Virginia Tech shootings, and the massacre at Sandy Hook Elementary School in Newtown, Connecticut) and leisure activities (e.g., an attack on Representative Gabrielle Giffords and an assembled crowd) being disrupted by shooters who kill and maim moviegoers and other civilians (Frank, 2014; Jenson, 2007; Wilshire, 2004). Cook and Ludwig (2000) estimate that gun violence in the U.S. costs the country $100 billion. Miller and Cohen have a higher estimate of $155 billion (including psychological costs and the adverse effect on quality of life). In 2016, there were 384 mass shootings of four or more people in the U.S., and in 2017 there were 346 mass shootings, which was one mass shooting a day over this two-year period (Galea et al., 2018). In reaction to the mass shootings in Las Vegas (Route 91 Harvest music festival on the Las Vegas Strip) and Orlando (Pulse nightclub shooting), the groundswell for greater public engagement with gun control initiatives shifted public discourse. More school shootings contributed to this trend, especially the school shooting in Parkland, Florida. Public debate continues to wax and wane post-shootings, with sustained conversation dying down even after the most tragic events. Public health professionals should play a role in national, state, and local efforts to prioritize a reduction in gun violence.

Violence in the Media Is Problematic

Media and healthcare researchers and policy makers recognize the dangers associated with violence in the media. Gun violence in the media is a part of the problem, and it contributes to the violence that exists in society. There is a pattern of gun aggression across the media, including television and video games, and the prevalence of gun violence depicted across various media platforms increases the likelihood that children, young adults, and others might imitate actions depicted in the media (Smith et al., 2004). Audiences are prey for media makers who use messaging embedded with implicit and explicit expressions of gun aggression. Audiences become desensitized to gun violence, as they are bombarded with repeated exposure to violence, coupled with blood and gore, which may foster emotional callousness to the lethality of shootings (Linz et al., 1984; 1988). Some people believe the media is to blame, while others do not (McGloin et al., 2015).

Still, some experts insist there is evidence that media, including video games, is a risk factor for aggressive behavior (Gentile & Bushman, 2012), and that it contributes to aggression more broadly (Greitemeyer & Mugge, 2014). The media is accused of priming audience members to react violently to circumstances or situations.

A lethal tool depicted as commonplace in these circumstances or situations is the firearm. According to CBS News (2018), twenty-two million U.S. children live in homes with a firearm, and in almost 50 percent of those residences, the guns have no trigger lock and are easily accessible. In these households, the Center for Injury Research and Policy indicated, parents believe their children do not know where the guns are located, but approximately 75 percent of the children know where the weapons are stored. Unfortunately, in Mississippi, one family learned about the dangers of gun aggression in the media through tragedy (CBS News, 2018):

> Monroe County officials say a 9-year-old boy shot his 13-year-old sister when she refused to hand over a video game controller. "He went over to the night stand where there was a gun and he came up behind her and shot her," says Sheriff Cecil Cantrell.
>
> Cantrell says the boy's mother was home when he retrieved the gun which was left unsecured in her bedroom. The boy's aunt said that he thought the gun was fake and unloaded. She adds that he's a straight-A student and the siblings got along well.

Healthcare researchers and experts are troubled by incidents like this, which is why they worked with policymakers to address weapons in homes throughout the U.S. As such, Objective 7.11 in the federal government's health and wellness plan, *Healthy People 2000*, was a goal to reduce by 20 percent the proportion of people who possess firearms and inappropriately store them (U.S. Department of Health and Human Services & Public Health Service, 1990, 1995). A decade later, *Healthy People 2010* Objective 15-4 addressed the issue of reducing loaded and unlocked firearms in households, which indicates that the issue continued to be an important health concern (U.S. Department of Health & Human Services, 2000). If the danger that youth will acquire an unsecured gun from home is not enough cause for concern, there are other ways for kids and young adults to acquire firearms.

Firearms are not toys. Desensitized children, youth, and adults must realize the lethality of these weapons. These weapons have age restrictions that impact the purchase of guns. Under federal law, an individual must be at least 21 to buy a handgun from a licensed dealer. However, if the gun is being purchased from a private, unlicensed seller, such as a neighbor, someone online, or at a gun show, the age limit is reduced to 18 (Wheeler, 2018). For long guns, including rifles like AR-15s and shotguns, an individual must be at least 18, but when long guns are purchased from an unlicensed seller, there is no minimum age (Wheeler, 2018). Firearms can also be obtained through illegal markets. Lenient oversight of licensed firearms dealers and little to no regulation of private sales between gun owners mean that guns move from the legal gun market to the illegal market (Wintemute, 2002). In this setting, inexpensive and poorly made small handguns are attractive to criminals and youth. Firearms are also obtained through purchases from a family member or acquaintance, as a loan or gift, through sharing arrangements and thefts (Cook & Pollack, 2017). With access to guns being so widespread, researchers are concerned that society's desensitization to gun aggression is an effect of media users' exposure to violence everywhere—acts of violence described on the radio, on television and online, and depicted in video games and movies. Narratives portrayed in video games, television shows, and movies provide reasons for users to justify violence against characters. Specifically, violent video games tend to justify violence for four reasons: (1) violence is condoned, because it serves a higher good (2) the enemy usually perpetrates heinous acts, (3) victims are commonly perceived as less worthy of protection, and (4) violent video games reward rather than sanction violence (Hartmann et al., 2014). There is abundant research affirming that exposure to images of guns can increase an individual's aggression (Carlson et al., 1990). The combination of guns and violent depictions in film creates an enhanced effect on a media user's level of aggression (Bushman et al., 2013).

When media users play a violent video game while using a gun controller, as they progress through the game, they encounter onscreen characters with guns, who pursue them and exhibit gun aggression. In this immersive environment, when media users are compelled to use the realistic looking firearm/gun controller to harm characters perceived to be a threat, they engage in the triple whammy of violence. A crucial finding of a study by McGloin et al. (2015) confirmed the triple whammy of violence (p. 291): significant support for the weapons priming hypothesis and suggests that the gun controller led to the formation of aggressive thoughts. Parents of underage media users need to provide greater awareness and education regarding gun safety in their households, and they need to exert parental control to reduce unintentional shootings. Eighty-nine percent of unintentional shooting deaths of children occur in the home, and parents are usually unaware that their children are playing with loaded guns (Li et al., 1996).

Media Agenda-Setting and Interventions Converge

Gun rights and gun control advocates recognize the media's ability to establish, reinforce, or refute a pro- or anti-gun agenda. Some media users are persuadable, while others are not. For some gun rights activists, any discussion of gun control is an attack on their culture and traditions. They perceive gun control activists and their media and legislative agendas as bad public policy and a personal affront (Hogan & Rood, 2015). Policy is affected by the public, and the public's attitudes can change or become recalcitrant after consumption of media content. All agenda-setters should consider the implications of gun safety-focused media content and media coverage on proponents of the Second Amendment and gun control legislation. "As a result, even if there were no right to bear arms, we should still not seek to substantially limit private ownership of guns unless we had good reason to think that would prevent serious harm" (LaFollette, 2000, p. 267). For many agenda-setters and stakeholders in and outside of the media who value public safety, the 1999 shooting at Columbine High School was the first shooting to play out before live audiences on cable news. The significance of this event was that it changed media coverage of shootings in the U.S. and stemmed the cultural shift in favor of the gun rights movement that began decades earlier. Ruth DeFoster (2010) addresses this turn of events:

> It was, in many ways, an analog to the paradigm shift that accompanied news coverage of the first Gulf War—the exhaustive, cyclical, round-the-clock news coverage that followed the shooting represented a permanent change in public discourse about school shootings. Columbine marked a watershed in coverage of these kinds of tragedies.

The news media, in its agenda-setting function, sets parameters for public discourse about these shootings, piecing together a narrative underpinned by a particular construction of the world itself, a reality in which these shootings take place. As more school shootings went live and were shown on cable news, the media infused the ideology of gun safety into the narrative, weaving outrage and angst into the stories, with apathy being overridden by "enough is enough" (DeFoster, 2010).

The news media coverage of shootings in the U.S. is not uniform. Shootings that occur in the inner-city neighborhoods are oftentimes briefly mentioned, if they are mentioned at all (Parham-Payne, 2014). These neighborhoods are predominately Black and brown communities, where most of the population is African American or Hispanic. When these shootings are covered in the news, they rarely spark a call to action tantamount to the aftermath after the shootings in Columbine, Newtown, or Parkland. This differential treatment in media coverage plays an integral role in the incongruent response to these disparities. Between 1994 and 1999, African American minors were killed in school-associated events at a rate three times higher than their white counterparts (Anderson et al., 2001). CDC data examining a period from 1992 to 2006 juxtaposed an overall decline in school-associated homicides with higher rates of school-associated homicides in inner-city neighborhoods attended by predominately racial minorities (CDC, 2008). These inner-city children encounter a hostile environment that may produce a cyclical pattern of acts of violence (Martin et al., 2013). The news media compounds the problem these inner-city children encounter, since inner-city children watch media coverage of shootings in suburban areas and recognize that shootings at inner-city schools are not receiving the same breadth of coverage, which makes them wonder if the news media devalues their lives (Carpenter, 2012; Hill-Collins, 2000; Oliver, 2003).

The media is a powerful force in society. It impacts the news that media users consume, as well as the ideologies and narratives that shape their attitudes, and it can change or reinforce media users' behaviors. The media disseminates narratives to the public that are considered persuasive communication. These narratives reinforce or challenge ideologies that are nascent or pervasive in society. These narratives support gun rights and gun control, and the dueling ideologies and realities they endorse can provide safe harbor for supporters on both sides of the Second Amendment debate. Narratives consist of characters and messages that appeal to an audience, and they are embedded in entertainment. Media users interact with and learn from narratives while they play video games, watch television or movies, listen to music, or socialize on social media. Critics underscore the dangers that media poses for media users, yet they also should recognize that the media can be used to create awareness, educate, and persuade media users to change attitudes and behavior for their well-being and the wellness of their communities. There are a variety of ways for the media to aid public health professionals concerned about gun safety. PSAs are a popular narrative vehicle for public health professionals to deliver interventions to communities affected by gun aggression. The media enables PSAs to be delivered to the masses.

Traditional and new media platforms ranging from television to the Internet disperse PSAs and their narratives to media users and their networks. The PSAs that are compelling consist of relatable and trustworthy characters and engrossing stories. PSAs addressing gun violence that have been impactful on media users include those associated with Sandy Hook Promise, a national gun violence prevention organization formed after the school shooting at Sandy Hook Elementary School (Beer, 2016, 2017, 2018). Media platforms can boost the range of PSAs and the frequency of times media users consume PSA content. In 2017, in the aftermath of the shooting at the Route 91 Harvest music festival—the largest mass shooting in American history—the premiere episode of the revived MTV show *TRL* began with an anti-gun violence PSA (Weldon, 2017). Guests during the premiere episode included Ed Sheeran and DJ Khaled. DJ Khaled proclaimed, "We have to spread more love." DC Young Fly was standing onstage with his cohost, Tamara Dhia,when he addressed the Las Vegas shooting, saying, "For us, it hits hard because it took place at a concert packed with people of all ages coming together to share a common bond—the love of music." Another shooting that engrossed the public was the shooting of Jennifer Hudson's family. Hudson is a musical and film sensation known for her ascent from humble beginnings to stardom. Her rise in the entertainment business involved the loss and grief associated with losing multiple family members to gun violence. Over time, Hudson shared her experiences regarding the loss of her family. Her truth and authenticity gave her credibility with the public, and she uses her credibility when she wades into the debate between gun rights versus gun control. Hudson is a passionate advocate for stricter gun regulations, and she believes community engagement can mitigate gun violence.

Jennifer Hudson's Tragedy Is Too Common

One woman lost her four children to gun violence in Chicago. Here is her story, which is not uncommon in the inner city (Amnesty International, 2018):

> Ronnie, a 33-year-old aspiring music producer, was shot in the head while sitting in a parked car on the West Side of Chicago on 26 January 2013. On a television talk show a few weeks earlier, he had explained that he was a former gang member who had been in and out of jail, but was now mentoring young rappers, trying to keep them away from gang life. Jerome, aged 23, was shot and killed while using a payphone outside the Cabrini-Green public housing complex on 26 July 2000. Three months earlier, on 27 April, his 15-year-old sister, LaToya, had been standing in the lobby of a Cabrini-Green public housing complex when she was shot and killed by a 13-year-old boy. Five years before that, on 28 November 1995, 18-year-old Carlos was shot twice in the head by a classmate just blocks from their school, Jones Metropolitan High, in Chicago's South Loop.

This mother's story is a compelling one, but many Chicagoans have never heard it. Why? A story involving the loss of family members to violence is not uncommon in inner-city Chicago, but without media coverage, no one hears the story, and it remains hidden. One effective method for shining the spotlight on stories like the inner-city mother in Chicago involves a mediated, celebrity-driven narrative. The celebrity component of the mediated narrative increases the likelihood of sustained, intensive local and national coverage. The continuity of coverage over longer periods of time rein-forces awareness about gun violence and prolongs the time an individual considering a need for change has to actually change. Jennifer Hudson is a Chicago native who can relate to the loss of a family member and has experienced secondary victimization.

In 2004, Fox's *American Idol* launched Hudson into stardom during its third season. She was a finalist on the show, and it helped her gain exposure and a fan base. In 2005, she beat out hundreds of competitors to win the role Effie White in the film adaptation of the Broadway musical *Dreamgirls*. For the role of Effie White, Hudson won a Golden Globe and an Oscar in the Best Supporting Actress category. In 2008, she appeared in the film *Sex and City*. Unfortunately, in 2008, Hudson's mother, brother, and nephew were killed by her estranged brother-in-law. According to the *Chicago Tribune* (2008), Hudson's brother-in-law was William Balfour. A parolee for a 1999 attempted murder conviction, Balfour fired shots through a door, which struck Hudson's brother, Jason. Balfour then entered the house and continued to fire, hitting Hudson's mother, Darnell Donerson, when she entered the room. Balfour fled the scene and went to the apartment of his pregnant girlfriend. Authorities issued an Amber Alert for Julian King, the seven-year-old son of Hudson's sister, Julia. When the police arrested Balfour, Julian was not with him.

On Saturday, October 25, 2008, Hudson identified the bodies of her brother and mother at the Cook County medical examiner's office. On Monday, October 27, Julian's body was discovered in the back of Jason Hudson's Chevrolet Suburban, his body slumped over in the back seat with a bullet to the head. The police found the murder weapon, a stolen gun, in an alley a block from Julian's dead body (*Chicago Tribune*, 2008). The ATF traced the recovered gun to its original owner in Michigan, who reported the firearm as stolen (*Chicago Tribune*, 2008). Despite the turmoil Hudson was enduring, she won her first Grammy in 2009 for her debut album and garnered more coveted movie roles, including *The Secret Life of Bees*.

In 2012, Balfour received three consecutive life sentences without possibility for parole plus 120 years (CNN, 2012). During the trial, Hudson was the first of more than 80 witnesses, and on the witness stand, she broke down as she talked about her family. Prosecutors asserted during the trial that Balfour was married but separated from Hudson's sister, Julia, and that he was jealous and angry over his failing marriage (Izadi, 2018). After the verdict, Anita Alvarez, then State's Attorney for Cook County, Illinois, said, "This significant sentence is appropriate given the heinous and inhumane nature of these crimes which demanded the full force of justice" (CNN, 2012).

Many residents in the area where the shooting occurred were surprised Hudson's family was the target, but many inner-city natives on the South Side and West Side were familiar with shooting deaths. Chicago's Englewood neighborhood where Hudson grew up is also where NBA superstar Derrick Rose and comedian and actor Bernie Mac grew up. It is one of the neighborhoods in Chicago confronting higher rates of violence, unemployment, and health disparities (*Tell Me More* from NPR News, 2012). In Chicago, neighborhoods like Englewood are mostly African American or Latino, poor, segregated, and under-resourced. In 2012, on *Oprah's Next Cha*pter, Hudson revealed how the tragic murders of her mother, brother, and nephew impacted her:

> It literally takes a part of you. My mother always told me, no matter Jenny, no matter how negative things are, you always find the positive. When you lose a loved one, you don't want to see a birthday come. How can I turn something so negative into a positive.

Hudson's nephew, Julian, was murdered when he was seven years old, and in honor of his birthday on August 14, Hudson began the Julian D. King Gift Foundation Hatch Day Celebration, which was formally recognized by then Chicago mayor Rahm Emanuel in 2012. In recognition of Hatch Day, in 2012, children at the Salvation Army Ray and Joan Kroc Corps Community Center received free school supplies to help with their education.

In a 2014 interview with the *Observer Magazine*, Hudson discussed her struggles with being overweight, growing up in a crime-ridden neighborhood, stardom in music, film, and business, and the shooting of her family members and the ensuing trial (Thorpe, 2014). Hudson told the *Observer*, "I have definitely seen the highest of the highs and the lowest of the lows." She continued, "You don't know how strong you are until you are placed in that kind of moment." She poignantly addressed her faith and how relying on the memory of her mother helped her: "There would be no point in faith if it wasn't tested. My mother always told me no matter how negative your life seems to be, you must always look for a positive. In many ways the trial was the most dreadful part of it all. But again I know my mother would not have wanted us to miss a beat, so we were there every day." The birth of Hudson's son, David, saved her from despair (Messer, 2015). Hudson stated, "I went from being an aunt, having a mom, and being a mom, and raising my own child. I tell David all the time, 'You saved my life.'" In a *W Magazine* interview with Vanessa Lawrence (2015), Hudson talked about being approached by director Spike Lee to play the mother of a young girl killed by gunfire in the movie *Chi-Raq*. Hudson revealed, "But when I really thought about it, I understood why he came to me and I thought, 'You know what? It's worth me telling my story so that hopefully no one else has a story like this to tell.'" Hudson's activism transcends her art, beyond addressing gun violence in film, she attends reform rallies to champion gun reform.

In 2018, Hudson joined Paul McCartney, Common, Miley Cyrus, Amy Schumer, and other celebrities at student gun reform rallies. The protests were deeply personal for teenage survivors of shootings and for celebrities like Hudson, who had been personally affected by gun violence (Elber, 2018). During the March for Our Lives rally in Washington, D.C., Hudson performed "The Times They Are A-Changin'," and alluded to the shooting deaths of her mother, brother, and nephew. When encouraging the vast crowd to join her in song, she declared, "We've all lost somebody. We've all got a purpose and we want what? We want change." Hudson appeared tearful during her performance, which was backed by members of a Washington choir and survivors of the shooting at Marjory Stoneman Douglas High School in Parkland, Florida, which took place on February 14, 2018. Parkland students and students from across the country led rallies attended by hundreds of thousands of people in cities across the U.S. According to *The Washington Post* (2018), after Hudson closed out the march, she stated, "A day like this is almost like reliving it, over and over again." In an interview on the *Van Jones Show* (2018) after the March for Our Lives rally in Washington, D.C., Hudson told the host, "It is almost impossible to understand what victims, the families, are going through, what they feel, or even to be able to relate to a situation like this unless you've been in it. So for people who are watching … know that it can be anybody. It can happen to anybody." Celebrities like Hudson helped attract attention to rallies in the nation's capital and cities throughout the U.S. The families that were impacted by losing a loved one spoke at the rallies, which resonated with the celebrities and non-celebrities in attendance.

These family members are victims too, and their messages to the public affected media users listening or watching news coverage via platforms on radio, print, television, or online. Hudson was affected by a clip of a grieving Lori Alhadeff, whose daughter was killed in the Parkland shooting (Izadi, 2018). In the clip, Alhadeff yells into the camera, "I just spent the last two hours putting the burial arrangements for my daughter's funeral, who is 14! President Trump, please do something! Do something, action! We need it now! These kids need safety, now!" Hudson reacted:

> She was screaming out. I understand every inch of her frustration…. She's angry, for one, because this is nonsense. Then, two, no one understands. She's pouring out. I could hear it. I knew where it came from…. It's like reliving it. And I was like, unfortunately, "Welcome to my club." My heart completely went out to her. I was like, "You're not alone. I understand everything you're feeling."

According to the *Star Tribune* (2018), after the march, Hudson was moved by her participation, sharing, "My mother always taught us the importance of helping others and giving back. More than anything, we need to support our youth as they truly are the future." In June 2018, Hudson continued her support for youth against gun violence when she joined Chance the Rapper, Parkland survivors, and others for the annual peace march organized by St. Sabina Catholic Church on Chicago's South Side. For the previous 10 years, the event had marked the end of the school year for Chicago Public Schools, bringing together the community in solidarity against gun violence (NBC Chicago, 2018). The rally kickstarted Parkland survivors' voter turnout initiative called March for Our Lives: Road to Change, a multistate bus tour to encourage young people to register to vote in the 2018 midterm elections. Gallup reported on October 17, 2018, that 61 percent of Americans favored stricter laws on the sale of firearms. The year 2018 reflects the highest percentage in favor of tougher firearms laws in two or more decades.

Hidden Narrative: Beyond Awareness, Healthcare Professionals Have Something to Say

On December 2, 2015, the day after a mass-casualty shooting in San Bernardino, California, which took the lives of 14 health department workers, the U.S. Senate voted down a bipartisan amendment that would have expanded background checks for firearm sales at gun shows and online sales (Wahowiak, 2016). The divide between senators regarding the issues of gun rights and gun safety prevented the passage of stricter gun control measures. The divisions that persist in the public exist in Congress and among public health professionals. Even as public health professionals are gunned down in mass shootings, some healthcare professionals own firearms and are skeptical about the government establishing additional regulations on gun ownership. The polarization of viewpoints regarding firearms in our personal and professional lives has implications for public health and society at large. In a survey, *MD Magazine* asked readers questions pertaining to gun control, and 928 physicians answered the questions (Scott & Kaltwasser, 2016). More than half of the poll's physician respondents owned guns, and almost 67 percent of them used firearms for protection. Over 90 percent of respondents wanted increased background checks. Additional survey results showed that 69 percent of physicians supported a ban on assault weapons and slightly more than 60 percent favored limits on magazine sizes.

Whether as researchers, members of a patient treatment team, or victims of gun violence, healthcare professionals are on the front lines of the gun violence epidemic. "When a new disease, particularly an infectious disease, enters the community … we have a mechanism to anticipate it, track it, get our arms around it," said Dr. Georges Benjamin, the executive director of the American Public Health Association (Kodjak, 2017). Dr. Benjamin maintained, "We do that when we have measles, mumps, chicken pox, zika. But firearm-related death and disability, we don't." He continued, "Firearms are a tool, and … a consumer product. And unlike other consumer products, we're not working hard to make that consumer product safer." Society needs research-generated knowledge that could lead to better enforcement, guidelines, prevention, and interventions that reduce the toll of gun injuries without cutting off access to guns. Firearms are among the least well-studied contributors to population health (Galea et al., 2018). Furthermore, "the lack of high-quality studies examining such best practices for firearm safety screening limits the ability to derive consensus guidelines for clinicians and again highlights the need for additional well-funded research" (Roszko et al., 2016). Another concern of professionals in public health is the effect that a lack of funding for research and scholarship has on opportunities for a new generation of junior scholars who are essential to a national brain trust for combating the firearm violence crisis (Galea et al., 2018).

Healthcare professionals are limited by the actions of legislative bodies and foundations, yet there is still much they can do. Physicians are well positioned to be mindful of a patient's right to bear arms while promoting patient firearm safety. Physicians must be knowledgeable if they practice in a gun owner comfort zone, which enables states to levy legal sanctions against physician-initiated gun conversations. In 2011, Florida became the first state to pass a law prohibiting physicians from asking their patients if they own guns (Parent, 2016). The Florida law, known as the Firearm Owners' Privacy Act (FOPA), and others based on its precedent are predicated on the assumption that gun safety is not a physician's responsibility. Gun control activists fought Florida in court to overturn the law, ultimately having it reversed in 2015 by the 11 judges sitting *en banc* on the 11th Circuit Court of Appeals (Hiltzik, 2017). Many physicians believe their duties span personal health, public health, and safety spheres. To fully address these duties, they need flexibility in addressing private patient matters (Parent, 2016). These physician-patient discussions about safe gun practices must not be motivated by or convey disapproval of gun ownership.

The pushback against beliefs and policies like those associated with FOPA emphasizes that physicians and their professional and community partners must identify best practices for firearm safety, guidelines, and screenings in states such as Florida. Otherwise patients, families, and communities will suffer a loss of effective and respectful life-saving interventions. Examples of interventions relying on doctor-patient communication regarding a variety of issues including gun safety are Baltimore's Safe Streets program (Hsu, 2016), the R. Adams Cowley Shock Trauma Center's Baltimore Violence Intervention Program (University of Maryland Medical Center, 2021), Syracuse's Trauma Response Team (Jennings-Bey et al., 2015), Ventura County, California's Operation PeaceWorks (Duncan, Waxman, Romero, & Diaz, 2014), and the Boston Gun Project (Tita et al., 2010). The best known of these interventions is probably the Boston Gun Project, also known as Operation CeaseFire, which has been adapted by other urban areas to reduce violent crime, including gun violence.

REFERENCES

Amnesty International. (2018). *In the line of fire: Human rights and the U.S. gun violence crisis.* https://www.amnestyusa.org/wp-content/uploads/2018/09/Gun-Report-Full_16.pdf.

Anderson, M., Kaufman, J., Simon, T.R., Barrios, L., Paulozzi, L., Ryan, G., Hammond, R., Modzeleski, W., Feucht, T., Potter, L., & School-Associated Violent Deaths Study Group (2001). School-associated violent deaths in the United States, 1994–1999. *JAMA, 286(21),* 2695–2702. https://doi.org/10.1001/jama.286.21.2695.

Beer, J. (2016, December 6). Why "Evan" works: Behind the incredible Sandy Hook Promise PSA. *Fast Company.* https://www.fastcompany.com/3066273/why-evan-works-behind-the-incredible-sandy-hook-promise-psa.

Beer, J. (2017, December 12). New gun violence PSA looks ahead to tomorrow's school shooting. *Fast Company.* https://www.fastcompany.com/40506631/new-gun-violence-psa-looks-ahead-to-tomorrows-school-shooting.

Beer, J. (2018, March 22). This PSA focuses on "The Other Side" of gun violence. *Fast Company.* https://www.fastcompany.com/40548394/this-psa-focuses-on-the-other-side-of-gun-violence.

Bream, J. (2018, May 5). Jennifer Hudson talks gun violence, Aretha Franklin and rare Minneapolis concert. *Star Tribune.* https://www.startribune.com/jennifer-hudson-talks-gun-violence-aretha-franklin-and-rare-minneapolis-concert/481676531/.

Boser, B.L., & Lake, R.A. (2014). "Enduring" incivility: Sarah Palin and the Tucson tragedy. *Rhetoric & Public Affairs 17(4),* 619–651. https://doi.org/10.14321/RHETPUBLAFFA.17.4.0619.

Buchanan C. (2011). The health and human rights of survivors of gun violence: Charting a research and policy agenda. *Health and Human Rights, 13(2),* E50–E63. https://www.hhrjournal.org/2013/08/the-health-and-human-rights-of-survivors-of-gun-violence-charting-a-research-and-policy-agenda/.

Bushman, B.J., Jamieson, P.E., Weitz, I., & Romer, D. (2013). Gun violence trends in movies. *Pediatrics, 132(6),* 1014–1018. https://doi.org/10.1542/peds.2013-1600.

Carlson, M., Marcus-Newhall, A., & Miller, N. (1990). Effects of situational aggression cues: A quantitative review. *Journal of Personality and Social Psychology, 58(4),* 622–633. https://doi.org/10.1037/0022-3514.58.4.622.

Carpenter, T. (2012). Construction of the crack mother icon. *Western Journal of Black Studies, 36(4),* 264–275.

CBS News. (2018, March 19). *3 out of 4 children in homes with guns know where the firearms are kept.* https://www.cbsnews.com/news/3-out-of-4-children-in-homes-with-guns-know-where-the-firearms-are-kept/#.

Center for Disease Control & Prevention. (2008). *School-associated student homicides—United States, 1992–2006.* https://www.cdc.gov/mmwr/preview/mmwrhtml/mm5702a1.htm#.

CNN Wire Staff. (2012, July 24). *Killer of Jennifer Hudson relatives gets three life sentences without parole.* CNN. https://www.cnn.com/2012/07/24/justice/illinois-hudson-murder-trial/index.html.

Collins, L.J. (2014). The Second Amendment as demanding subject: Figuring the marginalized subject in demands for an unbridled second amendment. *Rhetoric & Public Affairs, 17(4)*, 737–756. https://doi.org/10.14321/rhetpublaffa.17.4.0737.

Cook, P.J. (2013). The great American gun war: Notes from four decades in the trenches. *Crime and Justice, 42(1)*, 19–73. https://doi.org/10.1086/670397.

Cook, P.J., & Ludwig, J. (2000). *Gun violence: The real costs*. Oxford University Press.

Cook, P.J., & Pollack, H.A. (2017). Reducing Access to Guns by Violent Offenders. *RSF: The Russell Sage Foundation Journal of the Social Sciences 3(5)*, 2–36. https://doi.org/10.7758/RSF.2017.3.5.01.

Cordeiro, M. (2018, January 29). Florida gun violence prevention group releases PSA featuring Pulse community. *Orlando Weekly*. https://www.orlandoweekly.com/Blogs/archives/2018/01/29/florida-gun-violence-prevention-group-releases-psa-featuring-pulse-community.

Cron, T. (1986). The Surgeon General's workshop on violence and public health: Review of the recommendations. *Public Health Reports, 101(1)*, 8–14.

DeFoster, R. (2010). American gun culture, school shootings, and a "frontier mentality": An ideological analysis of British editorial pages in the decade after Columbine. *Communication, Culture & Critique, 3(4)*, 466–484. https://doi.org/10.1111/j.1753-9137.2010.01081.x.

Duncan, T.K., Waxman, K., Romero, J., & Diaz, G. (2014). Operation PeaceWorks: A community program with the participation of a Level II trauma center to decrease gang-related violence. *The Journal of Trauma and Acute Care Surgery, 76(5)*, 1208–1213. https://doi.org/10.1097/TA.0000000000000179.

Elber, L. (2018, March 24). Stars affected by violence join students' gun-reform rallies. *Chicago Tribune*. https://www.chicagotribune.com/entertainment/ct-celebrities-gun-reform-rallies-20180324-story.html.

Frank, D.A. (2014). Facing Moloch: Barack Obama's national eulogies and gun violence. *Rhetoric & Public Affairs, 17(4)*, 653–678. https://doi.org/10.14321/rhetpublaffa.17.4.0653.

Galea, S., Branas, C.C., Flescher, A., Formica, M.K., Hennig, N., Liller, K.D., Madanat, H.N., Park, A., Rosenthal, J.E., & Ying, J. (2018). Priorities in recovering from a lost generation of firearms research. *American Journal of Public Health, 108(7)*, 858–860. https://doi.org/10.2105/AJPH.2018.304436.

Gallup. (2018). *Six in 10 Americans support stricter gun laws*. https://news.gallup.com/poll/243797/six-americans-support-stricter-gun-laws.aspx.

Gentile, D.A., & Bushman, B.J. (2012). Reassessing media violence effects using a risk and resilience approach to understanding aggression. *Psychology of Popular Media Culture, 1(3)*, 138–151. https://doi.org/10.1037/a0028481.

Greitemeyer, T., & Mugge, D.O. (2014). Video games do affect social outcomes: A meta-analytic review of the effects of violence and prosocial video game play. *Personality and Social Psychology Bulletin, 40(5)*, 578–589. https://doi.org/10.1177/0146167213520459.

Hartmann, T., Krakowiak, K.M., & Tsay-Vogel, M. (2014). How violent video games communicate violence: A literature review and content analysis of moral disengagement factors. *Communication Monographs, 81(3)*, 310–332. https://doi.org/10.1080/03637751.2014.922206.

Hill-Collins, P. (2000). *Black feminist thought*. Routledge.

Hiltzik, M. (2017, February 17). An appeals court overturns Florida's gag law preventing doctors from asking about guns in the home. *Los Angeles Times*. https://www.latimes.com/business/hiltzik/la-fi-hiltzik-florida-guns-20170217-story.html.

Hogan, J.M., & Rood, C. (2015). Rhetorical studies and the gun debate: A public policy perspective. *Rhetoric & Public Affairs, 18(2)*, 359–372. https://doi.org/10.14321/rhetpublaffa.18.2.0359.

Hsu, A. (2016, April 8). *Baltimore sees hospitals as key to breaking a cycle of violence*. NPR. https://www.npr.org/sections/health-shots/2016/04/08/473379238/baltimore-sees-hospitals-as-key-to-breaking-a-cycle-of-violence#.

Izadi, E. (2018, March 25). "It can happen to anybody": Jennifer Hudson on gun violence and her personal tragedy. *Washington Post*. https://www.washingtonpost.com/news/arts-and-entertainment/wp/2018/03/25/it-can-happen-to-anybody-jennifer-hudson-on-gun-violence-and-her-personal-tragedy/.

Jennings-Bey, T., Lane, S.D., Rubinstein, R.A., Bergen-Cico, D., Haygood-El, A., Hudson, H., Sanchez, S., & Fowler, F.L. (2015). The trauma response team: A community intervention for gang violence. *Journal of Urban Health, 92(5)*, 947–954. https://doi.org/10.1007/s11524-015-9978-8.

Jenson, J.M. (2007). Aggression and violence in the United States: Reflections on the Virginia Tech shootings, *Social Work Research, 31(3)*, 131–134. https://doi.org/10.1093/swr/31.3.131.

Jones, V. [Cable News Network]. (2018, March 24). *Van Jones Show: Jennifer Hudson—Gun violence can happen to anybody* [Video]. YouTube. https://www.youtube.com/watch?v=YsGSQ_nzSI4.

Kodjak, A. (2017, November 15). *What if we treated gun violence like a public health crisis?* NPR. https://www.npr.org/sections/health-shots/2017/11/15/564384012/what-if-we-treated-gun-violence-like-a-public-health-crisis.

LaFollette, H. (2000). Gun control. *Ethics, 110(2)*, 263–281. https://doi.org/10.1086/233269.

Lawrence, V. (2015, December 9). Jennifer Hudson sounds off on gun control. *W Magazine.* https://www.wmagazine.com/story/jennifer-hudson-color-purple.

Li, G., Baker, S.P., Discala, C., Fowler, C., Ling, J., & Kelen, G.D. (1996). Factors associated with the intent of firearm-related injuries in pediatric trauma patients. *Archives of Pediatric & Adolescent Medicine, 150*, 1160–1165.

Linz, D.G., Donnerstein, E., & Penrod, S. (1984). The effects of multiple exposures to filmed violence against women. *Journal of Communication, 34(3)*, 130–147. https://doi.org/10.1111/j.1460-2466.1984.tb02180.x.

Linz, D.G., Donnerstein, E., & Penrod, S. (1988). Effects of long-term exposure to violent and sexually degrading depictions of women. *Journal of Personality and Social Psychology, 55(5)*, 758–768. https://doi.org/10.1037/0022-3514.55.5.758.

Maragos, A. (2018, June 16*). Celebrities, Parkland students kick off rally, March for Peace in Chicago.* NBC Chicago. https://www.nbcchicago.com/news/national-international/parkland-chicago-st-sabina/147249/.

Martin, L., Revington, N., & Seedat, S. (2013). The 39-item child exposure to community violence (CECV) scale: Exploratory factor analysis and relationship to PTSD symptomatology in trauma-exposed children and adolescents. *International Journal of Behavioral Medicine, 20(4)*, 599–608. https://doi.org/10.1007/s12529-012-92690-7.

McGloin, R., Farrar, K.M., & Fishlock, J. (2015). Triple whammy! Violent games and violent controllers: Investigating the use of realistic gun controllers on perceptions of realism, immersion, and outcome aggression. *Journal of Communication, 65(2)*, 280–299. https://doi.org/10.1111/jcom.12148.

Messer, L. (2015, October 7). *Jennifer Hudson opens up about her family's murders.* ABC News. https://abcnews.go.com/Entertainment/jennifer-hudson-opens-familys-murders/story?id=34309912.

Miller, T.R., & Cohen, M.A. (1997). Costs of gunshot and cut/stab wounds in the United States, with some Canadian comparisons. *Accident Analysis and Prevention, 29(3)*, 329–341. https://doi.org/10.1016/s0001-4575(97)00007-9.

Oliver, M.B. (2003). African American men as "criminal and dangerous": Implications of media portrayals of crime on the "criminalization" of African American men. *Journal of African American Studies, 7(2)*, 3–18. https://doi.org/10.1007/s12111-003-1006-5.

Parent, B. (2016). Physicians asking patients about guns: Promoting patient safety, respecting patient rights. *Journal of General Internal Medicine, 31(10)*, 1242–1245. https://doi.org/10.1007/s11606-016-3694-2.

Parham-Payne, W. (2014). The role of the media in the disparate response to gun violence in America. *Journal of Black Studies, 45(8)*, 752–768. https://doi.org/10.1177/0021934714555185.

Roszko, P.J., Ameli, J., Carter, P.M., Cunningham, R.M., & Ranney, M.L. (2016). Clinician attitudes, screening practices, and interventions to reduce firearm-related injury. *Epidemiologic Reviews, 38(1)*, 87–110. https://doi.org/10.1093/epirev/mxv005.

Scott, G., & Kaltwasser, J. (2016, January-18). *MD Poll: Majority of doctors own guns, want tighter controls.* MD Magazine. https://www.hcplive.com/view/md-poll-majority-of-doctors-own-guns-want-tighter-controls.

Small Arms Survey (2007). *Small arms survey 2007: Guns and the city.* Cambridge University Press.

Smith, S.L., Lachlan, K., Pieper, K.M., Boyson, A.R., Wilson, B.J., Tamborini, R., & Weber, R. (2004).

Brandishing guns in American media: Two studies examining how often and in what context firearms appear on television and in popular video games. *Journal of Broadcasting & Electronic Media*, 48(4), 584–606. https://doi.org/10.1207/s15506878jobem4804_4.

Tell Me More (2012, May 14). *Is Jennifer Hudson's tragedy all too common?* NPR. https://www.npr.org/2012/05/14/152673032/is-jennifer-hudsons-tragedy-all-too-common.

Thorpe, V. (2014, July 27). Jennifer Hudson tells of trauma of gun attack on her family. *The Guardian*. https://www.theguardian.com/culture/2014/jul/27/jennifer-hudson-tells-of-gun-attack-family.

Tita, G. Reley, K.J., Ridgeway, G., Grammich, C., Abrahamse, A.F., & Greenwood, P.W. (2010). *Reducing gun violence: Results from an intervention in East Los Angeles*. RAND Corporation.

Tribune Staff. (2008, November 10). Updated: Timeline in the murders of Jennifer Hudson family members. *Chicago Tribune*. https://www.chicagotribune.com/chi-jennifer-hudson-murders-timeline-story.html.

Understanding and improving health, 2nd ed. U.S. Government Printing Office. https://www.healthypeople.gov/2010/Document/pdf/uih/2010uih.pdf.

United States Department of Health and Human Services. (1990). Healthy people 2000: National health promotion and disease prevention objectives. Publication PHS 91-50213. https://files.eric.ed.gov/fulltext/ED332957.pdf.

United States Department of Health and Human Services. (1995). Healthy people 2000: Midcourse review and 1995 revisions. Publication PHS 91-50213. https://files.eric.ed.gov/fulltext/ED332957.pdf.

United States Department of Health and Human Services. (2000). Healthy people 2010:

Violence Intervention Program (VIP)—Baltimore. (2021). University of Maryland Medical Center. https://www.umms.org/ummc/health-services/shock-trauma/center-injury-prevention-policy/violence/intervention-program.

Wahowiak, L. (2016). Public health taking stronger approach to gun violence: APHA, Brady team up on prevention. *The Nation's Health, 45(10)*, 1–10. https://www.thenationshealth.org/content/45/10/1.3

Weldon, S. (2017, October 2). TRL debut begins with anti-gun violence PSA following deadly Las Vegas shooting. *Entertainment Weekly*. https://ew.com/tv/2017/10/02/trl-gun-violence-psa-las-vegas-shooting/.

Wheeler, L. (2018, February 22). What are the legal ages for buying guns? *The Hill*. https://thehill.com/homenews/politics-101/375154-what-are-the-current-age-restrictions-on-guns.

Wilshire, P. (2004). Presentation and representation in Michael Moore's *Bowling for Columbine*. *Australian Screen Education, 35*, 91–95.

Winett, L.B. (1998). Constructing violence as a public health problem. *Public Health Reports, 113(6)*, 498–507.

Winfrey, O. [Oprah Winfrey Network]. (2012, September 9). *Oprah's Next Chapter: How the murders of Jennifer Hudson's family members affected her* [Video]. Oprah.com. http://www.oprah.com/own-oprahs-next-chapter/how-the-murders-of-jennifer-hudsons-family-affected-her-video#ixzz5QpVo033r.

Winkler, A. (2011). *Gunfight: The battle over the right to bear arms in America*. W.W. Norton.

Wintemute G.J. (2002). Where the guns come from: The gun industry and gun commerce. *The Future of children, 12(2)*, 54–71. https://doi.org/10.2307/1602738.

6

Home Invasion
and Celebrities Who
Lived to Talk About It

According to a study conducted by the United States Department of Justice (2013) regarding household burglary between 1994 and 2011, the largest proportion of burglaries involved someone with no legal right to be in the residence who entered without use of force. The National Council for Home Safety and Security reports that there are approximately 2.5 million burglaries a year, meaning one burglary every 13 seconds, with 66 percent of those being home break-ins (Alarms.org, 2019). Items taken during completed burglaries include cash and checks, credit and bank cards, purses and wallets, appliances and electronics, silver, china, art objects, stamps or coins, various other personal portable objects, tools, and miscellaneous equipment (U.S. Department of Justice, 2013). Homeowners care about the loss of their possessions, but there are other considerations that are more important. The intensity of feelings aroused by having your home invaded or burglarized is staggering (Maguire, 1980, pp. 265–266):

> Person No. 539. I shall never forget it because my privacy has been invaded. I have worked hard all my life and had my nose to the grindstone ever since and this happens. Now we can't live in peace. I have a feeling of "mental rape." I feel a dislocation and disruption of private concerns. I have destroyed everything they touched. I feel so extreme about it.
>
> Person No. 629. I'll never get over the thought that a stranger had been in here while we were in bed … the idea that a stranger, who could be one of those horrible revolting creatures, has been mauling my things about.
>
> Person No. 976. They had gone through all my clothes. I felt a real repulsion—everything felt dirty. I wanted to move—I had nightmares, and it still comes back even now.
>
> Person No. 1010. It's the next worst thing to being bereaved; it's like being raped.

Oftentimes, the invasion of personal space undercuts a sense of privacy and fosters a sense of lack of control. The rhetoric and terminology used in the safety and security industry, law enforcement, and violence prevention research address similarities and conflicting assumptions regarding commonly held understandings of home. Home and house are interchangeable—they are understood as "a physical entity with identifiable interior and exterior conditions, and a place of security and privacy" (Waghorn, 2009, p. 262). Home invasion entails the physical structure where the owner resides, as well as the spatial and cultural references that extend the parameters for home beyond a physical entity (Waghorn, 2009). An unlawful breach of the physical, spatial, or cultural references of a home or house is home invasion. Anything taken without permission of the owner from the physical, spatial, or cultural boundaries of the home or house is burglary. In the U.S., in common law, burglary involves the breaking and entering of the dwelling of another with intent to commit a felony or petit larceny (Perkins, 1969, p. 212). Breaking involves breach or opening of a dwelling structure through nefarious means, including disabling or putting aside any material part of the structure intended as security against intrusion (Shover, 1991). "The entry may be by force ... or it may be through an unlocked door or an open window. As long as the person entering had no legal right to be present in the structure..." (Bureau of Justice Statistics 1989, p. 126). The law regarding burglary has evolved over the years to include all variations of attempted and unlawful entry regardless of how it is accomplished. The U.S. criminal codes have also evolved over the years to include degrees of burglary, which are dependent on whether the burglarized structure was occupied when entered, whether the perpetrator was armed, the time of day, and whether any victims were assaulted (Shover, 1991). According to *Cost of Crime: A Systematic Review* (2015), owners of compromised structures endure substantial economic costs associated with burglary, and their neighbors and communities also endure societal costs, with implications for various industries, such as insurance, security, and healthcare, among others.

Burglary is also referred to as robbery. The Criminal Justice Information Services Division (2010) of the U.S. Department of Justice relies on the FBI's definition of robbery, which is the taking or attempting to take anything of value from the care, custody, or control of a person or persons by putting the victim in fear, threat of force, use of force or violence, or some combination of these behaviors. The most common tools for breaking in are pry bars, pliers, screwdrivers, and little hammers (Alarms.org, 2019). Burglars tend to be young males who are amateurs and acting out of desperation (Alarms.org, 2019; Mullin & Wright, 2003; Sorensen, 2003; Weisel, 2002). Sometimes the social networks these burglars operate in facilitate their criminal activity. Within these networks, attentive burglars learn how to victimize property owners, developing an understanding of house layouts and the likely locations of the most valuable objects, as well as planned routes for escape (Robson, 2015). More experienced burglars are not afflicted with indecision, instead operating on a skilled "automatic pilot" that enables them to quickly exploit vulnerabilities in safety and security. Amateur burglars who are desperate are more dangerous than experienced burglars. In Kleck and Jackson's (2016) study of criminal cases focused specifically on robbery and burglary taken from the Survey of Inmates in State and Federal Correctional Facilities (SISPCF) 2004 (U.S. Department of Justice, 2007), an in-person survey of a national probability sample of prison inmates interviewed by employees of the U.S. Bureau of the Census, which found that unemployment was five times more common among robbers and burglars than among nonoffenders.

Do Safety and Public Health Advocates Understand Home Invasion?

Theoretical underpinnings for explaining safety and security within the context of home invasion, robbery, and burglary focus on three factors. The first factor involves understanding the environment in which breaking and entering occurs. The second factor entails assessment of the psychological well-being of the victimized property owner. The third factor pertains to the public health perspective the media plays in its coverage of violence associated with property crime. These factors are researched in a variety of fields or disciplines, including criminology, public health, journalism, and communication studies. This chapter examines pertinent ideas in these fields and disciplines. There is an effort to identify connections between concepts which together form a more complete understanding of what happens before and during a home invasion, how to cope in the aftermath of such a horrendous event, and how to prevent it from happening again. Public health professionals along with other experts can use of all these ideas in multipronged interventions, with the goal of mitigating danger and alleviating the symptoms associated with a traumatic experience.

Offenders and perpetrators surveil areas to determine if they are an estimated lower risk of detection and arrest. Areas with a high proportion of detached single-family houses are attractive for home invasion, because they can be entered directly from the street, and they usually have multiple access points (Bernasco, 2006). According to Hakim et al. (2001), a detached single-family house located within a quarter of a mile of an exit from a major thoroughfare with the following characteristics is a target for home invasion and burglary or robbery: (1) adjacent to woods or a playground, (2) no alarm nor a motion sensor or timer to turn lights on and off at night, (3) no car parked in the driveway, and (4) the homeowner does not have a neighbor to pick up mail and newspapers when away. In addition to the entity constituting the domicile, criminology theories consider spatial and temporal dimensions. These theories have been refined over time to address repeat and near-repeat burglaries and victimization. Cohen and Felson (1979) discuss Routine Activities Theory to help explain the decision-making of perpetrators. According to this theory, crimes are an outcome of the convergence of a likely offender, a suitable target, and the absence of a capable guardian. The absence of one or more of these things in a particular space and time prevents a criminal act such as a home invasion or burglary from happening. More law enforcement in an area around times of heightened criminal activity can mitigate crime rates. Whether there are fewer offenders in an area at a specific time or fewer suitable targets in places where offenders congregate, fewer of either will make a difference.

The Routine Activities Theory explains the occurrence of criminal events, but it does not address the decision-making process for offenders and perpetrators. This decision-making process is addressed by the Rational Choice Theory, which is rooted in the assumption that offenders and perpetrators consume goods and participate in activities that they believe fulfills a need or desire (Clarke & Cornish, 1985; Groff, 2007). The theory is predicated on the claim that all people can comprehend a wide variety of factors prior to making a decision. Nonetheless, its assumptions are utilized in many fields, including criminology, and it oftentimes complements the Routine Activities Theory (Herrnstein, 1990). A criminologist relying on Rational Choice Theory who examines the reasoning behind an offender's or perpetrator's behavior seeks to understand the opportunities, costs, and benefits attached to each criminal act (Cornish & Clarke, 1987). For instance, a reduced travel distance to and from a target area, as well as between target areas, are factors in a burglar's cost-benefit analysis about which target area to choose for home invasion and robbery. Burglars have limited mobility, so they commit their offenses close to known territory, including their neighborhood and the surrounding area. They must consider carrying stolen items away from the scene of the crime. According to Rational Choice Theory, burglars will act when the opportunity presents itself, especially when a target area consists of neighborhoods with proximity to concentrations of restaurants, bars, and clubs, which serve as meeting points for offenders to congregate (Bernasco, 2006). Concentration of facilities are addressed in greater depth in the behavioral ecology theory known as optimal foraging (also known as Optimal Foraging Theory; Krebs & Davies, 1987, p. 64–66).

Optimal Foraging Theory is used to understand the spatial-temporal pattern of home invasion, burglary, or robbery, and to discern how burglars determine when intrusion into someone's home will maximize their reward while minimizing risk of getting caught. A key assumption of the theory is that the time of day or time of the year in a particular neighborhood or part of a city is of interest to a burglar, who realizes timing is a crucial factor in determining when to forage for an object of interest (Brantingham & Tita, 2008; Johnson et al., 2007; Fielding & Jones, 2012). Ultimately, for "…optimal foraging offenders who create these patterns of burglaries which are close in space and time and are the work of the same (by definition repeat) offender(s)" timing (e.g., day or night, a specific time of the month or year, etc.) the home invasion, burglary, or robbery in neighborhoods or areas where deployable police resources are lacking means a reduced risk of detection (Fielding & Jones, 2012, p. 31). In the U.S., foragers are wary of security systems. However, only 17 percent of houses have a system in place, resulting in the remaining 83 percent of houses being 300 percent more likely to be burglarized (Alarms.org, 2019). Even when property owners are not reluctant to acquire a security system there is a silver lining for foragers because when they visit a neighborhood with signs and stickers indicating which properties have a security system, properties without security systems also stand out. According to the National Council for Home Safety and Security, some property owners do not acquire a security system because they are costly, less dependable than a dog, and give property owners anxiety due to system instillation, use, and maintenance (Alarms.org, 2019).

Anxiety is a problem for homeowners after a breaking and entering. Adjustment disorder (AjD) is among the most diagnosed mental health conditions in clinical practice (Casey, 2014; Evans et al., 2013), with higher prevalence of AjD among homeowners who have experienced a home invasion, burglary, and robbery. According to the American Psychiatric Association (2013) and the World Health Organization (1992), AjD is a transient maladaptive or pathological reaction to an identifiable stressor which emerges within one month of a stress event. Home invasion, burglary, and robbery are the stressful events for homeowners experiencing AjD—these victims feel their privacy has been violated and feel anxiety, hypervigilance, anger, hostility, and sadness (Beaton et al., 2000). AjD can lead to significant social impairments. Within an occupational context, 37 percent of AjD patients who received treatment did not fully return to work within three months (Van der Klink et al., 2003). "Symptoms include otherwise normative behaviors that manifest more intensely than usually expected when an individual confronts such a stressor" (Bachem & Maercker, 2016, p. 398), such as attempts to avoid thoughts and feelings associated with the burglary and concerns that it will reoccur. Victims who experience anxiety, depression, shock, anger, fear, sleeplessness, exhaustion, and confusion six months following a burglary usually manifest persistent post-traumatic stress reactions (Chung et al., 2014). To be diagnosed with post-traumatic stress disorder (PTSD) in the aftermath of a burglary, the victim needs to have experienced actual or threatened death or serious injury or a threat to the physical integrity of oneself or others during the event (APA, 1994). Personal experiences shape property owners' reactions to home invasion, burglary, and robbery, but other experiences matter too.

The media coverage of home invasion affects property owners' perceptions of burglary and robbery. News media affects media users' emotions and feelings associated with their susceptibility to property crimes. When journalists report on property crimes and related violence from law enforcement or criminal justice perspectives, their coverage punctuates events such as burglaries into somewhat isolated episodes. The harm associated with this coverage is that media users consume information on media platforms ranging from television to social media, and they only decode enough information to increase their fear of violence. They develop a fatalistic attitude toward crime and violence. Emergent from this coverage is the sentiment that violence is inevitable, and there is little the public can do to counteract it. In response to the fatalistic attitude embodied in the news media, interventionists suggest an alternative perspective, which entails emphasis on reporting criminal and violent acts including home invasion, burglary, and robbery within the context of public health (Rodgers & Thorson, 2001). "Further ... crime and violence reporting was framed predominately as isolated events, and not patterns that were caused by factors that should themselves be examined for their potential impact on prevention" (Rodgers & Thorson, 2001, p. 178).

From a narrative or framing point of view, facts matter, and how those facts are portrayed matters. Print, broadcast, and social media provide a means for publicizing salacious facts about criminal events that enable a shift in public attention away from more insightful observations of systemic factors and patterns in crime stories and other narratives. The overrepresentation of salacious facts about violent acts within episodic narration masks the social and environmental characteristics that predispose an individual to commit home invasion, burglary, or robbery. Media coverage in these instances frame property crimes as law enforcement or criminal justice issues instead of as socioeconomic, violence prevention, and public safety issues. Oftentimes, the media's framing of crimes, including homicide, domestic violence, and property crimes, does not fully serve the public interest, because coverage is narrowcast as infotainment. Media studies experts agree that framing in these circumstances has implications (Rodgers & Thorson, 2001, p. 178):

The result is that readers are left with the impression that crime occurs because of "bad" people. The inference waiting to be made is that there can be no solutions—except to punish—and prevention is not at all part of the picture. Interestingly, the one place where we would expect to find crime placed into context was in follow-up stories. Unfortunately, we observed little reporting about the causes and consequences of crimes—the kind of reporting one might expect from follow-up stories. Follow-ups were, in fact, less likely than first-time stories to contain this kind of information. On average, about one public health fact was present in every crime story analyzed.

The next section of the chapter addresses celebrity narratives involving encounters with property crime, specifically incidents of home invasion, burglary, and robbery. These narratives rely on repetition of public health facts, which have the propensity to produce effects on news consumers.

Celebrities Encounter Home Invasion

Celebrities are targeted by stalkers, burglars, robbers, and other offenders who want their livelihood—to take their fortune, maybe steal their spotlight, and in some cases ensnare celebrities in a world of turmoil. Many celebrities have an online presence. Paparazzi track celebrity whereabouts, and fans in the social media age check their favorite celebrities' status updates regarding their location and itinerary. Many celebrities who are used to public scrutiny and who have the means take precautions to ensure the well-being and safety of themselves and their families. Actresses such as Gwyneth Paltrow and Sandra Bullock have dealt with stalkers who invade their private spaces, despite the efforts of their personal security teams, high-tech camera security systems, panic room safety doors, and even an attack dog (Fisher, 2017). According to a police search warrant, in 2014, a man presumably scaled a chain-link fence topped with barbed wire to get into Bullock's house (Leopold, 2014). When the police arrived, the intruder was screaming, "Sandy, I'm sorry. Please don't press charges." Apparently, the intruder had a notebook with photographs of the actress and handwritten notes, one of which read, "I will forever be thinking of you and (Bullock's son) Louie, my son, as you are my wife by law, the law of God and you belong to me and me to you." When police searched the intruder's home, they found many weapons, including a half-dozen illegal machine guns (Leopold, 2014).

Fans were shocked to find out: "At 1 AM she hears a loud banging inside the house. Bullock goes to her bedroom door to close and lock it and she sees Corbett [the stalker] right there in the hallway wearing dark clothing." Authorities were not lenient toward Corbett, and the intruder was charged with stalking, burglary, and possessing an illegal firearm (Kornowski, 2014). A well-known example of home invasion for an unidentified reason involved Taylor Swift. Police found a ladder leading up to a window that an intruder had broken to gain access to Swift's New York City home. Once inside, the intruder took a shower then had a nap. The intruder had been arrested at the same address earlier in the year for allegedly using a shovel to break in the front door. The intruder was charged with felony stalking, burglary, criminal mischief, and criminal trespass (Millington, 2018). Sometimes home invasions involving celebrities are because of their fame instead of their possessions. In the moment, a celebrity encounters a deranged person. They do not know why the person is in their home. Perhaps the offender is an overzealous fan, maybe a stalker, or maybe the person is willing to harm them for an unidentified reason. In these moments, celebrities are terrified like anyone else who experiences home invasion, especially when the breaking and entering occurs while they are at home.

Reality TV stars are not immune from home invasion, which Dina Manzo (*The Real Housewives of New Jersey*) and her partner found out when they returned home (ABC-7 Eyewitness News, 2017). When the couple entered the home, they were ambushed by two intruders who rushed toward them, with the couple being hit with a baseball bat and being punched. The intruders bound them together within the house and fled the scene with cash, jewelry, and other personal property. Both victims freed themselves and afterward were hospitalized and treated for facial injuries. The couple's lawyer issued the following statement (ABC-7 Eyewitness News, 2017):

> Dina and David are obviously shaken up from the traumatic and violent home invasion and robbery. No one should ever have to go through what they did. They are grateful to law enforcement and the other emergency responders and appreciate everyone's concern and well-wishes.

The rapper and actor LL Cool J confronted an intruder during a home invasion at his family residence in Sherman Oaks, California. Apparently, the intruder was unaware he was breaking and entering the home of a famous music artist. The intruder tripped the house's security system, which alerted LL Cool J, who went downstairs to investigate the commotion and found the intruder. He subdued the intruder, and his daughter called the police (Michaels, 2012).

During an interview with *Drink Champs* cohosts N.O.R.E. and DJ EFN (REVOLT TV, 2017), LL Cool J recalled his state of mind when he found an intruder in his house:

> Fighting for your life is not the same feeling as fighting in (other circumstances). I'm really scared, this is for keeps, I'm going to get it in, whatever it takes. It

was one in the morning, and the alarm pad went off. You know how you have an alarm, and it'll give you a minute to put your code in? I went to the keypad, and I'm looking at the keypad, like, family room? I'm thinking it's my daughter sneaking in, coming in late. When I was going towards the kitchen, he's coming out of the kitchen, and we're face to face. He's got all black on, he's got a big bag, the long Manson beard, boots. I'm terrified, it was freaky. We fought, he tried to rock for a minute. This is the part that's not fun. There was a point when I had to decide whether he should stay alive. I didn't know if he had anyone else with him. I had him on the ground on his stomach, finished, but I had to make that decision because I didn't know if he had someone upstairs.

LL Cool J and his family were not injured. The intruder suffered a broken nose, jaw, and ribs, according to a Los Angeles County District Attorney spokeswoman (Duke, 2012). Prosecutors charged the intruder with first degree burglary as a "third striker"—he had been convicted of voluntary manslaughter, auto theft, first degree burglary, and a petty theft. Because of these convictions, the intruder faced a term of 38 years in prison if convicted for the home invasion (Duke, 2012). During an interview with Oprah Winfrey after the incident, LL Cool J reflected on his encounter with the intruder (Podrazik, 2013):

> What was on my mind was what could have happened if I wasn't home. It wasn't one of those beat-your-chest moments. It was one of those grateful, thank God, gratitude moments that I was able to handle this situation, subdue this guy, wait for the police, get him out of here and everybody was safe. You know because if I wasn't here … house full of women, there's no telling what could have happened. He had bad intentions.

In an era of communication technology and social media, when smartphones and other devices are used to create online presence, which can give friends, and foes, even complete strangers a window into an individual's life, celebrities are learning the hard way to be careful with what they share online. Beginning in 2008, a rash of burglaries and robberies occurred in the L.A. area, and celebrity after celebrity was targeted. The perpetrators of this property crime spree later would be known as the Bling Ring. During their reign of terror, more than $3,000,000 in clothing and jewelry was stolen from Paris Hilton, Lindsay Lohan, Orlando Bloom, Brian Austin Green, and his then girlfriend Megan Fox, among others (Sales, 2000). The Bling Ring discovered celebrities' homes on Google Maps and celebrityaddressaerial.com and tracked the whereabouts of celebrities by checking celebrity or paparazzi social media posts and status updates (Sales, 2010). The Bling Ring consisted of a gang of well-off youth from "the Valley" who coveted the wardrobes of celebrities they admired. The members of the gang desired clothes, shoes, handbags, makeup, perfume, and underwear from designers such as Chanel, Gucci, Tiffany, Cartier, Prada, Marc

Jacobs, Dolce & Gabbana, Burberry, and Yves Saint Laurent (Sales, 2010). Some burglars in the Bling Ring stole to fuel their drug habits, while others surveilled celebrities and stole from them because they could. Paris Hilton's house was robbed five times between October and December of 2008 (Sales, 2010). Ultimately, authorities were able to rein in the Bling Ring, with celebrities aiding law enforcement by sharing their home surveillance videos, some of which were obtained by TMZ and broadcast on L.A.'s local news stations. Once images of the intruders were circulated in the media, the public provided tips regarding their identity, and law enforcement used Facebook to ascertain the "friends" and social network that comprised the Bling Ring.

The apprehension of the Bling Ring did not end the wave of burglaries and robberies afflicting celebrities. In 2017, between February and December, celebrities experienced home invasions from L.A. to London. Singer Alanis Morissette's house, located in a tony section of the Brentwood neighborhood of L.A., was invaded. Luckily, she and her husband were not home when burglars broke in and made off with a safe containing $2,000,000 in jewelry and other valuables (Winton, 2017). Simon Cowell, the former *American Idol* and *The X Factor* judge, was robbed while he and his family slept. Apparently, an intruder and burglar waited for Cowell's security guard to go to the restroom before he broke into Cowell's five-bedroom property in west London (Telegraph Reporters, 2017). The intruder had committed 58 offenses over two decades, including 37 convictions for burglary, and he put his skills to use when he entered Cowell's home through a patio door and stole jewelry and two passports. The burglar's DNA was found on gloves he dropped during his escape from the residence, as well as a handprint on a wall at the property. A jury of nine men and three women took less than 60 minutes to find him guilty (Telegraph Reporters, 2017).

Rapper A$AP Rocky's L.A. area home was also robbed in 2017. According to the radio station Power 92.3 Chicago, A$AP was not home, but others were affected:

> Sources say that the robbery was believed to be a targeted attack, possibly because A$AP Rocky posted a video to social media counting money in his home. They also stated that the Harlem rapper was not present at the time of the robbery but his sister was. The robbers held his sister at gunpoint while they proceeded to take property and jewelry from the rappers home. They tried to make off with A$AP's safe but were unable to get it open because his sister didn't know the combination. No harm was done to A$AP's sister but they left the safe in the driveway as they made away in their getaway car with 1.5 million dollars-worth of items they stole from the home.

The property crime spree continued throughout 2017, and celebrities were not immune from the crime wave. In December 2017, before the Billboard

Women in Music Awards, Kelly Clarkson mentioned during her chat with *Extra's* Renee Bargh that her house was "…robbed last night … materialistic things we didn't care about." She was disturbed by one detail: "The guy was in our kids' room … so that was a little weird" (Armstrong, 2017). Fortunately, Clarkson and her family were not home when the robbery occurred. Celebrity narratives like those of Sandra Bullock and Kelly Clarkson, LL Cool J and Simon Cowell, as well as the countless stories written in the media regarding the Bling Ring and its victims, were laced with public health facts in follow-up story after follow-up story. Media coverage about celebrities who experienced property crime, specifically, home invasion, burglary, and robbery consisted of prevention messages within storytelling about crime. These stories placed crime, prevention, health, and wellness into a violence awareness and prevention context.

Coping After Property Crime Victimization

The public is in danger. If you are not safe in your home, where are you safe? Crime victimization is an important health problem in the U.S. Epidemiological data indicates that 17.5 million property crimes (e.g., burglary theft, etc.) were committed against victims aged 12 and older in 2007, and an outcome of this behavior was injury and health-related problems (McCart et al., 2010). According to the Bureau of Justice Statistics (2010) special report, National Crime Victimization Survey: Victimization During Household Burglary, 27.6 percent of the time, a person is home while the burglary occurs, and 26 percent of those people are harmed—7.2 percent of burglaries result in someone being injured. Victimization contributes to admissions to emergency rooms. "During 1994 U.S. hospital emergency department (ED) personnel treated an estimated 1.4 million people for injuries from confirmed or suspected interpersonal violence" (Rand, 1997, p. 6), which includes rape/sexual assault, robbery, and assault (Centers for Disease Control, 1996). For households violently burglarized while someone was in the residence, about 12 percent faced an offender carrying a firearm (Catalano, 2010). Being home during a home invasion is a life-threatening situation.

In the aftermath of being targeted, victims experience traumatic stress. In order to cope with their trauma, they seek assistance from formal helpers (e.g., trained professionals, such as physicians, mental health workers, and law enforcement officials) and informal helpers (e.g., members of their social networks, including family and friends). Victims' satisfaction with the initial police response affects their ability to cope with trauma, AjD, and PTSD. Of utmost importance, "…the therapeutic or antitherapeutic impact of encounters with the legal system depends on how the individual perceives the quality of that encounter" (Kunst et al., 2013, p. 115). Victim satisfaction with police procedure is indicated with the following sentiments (Kunst et al., 2013, p. 113): (1) the police were polite, respectful, and courteous, (2) the police were approachable and friendly, (3) the police were professional, (4) the police were fair, (5) the police were helpful. According to Herman (2003), victim psychological well-being and satisfaction with the police investigation stage and later stages of the criminal justice process are impacted by their encounters with the legal system.

Once victims' encounters with the legal system end, they continue to deal with the lingering effects of their trauma. Victims still need treatment. Unfortunately, victims are confronted by barriers to treatment, such as limited availability of mental health services, lack of patients' resources, and fear of stigmatization, which elicit an impetus for traditional treatments and self-help interventions (Bachem & Maercker, 2016). Traditional treatments involve therapist contact. Untraditional treatments increasingly involve self-help as an unguided intervention paired with minimal to no therapist contact. According to the study *Self-Help Interventions for Adjustment Disorder Problems* (2016), a popular self-help intervention includes self-help manuals consisting of screening tests, information regarding applicable causes and symptoms for mental and emotional unwellness, a variety of approaches validated as treatments for PTSD, anxiety disorders, or depression, as well as exercises to mitigate symptoms which acerbate unwellness including preoccupations (e.g., constant rumination, excessive worry about the stressor) and failure to adapt (e.g., sleep disturbance, difficulties concentrating, loss of interest in previously enjoyable activities).

During the time it takes for an individual aided by formal and informal helpers to comprehend the magnitude of the victimization, too many victims experience repeat victimization (RV). For instance, a victim is still recovering from the initial burglary, and then the victim is burglarized again. Unfortunately, research indicates RV is a common occurrence (Laycock, 2001). Victimization is a predictor of further victimization at an individual as well as area level. These areas are known as "hot spots"—"an area that is the target of a higher than expected level of criminal activity" (Ratcliffe & McCullagh, 2001, p. 331). Victims in hot spots who experience RV are reintroduced to the trauma and encounters with police response and the criminal justice process. RV ensnares victims in a toxic cycle, which is why prevention of property crimes has become more imperative over time. According to *Criminology and Criminal Justice Senior Capstone Project* (2010), prevention includes Neighborhood Watch programs, rehabilitation and recidivism programs for offenders, interventions before crimes are committed, including early-childhood programs and drug and alcohol treatment programs, and policing agencies property crime prevention programs. According to *Burglary Revictimization: The Time Period of Heightened Risk* (1998), homeowners who are trying to prevent burglary and robbery should improve locks on doors and windows, eliminate spaces around a residence that obscure the visibility of entry points, add temporary and permanent alarms and lighting to ward off would-be offenders, and stay aware of offenses in the surrounding area.

In response to victimization and RV, government (e.g., public health and law enforcement officials) and private sector (e.g., security professionals) efforts may involve a prominent publicity element, informing residents of who or what area is vulnerable, how they are vulnerable, and addressing security measures and upgrades that should be implemented or that will be provided (Millie, 2008). The celebrity narratives discussed in this chapter are a crucial component of the publicity element. The celebrities are relatable and believable, and when they let down their guard, and reveal their vulnerabilities, media users pay attention. The spotlight on celebrity encounters with home invasion heightens awareness for potential victims, demonstrates how to survive the trauma of a break-in, and creates unwanted attention for would-be offenders and offenders.

References

ABC-7 Eyewitness News. (2017, May 16). Police: *"Real Housewives" star tied up, robbed during New Jersey home invasion.* ABC30.com. https://abc7ny.com/news/police-real-.

American Psychiatric Association. (2013). Diagnostic and statistical manual of mental disorders (5th ed.). (2013). APA.

Armstrong, M. (2017, December 1). Kelly Clarkson reveals her home was robbed: "Our whole house was bashed in." *Billboard.* https://www.billboard.com/index.php/articles/columns/pop/8054841/kelly-clarkson-home-robbed-women-in-music-interview.

Bachem, R., & Maercker, A. (2016). Self-help interventions for adjustment disorder problems: A randomized waiting-list controlled study in a sample of burglary victims. *Cognitive Behavior Therapy, 45(5),* 397–413. https://doi.org/10.1080/16506073.2016.1191083.

Beaton, A., Cook, M., Kavanagh, M., & Herrington, C. (2000). The psychological impact of burglary. *Psychology, Crime & Law, 6(1–2),* 33–43. http://doi.org/10.1080/10683160008410830.

Bernasco, W. (2006). Co-offending and the choice of target areas in burglary. *Journal of Investigative Psychology and Offender Profiling, 3(3),* 139–155. https://doi.org/10.1002/jip.49.

Brantingham, P., & Tita, G. (2008) Offender mobility and crime pattern formation from first principles. In L. Liu & J. Eck (Eds.), *Artificial crime analysis systems: Using computer simulations and geographic information systems* (pp. 193–208). Idea Press.

Bureau of Justice Statistics (1989). *Criminal victimization in the United States, 1987.* U.S. Department of Justice. https://www.bjs.gov/content/pub/pdf/cvus87.pdf.

Bureau of Justice Statistics (1997). *Violence-related injuries treated in hospital emergency departments.* United States Department of Justice. https://www.bjs.gov/content/pub/pdf/VRITHED.PDF.

Bureau of Justice Statistics. (2010). *National crime victimization survey: Victimization during household burglary.* United States Department of Justice. https://www.bjs.gov/content/pub/pdf/vdhb.pdf.

Bureau of Justice Statistics. (2013). *Household burglary, 1994–2011.* United States Department of Justice. https://www.bjs.gov/content/pub/pdf/hb9411.pdf.

Casey, P. (2014). Adjustment disorder: New developments. *Current Psychiatry Reports, 16(6)*, 1–8. http://doi.org/10.1007/s11920-014-0451-2.

Centers for Disease Control and Prevention. (1996). National hospital ambulatory medical care survey: 1994 emergency department summary. Vital and Health Statistics 275. https://www.cdc.gov/nchs/data/ad/ad275.pdf.

Chung, M.C., Stedmon, J., Hall, R., Marks, Z., Thornhill, K., & Mehrshahi, R. (2014). Posttraumatic stress reactions following burglary: The role of coping and personality. *Traumatology: An International Journal, 20(2)*, 65–74. https://doi.org/10.1037/h0099374.

Clarke, R., & Cornish, D. (1985). Modeling offenders' decisions: A framework for research and policy. *Crime Justice, 6*, 147–185. https://doi.org/10.1086/449106.

Cohen, L., & Felson, M. (1979). Social change and crime rate trends: A routine activity approach. *American Sociology Review, 44(4)*, 588–608. https://doi.org/10.2307/2094589.

Cornish, D., & Clarke, R. (1987). Understanding crime displacement: An application of rational choice theory. *Criminology, 25(4)*, 933–948. https://doi.org/10.1111/j.1745-9125.1987.tb00826.x.

Criminal Justice Information Services Division. (2010). *FBI—robbery*. FBI's Uniform Crime Reporting (UCR) Program. https://ucr.fbi.gov/crime-in-the-u.s/2010/crime-in-the-u.s.-2010/violent-crime/robberymain.

Duke, A. (2012, August 24). *"Mama said knock you out": LL Cool J broke burglary suspect's nose, jaw, ribs*. CNN. https://www.cnn.com/2012/08/23/showbiz/ll-cool-j-burgar.

Evans, S.C., Reed, G.M., Roberts, M.C., Esparza, P., Watts, A.D., Correia, J.M., Ritchie, P., Maj, M., & Saxena, S. (2013). Psychologists' perspectives on the diagnostic classification of mental disorders: Results from the WHO-IUPsyS Global Survey. *International Journal of Psychology, 48(3)*, 177–193. https://doi.org/10.1080/00207594.2013.804189.

Fielding, M., & Jones, V. (2012). "Disrupting the optimal forager": Predictive risk mapping and domestic burglary reduction in Trafford, Greater Manchester. *International Journal of Police Science & Management, 14(1)*, 30–41. https://doi.org/10.1350/ijps.2012.14.1.260.

Fisher, G. (2017, September 8). *High-risk, high-expense security for celebrities plagued by stalkers*. CBS News. https://www.cbsnews.com/news/high-risk-high-expense-security-for-celebrities-like-gwyneth-paltrow-sandra-bullock-plagued-by-stalkers/.

Groff, E. (2007). Simulation for theory testing and experimentation: An example using routine activity theory and street robbery. *Journal of Quantitative Criminology, 23(2)*, 75–103. https://doi.org/10.1007/s10940-006-9021-z.

Hakim, S., Rengert, G.F., & Shachmurove, Y. (2001). Target search of burglars: A revised economic model. *Papers in Regional Science, 80(2)*, 121–137. https://doi.org/10.1111/j.1435-5597.2001.tb01791.x.

Herman, J.L. (2003). The mental health of crime victims: Impact of legal intervention. *Journal of Traumatic Stress, 16(2)*, 159–166. https://doi.org/10.1023/A:1022847223135.

Herrnstein, R. (1990). Rational choice theory: Necessary but not sufficient. *American Psychologist, 45(3)*, 356–367. https://doi.org/10.1037/0003-066X.45.3.356.

internscbc. (2017, May 17). *A$AP Rocky's home involved in armed robbery!* Power 92 Chicago. http://web.archive.org/web/20170519010838/https://www.power92chicago.com/2017/05/17/aap-rockys-home-involved-in-armed-robbery/.

Johnson, S.D., Bernasco, W., Bowers, K.J., Elffers, H., Ratcliffe, J., Rengert, G., & Townsley, M. (2007). Space-time patterns of risk: A cross national assessment of residential burglary victimization. *Journal of Quantitative Criminology, 23(3)*, 201–219. https://doi.org/10.1007/s10940-007-9025-3.

Kleck, G., & Jackson, D. (2016). What kind of joblessness affects crime? A national case-control study of serious property crime. *Journal of Quantitative Criminology, 32(4)*, 489–513. https://doi.org/10.1007/s10940-016-9282-0.

Kornowski, L. (2014, July 15). *Sandra Bullock faced stalker in home invasion, search warrant reportedly reveals*. HuffPost. https://www.huffpost.com/entry/sandra-bullock-faced-stalker-home-invasion_n_5586942.

Krebs, J., & Davies, N. (1987). *An introduction to behavioral ecology*. Oxford University Press.

Kunst, M.J., Rutten, S., & Knijf, E. (2013). Satisfaction with the initial police response and development of posttraumatic stress disorder symptoms in victims of domestic burglary. *Journal of Traumatic Stress, 26(1)*, 111–118. https://doi.org/10.1002/jts.21774.

Laycock, G. (2001). Hypothesis-based research: The repeat victimization story. *Criminal Justice, 1(1)*, 59–82. https://doi.org/10.1177/1466802501001001004.

Leopold, T. (2014, July 15). *Sandra Bullock came face-to-face with stalker in her own home.* CNN. https://www.cnn.com/2014/07/15/showbiz/celebrity-news-gossip/sandra-bullock-Stalker.

Maguire, M. (1980). The impact of burglary upon victims. *The British Journal of Criminology, 20(3)*, 261–275. https://doi.org/10.1093/oxfordjournals.bjc.a047171.

McCart, M.R., Smith, D.W., & Sawyer, G.K. (2010). Help seeking among victims of crime: A review of the empirical literature. *Journal of Traumatic Stress, 23(2)*, 198–206. https://doi.org/10.1002/jts.20509.

Michaels, S. (2012, August 23). LL Cool J detains intruder at his home. *The Guardian.* https://www.theguardian.com/music/2012/aug/23/ll-cool-j-intruder.

Millie, A. (2008). Vulnerability and risk: Some lessons from the UK Reducing Burglary Initiative. *Police Practice and Research, 9(3)*, 183–198. https://doi.org/10.1080/15614260701797512.

Millington, A. (2018, April 23). *Taylor Swift's stalker reportedly broke into her house, took a shower, then fell asleep.* Business Insider. https://www.businessinsider.com/taylor-swift-stalker-broke-into-her-house-took-a-shower-then-fell-asleep-2018-4housewives-star-tied-up-robbed-during-home-invasion/1994454/.

Mullins, C.W., & Wright, R. (2003). Gender, social networks, and residential burglary. *Criminology, 41(3)*, 813–840. http://dx.doi.org/10.3886/ICPSR06148.

National Council for Home Safety and Security. (2019). *Burglary statistics.* https://www.alarms.org/burglary-statistics/.

Perkins, R.M. (1969*). Criminal law (2nd ed.).* Foundation Press.

Podrazik, J. (2013, January 26). *LL Cool J: Intruder who broke in "had bad intentions" (VIDEO).* HuffPost. https://www.huffpost.com/entry/ll-cool-j-intruder_n_2550509.

Portland State University Criminology and Criminal Justice Senior Capstone. (2010). *Prevention of residential burglary: A review of the literature.* Criminology and Criminal Justice Senior Capstone Project. https://pdxscholar.library.pdx.edu/cgi/viewcontent.cgi?article=1002&context=ccj_capstone.

Ratcliffe, J., & McCullagh, M.J. (2001). Chasing ghosts? Police Perception of High Crime Areas. *British Journal of Criminology, 41(2)*, 330–341. https://doi.org/10.1093/bjc/41.2.330.

REVOLT TV. (2017, August 2). *LL Cool J gives "Drink Champs" a play-by-play of fighting a burglar in his home.* https://www.revolt.tv/2017/8/2/20819848/ll-cool-j-gives-drink-champs-a-play-by-play-of-fighting-a-burglar-in-his-home.

Robinson, M.B. (1998). Burglary revictimization: The time period of heightened risk. *British Journal of Criminology, 38(1)*, 78–87. https://doi.org/10.1093/OXFORDJOURNALS.BJC.A014229.

Robson, D. (2015, June 18). *The strange expertise of burglars.* BBC. https://www.bbc.com/future/article/20150618-the-strange-expertise-of-burglars.

Rodgers, S., & Thorson, E. (2001). The reporting of crime and violence in the *Los Angeles Times*: Is there a public health perspective? *Journal of Health Communication, 6(2)*, 169–192. https://doi.org/10.1080/10810730120636.

Sales, N.J. (2010, March 1). The suspects wore louboutins. *Vanity Fair.* https://archive.vanityfair.com/article/share/e9cc0cc3-dbf1-4fab-8367-5fc7c05608e6.

Shover, N. (1991). Burglary. *Crime and Justice, 14*, 73–113. https://doi.org/10.1086/449184.

Sorenson, D.W.M. (2003). *The Nature and Prevention of Residential Burglary: A Review of the International Literature with An Eye Toward Prevention in Denmark.* Denmark's Ministry of Justice. https://www.justitsministeriet.dk/sites/default/files/media/Arbejdsomraader/Forskning/Fo rskningspuljen/2011/2003/The_Nature_and_Prevention_of_Residential_Burglary.pdf.

Telegraph Reporters. (2017, February 28). Serial burglar guilty of "terrifying" raid on Simon Cowell's house. *The Telegraph.* https://www.telegraph.co.uk/news/2017/02/28/serial-burglar-guilty-terrifying-raid-simon-cowells-house/.

Van der Klink, J.J.L., Blonk, R.W.B., Schene, A.H., & Van Dijk, F.J.H. (2003). Reducing long term sickness absence by an activating intervention in adjustment disorders: A cluster randomized controlled design. *Occupational and Environmental Medicine, 60(6)*, 429–437. http://doi.org/10.1136/oem.60.6.429.

Waghorn, K. (2009). Home invasion. *Home Cultures, 6(3)*, 261–286. https://doi.org/10.2752/174 063109X12462745321507.

Weisel, D.L. (2002). *Problem-oriented guides for police: Burglary of single family houses*. Office of Community Oriented Policing Services, United States Department of Justice. https://live-cpop.ws.asu.edu/sites/default/files/problems/pdfs/Burglary_of_Single-Family_Houses.pdf.

Wickramasekera, N., Wright, J., Elsey, H., Murray, J., & Tubeuf, S. (2015). Cost of crime: A systematic review. *Journal of Criminal Justice, 43(3)*, 218–228. https://doi.org/10.1016/j.jcrimjus.2015.04.009.

Winton, R. (2017, February 14). Alanis Morissette's Brentwood home is burglarized; thieves take safe containing $2 million in jewelry. *Los Angeles Times*. https://www.latimes.com/local/lanow/la-me-ln-alanis-jewels-burglars-20170214-story.html.

World Health Organization (1992). The ICD-10 classification of mental and behavioral disorders: Clinical description and diagnostic guidelines. WHO Press. https://apps.who.int/iris/bitstream/handle/10665/37958/9241544228_eng.pdf?sequence=8&isAllowed=y.

7

"No" to Sexual Misconduct
#MeToo and #TimesUp Campaigns in Hollywood

Before the era of the #MeToo and #TimesUp Campaigns, many alleged victims were silenced. Various industries ooze toxic masculinity, which places everyone, especially women, in danger (Burkhart et al., 1994; Harris & Edwards, 2010). Scrutiny of the entertainment industry in the United States offers insight into the changing landscape of sexual misconduct in society. The decision-makers who influence whether an aspiring entertainer or performer gets a role on a star-making production includes well-known producers and actors. Sometimes talent is not enough to get you the part. What if there is an expectation of something in return, a quid pro quo? The demands of these decision makers are sometimes described as too demanding, demeaning, or unreasonable. If quid pro quo harassment or sexual assault happens, the behavior is criminal.

Preventative initiatives should be a priority to mitigate the adverse effects of sexual misconduct, including sexual harassment and sexual assault. Outreach regarding sexual misconduct must consider the changing landscape. Sexual misconduct does not stop offline with the popularity of social networking sites (SNS). In late 2014, Australian gamer journalist Alanah Pearce received a Facebook message stating, "i'll rape u if I ever see u cunt" (cited in True, 2014). Cyber-harassment is common, and for many women online, experiencing rape threats and sexualized vitriol can be an everyday occurrence (Jane, 2014a, 2014b, 2015). Furthermore, the perpetrators and recipients of offline and online sexual misconduct are not only adults but adolescents. Pearce received abuse through public Facebook pages, and she determined that some of the perpetrators were adolescents (Pearce cited in True, 2014). Studies indicate that 4 to 38 percent of adolescents (13–18 years) encountered sexual harassment in cyberspace, and girls were harassed more than boys, with both genders experiencing emotional, educational, and health problems due to their experiences (Hill, 2011; Mitchell et al., 2014). Cyberspace provides adolescents and adults with another place to encounter a wide range of unwelcome verbal and explicitly sexual and gender-degrading comments (Barak, 2005). Despite the prevalence of offline and online sexual misconduct, some women refuse to be discouraged. They are savvy in this hashtag-oriented, social media–saturated society, and understand SNS brings people together across time and space, which enables them to share stories with strangers online and offline.

The #NotOkay movement began in October 2016 and focused attention on the effects of sexual harassment and sexual assault on American women. Over 1,000,000 women tweeted using the hashtag #NotOkay, bringing exposure to their experiences with sexual discrimination, which involved abuse at the hands of coworkers (Leung, 2017). Prior to the hashtag #NotOkay, the seeds of activism were planted by Tarana Burke, who in 2007 penned letters to celebrity sexual abuse survivors including Queen Latifah, Mary J. Blige, Gabrielle Union, Fantasia, and Missy Elliott, in search of recognition from them and other like-minded Black women to support the notion that all women could triumph over their abusers. Just Be Inc., the advocacy organization Burke founded, launched the "Me Too" mantra, which later became the #MeToo movement. Actresses such as Alyssa Milano, outraged by sexual harassment and assault faced by women at large, especially actresses in the entertainment industry, used #MeToo to respond to bombshell abuse allegations made against storied Hollywood producer Harvey Weinstein—within days more than 12 million people used the hashtag or liked or commented on it across social media platforms Facebook and Twitter (Millner, 2018). Hundreds of Hollywood women came together in January 2018 to launch Time's Up, a massive initiative to combat workplace sexual harassment, which entailed (Mohan, 2019, p. 1):

> Over the last year, the group has wielded its star power to gather nearly $25 million in donations for its defense fund, which provides legal aid to lower wage workers who are subject to sexual misconduct; the fund has already dedicated $6 million to 100 legal cases and investigations. Time's Up has also spawned multiple affiliates that are spreading the organization's mission to other industries—advertising and tech, for example.

Actresses came forward to assert "me too" and "times up," including Ashley Judd, Gwyneth Paltrow, and Salma Hayek. These women seek restitution. Their online activism is part of a comprehensive strategy to tell their stories and fight back. These trailblazers have harnessed the connectivity of SNS to forge an online and offline movement to combat sexual misconduct. Despite detractors, the tide is turning, and justice will not be denied.

According to the peer-reviewed journal article "Sexual Harassment and Corporate Law" (2018) in the *Columbia Law Review*, workplace "sexual harassment" emerged in legal and lay lexicons in the 1970s, with an influx in use during the 1990s amid the sexual misconduct scandals involving Supreme Court nominee (later Justice) Clarence Thomas and President Bill Clinton. In 1975, Lin Farley coined what would become an in-use definition for sexual harassment, which is "[a]ny repeated and unwanted sexual comments, looks, suggestions, or physical contact that you find objectionable or offensive and causes you discomfort on your job" (Hemel & Lund, 2018, p. 1594). In 1979, Catharine MacKinnon's legal analysis identified two components of sexual harassment in the workplace: condition of work, known now as "hostile environment," and "quid pro quo." Condition of work pertains to unwanted sexual attention, verbal or behavioral. Cooper (1985) ascribes four of the six levels of sexual harassment to a "hostile environment," including compliments indicating (1) "the lecher's" aesthetic appreciation for the victim, (2) unwanted social touching, (3) foreplay harassment, and (4) sexual abuse. Perpetrators of sexual harassment and sexual assault take advantage of workplace settings, recognizing that verbal and nonverbal communication are used to complete work and engage in sexual misconduct. Oftentimes, victims of sexual harassment encounter use of words or language as acts of coercion or aggression.

In 1980, the Equal Employment Opportunity Commission (EEOC) added sexual harassment as a form of sex discrimination in the workplace, violating Title VII of the Civil Rights Act of 1964, which forbid employers from discriminating based on race, color, religion, sex, or national origin. This legal requirement focuses on whether the rejection of unwelcome behavior explicitly or implicitly affects an individual's employment, unreasonably interferes with someone's work performance, or creates an intimidating, hostile, or offensive work environment (EEOC, 2002). In 1993, in *Harris v. Forklift Inc.*, the Supreme Court decided in addition to what the victim deemed abusive, if a "reasonable person" would perceive behaviors as sexual harassment, then an employer should be held accountable. Throughout the 1990s, employers adopted sexual harassment policies (Dobbin & Kelly, 2007). These policies admonish perpetrators of unwanted sexual or sexist attention in virtually any location. The number of sexual harassment charges filed with the EEOC and state and local Fair Employment Practices agencies between 1994 and 2005 averaged slightly over 14,000 annually, with monetary resolutions averaging $38 million (EEOC, 2006). Sex discrimination and sexual violence are variations of sexual misconduct that remain a critical health concern. Sexual violence is also known as sexual assault or rape, and it occurs without explicit consent of the recipient (Office of Violence Against Women, 2021). Sexual assault or rape involve unwanted or nonconsensual touching, kissing, sexual contact, or sexual intercourse, including while incapacitated (Brown, 2018). The conceptualization for sexual assault explicates the relationship between agency in the perpetration of these acts and being pressured or forced to have sexual contact (George et al., 1992; Kelly et al., 1996). Victimization usually involves a perpetrator known by the victim, such as a current or former intimate partner or acquaintance (Black et al., 2011). Sexual assault occurs frequently in the U.S., yet few cases are reported for fear of stigmatization.

Who Decided Labels Matter?

Communication scholars focus less on psychological and behavioral conceptualizations of sexual harassment and more on the language of sexual harassment. To foreground victim experiences with the language of sexual harassment, a discursive examination focuses on narrative reports of sexual harassment, giving voice to victims, merging their personal narratives within societal and organizational history (Clair, 1993, 1994). Personal narratives are generalized, first-person, and retroactive accounts give voice to victims' experiences. When there is a pattern of experiences among victims within a workplace setting or industry, personal narratives contribute to a grand narrative about a culture of victimization. The culture of victimization enables a hostile environment to take hold, which ensnares many unsuspecting victims. To cope with the hostile environment, many victims seek support.

One way for victims to make sense of their experiences is to compare their traumatic experiences with other individuals. Initially, many women may not believe they have been victimized, especially if the "politically correct" labels used in society do not reflect their experiences with sexual misconduct. Women who speak up may find it difficult to articulate their experiences with sexual misconduct, which Clair (1993) characterized as denotative hesitancy. In addition to this dissonance, using words such as survivor instead of victim or sexual assault instead of rape can create uncertainty regarding how to describe one's experiences to others. Sometimes there is a hesitancy to tell family and friends about nonconsensual sex or to participate in counseling, which leaves many victims without a space to advance a nuanced vocabulary regarding their experiences (Harris, 2011), the aftermath being the imposition of patriarchal norms upon women's experiences. Beliefs and norms vary across regions of the world. However, in many cultures, they are more restrictive of what women do, especially during interactions perceived as flirtatious or sexual. In some countries, there is palpable fear that revealing information about sexual activity to others will adversely impact a women's familial and cultural standing in society.

Myths in these regions emphasize the male gaze, framing encounters from a man's perspective, and shifting the responsibility for flirtatious or sexual encounters to women if something goes wrong. Who is responsible when men in South Africa suffering from AIDS rape virgin girls to be "cured?" Who is to blame in India when women who are sexually harassed or assaulted are victim-shamed, because they were perceived as displaying their bodies and indulging in obscene activities? Does the woman or the violator deserve support in the United States, when there is a myth that women ask to be raped if they exhibit certain behavior such as wearing revealing clothing, walking alone at night, or engaging in intimate behavior? These questions are posed and critically analyzed in "A Critique of Causes and Measures of Rape: A Systematic Review of Literature" (2018), where the researchers examine the cumulative effects of patriarchy and hegemony on women throughout the world. An outcome of hegemonic, patriarchal cultures in many societies is the emergence of a culture of rape (Berkowitz, 1994; Capraro, 1994), which is used as an instrument to subjugate women (Brownmiller, 1975). In response to these myths, many women succumb to pressure, coercion, or force, and submit to men. Without narratives to challenge the status quo, nothing changes. Celebrities who have experienced sexual misconduct, who are willing to share with the public what happened, are in a position to challenge the status quo. Celebrity narratives resonate with fans, the media, and society at large, so how celebrities behave when they encounter sexual misconduct sets an example for other women.

Celebrity narratives regarding sexual harassment or sexual assault can be helpful to these women, because the information provided by these celebrities could mitigate uncertainty about how to describe feelings or trauma. Over the last few years, female celebrity narratives highlighted the need to examine how women come to claim certain labels over others, including whether a lecher is called a perpetrator, abuser, or rapist, or the act is referred to as having sex, forced intercourse, or sexual assault, and if women experiencing the trauma self-identify as victims, survivors, or both. Furthermore, celebrity narratives could help women who experience sexual misconduct share stories outside normative restrictions, considering "...societal discourses will help determine how she understands and speaks about experience" (Koelsch, 2014, p. 14). Within the context of sexual assault, the power of naming and giving meaning to words is empowering, and in a supportive environment, women who have encountered problematic sexual episodes can determine if they label themselves as victims or survivors (Averill & Nunley, 1992; Carosella, 1995; Young & Macquire, 2003). When celebrity and non-celebrity victims or survivors use their voices, their stories resonate with other women. They create agency for themselves and reclaim control. The underlying message in these narratives is that together women can empower one another and make their own choices.

These narratives affect the men in women's lives. Men and women define sexual harassment differently, and men struggle to define what behavior crosses the line between flirtation or rudeness and sexual harassment. When men are uncertain about how to respond in these circumstances or are unsure about what to do when they learn that the women in their lives are dealing with sexual misconduct, their lack of comprehension often results in a failure to respond (Leung, 2017). Celebrity narratives of victims and survivors of sexual harassment and sexual assault can inform men and move men off the sidelines regarding these issues. Kelley and Thibaut (1978) suggest that individuals in relationships are outcome interdependent, and that relational partners should be concerned with the well-being of each other. In these relationships, women are a source of positive outcomes for men, and men should realize that whatever potentially threatens the women in their lives indirectly threatens the rewards the men experience. Women need to feel comfortable sharing stories about their experiences with sexual misconduct with the men in their lives. Otherwise, these men cannot provide them with adequate support. "If worrying about the safety of a partner becomes too 'costly' in terms of the cost/rewards ratio … then one person should be motivated to talk with the other to ensure their safety" (Morrison, 2005, p. 252). Women also need to provide support to boys and men in their lives who experience sexual misconduct, especially since they may not seek counseling because of the stigma associated with being harassed or assaulted by a female perpetrator. According to the book *A Review of the Literature on Sexual Assault Perpetrator Characteristics and Behaviors* (2015), there are too few studies that examine female sexual assault perpetrators: "there is currently little consensus on the characteristics or behaviors of female sexual assault perpetrators, especially those that offend against other adults" (p. 40–41).

Framing and Sexual Misconduct

Sexual misconduct is perceived differently depending on an individual's gender. Perception is affected by cultural beliefs, values, and norms. Culture contributes to the psychological frames that exclude certain messages and include others. According to Bateson (1972), a psychological frame delimits messages or meaningful actions and affects the evaluation of a message. Moreover, whatever is included inside the frame is interpreted differently than whatever is outside of it. Men's and women's perceptions of their experiences with sexual misconduct are impacted by male-dominated framing of flirtation, touching, and sexual interactions in many regions of the world. Male-dominated societies tend to marginalize women's experiences with sexual harassment and sexual assault. Sexual misconduct is socioculturally constructed, and perceptions of sexual discrimination and sexual assault are mediated by a variety of factors, including gender power equations, moral values, and attitudes toward violence. In many industries in the U.S., women are excluded from positions of power. This exclusion makes some industries more susceptible to a sexual harassment and rape-prone culture. These cultures make it easier to restrict women's freedom and increase the prevalence of their objectification. When these cultures have rigid sex-role systems, they show higher sexual violence (Kalra & Bhugra, 2013). The MeToo hashtag started in the U.S. and became a global phenomenon because women in every region throughout the world confront male-dominated framing, marginalization, and sexual misconduct in their personal lives, at work, offline, and online. The *Scandinavian Journal of Primary Health Care* (2018) recognizes how female professionals including actresses, politicians, scientists, artists, and doctors are coming forward via SNS and offline to share their stories. Reporting in *Times Magazine* (2018) indicates that in China, South Korea, India, and beyond, the #MeToo movement has galvanized women's rights activists and survivors, and ordinary citizens are initiating grassroots efforts, such as #BabaeAko (I Am a Woman) in the Philippines, #WithYou in Japan, and #DontTellMe-HowToDress in Thailand.

In the U.S., within the timeframe of the #NotOkay and #MeToo movements, between 2017 and 2018, shareholders of Signet Jewelers, 21st Century Fox, Liberty Tax, Wynn Resorts, National Beverage Corp., CBS, Papa John's, and Nike sued corporate directors and officers related to reported sexual misconduct at those companies (Hemel & Lund, 2018). In corporate America, men in power often "control access to a woman's future—and to her physical, psychological, spiritual, economic and intellectual well-being" (Rutter, 1989, p. 23). Women trust these men and perceive them as mentors, supervisors, bosses, colleagues, or friends. Female employees or subordinates rely on verbal and nonverbal communication between themselves and their employers or supervisors to build rapport and professional relationships. Perpetrators use the same communication as a conduit through which sexual harassment is expressed (Keyton & Menzie, 2007). Being the recipient of inappropriate verbal or nonverbal communication destroys trust built over time. Sexual harassment and sexual assault within institutions also undermines morale, in part by eroding trust.

Shareholders examining their companies are suing corporate fiduciaries that engage in sexual misconduct because of the perceived effects on organizational morale, productivity, value, and compliance with the law. The article "Sexual Harassment and Corporate Law," which was published in the *Columbia Law Review*, specifies the conditions under which shareholders hold corporate fiduciaries accountable including: shareholders of Signet Jewelers took action against its then CEO for misleading investors about a culture of sexual harassment; after the departures of Fox News CEO Roger Ailes and broadcaster Bill O'Reilly, shareholders filed a derivative action against Ailes's estate and the directors of what was Fox News's parent company 21st Century Fox; the Philadelphia-based pension fund filed a derivative lawsuit against Liberty Tax because its former CEO, John Hewitt, was revealed in news reports to have used company resources to fund his romantic liaisons; news reports also got the former Wynn Resorts CEO Steve Wynn in trouble for a purported decades-long pattern of sexual harassment; shareholders sued National Beverage Corp. for alleged false and misleading statements they believed concealed CEO Nick Caporella's sexual harassment of pilots on a corporate jet; as well as shareholder lawsuits against the then CEOs of CBS and Papa John's; additionally, Nike shareholders sued in Oregon state court alleging a "boys' club culture" that contributed to bullying, sexual harassment, and gender discrimination of female employees.

Corporate America is not unique, with sexual misconduct scandals rocking the U.S. military and Congress. Rates of military sexual assault (MSA) are alarmingly high, even though MSA is underreported and underestimated (GAO, 2008). Barriers to reporting MSA include fears of confidentiality breaches or retaliation, shame, being denied clearances, betraying one's group, being negatively judged by peers and superiors, and being revictimized (U.S. Air Force, 2004). Barriers to reporting in Congress include that for most of its history, it had exempted itself and its legislative branch employees from workplace discrimination laws (Congressional Research Service, 2018). The Congressional Accountability Act of 1995 (CAA) changed the legal landscape by extending antidiscrimination laws to the legislative branch. The CAA did not prevent the perception of wrongdoing since "criticism has been raised about the CAA's allowance for confidential settlements with victims, payments for those settlements with taxpayer funds, and the CAA's provision for mandatory counseling and mediation in response to a complaint" (Congressional Research Service, 2018, p. 2). A year after the #MeToo movement went viral, the Politico (2018) headline "Congress reaches deal to curb sexual harassment on Capitol Hill" addressed bipartisan reforms to overhaul the broken process for addressing sexual harassment complaints. Many pundits and media users found it disturbing that these changes only happened after a series of sexual misconduct scandals created a PR nightmare for Congress.

Celebrities Embrace #MeToo and #TimesUp

During the 2018 Golden Globe Awards ceremony, celebrities shocked the public by bringing activists as their guests. Many well-known and respected actresses brought supporters of the Time's Up initiative. Laura Dern, Amy Poehler, Susan Sarandon, Meryl Streep, Emma Stone, Emma Watson, Michelle Williams, and others used the red carpet and the awards show to provide their guests with international media coverage to address the necessity for fair treatment of women in entertainment, other industries, and society at large (McGirt, 2018). When reporters sought Michelle Williams for commentary, she was eager to shift attention from herself to her guest, Tarana Burke, the founder of the #MeToo movement and senior director of Girls for Gender Equity. Burke posted a joint statement from activists about their participation in the event. It read, in part (McGirt, 2018, p. 2):

> Too much of the recent press has been focused on perpetrators and does not adequately address the systemic nature of violence including the importance of race, ethnicity and economic status in sexual violence and other forms of violence against women. Our goal in attending the Golden Globes is to shift the focus back to survivors and on systemic lasting solutions.

The other highlight of the award ceremony was Oprah Winfrey, the first African American woman to win the Cecil B. DeMille Award. Oprah was thrilled to win the award, and she used her acceptance speech to address the theme of the evening, #TimesUp (Zurawik, 2018). She stated:

> So I want all the girls watching here, now, to know that a new day is on the horizon! And when that new day finally dawns, it will be because of a lot of magnificent women, many of whom are right here in this room tonight, and some pretty phenomenal men, fighting hard to make sure that they become the leaders who take us to the time when nobody ever has to say "Me too" again.

She continued, "For too long women have not been heard or believed if they dare speak the truth to the power of those men. But their time is up. Their time is up." Rewind to the year before Oprah's DeMille Award speech: in October 2017, *New York Times* journalists Jodi Kantor and Megan Twohey revealed multiple allegations of sexual harassment against Harvey Weinstein. Outcomes of the article included the resignations of four members of the all-male board at Weinstein Company and the firing of Weinstein. In a separate 10-month investigation led by Ronan Farrow, which corroborated the findings of the *Times* report, Farrow was told by 13 women that between the 1990s and 2015 Weinstein sexually harassed or assaulted them (Farrow, 2017a). Hollywood is still grappling with the fallout of the Weinstein allegations.

Weinstein cofounded the production-and-distribution companies Miramax and the Weinstein Company. He helped reinvigorate independent film production and distribution with films like *The King's Speech*, *The Crying Game*, *Pulp Fiction*, *The English Patient*, *Shakespeare in Love*, and *Sex, Lies, and Videotape*. He facilitated the convergence of promising scripts, directors, and actors, with his films garnering more than 300 Oscar nominations. During awards season, he was thanked by countless people, ranking just after Steven Spielberg and right before God (Farrow, 2017a). Beyond the adulation, many people in the industry were fearful of him. Why? Despite the allure of working on a Weinstein project in Hollywood, some actresses had horrible experiences with Weinstein. Once allegations surfaced in the media pertaining to sexual harassment and sexual assault, these women had to make gut-wrenching decisions about sharing their stories with their peers, their industry, and the public.

Lupita Nyong'o first met Weinstein in 2011 while attending Yale Drama School. She was aware of his reputation as a bully, and she had her own experience with him, but she remained silent. She acknowledged "joining in the conspiracy of silence that has allowed this predator to prowl for so many years" (Abrams, 2017). The Academy Award winner and star of *Black Panther*, continued, "I have felt such a flare of rage that the experience I recount below was not a unique incident with me, but rather part of a sinister pattern of behavior." One of her incidents with him happened at a dinner with Weinstein in a private hotel room: "He told me not to be naïve. If I wanted to be an actress, then I had to be willing to do this sort of thing." When she expressed no interest in his advances, he became cold and threatened her (Abrams, 2017). Nyong'o wants women to speak out about their experiences with predators, so they can "regain that power." In a 2018 interview with Howard Stern, Gwyneth Paltrow said that Weinstein sexually harassed her in a hotel room in 1995, asking her to give him a massage (Desta, 2018). Although Weinstein would later deny the allegation, Paltrow—an Academy Award winner and the star of *Iron Man*—insisted that she told then boyfriend Brad Pitt about the incident: "I told [Pitt] right away and I was very shaken by the whole thing." Pitt decided to confront Weinstein when all three were attending the opening of *Hamlet* on Broadway. Paltrow was thankful for Pitt's intervention, where he did the "...equivalent of throwing him against the wall, energetically," Paltrow recalled. She continued, "It was so fantastic. He leveraged his fame and power to protect me at a time when I didn't have fame or power yet. He said, 'If you ever make her feel uncomfortable again, I'll kill you,' or something like that." In his 2017 exposé in *The New Yorker* addressing allegations about Weinstein, Ronan Farrow stated that women struggled with whether to speak publicly, and that advice from friends, loved ones, and colleagues was a deciding factor.

Rosie Perez urged friend Annabella Sciorra to self-disclose to the public her own experience with sexual assault. Perez remembers, "I told her, 'I used to tread water for years. It's fucking exhausting, and maybe speaking out, that's your lifeboat. Grab on and get out.'" Perez recalled, "I said, 'Honey, the water never goes away. But after I went public, it became a puddle and I built a bridge over it, and one day you're gonna get there, too.'" Sciorra, who received an Emmy nomination for her role in *The Sopranos*, listened to her friend, and agreed to share her story during a phone conversation with Farrow. Farrow (2017) stated:

> Sciorra called me. The truth, she said, was that she had been struggling to speak about Weinstein for more than twenty years. She was still living in fear of him, and slept with a baseball bat by her bed. Weinstein, she told me, had violently raped her in the early 1990s, and over the next several years, sexually harassed her repeatedly.

The notoriety associated with making public allegations against Weinstein was alarming to Sciorra. She recognized that "going public" was a life-altering experience that marked her as a sexual assault victim. "Now when I go to a restaurant or to an event, people are going to know that this happened," she said. "They're gonna look at me and they're gonna know. I'm an intensely private person, and this is the most unprivate thing you can do." Actress Daryl Hannah can empathize with Sciorra; she also experienced trauma because of Weinstein, and she decided to speak out and add her voice to the public outcry.

Hannah explained, "You get dragged into the gutter of nastiness and pettiness and shame and all of these things, and it sometimes seems healthier and wiser to just move on with your life and not allow yourself to be re-victimized." Weinstein is a man whose behavior made Hannah feel unsafe, who in one moment asked her if he could touch her breasts, and in other moments made her feel cornered and desperate. Hannah recounts instances where Weinstein pounded on her hotel room door, and she escaped out a back entrance. She also barricaded herself in her room using furniture (Farrow, 2017b). Weinstein reacted to the public outcry by issuing denials. Weinstein or a spokesperson issued an absolute denial or statement, such as this one (Farrow, 2017a): "Any allegations of non-consensual sex are unequivocally denied by Mr. Weinstein. Mr. Weinstein has further confirmed that there were never any acts of retaliation against any women for refusing his advances." Weinstein had a chance to address the allegations and public outcry in court. His accusers were floored when he surrendered to authorities in New York. In response to the scene, Rose McGowan, Weinstein's most vociferous critic, told journalist Megyn Kelly, "I can say this, the man who pinned me down had handcuffs on him today."

McGowan was one of more than 80 women to go public with allegations of sexual misconduct against Weinstein, and Weinstein would be charged with first- and third-degree rape and committing a criminal sexual act in the first degree from incidents with two separate women (Stelter, 2018). Weinstein reached a settlement with McGowan when she was 23 years old, after "an episode in a hotel room" during a film festival (Townsend, 2017). In 1997, McGowan had reached a $100,000 settlement with Weinstein, but that agreement did not include a confidentiality clause (Dominus, 2017). Apparently, with *The New Yorker* investigation looming, someone close to Weinstein reached out to a lawyer for McGowan to offer her hush money in exchange for signing a nondisclosure agreement (Dominus, 2017). No agreement was signed, and McGowan would continue to use her sizeable platform on Twitter to speak out against sexism within the entertainment industry. McGowan asserted, "They blame the victim, they do all that shit. People are bred to be scared. They are bred to put fear into people and that's what they do, they're bred to put fear into the publishers and lawyers and they overreach it, and I'm going to do what I can and come out as hard as I can."

A grand jury in New York indicted Weinstein on charges of rape and criminal sex. Perhaps Weinstein's downfall will allow victims to heal. Some of them lost their careers or had their careers severely damaged because they refused Weinstein's advances. Rosanna Arquette, best known for her roles in *Pulp Fiction* and *Desperately Seeking Susan*, told NPR's Mary Louise Kelly that she believes Weinstein may have been responsible for sabotaging her career. Why? "Arquette says she rejected Weinstein at the Beverly Hills Hotel in the early 1990s, when she went there to pick up a script and have dinner with him. She says that he came to the door in a white bathrobe, asking for a massage, and that he grabbed her hand and tried to force her to touch his erect penis. She says that she jerked her hand away and said 'No,' and that he told her she was 'making a very big mistake'" (Edes & Kelly, 2018). Arquette said, "You have the most powerful businesspeople in the world protecting [Weinstein] for years." She continued, "Roles started to disappear, and new opportunities didn't seem to come." She believes Weinstein has had her and other women spied on (Wagmeister, 2019). She does not have an agent and believes she is still blackballed in the industry. Arquette is the highest-profile actress to appear in the Weinstein documentary, *Untouchable*, which involves former colleagues and victims discussing Weinstein's rise and fall (Wagmeister, 2019). Arquette is not shy about sharing her thoughts on the industry, insisting, "There's a lot of people that made a lot of money from him, and continue to. There's a boys club that protects the boys. He's just one of many men, as we're seeing more and more men being exposed for their awful behavior and their abuse of power." In exasperation, she continued, "There are a lot more women, and a lot of lives and careers have been destroyed."

In 1996, 28-year-old Mira Sorvino won an Academy Award for her breakout role in *Mighty Aphrodite*. A few years later, people noticed her absence in Hollywood. Where had she gone? Sorvino attributed Weinstein as a factor when she stated, "…I definitely felt iced out and that my rejection of Harvey had something to do with it." She affirmed that Weinstein sexually harassed her and tried to coerce her into a physical relationship (Arkin, 2017). Director Peter Jackson confirmed long-running rumors that Weinstein steered him away from casting Sorvino and actress Ashley Judd in the *Lord of the Rings* franchise (Arkin, 2017). Jackson stated, "At the time, we had no reason to question what these guys were telling us. But in hindsight, I realize that this was very likely the Miramax smear campaign in full swing." Sorvino reacted to Jackson's comments on Twitter: "Just seeing this after I awoke, I burst out crying. There it is, confirmation that Harvey Weinstein derailed my career, something I suspected but was unsure. Thank you Peter Jackson for being honest. I'm just heartsick." Alyssa Rosenberg, a culture columnist for *The Washington Post*, addressed how actresses were blackballed: "I think it's important for people to remember that Hollywood is a project-based industry." She elaborated, "If someone can stop you from getting work for a year or two years, you can fall out of the industry entirely. You're sort of always interviewing for [for work]." In 2017, in an in-depth article in *Time*, Sorvino wrote about her experience and the experiences of many women. She demanded:

> It is time for the culture to shift—the age-old tradition of the monied and powerful imposing themselves sexually on the vulnerable and the weak. The Droit du Seigneur must end. And it must end now. This is not a partisan issue. It is not relegated to Hollywood, or red or blue states. Almost every woman I know has some harrowing tale of harassment or sexual assault, and almost every one of them has not gone public for a variety of reasons, including shame and fear.
>
> I am here to encourage a mass speaking-out. The atmosphere of impunity for predators who see it as their right to create climates of sexual intimidation, workplaces, campuses or even homes which are not meritocracies but transactional spaces where in order to keep one's job or wellbeing one must somehow endure or comply with these unlawful advances, must be shut down. Victim-shaming must be quelled, and the real evildoers called out and punished to the fullest extent of the law.

In 2015, as part of Variety's "Power of Women" issue, Ashley Judd shared a story she'd never revealed to the public about being sexually harassed by a mogul from a rival studio. Judd explained what transpired: "He was stealth and expert about it. He groomed me, which is a technical term…." He suggested that she meet him at his hotel for something to eat. When she arrived, he lured her into his room, asking her to help him pick out what he would wear. Judd acknowledged the bargaining that followed: his remarks were come do this or that, which she responded to with "no, no, no." Banter would ensue. Judd wanted out of the room without falling prey to his advances. She got out but was never offered a movie from his studio. Judd understood, "When I kept saying no to everything, there was a huge asymmetry of power and control in that room." In 2017, Judd revealed in a television interview with Diane Sawyer that Weinstein was the mogul from the rival studio. In an interview with *BBC Hardtalk*'s Stephen Sackur (2018), Judd stated, "He has not denied that he harassed me. And in fact, he has apologized for it. In my particular example, what he said, and this is a direct quote, 'he didn't land a glove on me,' and he didn't because as you noticed, I was able to flee the room, but he absolutely harassed me, he abused his power, and he lorded it over me, this imbalance between us, um with with vitriol and abuse of charm for two years." Judd talked with her parents about naming Weinstein, and she mentioned that her mother, singer Naomi Judd, told her to "go get him." By sharing her story in interviews and on social media, Judd contributed to the #MeToo movement and helped liberate herself and other women from the toxic shame that perpetrators put onto their victims (Effron, 2017). In the aftermath, Weinstein was expelled by the Academy of Motion Picture Arts and Sciences.

In April 2018, Judd sued Weinstein, insisting that his behavior harmed her career. Director Peter Jackson's recollection that false information provided by Weinstein led to Judd being removed from a casting list for the *Lord of the Rings* franchise confirmed for Judd that "something unseen was holding her back from obtaining the work she wanted, and had been doing so for decades." In a tweet, Judd thanked Jackson for coming forward and revealing what really happened: "Peter & Fran had me in—showed me all the creative, the boards, costumes, everything. They asked which of the two roles I preferred, and then I abruptly never heard from them again. I appreciate the truth coming out. Thank you, Peter." Judd's lawsuit, if victorious, could clarify sexual harassment protections for those in nontraditional business relationships. While Judd was not Weinstein's employee, she claims that she had a continuing business relationship with him, because she had already been cast in his film *Smoke* and was summoned to his hotel room to discuss roles in additional projects (Barnes, 2018). Furthermore, Judd is suing Weinstein for defamation and sexual harassment and for violating California's Unfair Competition law.

In *Town and Country Magazine* (2018), Salma Hayek interviewed Judd about the Weinstein allegations and revealed that she, too, had evaded his advances. In an op-ed piece in *The New York Times*, Hayek expounded upon her experience with Weinstein:

I don't think he hated anything more than the word "no." The absurdity of his demands went from getting a furious call in the middle of the night asking me to fire my agent for a fight he was having with him about a different movie with a different client to physically dragging me out of the opening gala of the Venice Film Festival, which was in honor of *Frida,* so I could hang out at his private party with him and some women I thought were models but I was told later were high-priced prostitutes. The range of his persuasion tactics went from sweet-talking me to that one time when, in an attack of fury, he said the terrifying words, "I will kill you, don't think I can't." When he was finally convinced that I was not going to earn the movie the way he expected, he told me he had offered my role and my script with my years of research to another actress. In his eyes, I was not an artist. I wasn't even a person. I was a thing: not a nobody, but a body.

Weinstein's lawyers issued a denial of Hayek's allegations: "All of the sexual allegations as portrayed by Salma are not accurate and others who witnessed the events have a different account of what transpired" (Oldham, 2018). Hayek took notice that Weinstein through surrogates disavowed the recounting of events by herself and Nyong'o, another woman of color. In response, Hayek asserted, "We are the easiest to get discredited." She continued, "It is a well-known fact. So he went back, attacking the two women of color, in hopes that if he could discredit us."

Eventually, Weinstein issued an apology to Hayek, which read: "Mr. Weinstein deeply apologizes to Ms. Hayek for any pain she has suffered as a result of his behavior or comments. Mr. Weinstein apologizes for his boorish behavior" (OWN, 2018). In 2018, Oprah Winfrey and Hayek discussed the statement over the phone after *Oprah's SuperSoul Conversations* at the Apollo Theater (OWN, 2018). Hayek told Winfrey that she accepted Weinstein's apology. Later in the conversation, Hayek mused, "Because, maybe if it was not for Harvey, all of these centuries of acceptance of this sexual harassment for women in the workplace wouldn't of come to the light and be examined like it is today." Winfrey responded, "Well, yes, had the fallout and the scandal in all of this." Some critics are concerned #MeToo and #TimesUp have swung the pendulum too far in the other direction. On *Good Morning America,* McGowan acknowledged that some members of the public are "sick of" hearing about allegations of abuse (Stelter, 2018). Her message for them is unapologetic: "Imagine how tired we are. Imagine how tired we are of it."

Role of Social Networks in Combating Sexual Misconduct

The most impactful social network impacting sexual misconduct in many societies is sexual misconduct prevention and education experts in government agencies and NGOs. International and national entities must engage stakeholders, who play a role in communities, families, and interpersonal and civic outreach. For instance, in the U.S., the CDC works to advance the primary prevention of sexual violence, to prevent violence before it begins. The CDC uses its Rape Prevention and Education Program (RPE) to fund grantees engaged in a range of activities that are culturally relevant and based on evidence. RPE grantees collect and analyze information in communities to make timely, data-driven decisions, such as implementing prevention strategies, engaging bystanders, educating youth, operating hotlines, working with state and local officials, and collaborating with partners to assess state and local organizations' evaluation capacity. The CDC is located within U.S. Department of Health and Human Services (HSS), which demonstrated it has a vested interest in combating sexual violence in 2011, when Challenge.gov hosted an online "Apps Against Abuse" competition collaboratively sponsored with the Office of Science and Technology Policy and the Office of the Vice President (Beaton, 2015). More than 30 apps were submitted. The European Union also infused technology into its prevention of sexual misconduct with the successful communication of an antiviolence policy on Twitter with the #SayNoStopVAW (Trillo, 2017). These experts work tirelessly to create and deploy preventive efforts, interventions, and outreach to civilians. The interconnected nodes or access points to care and support extend beyond the HHS, CDC, and their counterparts domestically and internationally.

Social networks ranging from family and friends to healthcare professionals, law enforcement, and judicial officers, as well as leadership in corporate suites, shareholders, and regulators, are essential to any comprehensive effort to mitigate sexual misconduct. These social networks affect the mental health and distress levels of victims and survivors (Campbell et al., 2009). They address a convergence of needs, including safety and protection, emotional needs (e.g., support, understanding, not being blamed), and medical triage and healthcare (Shahali et al., 2016). Specifically, family and friends provide advice and guidance to victims, who must make important decisions regarding whether to report sexual misconduct to employers, police, and doctors. Family and friends are among the individuals who are victims' first line of defense against the societal taboo or social stigma associated with sexual assault or rape prevalent in many societies and cultures (Lievore, 2005). When an individual survives the ordeal of sexual violence, immediate medical and law enforcement help are necessary.

The WHO (2003) provides these frontline workers with guidelines to improve professional health services for individuals (women, men, and children) who have been victimized by sexual violence. The WHO provides knowledge and skills for the management of victims, standards for the provision of care and forensic services to victims, and guidance on establishing or enhancing health and forensic services to victims. Police officers' responsiveness to sexual violence victims and survivors helps reduce secondary victimization. "Law enforcement officials, typically trained to get just the facts, can benefit from conducting interviews more slowly, doing more listening than talking, and recognizing that women facing the paradoxical situation of acquaintance rape may require more patience, more empathy, and more proactive listening during the interview process" (French, 2003, p. 315). When law enforcement determines that cyber harassment happens online, collaboration with social networking providers is necessary. The providers first evaluate content to ascertain if it violates their community standards, and if it does, delete violating content, sanction the harasser (e.g., providing a warning, suspending/blocking the account), or contacting and assisting law enforcement to stop cyber harassment (Chesney et al., 2009; Crawford & Gillespie, 2014; Perren, et al., 2012). Employers can take action to mitigate sexual harassment. Employers with governing boards and shareholders should empower them to be proactive and take corrective action when necessary. Boards should talk about any reported incidents of sexual harassment, examine their organizations' or industries' past responses to sexual harassment, demanding that management implement mandatory harassment training for workers at all levels, review procedures for handling complaints, ensure policies specify meaningful consequences for sexual harassment, and prioritize gender diversity and equity to counteract the pervasiveness of sexual harassment at work (Hemel & Lund, 2018). In the #MeToo era, shareholders are being more proactive in holding companies accountable for sexual harassment at work, and they are not afraid to pursue financial and legal recourse to emphasize that senior leadership should take sexual harassment seriously.

Every industry should work collaboratively with the public and private sectors to improve accountability for the development or lack thereof of preventive sexual misconduct and secondary victimization strategies. Despite the efforts of #MeToo and #TimesUp, some industries have a protracted problem with sexual misconduct, such as the U.S. military, but they cannot give up (Committee on Oversight and Government Reform, 2008; Merrill et al. 1998, 2001). Celebrated actresses were victimized in their industry like so many Americans. They joined the movements to say "me too" and "times up," and they directed their collective outrage toward the entertainment industry, which needs to make more progress before actresses believe sexual harassment and sexual assault are things of the past. Even when headlines about Weinstein and the allegations fade from the headlines, these movements to combat sexual misconduct will be judged by how effective they were in galvanizing reforms. These reforms are taking hold within and across industries in the U.S. and abroad.

Outside Hollywood, the global entertainment industry felt the shock-waves of these movements and in some instances more easily attained a more equitable workplace than their American counterpart. *Metro Magazine* (2018) highlights how Screen Australia's new *Code of Conduct to Assist the Prevention of Sexual Harassment* enforces the laws against sexual harassment and makes funding directly conditional on com-pliance: "it's the equivalent of posting giant neon billboards at every corner and threatening massive fines" (p. 116). Screen Australia joined forces with Screen Producers Australia and the Media, Entertainment & Arts Alliance to refine and restate procedures and efforts to prevent sex-ual harassment in the Australian entertainment industry (Siemienowicz, 2018). Change is coming within the entertainment industry, but what change looks like will vary because of cultural and societal differences in countries across the world. Perhaps what works in one place or in a specific industry will not be effective in another, so activists need to be flexible in order for reforms to take hold and mitigate sexual misconduct. Whatever happens, #MeToo and #TimesUp have inspired an uprising. The status quo must change.

REFERENCES

Abrams, A. (2017, October 20). "He told me not to be so naïve": Lupita Nyong'o says Harvey Weinstein sexually harassed her. *Time Magazine.* https://time.com/4990561/lupita-nyongo-harvey-weinstein-sexual-harassment/.

Arkin, D. (2017, December 15). *Peter Jackson seems to confirm Weinstein blacklisted Mira Sorvino, Ashley Judd.* NBC News. https://www.nbcnews.com/storyline/sexual-misconduct/peter-jackson-seems-confirm-harvey-weinstein-blacklisted-mira-sorvino-ashley-n830166.

Ashley Judd [@AshleyJudd]. (2017, December 15). *Peter & Fran had me in—showed me all the creative, the boards, costumes, everything. They asked which if the two roles I preferred, and then I abruptly never heard from hem again.* [Tweet]. Twitter. https://twitter.com/ashleyjudd/status/941768323812995077?lang=en.

Averill, J.R., & Nunley, E.P. (1992). *Voyages of the heart: Living an emotionally creative life.* The Free Press.

Back, C.J., & Freeman, W.C. (2018, February 7). *Addressing sexual harassment by modifying the congressional accountability act of 1995: A look at key provisions in H.R. 4924.* Congressional Research Service. https://www.everycrsreport.com/reports/LSB10067.html.

Barak, A. (2005). Sexual harassment on the internet. *Social Science Computer Review, 23(1),* 77–92. https://doi.org/10.1177/0894439304271540.

Barnes, B. (2018, April 30). Ashley Judd sues Harvye Weinstein, saying he harmed her career. *New York Times.* https://www.nytimes.com/2018/04/30/business/media/ashley-judd-harvey-weinstein-lawsuit.html.

Bateson, G. (1972). *Steps to an ecology of mind.* Ballantine.

Beaton, B. (2015). Safety as net work: "Apps against abuse" and the digital labor of sexual assault prevention. *Media Tropes e Journal, 5(1),* 105–124. file:///C:/Users/truma/Downloads/22127-Article%20Text-53406-1-10-20141104%20(1).pdf.

Berkowitz, A.D. (1994). Introduction. In A. Berkowitz (Ed.), *Men and rape: Theory, research, and prevention programs in higher education* (pp. 1–2). Jossey-Bass.

Black, M.C., Basile, K.C., Breiding, M.J., Smith, S.G., Walters, M.L., Merrick, M.T., Chen, J., & Stevens, M.R. (2011). *The national intimate partner and sexual violence survey (NISVS): 2010 summary report*. National Center for Injury Prevention and Control, Centers for Disease Control and Prevention. https://www.cdc.gov/violenceprevention/pdf/nisvs_report2010-a.pdf.

Brown, T. (2018). Literacy narrative: Ways to write #MeToo. *Composition Studies 46(2)*, 189–91.

Brownmiller, S. (1975). *Against our will: Men, women and rape*. Simon & Schuster.

Burkhart, B.R., Bourg, S.E., & Berkowitz, A.D. (1994). Research on men and rape: Methodological problems and future directions. In A. Berkowitz (Ed.), *Men and rape: Theory, research, and prevention programs in higher education* (pp. 67–72). Jossey-Bass.

Campbell, R., Dworkin, E., & Cabral, G. (2009). An ecological model of the impact of sexual assault on women's mental health. *Trauma, violence & abuse, 10(3)*, 225–246. https://doi.org/10.1177/1524838009334456.

Capraro, R.L. (1994). Disconnected lives: Men, masculinity, and rape prevention. *New Directions for Student Services, 1994(65)*, 21–33. https://doi.org/10.1002/ss.37119946504.

Carosella, C. (1995). *Who's afraid of the dark? A forum of truth, support, and assurance for those affected by rape*. HarperCollins.

Chesney, T., Coyne, I., Logan, B., & Madden, N. (2009). Griefing in virtual worlds: Causes, casualties and coping strategies. *Information Systems Journal, 19*, 525–548. https://doi.org/10.1111/j.1365-2575.2009.00330.x.

Clair, R. (1993). The use of framing devices to sequester organizational narratives: Hegemony and harassment. *Communication Monographs, 60(2)*, 113–136. https://doi.org/10.1080/03637759309376304.

Clair, R.P. (1994). Resistance and oppression as a self-contained opposite: An organizational communication analysis of one man's story of sexual harassment. *Western Journal of Communication, 58*(4), 235–262. https://doi.org/10.1080/10570319409374499.

Committee on Oversight and Government Reform (2008, April). *Letter from Henry Waxman to the Honorable David Chu*. 110th Congress of the United States, House of Representatives. file:///C:/Users/truma/Downloads/485463.pdf.

Cooper, K. (1985). *Stop it now: How targets and managers can end sexual harassment*. Total Communication.

Crawford, K., & Gillespie, T. (2016). What is a flag for? Social media reporting tools and the vocabulary of complaint. *New Media & Society, 18(3)*, 410–428. https://doi.org/10.1177/1461444814543163.

Desta, Y. (2018, May 24). Gwyneth Paltrow reveals Brad Pitt threatened to "kill" Harvey Weinstein. *Vanity Fair*. https://www.vanityfair.com/hollywood/2018/05/gwyneth-paltrow-brad-pitt-harvey-weinstein.

Dobbin, F., & Kelly, E.L. (2007). How to stop harassment: The professional construction of legal compliance in organizations. *American Journal of Sociology 112(4)*, 1203–1243. https://doi.org/10.1086/508788.

Dominus, S. (2017, October 28). Refusing Weinstein's hush money, Rose McGowan calls out Hollywood. *New York Times*. https://www.nytimes.com/2017/10/28/us/rose-mcgowan-harvey-weinstein.html.

Edes, A., & Kelly, M.L. (2018, May 31). *Arquette: After rejecting Weinstein, "I had a completely different career."* NPR. https://www.npr.org/2018/05/31/615911004/arquette-after-rejecting-weinstein-i-had-a-completely-different-career#.

Effron, L. (2017, October 26). *How Ashley Judd fought off Harvey Weinstein's alleged sexual harassment*. ABC News. https://abcnews.go.com/Entertainment/ashley-judd-opens-diane-sawyer-harvey-weinstein-allegations/story?id=50717934.

Farrow, R. (2017a, October 23). From aggressive overtures to sexual assault: Harvey Weinstein's accusers tell their stories. *The New Yorker*. https://www.newyorker.com/news/news-desk/from-aggressive-overtures-to-sexual-assault-harvey-weinsteins-accusers-tell-their-stories.

Farrow, R. (2017b, October 27). Weighing the costs of speaking out about Harvey Weinstein. *The New Yorker*. https://www.newyorker.com/news/news-desk/weighing-the-costs-of-speaking-out-about-harvey-weinstein.

French, S.L. (2003). Reflections on healing: Framing strategies utilized by acquaintance rape survivors. *Journal of Applied Communication Research, 31(4)*, 209–319. https://doi.org/10.108 0/1369681032000132573.

George, L.K., Winfield, I., & Blazer, D.G. (1992). Sociocultural factors in sexual assault: Comparison of two representative samples of women. *Journal of Social Issues, 48(1)*, 105–125. https://doi.org/10.1111/j.1540-4560.1992.tb01160.x.

Greathouse, S.M., Saunders, J., Matthews, M., Keller, K.M., & Miller, L.L. (2015). *A review of the literature on sexual assault perpetrator characteristics and behaviors.* RAND Corporation. https://www.rand.org/content/dam/rand/pubs/research_reports/RR1000/RR1082/RAND_RR1082.pdf.

Harris v. Forklift, 510 U.S. 17 (1993).

Harris, III, F., & Edwards, K.E. (2010). College men's experiences as men: Findings and implications from two grounded theory studies. *Journal of Student Affairs Research and Practice, 47(1)*, 43–62. https://doi.org/10.2202/1949-6605.6085.

Hayek, S. (2017, December 12). Harvey Weinstein is my monster too. *New York Times.* https://www.nytimes.com/interactive/2017/12/13/opinion/contributors/salma-hayek-harvey-weinstein.html.

Hayek, S. (2018, March 1). Ashley Judd is reclaiming her time. *Town and Country Magazine.* https://www.townandcountrymag.com/leisure/arts-and-culture/a18729402/ashley-judd-interview-salma-hayek-april-2018/.

Haynes, S., & Chen, A.H. (2018, October 29). #MeToo heads east. *Time Magazine.* https://time.com/5428182/metoo-heads-east/.

Hemel, D., & Lund, D.S. Sexual harassment and corporate law. *Columbia Law Review, 118(6)*, 1583–1680. https://columbialawreview.org/content/sexual-harassment-and-corporate-law/.

Hill, C., & Kearl, H. (2011). *Crossing the line: Sexual harassment at school.* American Association of University Women. https://www.aauw.org/app/uploads/2020/03/Crossing-the-Line-Sexual-Harassment-at-School.pdf.

Jane, E.A. (2014a). "Your a ugly, whorish, slut." *Feminist Media Studies, 14(4)*, 531–546. https://doi.org/10.1080/14680777.2012.741073.

Jane, E.A. (2014b). "Back to the kitchen, cunt": Speaking the unspeakable about online misogyny. *Continuum—Journal of Media & Cultural Studies, 28(4)*, 558–570. https://doi.org/10.1080/10304312.2014.924479.

Jane, Emma A. 2015. Flaming? What flaming? The pitfalls and potentials of researching online hostility. *Ethics and Information Technology, 17(1)*, 65–87. https://doi.org/10.1007/s10676-015-9362-0.

Kalra, G., & Bhugra, D. (2013). Sexual violence against women: Understanding cross-cultural intersections. *Indian journal of psychiatry, 55(3)*, 244–249. https://doi.org/10.4103/0019-5545.117139.

Kelley, H.H., & Thibaut, J.W. (1978). *Interpersonal relations: A theory of interdependence.* Wiley.

Kelly, L., Burton, S., & Regan, L. (1996). Beyond victim or survivor: Sexual violence, identity, and feminist theory and practice. In L. Adkins & V. Merchant (Eds.), *Sexualizing the social: Power and the organization of sexuality* (pp. 77–101). Macmillan.

Keyton, J., & Menzie, K.A. (2007). Sexually harassing messages: Decoding workplace conversation. *Communication Studies, 58(1)*, 103–87. https://doi.org/10.1080/10510970601168756.

Koelsch, L.E. (2014). Sexual discourses and the absence of agency. *Women & Language, 37(2)*, 11–29. https://www.academia.edu/11609708/Sexual_Discourses_and_the_Absence_of_Agency.

Lamb, S. (1999). Constructing the victim: Popular images and lasting labels. In S. Lamb (Ed.), *New versions of victims: Feminists struggle with the concept* (pp. 108–138). New York University Press.

Leung, K. (2017). Microaggressions and sexual harassment: How the severe or pervasive standard fails women of color. *Texas Journalism on Civil Liberties & Civil Rights, 23(1)*, 79–102.

Levine, M., & Everett, B. (2018, December 12). *Congress reaches deal to curb sexual harassment on Capitol Hill.* Politico. https://www.politico.com/story/2018/12/12/congress-deal-sexual-harassment-bills-1060548.

Lievore, D. (2005). *No longer silent: A study of women's help-seeking decisions and service* responses to sexual assault. *A report prepared by the Australian Institute of Criminology for the Australian Institute of Criminology for the Australian Government's Office for Women*. Australian Institute of Criminology. https://www.aic.gov.au/sites/default/files/2020-05/no-longer-s ilent-a-womens-help-seeking-decisions-and-service-responses-to-sexual-assault.pdf.

McGirt, E. (2018, January 8). raceAhead: The #MeToo stars shine at The Golden Globes. *Fortune*. https://fortune.com/2018/01/08/oprah-golden-globes-speech-raceahead/.

Merrill, L.L., Newell, C.E., Milner, J.S., Koss, M.P., Hervig, L.K., Gold, S.R., Rosswork, S.G., & Thornton, S.R. (1998). Prevalence of premilitary adult sexual victimization and aggression in a Navy recruit sample. *Military Medicine, 163(4)*, 209–212. https://doi.org/10.1093/milmed/163.4.209.

Merrill, L.L., Thomsen, C.J., Gold, S.R., & Milner, J.S. (2001). Childhood abuse and premilitary sexual assault in male Navy recruits. *Journal of Consulting and Clinical Psychology, 69(2)*, 252–261. https://doi.org/10.1037//0022-006x.69.2.252.

Millner, D. (2018, October 25). The movement & the future: Tarana Burke. *Essence*. https://www.essence.com/magazine/tarana-burke-profile-november-2018/.

Mira Sorvino [@MiraSorvino]. (2017, December 15). *Just seeing this after I awoke, I burst out crying. There it is, confirmation that Harvey Weinstein derailed my career* [Tweet]. Twitter. https://twitter.com/mirasorvino/status/941689525960556544?lang=en.

Mitchell, K.J., Ybarra, M.L., & Korchmaros, J.D. (2014). Sexual harassment among adolescents of different sexual orientations and gender identities. *Child Abuse & Neglect, 38(2)*, 280–295. https://doi.org/10.1016/j.chiabu.2013.09.008.

Mohan, P. (2019, February 28). The #TimesUp movement is coming to healthcare. *Fast Company*. https://www.fastcompany.com/90313343/the-timesup-movement-is-coming-to-health-care.

Morrison K. (2005). Motivating women and men to take protective action against rape: Examining direct and indirect persuasive fear appeals. *Health communication, 18(3)*, 237–256. https://doi.org/10.1207/s15327027hc1803_3.

Office of Violence Against Women. (2021). *Victims of sexual violence: Statistics*. United States Department of Justice. https://www.justice.gov/ovw/sexual-assault.

Oldham, S. (2018, May 13). Salma Hayek says Harvey Weinstein only responded to her and Lupita Nyong'o's harassment claims because women of color are easier to discredit. *Variety*. https://variety.com/2018/film/news/salma-hayek-says-harvey-weinstein-only-re sponded-to-her-and-lupita-nyongos-harassment-claims-because-women-of-color-are-easier-to-discredit-1202808828/.

Perren, S., Corcoran, L., Cowie, H., Dehue, F., Garcia, D., Mc Guckin, C., Sevcikova, A., Tsatsou, P., & Vollink, T. (2012). *Tackling cyberbullying: Review of empirical evidence regarding successful responses by students, parents, and schools. International Journal of Conflict and Violence, 6(2)*, 283–292. https://www.ijcv.org/index.php/ijcv/article/view/2919/pdf_58.

Rutter, P. (1989). *Sex in the forbidden zone*. Ballantine Books.

Sackur, S. [BBC News]. (2018, January 15). *Ashley Judd: I was not frightened of Harvey Weinstein—BBC News* [Video]. YouTube. https://www.youtube.com/watch?v=bA1U7QJL9XU.

Saguy, A. (2002). Sexual harassment in the news: The United States and France. *The Communication Review, 5(2)*, 109–141. https://doi.org/10.1080/10714420212478.

Setoodeh, R. (2015, October 6). Ashley Judd reveals sexual harassment by studio mogul. *Variety*. https://variety.com/2015/film/news/ashley-judd-sexual-harassment-studio-mogul-shower-1201610666/.

Shahali, S., Mohammadi, E., Lamyian, M., Kashanian, M., Eslami, M., & Montazeri, A. (2016). Barriers to healthcare provision for victims of sexual assault: A grounded theory study. *Iranian Red Crescent Medical Journal, 18(3)*, 1–7. https://doi.org/10.5812/ircmj.21938.

Siemienowicz, R. (2018, May 1). Scope: Screen industry news. Zero tolerance for screen-industry sexual harassment. *Metro Magazine*. https://search.informit.org/doi/10.3316/INFORMIT.646295999097388.

Sigurdsson E.L. (2018). #MeToo—A concern for general practice? *Scandinavian journal of primary health care, 36(1)*, 1–2. https://doi.org/10.1080/02813432.2018.1426153.

Singh, S., Sharma, E., & Dubey, M. (2018). A critique of causes and measures of rape: A systematic review of literature. *Language of India, 18(4)*, 293–307. http://www.languageinindia.com/april2018/sakshireviewrapeissuesfinal1.pdf.

Stelter, B. (2018, May 25). *Rose McGowan's message to Harvey Weinstein: "We got you."* CNN. https://www.cnn.com/2018/05/25/entertainment/rose-mcgowan-harvey-weinstein-megyn-kelly.

Townsend, M. (2017, October 14). Rose McGowan: "Hollywood blacklisted me because I got raped." *The Guardian.* https://www.theguardian.com/film/2017/oct/14/harvey-weinstein-rose-mcgowan-rape-film.

Trillo, T. (2017). Communicating anti-violence policy on Twitter: The European Commission and #SayNoStopVAW. *Styles of Communication, 9(1),* 9–24. https://hub.graceproject.eu/file/file/download?guid=5c501b00-1d63-40ea-8c6c-70d2a445c771.

True, E. (2014). The gaming journalist who tells on her internet trolls—to their mothers. *The Guardian.* https://www.theguardian.com/culture/australia-culture-blog/2014/nov/28/alanah-pearce-tells-on-her-internet-trolls-to-their-mothers.

United States Air Force. (2004). *Report concerning the assessment of USAF sexual assault prevention and response.* Department of the Air Force. https://www.sapr.mil/public/docs/reports/2004-annual-report.pdf.

United States Equal Employment Opportunity Commission. (2002). *Facts about sexual harassment.* https://www.eeoc.gov/fact-sheet/facts-about-sexual-harassment.

United States Equal Employment Opportunity Commission. (2006). *Sexual harassment charges EEOC & FEPAs combined: FY 1992-FY 2005.* https://www.eeoc.gov/statistics/sexual-harassment-chargeseeoc-fepas-combined-fy-1992-fy-1996.

United States Government Accountability Office. (2008). *DOD's and the Coast Guard's sexual assault prevention and response programs face implementation and oversight challenges.* https://apps.dtic.mil/sti/pdfs/ADA485714.pdf.

Wagmeister, E. (2019, January 25). Rosanna Arquette on backlash since speaking out against Weinstein: "I don't have an agent." *Variety.* https://variety.com/2019/film/news/rosanna-arquette-reveals-backlash-speaking-out-against-weinstein-1203118767/.

Winfrey, O. [Oprah Winfrey Network]. (2018, March 10). *Salma Hayek Pinault accepts Harvey Weinstein's apology | SuperSoul Conversations | OWN* [Video]. YouTube. https://www.youtube.com/watch?v=zMlSYUBghzA.

World Health Organization. (2003). *Guidelines for medico-legal care for victims of sexual violence.* WHO Press. https://apps.who.int/iris/bitstream/handle/10665/42788/924154628X.pdf?sequence=1.

Young, S.L., & Maguire, K.C. (2003). Talking about sexual violence. *Women and Language 26(2),* 40–51.

Zurawik, D. (2018, January 8). Oprah Winfrey Golden Globes speech a moving jolt of moral authority. *Baltimore Sun.* https://www.baltimoresun.com/opinion/columnists/zurawik/bs-fe-zontv-oprah-globes-20180108-story.html.

8

Taboo of Child Sexual Abuse and Celebrities Who Refuse to Remain Quiet

In September of 1998, police forces across the world banded together to bring down the Wonderland Club, an online child pornography ring spanning twelve countries. Club membership was contingent on possession of a digital library containing no less than 10,000 indecent images of minors. Members would circulate these photographs throughout the network by sending them from computer to computer as encrypted image files. The network eventually collapsed as the result of a worldwide criminal investigation, code-named Operation Cathedral, when over a hundred men suspected of being members were arrested

> —Passage from "Pedophiles in Wonderland: Censoring the Sinful in Cyberspace" in *The Journal of Criminal Law and Criminology*, 2008

In 2007, undercover reporters confirmed that Wonderland had reemerged as a place, with slides and swing sets, school rooms and rose-colored bedrooms, where children moved, spoke, and had sexual relations with adults in real time (Russell, 2008). These predators are a danger to children. Alarmingly, offenders can hide in plain sight, going undetected for years, and perhaps never getting caught. Even those who get arrested are found guilty for only a small percentage of the child abuse they have committed. Offenders usually know when to pursue, stop, and alter their sexual offending behaviors, which enables them to pursue multiple victims over prolonged periods of time without being discovered.

Offender typologies include child sexual abusers (CSA), pedophiles, and incest abusers, among others (Hudson, 2005). The average incarcerated pedophile reports being arrested for only one out of every 30 molestations (Musk et al., 1997). Even more jaw-dropping are the facts that the average nonincarcerated pedophile molests 117 youngsters, and that pedophiles who molest boys have an average of 231 victims, versus an average of 23 for those who molest girls (Musk et al., 1997). In 1886, German psychiatrist Richard Freiherr von Krafft-Ebing coined the term "pedophile"—an individual who derives sexual gratification from contact with prepubescent children (McCartan, 2008; Silverman & Wilson, 2002). Most pedophiles are men (Howitt, 1995). Pedophiles are usually not strangers. They are more likely family members, lodgers, neighbors, or other adults from the immediate social environment of their victims (Primoratz, 1999). For girls, approximately 50 percent of offenders are family members, whereas for boys, 10 to 20 percent are relatives (Kendall-Tackett, 2001). Offenders engage in a variety of activities with minors, ranging from cuddling, caressing, and genital fondling to intercourse. A minor in the U.S. is anyone who is younger than 18 years old.

The U.S. is the same as other countries whose laws and regulations seek to create "fixed age of consent" for sexual practices. The problem is that there is no "uniform" age of consent across societies and cultures (Schaffner, 2002). In some Western societies, the age of consent for heterosexual sex is set at 15 or 16, and at these ages the "...assumption is that adolescents are, by and large, physically, and psychologically mature enough to be allowed to make their own decisions concerning sex" (Primoiratz, 1999, p. 101). In the U.S., the court cases *Roper v. Simmons, Graham v. Florida*, and *Miller v. Alabama* established the following distinctions between how juveniles under 18 engage in decision-making within the context of CSA and exploitation in comparison with adults: (1) a lack of maturity and an underdeveloped sense of responsibility, (2) a heightened susceptibility to negative influences and outside pressures, and (3) the fact that the character of a juvenile is more transitory and less fixed than that of an adult, resulting in "...the person under eighteen ... with a somewhat diminished capacity that will be eliminated with growth and maturity" (Leary, 2016, p. 129–130). Once a pedophile identifies a minor of interest, four preconditions are usually necessary before the grooming of the victim begins, including the motivation to sexually abuse, overcoming internal inhibitions, overcoming external inhibitions, and overcoming resistance of the minor (Finkelhor, 1984). During the beginning of the grooming process, the offender can experience cognitive distortions, such as the CSA is not hurting the minor, instead engendering "healthy" sexual exploration (O'Carroll, 1980). The outcome is that offenders justify their behavior and protect themselves from societal disapproval, avoid cognitive dissonance, and maintain their self-esteem (Milhaildes et al., 2004). Despite cognitive distortions, offenders are self-aware that they are sexually attracted to minors, and they understand that sexual practices with minors are illegal in most circumstances in many jurisdictions throughout the U.S. and in other countries.

Offenders can be manipulative, and oftentimes they have an awareness of how society perceives them, so their desire to not be identified as a threat explains their keen observational skills, reliance of adaptation, and their ability to groom victims (Hudson, 2005). Their behavior destroys the lives of their victims. A victim's ability to cope with trauma is influenced by characteristics of sexual abuse one experienced, personal characteristics, and characteristics of their homelife, and sources of support or lack thereof. These characteristics mediate the development of adverse outcomes in children who survive CSA. The immediate psychological consequences of CSA include shock, fear, anxiety, nervousness, guilt, symptoms of PTSD, denial, confusion, withdrawal, isolation, and grief (Institut national de santé publique du Québec, 2020). Additional consequences of sexual abuse exhibited in childhood involve maladjustment in school, delinquency, homelessness, running away from home, alcohol and drug use, gang involvement, teen pregnancy, sexually transmitted and blood-borne infections, and sexual revictimization and offences (Institut national de santé publique du Québec, 2020). Abused children carry their mental and physical scars into adulthood, with ramifications for their sexual and physical health, psychological health, and relational and marital well-being, and for women, specific concerns related to the perinatal period and parental process (Campbell et al., 2009; DiLillo & Damashek, 2003; Dube et al., 2005; Elliott et al., 2004; MacMillan, 2000). Oftentimes, the ramifications of CSA are not discussed. Society's recent memory regarding the priest abuse scandal in the Catholic Church (Dixon, 2004; Stevens et al., 2018), as well as the "Sandusky scandal" at Pennsylvania State University, have focused greater media attention and public scrutiny of CSA in the U.S. and around the world (Brady & Carey, 2011; *Centre Daily Times*, 2021; Solomon, 2011; Thompson, 2012). In response to the public outcry about pedophilia and CSA, more adult survivors are coming forward and seeking justice.

This chapter addresses the CSA Anthony Edwards experienced in his youth, and how he found the courage to speak out. Anthony Edwards wants children and adults who have confronted CSA to know they can transition from victim to survivor. Edwards is a well-known actor who portrayed Dr. Mark Greene on the NBC television show *ER*. Many fans do not know that a man who served as a mentor to a pubescent Edwards and his group of childhood friends is an accused pedophile, whom Edwards and others claim took advantage of them. After Edwards wrote an essay that was published on *Medium* accusing a famous theatrical writer/producer of molesting him and raping one of his friends, seven others from their theater group told the *Los Angeles Times* that their former mentor molested or attempted to molest them. The men are no longer remaining quiet, and the media coverage of their stories brings into our public consciousness an issue many would rather not discuss.

Theoretical Background for CSA Research

Societal awareness about CSA increased dramatically throughout the 1970s and was predicated on stronger reporting laws and new research focused on the prevalence and harmful effects of CSA. The U.S. had established its first nationwide system of government-sponsored child protection by the end of the 1970s (Myers, 2008). Surveillance of CSA in the U.S. and abroad indicates that it happens in communities in every county, state, and country. Sadly, 12.7 percent of all children experience sexual abuse, with girls being two to three times as likely as boys to be sexually abused in Asia, Europe, and North America (Stoltenborgh et al., 2011). Recently, a higher prevalence for girls was found in some African nations (Sumner, et al., 2015). Many adults have their first encounters with sexual violence during childhood or adolescence. Population-based studies in diverse locations such as Cameroon, the Caribbean, Peru, New Zealand, South Africa, and Tanzania have reported high rates of forced sexual initiation (WHO, 2003). Recent research indicates that almost 20 percent of women and 8 percent of men across 22 countries experience sexual abuse before the age of 18 (Pereda, 2009). Community studies indicate that both boys and girls experience sexual abuse within homes and institutional or community settings outside of their school or university, most often by trusted adults (Brown, 2009). Abuse that occurs in institutional settings can be classified as individual abuse, program or sanctioned abuse, and system abuse (Plann, 2008). Individual abuse involves acts committed by an individual or by individuals, and it may be of a physical, emotional, or sexual nature. Program or sanctioned abuse is committed by an institution with the administration's approval—these practices violate normative behavior, and punishments are reprehensible. System abuse is when the system (e.g., government, NGO, etc.) is overtaxed due to inadequate management, planning, or resources, and unable to guarantee the safety and well-being of its people.

Within home, institutional, and community settings, predators use luring communication to entrap minors. The Luring Communication Theory (LCT) posits five propositions to explain how perpetrators use luring communication (Olsen et al., 2007). The first proposition involves the perpetrator gaining access to a minor, followed by the entrapment of the victim and the development of an ongoing sexual relationship. The second proposition maintains that luring communication is only successful if the perpetrator cultivates deceptive trust on the part of the victim. The perpetrator is more capable of controlling the victim physically and emotionally when he has identified the characteristics of the victim that need to be manipulated, the buttons to push, to enable exploitation. Once entrapment ensues, and deceptive trust is created, the third proposition is activated, whereby the perpetrator uses three interdependent processes—grooming, isolating, and approach—to reinforce and sustain the relationship. A communication process ensues, with the perpetrator attempting to establish a relationship with a minor, deploying messages that will obtain the minor's attention and persuade the minor to accept the perpetrator's relationship definition.

Throughout the luring communication, sexual coercion is used. Sexual coercion involves the perpetrator engaging in compliance-gaining tactics to influence the sexual cooperation or compliance of the minor (Olsen et al., 2007). Sexual coercion can be perceived as game-playing that is annoying, harassing, or unpleasant but not dangerous (Spitzberg et al., 2001). Sexual coercion is a risky endeavor for the perpetrator, which is why perpetrators prefer that it occurs in relatively private contexts. The perpetrator wants their luring and sexual coercion to take place away from public observance or interference (Spitzberg et al., 2001). By building deceptive trust, the perpetrator "…is able to communicatively groom and isolate the child…" to "…accept subtle sexual advances. In turn, the isolation, grooming, and approaches reinforce the trust, and the cycle continues as sexual contact begins" (Olsen et al., 2007, p. 247). The fourth proposition addresses the entrapment cycle and the mediating effect of communicative responses of victim and perpetrator on the viability of a prolonged sexual relationship. The fifth proposition accounts for luring communication in the entrapment cycle being influenced by a variety of contexts, including time, culture, and power and control (Olsen et al., 2007). The trauma does not end when the CSA stops—the fallout continues. Victims of CSA are more likely than their non-abused counterparts to experience depression, substance abuse, post-traumatic stress disorder (PTSD), and suicide in adulthood (WHO, 2018). Minors who have engaged in sexual encounters with offenders have their perspective of what transpired. "Subjectively, the sexual contact may be experienced as entirely pleasant, as unpleasant but relatively inconsequential, as a painful experience that can be overcome, or as a trauma that dominates a person's life" (Nelson & Oliver, 1998, p. 572). The only way anyone knows how victims feel is to let them speak for themselves.

In the study "Locating the Voice of Logic: Disclosure Discourse of Sexual Abuse," children told researchers they were strategic about telling or withholding information about the sexual coercion they experienced (Petronio et al., 1997). This assertion is at the core of Communication Privacy Management (CPM), which posits that there is a tension between revealing and concealing private information, so that individuals who self-disclose information must create and regulate the privacy boundaries between themselves and those to whom they disclose (Kennedy-LighPetronio et al., 2012; Petronio, 2007). CPM relies on five major criteria, including cultural, gendered, motivational, contextual, and risk to determine what information crosses the threshold between private and public information. Some victims need tacit permission from others to disclose their abuse. Full disclosure is not given instantaneously; instead, many victims rely on incremental disclosure to test the viability of ultimately revealing that they were abused, who abused them, how they were abused, and where they were abused. There is consideration for others, and how they will be impacted, as well as a determination of the consequences for self-disclosure.

Some disclosure consequences include ostracism and isolation for the discloser, the receiver, or both parties in situations involving a high-risk disclosure (Durham, 2008; Greene & Faulkner, 2002). Victims who self-disclose have determined they can trust the recipient of the information about CSA to maintain boundary coordination. Recipients of victim self-disclosures should be supportive, respectful, and nonjudgmental, recognizing that the victim may rely on the recipient for support or access to aid (Durham, 2008; Petronio, 2002; Petronio et al., 1996; Plueretti & Chesebro, 2015). When recipients are prosecutors, they rely on victims' and survivors' testimony as corroborating evidence. Cases lacking strong evidence (e.g., confession, physical evidence, eyewitness) are twice as likely to fail than those with a corroborating witness (Walsh et al., 2008). Victims and survivors of CSA rely on the media and the criminal justice system to hold perpetrators and offenders accountable. Understanding the portrayal of their stories in the press, in social media, as testimony in investigations and on the witness stand improves the chance of successful prosecution.

Anthony Edwards Speaks Out about Friendship Group's CSA

The staff of Vox created a list of 263 celebrities, politicians, CEOs, and others who have been accused of sexual misconduct since April 2017 (Vox, 2019). Gary Goddard—a writer, producer, director, and businessman—was included on the list. Once allegations of him sexually abusing eight men when they were minors were covered in the media, Goddard took a leave of absence from the entertainment design firm The Goddard Group. Acclaimed actor Anthony Edwards is one of the men who accused Goddard of molesting him (Jensen, 2017). Edwards, who appeared in the films *Fast Times at Ridgemont High, Revenge of the Nerds,* and *Top Gun,* considered Goddard a mentor and friend in his youth. Edwards acknowledges that Goddard was present when his own father was emotionally unavailable. He believes Goddard used the void left by his father to manipulate him (Jensen, 2017). Goddard was a successful former theater prodigy, who returned to Santa Barbara throughout his 20s to direct and mentor child actors in his hometown. Goddard vowed to bring the most talented among the devoted boys, referred to a "Goddardites," to Hollywood (Roberts, 2017). According to Edwards, Goddard wanted something from the boys, and he made advances ranging from "straying hands on thighs during lulls in a production or fondling in a darkened Disneyland ride, to repeated incidents of sexual abuse during a troupe's overnight stays in a statewide tour" (*Los Angeles Times,* 2017). Goddard was known in his hometown for directing youth productions, including *Oliver!* and *Jesus Christ Superstar.* The boys in his productions looked up to him. "He was king of magical and exciting," said former actor Bret Douglas Nighman, who met Goddard when he was 13 (Roberts, 2017). Former actor Mark Driscoll remembered Goddard as "the most important person in my life." As time went on, the CSA haunted the actors, and they had to speak out.

Edwards spoke out on in an autobiographical exposé published on the website *Medium* on November 10, 2017. Edwards met Goddard when he was 12 years old. Goddard became a dominant force in Edwards' life, and he was emotionally available as a mentor in ways Edwards' father was not—Edwards' father suffered from undiagnosed PTSD from World War II. Goddard taught Edwards the craft of acting, the importance of studying, and, more importantly, was a friend. Edwards was a Goddardite, so contemplate his state of mind when he was confronted:

> When I was 14 years old, my mother opened the door for me to answer honestly about the rumors she had heard about Gary Goddard—who was my mentor, teacher and friend—being a pedophile. I denied it through tears of complete panic. To face that truth was not an option as my sense of self was completely enmeshed in my gang of five friends who were all led by this sick father figure.

Edwards called the man who was his teacher, friend, and mentor sick. He explained why:

> One of the most tragic effects of sexual abuse in children is that the victims often feel deeply responsible—as if it is somehow their fault. With their sick form of control, abusers exploit a child's natural desire to bond. The victims are required to play by the abuser's rules, or else they are "out"—banished from the

only world they know. Abusers are successful when they keep control of that little world—a world that is based on fear. The use of fear to control and manipulate can be both obvious and subtle. Abusers will often use the word "love" to define their horrific actions, which constitutes a total betrayal of trust.

Nighman wrote his own essay on *Medium* on November 17, 2017. In the essay, Nighman recalled an event that took place in 1977 that was traumatic for Edwards and himself: "…when Tony was about to turn fifteen and I was getting close to turning sixteen, Gary Goddard directed California Youth Theater's production of 'Peter Pan.' The show would open in Santa Barbara, and then it would tour up and down the California coast." Edwards had been in Goddard productions in previous years, and Goddard had gained his trust. Both Edwards and Nighman were cast in *Peter Pan*. Once the show departed Santa Barbara for its tour, the CSA began. Nighman explains:

> One night while on tour I awoke to find Goddard trying to get into my bed, under my covers and into my underwear. I fought him off and pushed him away. Although it was dark I saw him force his way into Tony's bed—which was about twelve feet from mine. I thought that Tony would fight him off too. I lay in my bed with my heart pounding and listened as one of my best friends who I loved got sexually molested. I was scared, in shock, heartbroken and confused. I felt like I betrayed Tony for doing nothing. I was certain that Tony was straight, and I couldn't figure out why he would let this man touch him.
>
> It wasn't until I read Tony's story that he wrote and posted on *Medium* in which he said that his relationship with Goddard started at age twelve, and the sexual abuse started before he was fourteen, that it finally made sense why Tony didn't push him away as I did. I realized that, of course, it had happened to him before. Tony had been groomed and sexually abused for years by this pedophile who we thought was our friend and mentor.

Driscoll confirmed that Goddard repeatedly sexually abused him over a three-year period, and four Santa Barbara classmates told the *Los Angeles Times* that Driscoll informed them of the CSA during a get-together two decades ago (Garcia-Roberts, 2017). Nighman confirmed that Goddard attempted to molest him on four occasions by the time he was 16. Nighman's childhood friend Mark Daly, now an attorney in Denver, remembers Nighman telling him about Goddard trying to fondle him during a touring production of *Peter Pan* (Garcia-Roberts, 2017). Nighman went on *The Dr. Oz Show* on December 7, 2017, to affirm his recollection of events as stated in his story posted on *Medium*. Edwards, Nighman, and Driscoll were among a group of young actors who have come forward to address their experiences with Goddard. In response to the allegations, Goddard's press representative, Sam Singer, initially released the following statement: "Gary first met Anthony more than 40 years ago. Gary was a mentor, teacher, and a friend to Anthony, which makes this story all the more disturbing to him. As to the allegations that Mr. Edwards made in his post today, I can unequivocally deny them on Gary's behalf" (Jensen, 2017). Another denial from a Goddard spokesman was issued regarding Nighman's allegations. As more accusers and allegations surfaced and were confirmed by other Goddardites, their friends, and family members, Singer issued another statement: "We stand by our statement denying the allegations by Anthony Edwards against Gary Goddard. This new post by Brett Douglas Nighman makes equally false claims against Mr. Goddard" (Otterson, 2017). By the end of 2017, in the aftermath of the allegations, The Goddard Group announced that Taylor Jeffs, then the company's director of design, would take over Goddard's duties. Furthermore, in a statement from then Chief Operating Officer Barry Kemper, Goddard's stepping down would allow the company and its employees to "continue their projects undistracted by recent allegations made against him" (Martin, 2017). Edwards and other Goddardites are survivors, yet they live with their experiences every day.

Edwards told *The Daily Beast* that he was not molested daily, and that the abuse occurred as he became immersed in theater and acting. Over time, Edwards developed "survival techniques," as he called them, such as avoiding staying overnight with Goddard, and eventually he "worked his way away" from him (Teeman, 2018). Now he realizes he compartmentalized the trauma associated with his CSA, and as a result he developed PTSD. Edwards shared his CSA experiences in therapy and a men's group:"I thought, 'There is no shame here,'" Edwards explained. He continued, "It happens to one in six men, perhaps this is a way to try and shake some of the stigma off." The allegations being made publicly gave victims a voice, and the media coverage focused attention on an issue, CSA, that is not regularly discussed in society. Despite California's statute of limitations preventing Edwards from obtaining the prosecution of Goddard, Edwards understood that he could make a difference:

> …but there was no reason to carry on covering up and maintaining that secrecy, which was also part of the code of co-dependency, part of the culture of abuse. You hear the same thing around alcoholism: people staying silent, and ending up denying the truth. Mariska Hargitay [his friend, and ex–*ER* and *Law and Order: SVU* colleague] told me to take care of myself first. That's where the journey started.

Edwards is focused on healing. He hopes his story helps inspire victims and survivors of CSA to empower themselves. In 2018, Edwards joined the board of 1in6, which is comprised of program leaders and academic experts on sexual abuse, violence, and public health. In addition to performing regular board duties, Edwards will grow the organization's awareness initiative, including participating with 1in6 staff in presentations on sexual abuse, violence, and public health (1in6.org, 2018). 1in6 issued a statement regarding Edwards : "He will be an exceptional advocate for male survivors, bringing an articulate voice and well-known face to an issue that is often unseen and unspoken." Edwards imparted valuable insight into his perspective moving forward: "Only after I was able to separate my experience, process it, and put it in its place could I accept this truth: My abuse may always be with me, but it does not own me." Edwards told *The Daily Beast* (2018) that he wanted people to know: "There are so many people who have suffered so much more. It felt good to share, and good to talk. I've had a really, gratefully blessed life. I have a wonderful career, four beautiful children, I have so much to be thankful for."

Safeguarding Against CSA

People are made uncomfortable by the topic of sex. Sex involving minors escalates the discomfort, with conversation fraught with panic, as parents broach the subject with children, or families have discussions with healthcare experts and educators. Social mores dictate that sex involving minors is discouraged, yet it happens. Minors observe social norms regarding sex and how peers and adults talk about it—the outcome is reluctance to discuss sex with family and friends, to self-censor, and censor others, which undercuts comprehensively personal, familial, and public health approaches to practicing safe sexual practices and preventing sexual abuse. Within this context, abhorrent acts such as CSA are considered taboo. Therefore CSA becomes a topic no one wants to discuss. Without someone willing to engage in discourse about CSA, specifically, a discussion initiated by someone who has survived it, most people will remain unaware or ignorant of the ramifications of CSA. Anthony Edwards and other former Goddardites spoke out to give voice to their childhood experiences, to give children who endure CSA visibility, and to provide survivors like themselves, many of whom remain voiceless, representation in a national and international dialogue that is overdue. If this discourse does not foster discussions between those who have been abused and their family and friends, or engender greater community engagement with victims and survivors, CSA becomes a topic many people will never understand. The consequences of not understanding are dire.

Lacking understanding, society finds itself in an environment where perpetrators, offenders, and reoffenders thrive. "It is not uncommon in the wake of a child abuse tragedy for relatives, friends, and neighbors to reveal that they had a concern about the safety of the child but failed to report it.

Even professionals who are mandated to report often fail to do so" (Pence & Wilson, 1994, p. 72). An offender can have many victims before getting caught, and this individual is susceptible to reoffending. What are victims to do in this environment? Some victims succumb to adverse health conditions ranging from drug addiction to self-harm. According to the WHO (2014), CSA is among 24 global risk factors that affect the global burden of disease. CSA is a risk factor for four serious mental health disorders with disability and costs of greater than or equal to $70 billion, including schizophrenia, bipolar disorder, drug abuse/dependence, and major depressive disorder (Cutajar et al., 2010; Eaton et al., 2008; Molnar et al., 2001). Despite the impact of CSA, the CDC (2010) reported only 20 percent of public health agencies in all 50 states and the District of Columbia offered CSA prevention programs.

Oftentimes, survivors of CSA endure PTSD. Even when the abuse ends, the trauma persists. CSA destroys lives, so safeguarding against it is imperative. "Child sexual abuse investigations may involve child protection, licensing authorities, prosecutors, and county, state, and federal law enforcement personnel" (Pence & Wilson, 1994, p. 75). Various stakeholders, including law enforcement, prosecutors, doctors, and mental health providers, must work together to bring perpetrators and offenders to justice and to provide care to survivors. One area where stakeholders recognize a need for reform is agreeing on appropriate language involving child abuse and exploitation. Otherwise, the data collected, the strategic response designed, the legislation implemented, and the interventions conceived will be impaired (Leary, 2016). Once accurate language is negotiated and agreed upon, governments must use it in all phases of a criminal occurrence, including the reporting, investigating, and prosecuting of CSA, as well as during the surveillance of offenders (Leary, 2016). Once this reform is completed nationally and internationally, it could be transformative.

There is acknowledgment that progress takes time. In the U.S., it took 20 years for government reforms to create and strengthen sex offender registries. The Jacob Wetterling Crimes Against Children and Sexually Violent Offender Registration Act, a component of the Federal Violent Crime Control and Law Enforcement Act of 1994, requires states to create sex offender registries (Meiners, 2015). In 1996 and 2006, additional laws were passed, specifically Megan's Law, and its augmentation, the Adam Walsh Child Protection and Safety Act (SORNA). Together these laws require individuals convicted of sexual offenses (including in juvenile systems) ranging from public indecency and lewdness to aggravated assault, to register in the jurisdiction where they live, work, and attend school, with this information compiled into national and state sex offender registries to be accessible to the public online (Wright, 2003). Now these sex offender registries play an outsized role in the mitigation of CSA.

Another area where reform is necessary is the underestimation of the importance of empathy. Stakeholders must have empathy for victims and survivors in order to understand them. If victims believe support providers do not care about them or are being disingenuous, they will not put their trust in outreach meant for their well-being. "Empathy is a skill which enables understanding of another person's experience, and appropriate responses and behaviors" (Matthews & Collin-Vézina, 2016, p. 6). Two stakeholders who need to express empathy in dealing with victims include doctors and police officers. Victims need doctors and law enforcement to be willing to imagine the abused minor's perceptions, needs, and trauma, while avoiding behavior that induces profound stress for some victims (Greeson et al., 2016; Thomas & Humphery, 2014). If victims and survivors have positive, reaffirming experiences with doctors and law enforcement, they are more receptive to therapy and treatment. Research indicates that outcomes were better for sexually abused minors who participated in psychological treatment than when no professional treatment intervention was provided (Hetzel-Riggin et al., 2007). Psychotherapy treatment improved survivors' self-esteem and overall functioning (Harvey & Taylor, 2010; Finkelhor & Berliner, 1995; Putnam, 2003; Saywitz et al., 2000).

Traditionally, CSA initiatives and reforms focus on clinical intervention and criminal redress. However, there should be less of a reactive approach and more focus on prevention. In research published in *Public Health Reports*, in the conclusions section of "The Need for a Comprehensive Public Health Approach to Preventing Child Sexual Abuse" (2014), experts provided recommendations that stakeholders should follow (p. 227):

> There are many reasons to champion a comprehensive public health approach to CSA prevention. Most fundamentally, it is simply more humane to prevent CSA than to address abuse after it occurs. The public health approach emphasizes the importance of such prevention within the context of scientific rigor, rational discourse, and multidisciplinary collaboration. Achieving a national public health approach to CSA prevention will require a sustained focus on further reducing CSA policy resistance, encouraging national leadership, and identifying sustainable resources, all of which appears within reach.

REFERENCES

Alling, M. (2018, April 17). *Actor Anthony Edwards joins board of 1in6, a national nonprofit serving men who have experienced sexual abuse or assault.* 1in6.org. https://1in6.org/2018/04/actor-anthony-edwards-joins-board-1in6-national-nonprofit-serving-men-experienced-sexual-abuse-assault/#.

Brady, E., & Carey, J. (2011, November 8). Penn State sex abuse scandal chips at Joe Paterno's legacy. *USA Today.* http://unh.edu/ccrc/news/USAToday-PennStateSexAbuseScandal.pdf.

Brown, D.W., Riley, L., Butchart, A., Meddings, D.R., Kann, L., & Harvey, A.P. (2009). Exposure to physical and sexual violence and adverse health behaviors in African children: Results from the Global School-based Student Health Survey. *Bulletin of the World Health Organization, 87(6),* 447–455. https://doi.org/10.2471/blt.07.047423.

Campbell, R., Dworkin, E., & Cabral, G. (2009). An ecological model of the impact of sexual assault on women's mental health. *Trauma, violence & abuse, 10(3),* 225–246. https://doi.org/10.1177/1524838009334456.

Centers for Disease Control and Prevention (2010). *Findings from the 2009 child maltreatment prevention environmental scan of state public health agencies.* https://www.cdc.gov/violenceprevention/pdf/phli_cm_environmental_scan-a.pdf.

Cutajar, M.C., Mullen, P.E., Ogloff, J.R., Thomas, S.D., Wells, D.L., & Spataro, J. (2010). Schizophrenia and other psychotic disorders in a cohort of sexually abused children. *Archives of General Psychiatry, 67(11),* 1114–1119. https://doi.org/10.1001/archgenpsychiatry.2010.147.

DiLillo, D., & Damashek, A. (2003). Parenting characteristics of women reporting a history of childhood sexual abuse. *Child Maltreatment, 8(4),* 319–333. https://doi.org/10.1177/1077559503257104.

Dixon, M.A. (2004). Silencing the lambs: The Catholic Church's response to the 2002 sexual abuse scandal. *Journal of Communication and Religion, 27(1),* 63–86.

Dube, S.R., Anda, R.F., Whitfield, C.L., Brown, D.W., Felitti, V.J., Dong, M., & Giles, W.H. (2005). Long-term consequences of childhood sexual abuse by gender of victim. *American Journal of Preventive Medicine, 28(5),* 430–438. https://doi.org/10.1016/j.amepre.2005.01.015.

Durham, W.T. (2008). The rule-based process of revealing/concealing the family planning decisions of voluntarily child-free couples: A communication privacy management perspective. *Communication Studies, 59(2),* 132–147. https://doi.org/10.1080/10510970802062451.

Eaton, W.W., Martins, S.S., Nestadt, G., Bienvenu, O.J., Clarke, D., & Alexandre, P. (2008). The burden of mental disorders. *Epidemiologic Reviews, 30,* 1–14. https://doi.org/10.1093/epirev/mxn011.

Edwards, A. (2017, November 10). *Yes mom, there is something wrong: From victim to survivor.* Medium. https://medium.com/@anthonyedwards/yes-mom-there-is-something-wrong-f2bcf56434b9.

Elliott, D.M., Mok, D.S., & Briere, J. (2004). Adult sexual assault: Prevalence, symptomatology, and sex differences in the general population. *Journal of Traumatic Stress, 17(3),* 203–211. https://doi.org/10.1023/B:JOTS.0000029263.11104.23.

Finkelhor, D. (1984). *Child sexual abuse: New theory and research.* Free Press.

Finkelhor, D., & Berliner, L. (1995). Research on the treatment of sexually abused children: A review and recommendations. *Journal of the American Academy of Child and Adolescent Psychiatry, 34(11),* 1408–1423. https://doi.org/10.1097/00004583-199511000-00007.

Garcia-Roberts, G. (2017, December 20). Hollywood producer Gary Goddard accused of sexual misconduct by 8 former child actors. *Los Angeles Times.* https://www.latimes.com/business/la-fi-ct-goddard-accusers-20171220-story.html.

Greene, K., & Faulkner, S.L. (2002). Expected versus actual responses to disclosure in relationships of HIV-positive African American adolescent females. *Communication Studies, 53(4),* 297–317. https://doi.org/10.1080/10510970209388595.

Greeson, M.R., Campbell, R., & Fehler-Cabral, G. (2016). "Nobody deserves this": Adolescent sexual assault victims' perceptions of disbelief and victim blame from police. *Journal of Community Psychology, 44(1),* 90–110. https://doi.org/10.1002/jcop.21744.

Harvey, S.T., & Taylor, J.E. (2010). A meta-analysis of the effects of psychotherapy with sexually abused children and adolescents. *Clinical Psychology Review, 30(5),* 517–535. https://doi.org/10.1016/j.cpr.2010.03.006.

Hetzel-Riggin, M.D., Brausch, A.M., & Montgomery, B.S. (2007). A meta-analytic investigation of therapy modality outcomes for sexually abused children and adolescents: An exploratory study. *Child Abuse & Neglect, 31(2),* 125–141. https://doi.org/10.1016/j.chiabu.2006.10.007.

Howitt, D. (1995). *Pedophiles and sexual offenses against children.* Wiley.

Hudson, K. (2005). *Offending identities: Sex offenders' perspectives of their treatment and management.* Willan.

Institut national de santé publique du Québec (2020). *Media information kit on sexual assault.*

The Ministère des Communications, de la Culture et de la Condition feminine. https://www.inspq.qc.ca/en/sexual-assault/understanding-sexual-assault/consequences.

Jensen, E. (2017, November 10). Former "ER" star Anthony Edwards says Gary Goddard molested him "for years." *USA Today*. https://www.usatoday.com/story/life/people/2017/11/10/anthony-edwards-says-gary-goddard-molested-him-for-years/852778001/.

"Jerry Sandusky scandal." (2021). *Centre Daily Times*. https://www.centredaily.com/news/local/education/penn-state/jerry-sandusky/.

Kendall-Tackett, K. (2001). *The hidden feelings of motherhood. Coping with mothering stress, depression, and burnout*. New Harbinger.

Kennedy-Lightsey, C.D., Martin, M.M., Thompson, M., Himes, K.L., & Clingerman, B.Z. (2012). Communication privacy management theory: Exploring coordination and ownership between friends. *Communication Quarterly, 60(5)*, 665–680. https://doi.org/10.1080/01463373.2012.725004.

Leary, M.G. (2016). The language of child sexual abuse and exploitation. In C.B. Hessick (Ed.), *Crime, language, and social consequences* (pp. 109–144). University of Michigan Press.

Letourneau, E.J., Eaton, W.W., Bass, J., Berlin, F.S., & Moore, S.G. (2014). The need for a comprehensive public health approach to preventing child sexual abuse. *Public Health Reports, 129(3)*, 222–228. https://doi.org/10.1177/003335491412900303.

Macmillan, R. (2000). Adolescent victimization and income deficits in adulthood: Rethinking the costs of criminal violence from a life-course perspective. *Criminology, 38(2)*, 553–588. https://doi.org/10.1111/j.1745-9125.2000.tb00899.x.

Martin, H. (2017, November 28). Gary Goddard, accused by Anthony Edwards of sexual assault, takes leave from his company. *Los Angeles Times*. https://www.latimes.com/business/la-fi-ct-gary-goddard-20171128-story.html.

Mathers, C., Stevens, G., & Mascarenhas, M. (2009). *Global health risks: Mortality and burden of disease attributable to selected major risks*. World Health Organization. https://apps.who.int/iris/bitstream/handle/10665/44203/9789241563871_eng.pdf?sequenc e=1&isAllowed=y.

Mathews, B., & Collin-Vézina, D. (2016). Child sexual abuse: Raising awareness and empathy is essential to promote new public health responses. *Journal of Public Health Policy, 37(3)*, 304–314. https://doi.org/10.1057/jphp.2016.21.

McCartan, K.F. (2008). Current understandings of pedophilia and the resulting crisis in modern society. In J. Caroll & M. Alena (Eds.), *Psychological sexual dysfunctions* (pp. 51–84). Nova Biomedical.

Meiners, E.R. (2015). Offending children, registering sex. *Women's Studies Quarterly 43(1)*, 246–263. https://doi.org/10.1353/wsq.2015.0021.

Mihailides, S., Devilly, G.J., & Ward, T. (2004). Implicit cognitive distortions and sexual offending. *Sexual Abuse: Journal of Research and Treatment, 16(4)*, 333–350. https://doi.org/10.1177/107906320401600406.

Molnar, B.E., Buka, S.L., & Kessler, R.C. (2001). Child sexual abuse and subsequent psychopathology: Results from the National Comorbidity Survey. *American Journal of Public Health, 91(5)*, 753–760. https://doi.org/10.2105/ajph.91.5.753.

Musk, H., Swetz, A., & Vernon, M. (1997). Pedophilia in the correctional system. *Corrections Today, 59(5)*, 24–29.

Myers, J.E.B. (2008). A short history of child protection in America. *Family Law Quarterly, 42(3)*, 449–463. https://us.sagepub.com/sites/default/files/upm-binaries/35363_Chapter1.pdf.

Nelson, A., & Oliver, P. (1998). Gender and the construction of consent in child-adult sexual contact: Beyond gender neutrality and male monopoly. *Gender & Society, 12(5)*, 554–577. https://doi.org/10.1177/089124398012005004.

Nighman, B. (2017, November 17). *Anthony Edwards is telling the truth—Gary Goddard is a pedophile*. Medium. https://medium.com/@bretnighman/anthony-edwards-is-telling-the-truth-2a54c2bde848.

O'Carroll, T. (1980). *Pedophilia: The radical case*. Peter Owen.

Olson, L., Daggs, J.L., Ellevold, B.L., & Rogers, T.K. (2007). Entrapping the Innocent: Toward a Theory of Child Sexual Predators' Luring Communication. *Communication Theory, 17(3)*, 231–251. https://doi.org/10.1111/j.1468-2885.2007.00294.x.

Otterson, J. (2017, November 20). Fellow actor backs Anthony Edwards molestation claims against producer Gary Goddard (updated). *Variety*. https://variety.com/2017/tv/news/anthony-edwards-gary-goddard-sexual-molestation-2-1202619538/.

Oz, M. [The Dr. Oz Show]. (2017, December 2). *Oz exclusive: More victims of Anthony Edwards' alleged abuser speak out* [Video]. Doctoroz.com. https://www.doctoroz.com/episode/oz-exclusive-more-victims-anthony-edwards-alleged-abuser-speak-out.

Pence, D.M., & Wilson, C.A. (1994). Reporting and investigating child sexual abuse. *The Future of Children, 4(2)*, 70–83. https://doi.org/10.2307/1602524.

Pereda, N., Guilera, G., Forns, M., & Gómez-Benito, J. (2009). The prevalence of child sexual abuse in community and student samples: A meta-analysis. *Clinical Psychology Review, 29(4)*, 328–338. https://doi.org/10.1016/j.cpr.2009.02.007.

Petronio, S. (2002). *Boundaries of privacy: Dialectics of disclosure*. State University of New York Press.

Petronio, S. (2007). Translational research endeavors and the practices of communication privacy management. *Journal of Applied Communication Research, 35(3)*, 218–222. https://doi.org/10.1080/00909880701422443.

Petronio, S., Flores, L.A., & Hecht, M.L. (1997) Locating the voice of logic: Disclosure discourse of sexual abuse. *Western Journal of Communication, 61(1)*, 101–113. https://doi.org/10.1080/10570319709374565.

Petronio, S., Reeder, H.M., Hecht, M.L., & Mon't Ros-Mendoza, T. (1996). Disclosure of sexual abuse by children and adolescents. *Journal of Applied Communication Research, 24(3)*, 181–199. https://doi.org/10.1080/00909889609365450.

Plann, S. (2008). "Bad things": Child abuse and the nineteenth-century Spanish National School for the Deaf and Blind. *Sign Language Studies, 8(2)*, 181–210. https://doi.org/10.1353/sls.2008.0002.

Primoratz, I. (1999). Pedophilia. *Public Affairs Quarterly, 13(1)*, 99–110.

Putnam, F.W. (2003). Ten-year research update review: Child sexual abuse. *Journal of the American Academy of Child and Adolescent Psychiatry, 42(3)*, 269–278. https://doi.org/10.1097/00004583-200303000-00006.

Russell, G. (2008). Pedophiles in wonderland: Censoring the sinful in cyberspace. *Journal of Criminal Law & Criminology, 98*, 1467–1499. https://scholarlycommons.law.northwestern.edu/cgi/viewcontent.cgi?article=7310&conte xt=jclc.

Saywitz, K.J., Mannarino, A.P., Berliner, L., & Cohen, J.A. (2000). Treatment of sexually abused children and adolescents. *American Psychologist, 55(9)*, 1040–1049. https://doi.org/10.1037/0003-066X.55.9.1040.

Schaffner, L. (2002). An age of reason: Paradoxes in the U.S. legal construction of adulthood. *International Journal of Children's Rights, 10*, 201–232.

Silverman, J., & Wilson, D. (2002). *Innocence betrayed: Pedophilia, the media and society*. Polity.

Solomon, G. (2011, November 21). *Slow to React*. American Journalism Review. https://ajrarchive.org/article.asp?id=5178.

Spitzberg, B.H., Marshall, L., & Cupach, W.R. (2001) Obsessive relational intrusion, coping, and sexual coercion victimization. *Communication Reports, 14(1)*, 19–30, https://doi.org/10.1080/08934210109367733.

Stevens, J.M., Arzoumanian, M.A., Greenbaum, B., Schwab, B.M., & Dalenberg, C.J. (2019). Relationship of abuse by religious authorities to depression, religiosity, and child physical abuse history in a college sample. *Psychological trauma: Theory, research, practice and policy, 11(3)*, 292–299. https://doi.org/10.1037/tra0000421.

Stoltenborgh, M., van Ijzendoorn, M.H., Euser, E.M., & Bakermans-Kranenburg, M.J. (2011). A global perspective on child sexual abuse: Meta-analysis of prevalence around the world. *Child Maltreatment, 16(2)*, 79–101. https://doi.org/10.1177/1077559511403920.

Sumner, S.A., Mercy, A.A., Saul, J., Motsa-Nzuza, N., Kwesigabo, G., Buluma, R., Marcelin, L.H., Lina, H., Shawa, M., Moloney-Kitts, M., Kilbane, T., Sommarin, C., Ligiero, D.P., Brookmeyer, K., Chiang, L., Lea, V., Lee, J., Kress, H., Hillis, S.D., & Centers for Disease Control and Prevention (2015). Prevalence of sexual violence against children and use of social services—seven countries, 2007–2013. *Morbidity and Mortality Weekly Report, 64(21)*, 565–569. https://www.ncbi.nlm.nih.gov/pmc/articles/PMC4584766/pdf/565-569.pdf.

Teeman, T. (2018, April 17). *ER's star Edwards: I don't see my childhood sexual abuse as a "tragedy."* The Daily Beast. https://www.thedailybeast.com/er-star-anthony-edwards-i-dont-see-my-childhood-sexual-abuse-as-a-tragedy.

Thomas, J., & Humphery, S. (2014). Safeguarding children: A challenge to doctors. *BMJ, 349*, g5898. https://doi.org/10.1136/bmj.g5898.

Thomas, T. (2005). *Sex crime: Sex offending and society* (2nd ed.). William.

Thompson, L. (2012). A preface to the chart "preferred terminology for sex trafficking and prostitution." *Social Work & Christianity, 39(4)*, 481–487. https://search.proquest.com/openview/13f85cd16a2deec84639640e5ee62c2b/1?pq-origsite=gscholar&cbl=40430.

Vox Staff. (2019, January 9). *A list of people accused of sexual harassment, misconduct, or assault: 263 celebrities, politicians, CEOs, and others who have been accused of sexual misconduct since April 2017.* Vox. https://www.vox.com/a/sexual-harassment-assault-allegations-list.

Walsh, W.A., Jones, L.M., Cross, T.P., & Lippert, T. (2010). Prosecuting child sexual abuse: The importance of evidence type. *Crime & Delinquency, 56(3)*, 436–454. https://doi.org/10.1177/0011128708320484.

World Health Organization. (2003). *Guidelines for medico-legal care for victims of sexual violence.* WHO Press. https://apps.who.int/iris/bitstream/handle/10665/42788/924154628X.pdf?sequence=1.

9

"Star" Athletes Use Videos
of Their Arrests
to Reveal Police Brutality

People derive meaning from how they look, and Black and non–Black people assign meaning to Black bodies. African Americans have a saying, the darker the berry, the sweeter the juice, celebrating their skin tone and features. However, in predominately white spaces, the more Afrocentric an African American's facial features, the more prone an African American is expected to be deviant (Eberhardt et al., 2006). It is disturbing that based on someone's appearance, body, clothing, or artifacts, their fellow citizens portend to know their character and how they will behave. Rarely do national narratives in the United States depict African Americans succeeding without assimilating or imitating whiteness. In Frantz Fanon's *Black Skin, White Masks* (2008), this sentiment is summarized: "To speak a language is to appropriate its world and culture. The Antillean who wants to be white will succeed, since he will have adopted the cultural tool of language" (p. 21). Even when Black bodies are perceived as imitating whiteness (i.e., that which is desirable in the U.S.), an imitation is oftentimes perceived as just that, an imitation. In the U.S., many Black people who have heritage in the country for generations, and those who have more recently immigrated, ponder: if we are all created equal, where are my inalienable rights?

In 2012, Jonathan Capehart used his *Washington Post* editorial on George Zimmerman's killing of Trayvon Martin to reflect upon a conversation he had with his mother when he was younger—the focus was on not talking back to police, not running in a public setting, and avoiding the appearance of suspicion. He contemplated: "After all, I was taught these things almost 20 years after Jim Crow by African Americans who experienced its soul-crushing force first hand…. So much has changed for the better since then. But then comes along Trayvon Martin to remind us that the burden of suspicion is still ours [i.e., black males] to bear. And the cost for taking our lives might be none."

Did Martin and countless other Black males and females die because of negrophobia? Shaun Gabiddon surmised in *Criminological Theories on Race and Crime* (2010) that negrophobia is an irrational fear of being victimized by Black people. Within the U.S., this irrational fear manifests in some white people, and this fear is an impetus for the shooting or harming of a Black person based on racial bias and stereotypes (Armour, 1997). Black people are maligned in the larger society, and they live in danger of being harmed under the slightest pretense (Gabiddon, 2010; Tonry, 2011). Various social and cultural institutions in the U.S. contribute to this toxic and dangerous environment for Black people. Scrutiny of this environment reveals that the media and law enforcement influence perceptions of Black people and directly affect how African Americans and other Black people in the U.S. are treated.

Media portrayals have been instrumental in the maligning of Black men. The media contributes to characterizations of how Black bodies will look and behave. Bryson's (1998) work addresses how these portrayals rely on stereotypes and caricatures, such as Black men as studs or imitators of whiteness (specifically white men). For media users, these characterizations can be visceral in nature, since they are triggers or "dog whistles" that elicit varied reactions. Lives hang in the balance when a Black male is perceived as dangerous because he is profiled as fitting "prototypes" of criminal suspects—both law enforcement and bystanders' reactions to his Black body could put his life in danger (Oliver et al., 2004). These characterizations are derived from perceptions of reality, although they may be divorced from the truth. When the news media and entertainment programmers (e.g., creators of print, television, film, and online representations) rely on less than flattering depictions of Black males, their "creative" content activates preexisting stereotypes and caricatures about Black males possessed by media users. The media influences the minds of everyone, from impressionable children and adolescents to persuadable young adults, their parents, and grandparents. Many people lack sufficient interaction with Black people to counteract media portrayals. Many urban, suburban, and rural areas in the U.S. are moderately to highly segregated residentially, reducing the likelihood of significant interaction between those who are racially and ethnically stereotyped and fellow citizens who are doing the stereotyping (Bonilla-Silva, 2009). The perceptions of "the Other" which are portrayed in the media create, confirm, or affirm stereotypes that may be the antithesis of who a Black person is.

This chapter addresses policy brutality and how law enforcement officers' reliance on stereotypes and caricatures of Black bodies, especially those associated with Black men as prototypes of criminal suspects, contributes to Black men being severely harmed, perhaps leading to loss of life, when they are involved in incidents with the police. During these incidents Black men perceived as imitators of whiteness in the mainstream media, such as successful Black male athletes who have attained fame, money, adulation, and status, endure police brutality like any other Black man. During these incidents, successful Black male athletes find that characteristics or behavior they are rewarded for while playing their sport endanger them when involved in an altercation with law enforcement. Stereotypes and caricatures of Black male bodies trump their celebrity status as successful male athletes. They are perceived as dangerous, and they too experience police brutality. Police brutality is defined as "the use of excessive physical force or verbal assault and psychological intimidation" (Walker, 2011, p. 579). Black people complain about experiencing police brutality more than their white counterparts (Smith & Holmes, 2003). Black people endure "driving while Black," meaning that they are stopped by police while driving a car more frequently than their white counterparts, and they underreport the frequency with which they are stopped because law enforcement perceives them as an unnatural fit with an affluent lifestyle (Tomaskkovic-Devey et al., 2006), whether it be driving an expensive car, or where they live, among other higher social desirability factors.

Caught on Tape

One tool that has been used to combat an escalation in police brutality against Black people is the taping and disseminating of recordings of their mistreatment in law enforcement encounters. The beating of Rodney King is one of the most infamous examples of police brutality caught on video in the twentieth century, and it shocked the nation when it was aired by the mainstream media in 1992. Lily Rothman (2016) reflected on how writer Touré noted in *Time* that what King experienced was not special: "What separated [the incident] from others was that 81 seconds of it was surreptitiously videotaped by a stranger, giving the world a look at the police coldly and cruelly beating a black man," he wrote. The cruelty continued into the 2000s and 2010s when Africans Americans and other people of color encountered police beatings and killings, including the murders of Sean Bell (shot at 50 times), Timothy Thomas, Amadou Diallo (shot at 40 times), Devin Brown (13 years old), Adolph Grimes (shot 12 times in the back), and Oscar Grant, and severe bodily harm experienced by Abner Louima, Gregory Lee-Bey, and Chad Holley (Chaney & Robertson, 2014, p. 109). In a world of iPhones and Twitter, bystanders can record footage and uploaded it to the Internet, so the world can be aware of what is happening in America. Many Americans were shocked that Eric Garner died while in police custody—many onlookers in person and via social media were convinced he was murdered before their eyes (TIME Video, 2014). Fast-forward to 2020, and the video recording of the police brutality George Floyd experienced. The public experienced a dying George Floyd's last moments. America and the world were left reeling after Floyd was heard on the over eight-minute video recording repeatedly exclaiming, "I can't breathe." The tragedy makes it clear that change is still needed.

These video recordings affect perceptions and interactions with law enforcement. Black people and other people of color want to avoid the police. Evidence indicates that Black youth recognize the "criminal" stigma associated with them, and they anticipate negative police behavior during their encounters with law enforcement (Brunson & Miller, 200; Carr et al., 2007; Fine et al., 2003; Hinds, 2007). Youth indicate that "more police makes it less safe; anything can happen with the police around," and "more police may mean lower rates of murder but more police brutality" (Fina et al., 2003, p. 2). Black youth on college campuses are like peers in neighborhoods across America, tired of the status quo, and receptive to concepts such as civic duty, advocacy, and activism. Their pleas for change are affirmed and amplified in the discourse of their social networks. These students' experiences with college administrators and other university stakeholders mirror the experiences their family and friends experience with law enforcement—marginality of Black people within institutions that form the bedrock of American society: "it is important to note the racialized history of exclusion…, integration, and battles against inequity that have inundated the institution's history" (Jones, 2017, p. 70). Black youth, youth of all backgrounds, and adults on- and off-campus, rely on hybridized online-offline networks to mediate interactions with law enforcement.

Social media platforms provide a connection between online and offline networks, and smartphones enable victims, bystanders, and other public and private entities to video record law enforcement encounters, upload them to social media, and spread awareness about police misconduct. It is "imperative for researchers to better understand how technology-embedded social movements navigate the diversity of information, narratives, and values, but most importantly, how social movements' utilization of these networks of information and technology can foster justice, equity, an democracy" (Tewksbury, 2018, p. 55). One group that has taken an outsized role in protesting police brutality is Black male athletes—men with hybridized online-offline networks that reach millions of fans and admirers, men with a platform they increasingly use to champion social justice. Scott Brooks (2016) detailed how Black male athlete activism is not new (p. 20):

One could begin with Tom Molineaux and his aspiration to be a prizefighter to purchase his freedom from slavery. Many have written about or studied Jack Johnson, another prizefighter who bucked the status quo and battled desegregating the heavyweight world championship. Of course, there's Muhammad Ali and his refusal to fight in the Vietnam War. And Ali's activism leads right into the Olympic Project for Human Rights and the broader statement by Black athletes including Jim Brown, Bill Russell, Kareem Abdul-Jabbar and others. A few more recent and relevant moments:

March 2012: LeBron James, Dwayne Wade and members of the 2012 Miami Heat post a photo on Twitter with hoodies and heads lowered in mourning for Trayvon Martin.

November 2014: Some players of the St. Louis Rams run out for introductions with their hands raised, in the "hands up, don't shoot" pose in solidarity with #BlackLivesMatter after Michael Brown's shooting death in nearby Ferguson, Missouri.

In the twenty-first century, athletes are in vogue. They have many adoring fans and social media followers. Black male athletes are popular among constituencies consisting of people with various gendered, racial, ethnic, national, educational, and socioeconomic identities. Millennials and members of Generation Z identify with Black male athletes because of what they represent: they are cultural icons who provide semiotic clues to how Blackness, the underdog in our American narrative, can be ascendant, entrepreneurial, and a success story—if they can make it, so can I (Mukherjee, 2006). These athletes resonate with Black people, especially Black youth, as a symbol of what is possible when you transcend your circumstances (other personas that resonate are the hip-hop mogul or the rap star). Black parents understand that their children see themselves in representations of Black athletes. For these reasons, when Black male athletes have a resolve in social justice and collective action, it is powerful.

When the experiences they address in their advocacy and activism are personal for themselves and their audiences, their candor and authenticity make them compelling spokespersons for change. Black male athletes who are successful at bringing about change partake in informed advocacy, "proceeding from knowledge of the U.S. legal system, laws, legal practitioners, and legal process and procedure" (Lynch & Mitchell, 1995, p. 10–11). Informed advocacy increasingly requires an acute understanding that social media influences the regional, national, and international news agendas. Informed advocacy on social media networks has the power to make memes and viral moments stories online, which become news carried offline through mainstream television, radio, or newspapers (Miladi, 2016). These Black male athletes, like activists around the world, are no longer mere observers or followers of news—they are shapers of the news. Their user-generated content about their experiences with police brutality becomes incorporated into news programs around the world. Black male athletes who upload video recordings of their and other Black people's violent encounters with police make it difficult for people to turn away from the truth and disrupt government's and mainstream media's information management and their political communication channels both locally and internationally. These athletes use their online and offline networks within and outside of policy and legal frameworks (Acosta, 2012; Reid, 2000), in and out of political work (Berry, 1999; Parks, 2008), ultimately relying on media users' perception of athletes' moral authority to speak on behalf of the countless Black men and women, fathers and mothers, and children, who die at the hands of police year after year.

Cultural and Political Effects of Transportation Media

Sarah Sharma (2008) conceptualizes the media through medium theory. She postulates that variations of mediums and media are not neutral, and depending on who uses them and how they are used, they produce cultural and political effects that have intended and unintended consequences for all parties involved. These parties include those driving or framing the message and those being driven or framed by it. This perspective of medium theory is applicable to traditional and social media, both being central technologies through which content creators and media users experience time and space. Sharma (2008) argues that medium theory assumes (p. 458):

> That the content is secondary to the spatial and temporal effects that are produced at the level of culture. It is in "medium theory" where questions of space, time, and the cultural and political effects of transportation media are central. In "medium theory" media are understood as environments in which social life unfolds.

Within this context the mediums and media not only contribute to reality, they create reality itself, and content creators and media users navigate the reality they both contribute to and manifest into being. Cyberculture and social media are the latest incarnation of this phenomenon, whereby people in the "real world" create avatars in virtual reality, in spaces such as *Second Life*, or fake online profiles for dating websites and apps, to engage with communicative partners who are either in on the fantasy or are being "catfished" as unsuspecting victims. The computer, smartphone, and other forms of communication and information technologies are conduits between the realities. They rely on electronic communication to transport content creators and willing and unwilling media users to social life they may or may not be prepared for. Technology enables users to cross back and forth across time zones and spaces with the click of a button, giving media users the ability to affect multiple realities in ways that were not possible 10 or 20 years ago. Ian Angus (1998) foresaw the implications of this new normal, noting a medium of communication "incorporates both a technology and a series of related social identities (or subject-position)" (p. 8). Cyberculture is the new normal, and social media platforms, websites, and apps allow more people now than at any other time in human history to tell their stories, create and share narratives from their vantage points, and side-step the gatekeepers who have always stood in their way at getting at the truth. Acknowledging that there are no "neutral" representations of identities in media content, content creators have an agenda in traditional and new media, in mainstream and alternative media. Black male athletes and their allies who challenge the status quo regarding police brutality straddle the duality between realities, between celebrity and adulation, and being phenotypically perceived as just another Black man, as the object of news and entertainment media coverage, and as content creators who use activism in various online-offline networks to advocate for change.

Professional and collegiate athletes recognize that their platform is unique. Other members of society have platforms, including politicians, other entertainers, and spiritual and religious leaders, but athletes seem more iconic because they are engrained in the public's psyche as an essential component of who we are. Many sports fans and non-fans have played sports before. Some of them excelled in the game, others watched in the stands, and many grew up in towns and cities in rural, suburban, or urban areas that covered the play-by-play moments of local sports heroes. Through sports, children can learn morals such as good sportsmanship, teamwork, the importance of character, and that winning is not all that matters. Americans and sports fans around the world associate some of the most important memories of their lives with sporting events. In the U.S., as Black men gained access and acceptance in collegiate and professional sports, Black male athletes received adulation as athletes, but when they addressed the ills faced by Black men in society, they historically faced less than receptive media and media users.

This reality and media landscape are changing, and social media is giving these athletes an opportunity to cultivate their messages, engage in dialogue with sports fans, and resonate with audiences online and offline. These athletes are increasingly a part of civic culture. Dahlgren (2009) explained how these civic cultures can have inherent cultural patterns of political participation—these patterns manifest in social media uses, including new arenas for engagement and participation in the blogosphere,

YouTube, Facebook, Twitter, TikTok, and Internet-based news organizations. Media users who engage one another on social media demonstrate cognitive and affective investment in civic culture (Dahlgren, 2009, p. 83). Some of them are compelled to contest perceived injustice (Castells, 2012; Howard et al., 2011), whether it be by joining online protests or participating in offline activism. In the 2000s and 2010s, social media platforms such as Facebook, Twitter, VKontakte, and Weibo globally spurred more civic engagement in Egypt, the U.S., Turkey, the United Kingdom, Russia, China, Hong Kong, Spain, Brazil, and Portugal (Al-Azm, 2011; Baumgarten, 2013; Branco, 2014; Castells, 2012; Eltantawy & Julie, 2011; Ho & Garrett, 2014; Lim, 2012). "Social network sites have changed not only the number of sustainable connections with other people but also the perception that it is plausible to relate with large numbers of people" (Cardoso et al., 2016, p. 3,912). Burkell et al. (2014) recognized that undergirding these online social networks are strong and weak ties, with more weak ties than their offline counterparts. Media users developed communalism online through sending messages, posting, chatting, and adding likes and comments to one another's walls (Cardoso, Lapa, & Di Fátima, 2016). To fully understand the implications of new media in civic culture, researchers should use these five distinct levels of analysis (Aday et al., 2010):

1. Level one is to transform (or not) individuals' attitudes and willingness to engage in political action.
2. Level two is to mitigate or exacerbate group conflict.
3. Level three is to facilitate collective action.
4. Level four is to help regimes to better spy on and control their citizens.
5. Level five is to garner international attention.

Activists are astute to recognize the galvanizing tool social media has become, and that it, along with their bodies, may not be perfect, "but sometimes they are enough" (DeLuca et al., 2012). Sometimes bodies and visual technologies of social media converge, and visual images of bruised and beaten bodies are elevated in eyewitness videos uploaded and streamed online. Once these eyewitness videos are in the public square, they can be used to further human rights as an investigative tool in advocacy work. They garner wider global media coverage than other records of abuse and misconduct, and they become a form of legal evidence in court rooms (Ristovska, 2016). Eyewitness videos are difficult for governments to use to manipulate the public, because media users can watch and listen to the video footage and determine for themselves what really happened. It is difficult for regimes to contain the fallout of eyewitness video once it has been posted and shared online. Once the eyewitness video is online, it diffuses through various online-offline networks, possibly going viral. Activists cannot underestimate the impact YouTube has on videos going viral and information about the video entering the mainstream media and public consciousness. Gauntlett (2011) sees YouTube as more than a video archive; it is a platform that seeks to create and foster community by encouraging "users to make comments, to subscribe, to give star ratings, to add friends and send messages, and to make videos responding to other videos" (p. 93).

Another important website and app for fostering public discourse, advocacy, and activism is Twitter. Twitter is a popular and effective means for discussing eyewitness videos online, and even if regimes are able to take a video down, tweets on Twitter provide real-time logistical coordination, information, information sharing, and discussion, which is difficult to eradicate or erase (Lotan et al., 2011). Twitter's global nature and ability to connect media users across time and space instantly through hashtags and retweets rattles authoritarian governments and secretive law enforcement agencies (Chaudhry, 2014). Activists use Twitter because it is: (1) quick, provides real-time information in 140 characters or less, (2) free, (3) personal, (4) highly mobile and resistant to government control, and (5) can be anonymous (Johnson et al., 2013, p. 126). These attributes have made Twitter a useful tool for activists around the world, including those who participated in the Arab Spring in the Middle East and protests in Hong Kong and the U.S. In the U.S., the #BlackLivesMatter movement began following the July 2013 acquittal of George Zimmerman for the murder of Trayvon Martin, and a year later, the movement protested the death of Michael Brown at the hands of violent acts by police (Langford & Speight, 2015). The #BlackLivesMatter movement persists as more Black men and women, boys, and girls, are killed by law enforcement.

In the study *Geographies of Pain: #SayHerName and the fear of Black Women's Mobility* (2016), research indicated that the #SayHerName movement has created awareness for Black women in ways other social media-related movements have not. The focus of #SayHerName is solely on the murder of Black women by law enforcement. Black women contend with pseudo-authoritarian officials and surveilling law enforcement agencies that seek to control their mobility. These actions do not exist in a vacuum, as similar efforts persist to control the movements of other marginalized groups (e.g., marginalized races, ethnicities, genders, sexualities, and classes). Black women who were murdered in transit by law enforcement, whether it be in cars, parking lots, or public streets, include Shantel Davis, Sharmel Edwards, Kendra James, LaTanya Haggerty, Shelly Frey, Tyisha Miller, Alexia Christian, and Sonji Taylor (Crenshaw, Ritchie, Anspach, & Gilmer, 2015). "As the popular news media situates anti–Black police violence largely within the experience of Black men, #SayHerName critiques this tendency by showing that Black women are strangely absent from this conversation" (Towns, 2016, p. 122). Unfortunately, for every Trayvon Martin, there is a Breonna Taylor. For every news story about Black lives adversely affected by police brutality, there are others that are ignored or are underreported. Far too often their stories are not present in news media coverage, and when they are represented in the news, how do content creators frame the narrative? Do they avert attention from the narrative to counternarratives? Perhaps public attention is shifted to the counternarratives of the "All Lives Matter" or the "Blue Lives Matter" movements, which downplay the complexity of identities that are victims of surveillance, oppression, systemic racism, and discrimination (Hoffman et al., 2016). Depending on media users' self-perceptions of these movements, counternarratives allow them to exhibit how they perceive dominant or alternative narratives that lampoon their own self-concepts.

Black Athletes Seek Accountability: Videoed Beatings Go Viral

Sports are America's pastime and a form of leisure that crosses cultural, social, ethnic, and racial lines. Children across the country become athletes and desire to be the "star" on their football, baseball, basketball, soccer, hockey, tennis, or golf teams. Some of these "star" athletes grow up to become local heroes, wunderkinds, and celebrities. They have fans who know them even when they know nothing about their sport. However, the fame these celebrities attain does not protect them from violence. Sometimes the violence they experience is perpetrated by those who are sworn to serve and protect them. In many instances, police single out these athletes as persons of interest because someone has committed a crime, and law enforcement's perception of these athletes is that they have characteristics similar to criminals.

Michael Bennett, who retired from the NFL in 2020, was playing for the Seattle Seahawks when he had an off-the-field encounter with police in Las Vegas in 2017. Media users who were not able to watch his live press conference about the encounter on September 6, 2017, can access it via YouTube (NFL YouTube Channel, 2017). The day after the encounter, Bennett took to Twitter to share a chilling letter about what transpired (Finley, 2017). He mentioned that after the Mayweather-McGregor fight in late August, he was heading back to his hotel ,when he heard gunshots. He explained that in the aftermath of the gunshots he was one of many bystanders who ran for safety, and that is when the police stopped him "for doing nothing more than simply being a black man in the wrong place at the wrong time." Bennett was forced to the ground. He told the media he felt profiled. Bennett's letter on Twitter elaborated on his experience: "As I laid on the ground, complying with his commands to not move, he placed his gun near my head and warned me that if I moved he would 'blow my f*****g head off' … terrified and confused … a second officer came over and forcefully jammed his knee into my back making it difficult for me to breathe … they then cinched the handcuffs on my wrists so tight that my fingers went numb." In a written statement to *HuffPost*, Black Lives Matter co-founder Patrisse Cullors reflected: "Michael Bennett and I met during Charleena Lyles' rally in August. He was clear that he is an activist first. I can't believe that a month later I am supporting him as a victim of police brutality." Cullors condemned the alleged assault of Bennet by police (Finley, 2017). Colin Kaepernick showed his support for Bennett when he stated publicly: "The violation that happened against my Brother Michael Bennett is disgusting and unjust. I stand with Michael and I stand with the people." Bennett appreciated the support from Cullors and Kaepernick. He also recognized that Black people alone cannot stop the injustice. He called on white NFL players to speak out against the injustices Black people face. Amid news media coverage of his encounter with the Las Vegas police, Bennett had to cope with the trauma associated with his experience and determine what he could do legally to hold law enforcement accountable.

Former NFL player Desmond Marrow's experience was more fraught than Bennett's. According to court documents from Marrow's lawyers, who are affiliated with the Atlanta chapter of Black Lives Matter, Marrow claims that after a white man threw a cup of coffee at his car while he was driving on Interstate 75, Marrow followed the car to the parking lot of a local Target to inquire about why the coffee was thrown (Callahan, 2018; Habersham, 2018). Marrow's lawyers, Andrea Boyd and Chris Stewart, insisted that a witness called 911 and erroneously reported that Marrow had a weapon (Habersham, 2018). In a Facebook post, Marrow disclosed the gruesome details of his encounter with police: "I had no type of weapon in my possession, I was arrested for having a gun that turned out to be my cell phone. During the arrest, the police knocked my teeth out, slammed me on my head and choked me out until I was unconscious." In the video, Marrow can be heard stating he is not fighting back, and the person capturing the video via cellphone is heard saying, "This is unbelievable." Instead of Henry County police apologizing for the mistreatment of Marrow, he was charged with felonies, including obstruction and making terroristic threats, as well misdemeanors, such as reckless and aggressive driving (Callahan, 2018; Habersham, 2018). Bennett's encounter in Las Vegas and Marrow's encounter in suburban Atlanta are not unique. Black men less famous than Bennett and Marrow have encounters with police in cities, in suburbia, and in rural towns and areas throughout the U.S. every day.

Officials in Milwaukee released a video showing officers using a stun gun on NBA player Sterling Brown over a parking violation. The chief of police declared the handling of the matter inappropriate, and the officers were disciplined (Smith & Hoffman, 2018). The 30-minute police body-camera video, which authorities initially refused to release to the public, showed a police officer confronting Brown as he emerged from a store. Brown's car was parked in a handicapped zone, "and the situation swiftly escalates into a confrontation with multiple officers and squad cars" (Smith & Hoffman, 2018). During the video, Brown does not appear to raise his voice or physically resist officers. A telling exchange occurs between one of the officers and Brown before he is tased with a stun gun: "I own this right here," an officer says at one point, with Brown responding, "You don't own me." The president of the Milwaukee branch of the N.A.A.C.P. called for changes to police department policies, adding, "For a person to go and have to be physically accosted at the hands of police for a parking citation speaks volumes." Milwaukee's major, Tom Barrett, said that "as a human being, I am offended by what I saw." He said: "Mr. Brown deserves an apology, and I am very sorry the Milwaukee police treated him in the fashion he was treated." During the NBA summer league, Brown shared his thoughts about his encounter with police with *The Undefeated* (Spears, 2018):

> I've questioned it a few times, just trying to brainstorm and figure out, "Why me?" But I got a platform that a lot of people don't have. And for the people that do have a platform that haven't experienced it, it's just something I got to take on and I just got to do it. I got to be that voice, and once it's time to actually step up and do something and put things into play, I can't look nowhere else but forward and try to make things happen.
>
> I was literally in and out. But I parked in a double handicap. I should have been given a ticket, no doubt about it. That has not justification to what escalated afterwards. So I did it, but what came after, you can't even compare it to what I should've gotten for what happened.

Brown spent several hours in jail, but he was released and never charged. Brown's NBA team, the Milwaukee Bucks, stated that they were "grateful for the services of good police officers," and that "incidents like this remind us of the injustices that persist." Brown decided to file a federal civil rights suit against the Milwaukee Police Department and the city, claiming his Fourth and Fourteenth Amendment rights were violated during his arrest and tasing, which resulted in the use of excessive force and wrongful arrest (Luthern & Barton, 2018). The lawsuit quotes extensively from the body camera footage of the altercation between Brown and police outside of a Walgreens and includes images of Facebook posts from one officer involved in the altercation, who appeared to mock Brown and share racist memes on the social media platform (Luthern & Barton, 2018). In response to the police altercation with Brown, the Fire and Police Commission requested an audit of the police department and demanded all body camera footage and all findings of the audit be submitted to the commission and the Common Council. In 2019, the city and Brown's attorney went to court to determine if a settlement could be reached, with Brown's attorney asserting any starting point for a settlement should include the city admitting to violations of Brown's constitutional rights (Luthern, 2019). The altercation involving Brown was not an anomaly—since 2015, the city had paid roughly $22 million in police misconduct lawsuits. Because the city is self-insured, citizens' taxes were used to pay the costs (Luthern & Barton, 2018). Whether or not oversight of these altercations occurs at the local, state, or national level, by commissions, councils, mayors, governors, or federal agencies, through civil lawsuits or criminal litigation, however these situations are resolved, the videotaped beatings or murders, the images and audio of what transpired can exist on social media indefinitely (Lynn, 2018). Once the genie is out of the bottle, it cannot be put back in.

Two TMZ cell-phone videos showed NBA star Thabo Sefolosha violently thrown to the ground by at least five New York City Police Department (NYPD) officers, hit with a retractable baton, and eventually led away limping in handcuffs (Penn, 2015). The police refuted Sefolosha's claims of police brutality and arrested him for disorderly conduct, resisting arrest, and obstruction of governmental administration. Sefolosha rejected multiple plea deals, and after deliberating for just 45 minutes, a jury exonerated him (Penn, 2015). Two weeks later, he announced that he was suing the police department for $50 million. Bennett, Marrow, Brown, Sefolosha, and their peers are standing up for themselves and for members of their communities who have had similar experiences but lack the fame to attract media scrutiny and greater accountability. Retired professional tennis player James Blake was also manhandled by police and wants to help others avoid a similar fate. A timestamped hotel surveillance tape shows a plainclothes NYPD officer who never showed a badge or identified himself tackle Blake, twist his arm, grab him by the neck, and throw him face-first onto the concrete. The officer thrust a knee into Blake's back as he slapped on handcuffs (Clarke, 2017). In the aftermath, Blake agreed not to sue the city, putting his focus on the public disciplinary trial of the police officer charged with using excessive force. He has written a book about his experience with police brutality, and he explores how athletes across sports have used their fame and influence to provide a voice on issues of social justice for decades.

The debate regarding when and how police use force during their interaction with the public has been in the headlines, and policing in urban communities has been an issue for generations. "Star" athletes are not immune to this issue and provide fans who have never witnessed a violent encounter with the police a peek inside the life of someone who feels unjustly targeted, abused, and stripped of their dignity. Fans who have had similar experiences as these athletes empathize with them and support their efforts to end police brutality. As these videoed beatings are shared on social media, discussed online and offline, and increasingly represented in news media coverage, they focus public attention on police brutality of Black people. Increasingly, the public, civic organizations, and local and state governments are urging the police to release body camera footage of these encounters.

The Need for Reform Is Overdue

The debate is over—police brutality is real. There are racial differences in police use of force. Regarding nonlethal use of force, evidence indicates Black Americans and Latin Americans are more than 50 percent more likely to experience some form of force in interactions with police: "Adding controls that account for important context and civilian behavior reduces, but cannot fully explain, these disparities" (Fryer, Jr., 2019, p. 1, 210). Furthermore, there needs to be an in-depth analysis of the root causes of excessive use of force by police applied to Black men, which results in "justifiable homicides" and murder. According to researchers Gilbert and Ray (2016), "justifiable homicides" involve excessive use of force by police that may result in homicides that are "deemed to be justified or excused and classified by the CDC as death by legal intervention" (p. 123). One root cause of excessive use of force by police applied to Black Americans are inadequate policies that fail to adequately protect Black Americans from aggressive and unnecessary violence—policing that treats civilians as enemy combatants instead of fellow Americans. This violence hurts people and communities. Police misconduct, violence, and brutality are a public health crisis in the U.S. Policy changes are needed to mitigate poor decision-making among officers. Opportunities exist for requiring different behaviors from law enforcement—specifically, local, county, and statewide police organizations—which would lessen the quantity and severity of the use of force incidents and improve health outcomes (Obasogie & Newman, 2017). Policy changes are crucial for creating conditions for decreasing violence and reducing adverse health impacts.

Since 2014, the Inter-American Commission on Human Rights has expressed serious concern over discriminatory police violence in the U.S. In a 2016 written submission on *Excessive Use of Force by the Police against*

Black Americans in the United States, the commission recognized that the murder of Eric Garner in New York and Michael Brown in Missouri are a part of a pattern of excessive force by police officers toward Black Americans and other persons of color. The commission expressed outrage that structural and legal deficiencies continue to underlie and feed disproportionate violence toward persons of color, and the issue of excessive force results in unjustified and unlawful killings that undermine many human rights. American and international standards of public health are inclusive of human rights, and healthcare organizations support violence prevention and violence mitigation. Together, five intersecting mechanisms at both the individual and community level help researchers discern an intelligible link between police brutality and excess morbidity among Black Americans (Alang et al., 2017, p. 2):

1. Fatal injuries that increase population-specific mortality rates.
2. Adverse physiological responses that increase morbidity.
3. Racist public reactions that cause stress.
4. Arrests, incarcerations, and legal, medical, and funeral bills that cause financial strain.
5. Integrated oppressive structures that cause systematic disempowerment.

As representatives of the state, law enforcement officials are given powers that can be misused to exacerbate factors (e.g., fatal injuries, adverse physiological responses, racist public reactions, arrests, incarcerations, and oppression) that contribute to the five intersecting mechanisms, including the power to use force and firearms, to arrest and detain, and to carry out searches or seizure (International Committee of the Red Cross, 2015). In democracies, the people bestow these powers upon law enforcement.

These policing powers should only be allowed to limit civilians' exercising of their rights and freedoms when necessary, to secure recognition and respect for the rights of others, for public order and the general welfare in a democratic society (International Human Rights Standards for Law Enforcement, 1997). "Because thinking about criminal procedure has tended to focus on the questions taken up by courts, the unfortunate result has been not just that *judges* have largely failed to consider the systemic requirements for democratic policing, but that most of the rest of us have, too" (Sklansky, 2005, p. 1,703). If the focus of the Supreme Court and lower courts has been on criminal procedure, is it surprising that less attention has been paid to racism in the criminal justice system and the ways local police practices can reinforce (or alleviate) patterns of domination? Where is the analysis of how police officers conduct criminal procedure and how courts react to the varied forces and conditions that police and civilians encounter within police culture, community culture, and convergent and divergent experiences (Bowers, 2017)? Attention should be focused on steps that can be taken to build trust between law enforcement and the communities of color they police: "…trust in the police depends on the police operating under rules and practices adopted openly, with ample opportunity for public input" (Sklansky, 2005, p. 1,828). The racial and gender factionalism between police officers and residents exists in police departments, yet many officers partake in the "blue is blue" culture, meaning they have one another's backs when in dangerous situations.

Despite "blue is blue" culture, division along the lines of race and gender contribute to communication, organizational, and community barriers within and outside of law enforcement. The fissures that exist because of the balkanization between minority and female officers and their peers is unfortunate but has created spaces for dissent and debate within police workforces. Within these spaces, reform is like a vine—it can germinate, grow, disperse, and take hold in areas where it had never existed, breaking down barriers to its existence: "reform that might otherwise have remained blocked by monolithic police opposition" brings a healthy dose of "'democratic oppositionalism' to the internal politics of law enforcement agencies" (Sklansky, 2005, p. 1,827). Reforms that emerge from democratic oppositionalism in police departments include civilian review, lobbying for restrictions on racial profiling, supporting reimposition of residency requirements, and calling on police departments to focus on the needs and interests of minority residents. Persons of color in law enforcement live in communities of color or have family or friends who live in communities of color, many of them having been racially profiled, and these relationships and experiences explain their empathy. If the culture of "blue is blue" can accept that it exists within larger, more encompassing local, county, statewide, and national cultures, perhaps it will become more receptive to the experiences of officers of color.

A force from outside of police departments compelling reform of the "blue is blue" culture comes from the federal government. Section 14141 of the Violent Crime Control and Law Enforcement Act of 1994 authorizes the U.S. Attorney General to sue local police departments that engage in a pattern or practice of violating constitutional and legal rights (Bell, 2017). The Department of Justice (DOJ) can use the threat of Section 14141 to reach an agreement with the agency to pursue reforms, or if litigation is necessary, to seek a consent decree, which mandates that actions be undertaken. Section 14141 is used during times of crises within local police departments, but conditions within local police departments and the toxicity between police and the communities they are sworn to serve can be very troublesome before the DOJ decides to use Section 14141 to intervene. Section 14141 is a helpful backstop, but other initiatives are needed beforehand for effective community policing to manifest. In 1994, the federal office of Community Oriented Policing Services (COPS) was established, and its purpose is to use federal funding to incentivize various reforms, such as attracting the most skilled officers to highest-need areas by assisting jurisdictions in providing higher wages for officers (Bell, 2017). Wage reforms are important because many officers secure secondary employment to supplement their income, and usually wealthier areas within a municipality or the private sector can afford to pay officers more than in highest-need areas. The wage reforms help level the playing field between lesser-need areas, which can afford to pay higher wages or overtime for sought-after policy academy graduates and officers, and highest-need areas, which traditionally lack the means to recruit and retain the most knowledgeable officers. Another concern that is real (Bell, 2017, p. 2136): "This dynamic sends a stark message that protecting wealthier areas is more lucrative than protecting higher-poverty areas. Secondary employment policies like these might even suggest, at least symbolically, that African American and poor lives truly lack value." If this imbalance and the stigmas associated with it continue to exist, worsening violence and higher crime rates in highest-need areas will persist. Wage reforms and other interventions must take into consideration the effects of policy changes on community policing and healthier partnerships between law enforcement and community stakeholders and their constituencies.

Over the years, interventions have been implemented to shift police practices away from deadly engagements and to disrupt practices that trivialize incessant police violence. Interventions are needed to retrain and reframe police determinations about which lives are valued physically and discursively and hold police accountable for who they perceive as worthy of life or death (Obasogie & Newman, 2016). Interventions need to address a multitude of issues that contribute to incessant police violence, such as overdispersal of OC spray (also known as pepper spray), excessive use of stun belts, stun guns and tasers, misuse of police dogs, use of dangerous restraint procedures, and police shootings (Amnesty International, 1999). Formal training for recruits and lauded community policing interventions like New York City's "Streetwise" program were meant to address some of these issues (Marks, 1999), but ultimately were unsuccessful at stymieing police brutality. What more can be done to stop police brutality? There is a need for measures that capture diverse policing outcomes and the importance of considering transactions with the public as an integral part of any measurement scheme (Mastrofski, 1999). Stephen Mastrofski (1999) purports that six domains of performance indicators aid in measuring the adequacy of police service to the community:

1. Attentiveness: A visible police presence.
2. Reliability: A quick, predictable response.
3. Responsiveness: Attempts to satisfy people's requests and explain reasons for actions and decisions.
4. Competence: Know how to handle criminals, victims, and the public.
5. Manners: Treat *all* people with respect.
6. Fairness: Equitable treatment for all—especially racial equality.

Sometimes law enforcement agencies, and departments can effectively use these domains to address the main concern communities have about policing: are police officers held accountable by communities for their service? When local police departments do an ineffective job using these domains, the local, county, state, and federal responses are necessary. The DOJ's Community Relations Service (CRS) is a federal response that seeks to prevent or resolve community conflicts and tensions arising from actions, policies, and practices perceived to be discriminatory because of race, color, or national origin (DOJ, 2003). The DOJ (2003) provides stakeholders additional guidance in *Principles of Good Policing: Avoiding Violence Between Police and Citizens*:

> CRS provides services, including conciliation, mediation, and technical assistance, directly to people and their communities to help resolve conflicts that tear at the fabric of an increasingly racially and ethnically diverse society. Police-citizen conflict accounts for a major portion of the disputes to which CRS responds. The agency provides a wide range of conciliation and technical assistance to help prevent or resolve disagreements over alleged police use of excessive force and other policing issues. CRS carries out most of its activities informally, but will conduct formal negotiations if the disputing parties believe that approach offers the best opportunity for reaching a mutually satisfactory settlement of their differences.

CRS and other tools for change are only useful when the body politic of America—people of every race, ethnicity, socioeconomic status, gender, sexual orientation, and domicile—take the reins of our democratic society. For public order and the general welfare of all people, police must comply with the public's demand for democratic policing. The videotaped police misconduct, beatings, and murders of unarmed Black men and women, whether they are "star" athletes or not, puts front and center in the American psyche the fact that incessant police violence exists today. If we all deserve equal treatment under the law, what are we doing about police brutality? No one is above the law. Police brutality is a stain on the fabric that binds all Americans together.

References

Acosta, R. (2012). Advocacy networks through a multidisciplinary lens: Implications for research agendas. *Voluntas, 23*, 156–181. https://doi.org/10.1007/s11266-011-9187-3.

Aday, S., Farrell, H., Lynch, M., Sides, J., Kelly, J., & Zuckerman, E. (2010). *Blogs and bullets: New media in contentious politics.* United States Institute of Peace. https://www.files.ethz.ch/isn/120788/pw65.pdf.

Alang, S., McAlpine, D., McCreedy, E., & Hardeman, R. (2017). Police brutality and Black health: Setting the agenda for public health scholars. *American Journal of Public Health, 107(5)*, 662–665. https://doi.org/10.2105/AJPH.2017.303691.

Al-Azm, S.J. (2011, Fall). The Arab Spring: Why exactly at this time? *Reason Papers, 33*, 223–229. https://reasonpapers.com/pdf/33/rp_33_18.pdf.

Amnesty International. (1999). *USA: Race, rights and police brutality.* Amnesty International. https://www.amnesty.org/download/Documents/144000/amr511471999en.pdf.

Angus, I.H. (1998). The materiality of expression: Harold Innis' communication theory and the discursive turn in the human sciences. *Canadian Journal of Communication, 23(1)*, 1–15. https://doi.org/10.22230/CJC.1998V23N1A1020.

Armour, J.D. (1997). *Negrophobia and reasonable racism: The hidden cost of being black in America.* New York University Press.

Baumgarten, B. (2013). Geração à Rasca and beyond: Mobilizations in Portugal after 12 March 2011. *Current Sociology, 61(4)*, 457–473. https://doi.org/10.1177/0011392113479745.

Bell, M.C. (2017). Police reform and the dismantling of legal estrangement. *The Yale Law Journal, 126*, 2054–2150. https://www.yalelawjournal.org/essay/police-reform-and-the-dismantling-of-legal-estrangement.

Berry, J.M. (1999). *The new liberalism: The rising power of citizen groups.* Brookings Institution Press.

Bonilla-Silva, E. (2009). *Racism without racists: Colorblind racism and the persistence of racial inequality in American.* Rowman & Littlefield.

Bowers, J. (2017). Annoy no cop. *University of Pennsylvania Law Review, 166*, 129–212. https://scholarship.law.upenn.edu/cgi/viewcontent.cgi?article=9603&context=penn_law_review.

Branco, M. (2014). *Brasil 2013: La calle y la presidenta [Brazil 2013: The street and the president].* La Vanguardia, El poder de las redes sociales. https://www.researchgate.net/profile/Gustavo-Cardoso-2/publication/301867379_Movilizacion_social_y_redes_sociales/links/572a5b0708ae2ef bfdbc1f6c/Movilizacion-social-y-redes-sociales.pdf.

Brooks, S. (2016). The fire this time: A context for understanding the Black male athlete protests at Missouri. *Phi Kappa Phi Forum, Summer*, 18–21.

Brunson, R.K., & Miller, J. (2006). Young Black men and urban policing in the United States. *British Journal of Criminology, 46(4)*, 613–640. https://doi.org/10.1093/bjc/azi093.

Bryson, S. (1998). Relationship between race and attitudes toward black men. *Journal of Multicultural Counseling and Development, 26(4)*, 282–294. https://doi.org/10.1002/j.2161-1912.1998.tb00205.x.

Burkell, J., Fortier, A., Wong, L., & Simpson, J.L. (2014). Facebook: Public space, or private space? *Information, Communication & Society, 17(8)*, 974–985. https://doi.org/10.1080/1369118X.2013.870591.

Callahan, Y. (2018, April 27). *Police caught on camera physically assaulting former NFL player Desmond Marrow.* The Root. https://www.theroot.com/police-caught-on-camera-physically-assaulting-former-nf-1825593736.

Capehart, J. (2012, March 18). Under "suspicion": The killing of Trayvon Martin. *Washington Post.* https://www.washingtonpost.com/blogs/post-partisan/post/under-suspicion-the-killing-of-trayvon-martin/2011/03/04/gIQAz4F4KS_blog.html.

Cardoso, G., Lapa, T., & Fátima, B.D. (2016). People are the message? Social mobilization and social media in Brazil. *International Journal of Communication, 10*, 3909–3930.

Carr, P.J., Napolitano, L., & Keating, J. (2007). We never call the cops and here is why: A qualitative examination of legal cynicism in three Philadelphia neighborhoods. *Criminology: An Interdisciplinary Journal, 45(2)*, 445–480. https://doi.org/10.1111/j.1745-9125.2007.00084.x.

Castells, M. (2012). *Networks of outrage and hope: Social movements in the Internet Age.* Polity.

Chaney, C., & Robertson, R.V. (2014). "Can we all get along?" Blacks' historical and contemporary (in)justice with law enforcement. *The Western Journal of Black Studies, 38(2)*, 108–122.

Chaudhry, I. (2014). #Hashtags for change: Can Twitter promote social progress in Saudi Arabia. *International Journal of Communication, 8*, 943–961. https://ijoc.org/index.php/ijoc/article/viewFile/2362/1111.

Clarke, L. (2017, September 7). James Blake, manhandled by police, wants to help others avoid that fate. *Washington Post.* https://www.washingtonpost.com/sports/tennis/james-blake-man-handled-by-police-wants-to-help-others-avoid-that-fate/2017/09/07/73617826-9018-11e7-84c0-02cc069f2c37_story.html.

Dahlgren, P. (2009). *Media and political engagement: Citizens, communication, and democracy.* Cambridge University Press.

DeLuca, K., Lawson, S., & Sun, Y. (2012). Occupy Wall Street on the Public Screens of Social Media: The Many Framings of the Birth of a Protest Movement. *Communication, Culture & Critique, 5(4)*, 483–509. https://doi.org/10.1111/j.1753-9137.2012.01141.x.

Eberhardt, J.L., Davies, P.G., Purdie-Vaughns, V.J., & Johnson, S.L. (2006). Looking deathworthy: Perceived stereotypicality of Black defendants predicts capital-sentencing outcomes. *Psychological Science, 17(5)*, 383–386. https://doi.org/10.1111/j.1467-9280.2006.01716.x.

Eltantawy, N., & Julie B.W. (2011). Social media in the Egyptian revolution: Reconsidering resource mobilization theory. *International Journal of Communication, 5*, 1207–1224. https://ijoc.org/index.php/ijoc/article/viewFile/1242/597.

Fanon, F. (2008). *Black skin, white masks.* Grove Press.

Fine, M., Freudenberg, N., Payne, Y., Perkins, T., Smith, K., & Wanzer, K. (2003). "Anything can happen with police around": Urban youth evaluate strategies of surveillance in public places. *Journal of Social Issues, 59(1)*, 141–158. https://doi.org/10.1111/1540-4560.t01-1-00009.

Finley, T. (2017, September 7). *NFL player Michael Bennett says police threatened to "blow my f*****g head off."* HuffPost. https://www.huffpost.com/entry/michael-bennet-police-brutality_n_59b00978e4b0b5e53102b4ad.

Fryer, R.G. (2019). An empirical analysis of racial differences in police use of force. *Journal of Political Economy, 127(3)*, 1210–1261. https://doi.org/10.1086/701423.

Gabbidon, S., & Greene, H.T. (2013). *Race and crime* (3rd ed.). Sage.

Gauntlett, D. (2013). *Making is connecting.* John Wiley & Sons.

Ghannam, J. (2011). *Social media in the Arab world: Leading up to the uprisings of 2011.* The Center for International Media Assistance. https://www.cima.ned.org/wp-content/uploads/2015/02/CIMA-Arab_Social_Media-Report-10-25-11.pdf.

Gilbert, K.L., & Ray, R. (2016). Why police kill Black males with impunity: Applying public health critical race praxis (PHCRP) to address the determinants of policing behaviors and "justifiable" homicides in the USA. *Journal of Urban Health: Bulletin of the New York Academy of Medicine, 93 Suppl 1*, 122–140. https://doi.org/10.1007/s11524-015-0005-x.

Habersham, R. (2018, April 30). Cop involved in ex-football player's arrest put on administrative duty after video surfaces. *Atlanta Journal-Constitution.* https://www.ajc.com/news/crime-law/thought-was-going-die-nfl-player-details-brutal-arrest/fDT4vH7lEktnRS1MIPOeLM/#.

Hinds, L. (2007). Building police—youth relationships: The Importance of procedural justice. *Youth Justice, 7(3)*, 195–209. https://doi.org/10.1177/1473225407082510.

Ho, W., & Garrett, D. (2014). Hong Kong at the brink: Emerging forms of political participation in the new social movement. In J.Y.S. Cheng (Ed.), *New trends of political participation in Hong Kong* (pp. 347–384). University of Hong Kong.

Howard, P.N., Duffy, A., Freelon, D., Hussain, M.M., Mari, W., & Maziad, M. (2011). *Opening closed regimes: What was the role of social media during the Arab Spring?* Project of Information Technology & Political Islam (ITPI). https://deepblue.lib.umich.edu/bitstream/handle/2027.42/117568/2011_Howard-Duffy-Freelon-Hussain-Mari-Mazaid_PITPI.pdf?sequence=1&isAllowed=y.

International Committee of the Red Cross. (2015). *International rules and standards for policing.* ICRC. https://www.icrc.org/en/doc/assets/files/other/icrc-002-0809.pdf.

Johnson, G.A., Tudor, B., & Nuseibeh, H. (2013). 140 characters or less: How is the Twitter mediascape influencing the Egyptian revolution? *Middle East Journal of Culture and Communication, 6(1)*, 126–148. https://doi.org/10.1163/18739865-00503006.

Jones, V. (2017). Marginality and mattering: Black student leaders' perceptions of public and private racial regard. *The Western Journal of Black Studies, 41(3 & 4)*, 67–80.

Langford, C.L., & Speight, M. (2015). #BlackLivesMatter: Epistemic positioning, challenges and possibilities. *Journal of Contemporary Rhetoric, 5(3/4)*, 78–89. http://contemporaryrhetoric.com/wp-content/uploads/2017/01/Langford_Speight_11_4.pdf.

Lim, M. (2012). Clicks, cabs, and coffee houses: Social media and oppositional movements in Egypt, 2004–2011. *Journal of Communication, 62(2)*, 231–248. https://doi.org/10.1111/j.1460-2466.2012.01628.x.

Luthern, A. (2019, October 10). "They violated his constitutional rights": New court filings in Sterling Brown lawsuit detail past officer misconduct. *Milwaukee Journal Sentinel.* https://www.jsonline.com/story/news/crime/2019/10/10/milwaukee-bucks-sterling-brown-lawsuit-details-police-misconduct/3918485002/.

Luthern, A., & Barton, G. (2018, June 19). Bucks rookie Sterling Brown's lawsuit shows police officer's racially charged Facebook posts. *Milwaukee Journal Sentinel.* https://www.jsonline.com/story/news/local/milwaukee/2018/06/19/bucks-rookie-sterling-brown-sue-milwaukee-police-who-tased-him/697716002/.

Lynch, R.S., & Mitchell, J. (1995). Justice system advocacy: A must for NASW and the social work community. *Social Work, 40(1)*, 9–12. https://doi.org/10.1093/sw/40.1.9.

Lynn, S. (2018, May 24). *Reaction to video of police using taser on Bucks' Sterling Brown.* Sporting News. https://www.sportingnews.com/us/nba/news/social-media-reaction-milwaukee-police-taser-sterling-brown-video/1b2vnwq5r9o06lrvcxk99gsj6b.

Marcus, N.C. (2016). From Edward to Eric Garner and beyond: The importance of constitutional limitations on lethal use of force in police reform. *Duke Journal of Constitutional Law & Public Policy, 12*, 53–106. https://scholarship.law.duke.edu/cgi/viewcontent.cgi?article=1117&context=djclpp.

Marks, A. (1999, May 13). NYPD as lab for reducing police brutality. *Christian Science Monitor.* https://www.csmonitor.com/1999/0513/p3s1.html.

Mastrofski, S.D. (1999). *"Policing for people."* Ideas in American Policing (seminar and publication series), Police Foundation. https://www.policefoundation.org/publication/policing-for-people/.

Miladi, N. (2016). Social media and social change. *Digest of Middle East Studies, 25(1)*, 36–51. https://doi.org/10.1111/dome.12082.

Mukherjee, R. (2006). The ghetto fabulous aesthetic in contemporary Black culture. *Cultural Studies, 20(6)*, 599–629. https://doi.org/10.1080/09502380600973978.

National Football League. [NFL YouTube Channel]. (2017, September 6). *Michael Bennett & Richard Sherman React to Bennett's Las Vegas Incident | NFL* [Video]. YouTube. https://www.youtube.com/watch?v=94OaisaO0Vg.

Obasogie, O., & Newman, Z. (2016). Black Lives Matter and respectability politics in local news accounts of officer-involved civilian deaths: An early empirical assessment. *Wisconsin Law Review, 2016(3)*, 541–574. https://repository.law.wisc.edu/s/uwlaw/media/77170.

Oliver, M.B., Jackson, R.L., II, Moses, N.N., & Dangerfield, C.L. (2004). The face of crime: Viewers' memory of race-related facial features of individuals pictured in the news. *Journal of Communication, 54(1)*, 88–104. https://doi.org/10.1111/j.1460-2466.2004.tb02615.x.

Parks, T. (2008). The rise and fall of donor funding for advocacy NGOs: Understanding the impact. *Development in Practice, 18(2)*, 213–222. https://doi.org/10.1080/09614520801899036.

Penn, N. (2015, October 29). GQ Exclusive: NBA star Thabo Sefolosha tells his story of assault by the NYPD. *GQ.* https://www.gq.com/story/thabo-sefolosha-nypd-assault#:~:text=Culture-,GQ%20Exclusive.

Reid, E.J. (2000). Understanding the word "advocacy": Context and use. In E.J. Reid (Ed.), *Structuring the inquiry into advocacy. Volume 1 of the seminar series nonprofit advocacy and the policy process.* The Urban Institute. https://www.urban.org/sites/default/files/publication/62271/309696-Structuring-the-Inquiry-into-Advocacy.PDF.

Ristovska, S. (2016) The rise of eyewitness video and its implications for human rights: Conceptual and methodological approaches. *Journal of Human Rights, 15(3)*, 347–360. https://doi.org/10.1080/14754835.2015.1132157.

Robert F. Kennedy Human Rights Global Justice Clinic NYU School of Law, International

Human Rights Law Clinic, UVA School of Law, & Hansford, J. (2015; updated 2016). *Excessive use of force by the police against Black Americans in the United States*. Inter-American Commission on Human Rights. https://rfkhumanrights.org/assets/documents/iachr_thematic_hearing_submission_-_excessive_use_of_force_by_police_against_black_americans.pdf.

Rothman, L. (2016, March 3). The police misconduct caught on tape before Rodney King. *Time Magazine*. https://time.com/4237832/citizens-filming-rodney-king/.

Sharma, S. (2008). Taxi as media: A temporal materialist reading of the taxi-cab. *Social Identities: Journal for the Study of Race, Nation and Culture, 14(4)*, 457–464. https://doi.org/10.1080/13504630802211910.

Sharma, S. (2014). *In the meantime: Temporality and cultural politics*. Duke University Press.

Sklansky, D.A. (2005). Police and democracy. *Michigan Law Review, 103*, 1699–1830.

Smith, B.W., & Holmes, M.D. (2003). Community accountability, minority threat, and police brutality: An examination of civil rights criminal complaints. *Criminology, 41(4)*, 1035–1063. https://doi.org/10.1177/0011128707309718.

Smith, M., & Hoffman, B. (2018, May 23). Video of Sterling Brown's arrest shows Milwaukee police using stun gun on N.B.A. player. *New York Times*. https://www.nytimes.com/2018/05/23/us/sterling-brown-milwaukee-police-taser.html.

Spears, M.J. (2018, July 13). *Sterling Brown's mindset during arrest: "Get home."* The Undefeated. https://theundefeated.com/features/sterling-browns-mindset-during-arrest-get-home/.

Tewksbury, D. (2018). Networking #Ferguson: An Ethnographic Study of Ferguson Protesters' Online-Offline Community Mobilization. *Democratic Communiqué, 27(2)*, 53–68.

Time Video. (2014, July 25). When fatal arrests are caught on camera. *Time Magazine*. https://time.com/3024396/fatal-arrests-police-camera/.

Tomaskovic-Devey, D., Wright, C., Czaja, R., & Miller, K. (2006). Self-reports of police speeding stops by race: Results from the North Carolina reverse record check survey. *Journal of Quantitative Criminology, 22(4)*, 279–297. https://doi.org/10.1007/s10940-006-9012-0.

Tonry, M. (2011). *Punishing race: A continuing American dilemma*. Oxford University Press.

Towns, A.R. (2015). The (racial) biases of communication: Rethinking media and blackness. *Social Identities, 21(5)*, 474–488. https://doi.org/10.1080/13504630.2015.1093469.

Towns, A.R. (2016). Geographies of pain: #SayHerName and the fear of Black women's mobility. *Women's Studies in Communication, 39(2)*, 122–126. https://doi.org/10.1080/07491409.2016.1176807.

United Nations High Commissioner for Human Rights, Centre for Human Rights. (1997). *International human rights standards for law enforcement: A pocket book on human rights for the police*. https://www.ohchr.org/documents/publications/training5add1en.pdf.

United States Department of Justice. (2003). *Principles of good policing: Avoiding violence between police and citizens*. Community Relations Service, DOJ. https://www.justice.gov/archive/crs/pubs/principlesofgoodpolicingfinal092003.pdf.

Walker, A. (2011). Racial profiling separate and unequal keeping the minorities in line-the role of law enforcement in America. *St. Thomas Law Review, 23(4)*, 576–619.

10

A Tale of Two Cities
and the Effects
of Community Violence
on Celebrity Natives

Every minute, someone, somewhere around the globe, is killed by a gun. The victim may have been walking down the street in Rio, Brazil; fleeing from armed guerrillas in Goma, Eastern Congo; or sitting in a living room in Indianapolis. The portability, affordability, and utility of small arms and light weapons have changed the arenas in which wars take place as well as dramatically increasing the lethality of violence in the domestic sphere (Farr, 2004, p. 16).

This quote is from Farr's (2004) essay "The New War Zone: The Ubiquitous Presence of Guns and Light Weapons Has Changed the Definitions of 'War,' 'Victim,' and 'Perpetrator.'" Farr's main argument is that war zones are no longer restricted militarized zones. Instead, war zones are in our communities and in our homes. But do communities willfully sign up for war at home? Enlisted personnel understand the risks, understand there is no guarantee that they will survive combat. War brings causalities. Those who survive are often injured emotionally, psychologically, and physically, and for their sacrifice, the government, family, friends, and the public devote considerable time and resources to ensure they are not forgotten. No one denies that their public health is affected by combat. As the new frontier for war moves closer to home, the stakeholders at the local, state, and federal levels must address the lethality of violence in communities and metropolitan areas.

Violence is an epidemic. Oftentimes, discussion of violence as a public health issue focuses on self-directed violence or interpersonal violence, yet this myopic attitude contributes to greater mortality. A 1979 Surgeon General's report identified violent behavior as a significant risk to health. Four years later, the Centers for Disease Control and Prevention (CDC) established the Violence Epidemiology Branch, which became the Division of Violence Prevention (CDC, 2011). The Division of Violence Prevention works with law enforcement and public health agencies to address the lethality of violence in communities throughout the U.S. Health experts and practitioners understand that to decrease the lethality of violence in communities, communities' anti-violence policies and mitigation efforts must underscore that there is greater recognition and comprehension of the connection between promoting health and preventing violence. Both public health and law enforcement are fields that respond to existing problems while simultaneously investing resources into prevention, the goal being to stop problems before they start (Schweig, 2014). Former Director of COPS Bernard K. Melekian stated in a 2012 letter to colleagues: "Law enforcement may not be aware of how often we already borrow or are inspired by strategies and practices from the public health field" (Wolf, 2012, p. iv). Melekian continued, "Long before a lieutenant in the New York City Transit Police Department revolutionized the profession by mapping violent crime hotspots in the subway system and creating what would become CompStat, a London doctor named John Snow began mapping and tracing the source of an 1854 cholera outbreak, thus founding the field of epidemiology" (Wolf, 2012, p. iv). Public health and public safety adopt similar strategies and tools, including data analysis, collaboration, community engagement, and problem solving. These agencies are among the stakeholders who must work together to keep violence from engulfing more communities. The public needs public health and public safety to uphold their communities, to mitigate, and ultimately end collective violence.

Stakeholders in urban and suburban neighborhoods across the United States and in metropolitan areas around the world understand that a plethora of factors affect collective violence in their communities. According to the World Health Organization (WHO), collective violence involves "...the instrumental use of violence by people who identify themselves as members of a group ... against another group or set of individuals, in order to achieve political, economic, or social objectives" (Krug et al., 2002, p. 215). Psychological violence, physical violence, sexual violence, and neglectful violence are embodied in collective violence. Collective violence involves organized violent crime, such as banditry and gang warfare, as well as state-perpetrated violence, such as genocide, repression, disappearances, torture, and other abuses of human rights. Moreover, collective violence perpetrated by gang violence, hooliganism, and police brutality impacts communities and manifests into murder, rape, assault, and battery (Dahlberg & Krug, 2002). A specific type of collective violence prevalent in the U.S. is community violence. Community violence consists of aggressive behavior outside the home among people who may or may not know one another (Voisin et al., 2016). Exposure to community violence is traumatic, and children too often are the victims, offenders, or witnesses to acts of aggression (e.g., muggings, robberies, burglaries, sexual assault, rape, use of weapons, and gang- or gun-related incidents).

The National Child Traumatic Stress Network (2021) defines community violence as "exposure to intentional acts of interpersonal violence committed in public areas by individuals who are not intimately related to the victim" (para. 1). Kliewer and Sullivan (2008) explain community violence as experiencing, seeing, or hearing about violence at home, school, or in the neighborhood. Each of these settings affects the others, compounding the trauma and amplifying a sense of despair. The trauma can lead to adjustment difficulties for children, adolescents, and young adults. There is a linkage between community violence, substance abuse, and wayward parental monitoring and youth sexual risk behaviors (Brady & Donenberg, 2006; Voisin et al., 2008, 2012, 2014). It is not shocking that traumatized youth seek validation, affection, approval, or intimacy from wherever they can get it.

Collective violence and community violence manifest into gun violence, and gun violence in turbulent communities intimidates residents, perpetuates misconceptions about "those people," and snuffs out meaningful reforms because stakeholders believe nothing will change. Gun violence is a threat to public health and safety, especially in low-income urban areas (Dahlberg & Mercy, 2009). In the U.S, homicide rates associated with firearms use are highest among teens and young adults 15 to 34 years of age, and among Black, American Indian/Alaskan Native, and Hispanic/Latinx populations. (CDC, 2020). Firearms-related homicide rates suggest elevated gun violence morbidity for these demographic groups, because youth recognize the "code of the street," and they understand that when individuals in their communities are threatened or when they are disrespected, cycles of retaliatory gun violence and repeated injury occurs (Anderson, 1999; Buss & Rashid, 1995; Rich & Grey, 2005; Sims et al., 1989). Nonfatal violent injury contributes to both physical and mental disability and accounts for substantial healthcare costs (CDC, 2002; Cook et al., 1999; Miller, Cohen, & Rossman, 1993; Mondragon, 1992; Tellez et al., 1995). "Violence in our communities is a serious public health issue, and as such, it is of great concern to hospitals that care for victims of violence and also prepare for possible mass events" (Bos et al., 2017, p. 2).

Hospitals provide critical and lifesaving services to victims, offenders, and witnesses. Hospitals are vital community stakeholders, whose anti-violence efforts and prevention and preparedness activities address the determinants of violence in turbulent communities, as well as respond appropriately when violence occurs (Bos et al., 2017). A 2017 report for the

American Hospital Association concluded that proactive and reactive violence response efforts cost U.S. hospitals and healthcare systems approximately $2.7 billion in 2016. The expenditure breakdown included $280 million related to preparedness and prevention to address community violence, $852 million in unreimbursed medical care for victims of violence, $1.1 billion in security and training costs to prevent violence within hospitals, and an additional $429 million for various related expenses. Hospitals are on the frontlines, as turbulent communities atrophied by violence seek a more optimistic future.

Two metropolitan areas that have been dealing with collective and community violence, which are the focus of this chapter, include South Central Los Angeles and surrounding suburban areas, including Compton, and the South Side and West Side neighborhoods of Chicago. In these urban areas, too many civilians are caught in the crossfire, and law enforcement practices make innocent bystanders feel underserved or victimized. The lethality of violence in these two metropolitan areas is covered in the news media, but the coverage is incomplete, as the more salacious attributes of incidents are often highlighted. These attributes are exploited by the media to entice media users to partake in the daily consumption of sensationalism. The purpose of sensationalism is for its source to elicit a reaction, whether it be more eyeballs on screens or more ears attentive to the cacophony of jeers, gossip, and insults. As long as media users are plugged in, influenced, primed, scared, intimidated, and riled up, one must wonder, does anyone realize the audience has become desensitized? The media is a business, and having more media users tuned in is good for business. The media understands that many people probably know someone who has been affected by collective or community violence, so when media users turn on the news, they can relate to the victims and maybe even the perpetrators. Sometimes—to the shock of fans and the public—the victim or perpetrator is a celebrity, upping the entertainment level or interest of the story. Celebrities may also be among the media users who are afraid after tuning in to media coverage of the latest shooting, beating, rape, or some other act of violence. Many celebrities are like their fans, some of whom grew up in metropolitan areas experiencing collective violence. When they visit family and friends, they learn about hooligans and gang members, as well as state-sponsored misconduct of law enforcement. Some celebrities reflect on their experiences with collective and community violence. They address how their notoriety does not shield them from the lethality of violence. This chapter examines narratives involving celebrities who have perpetrated or been victimized by violence and use their stories to make sense of the lethality of violence in communities. It becomes clear that if no one maintains control, collective violence can wreak havoc on people's lives.

Asking: Is the Trauma Related to Where or How I Grew Up?

People from different walks of life oftentimes have different experiences with the lethality of violence. Moore and Tonry's (1998) synthesis of key events that contribute to turbulent communities, especially urban communities, provides context for the youth violence epidemic in the U.S. In the 1970s and 1980s, employment opportunities in inner cities disappeared. Workers who once had jobs and disposable income no longer were able to buy goods and services that supported their community's small businesses. Workers and businesses that could relocate to survive left the inner cities. Families throughout these communities were under economic pressures that contributed to their breakup, leaving children in increasingly adverse conditions. Some youth joined gangs for affiliation and security. Gangs contributed to rivalries, fighting, and fear in communities, yet more youth joined them because it was a way to survive. In the mid- to late 1980s, as the crack cocaine epidemic ravaged communities plagued by escalating gang violence, gangs sold the drug to members of their communities, and they armed themselves with firearms for protection and to resolve business disputes. Violence beget further violence in these communities, as turf wars spurred the acquisition of guns out of self-protection, style, and status concerns. These turf wars were lethal, and rates of morbidity skyrocketed. Blumstein (1995) reported on how drug sellers in these communities and inner-city neighborhoods recruited juveniles, who were less vulnerable to the harsh punishments imposed by the adult criminal justice system, as cheap labor. These juveniles were provided with firearms and dispersed on blocks throughout their neighborhoods and communities, and whenever agitation or disputes surfaced, guns, rather than fists or other weapons, were used. Bjerregaard and Lizotte (1995) determined that youth who acquire guns for "protection" are significantly more likely to commit gun crimes and street crimes compared to youth who own guns for sport or who do not own firearms. They also found that gang members are more likely to own guns for "protection" than for sporting purposes. The possession of firearms and the willingness of owners to use them became emblematic of social identity and position in gangs and organized crime (Fagan & Wilkinson, 1998; Wilkinson & Fagan, 1996).

In the 1990s, community violence in the U.S. was rampant. Some experts characterized it as a public health epidemic (Bell & Jenkins, 1993). Urban adolescents were witnessing disturbingly high rates of community violence (Fitzpatrick & Boldizar, 1993; Osofsky et al., 1993; Richters & Martinez, 1993; Schwab-Stone et al., 1995). Schwab-Stone et al. (1999) reported 40 percent of urban adolescents had witnessed a shooting or stabbing within a one-year timeframe. Gorman-Smith et al. (2004) determined that virtually all urban adolescent boys they sampled in their research had witnessed at least three types of violence in their lifetimes. Moreover, Rosenthal (2000) indicated that 98 percent of urban adolescents had witnessed another person being victimized. When they witness someone being chased, threatened, attacked, wounded, or killed, they internalize these experiences. Despite the widely documented association between witnessing violence and perpetrating it (Farrell & Bruce, 1997; Miller et al., 1999)—a vicious cycle that can destroy individuals, families, and communities—not all adolescents in turbulent communities engage in violent acts. Researchers need to better understand the effects of community violence on residents of a neighborhood, especially the implications for youth, some of whom become violent, while having peers despite exposure to a high-risk environment, who become resilient (Brookmeyer et al., 2005). How did these youth achieve adaptive success? Understanding community violence is imperative for the American and global public healthcare system.

According to Stock et al. (2016), a six-month NBC Bay Area investigation found growing economic disparity in Oakland, which scientists believe contributes to continuing violent crime in some parts of the city. East and West Oakland are among areas with double-digit unemployment, low education levels, and tens of thousands of residents living below the poverty line. Average income in these neighborhoods was only slightly more than half the citywide average. In the reporting about findings of the investigation, Dr. Howard Pinderhughes, an area professor whose work concentrates on the prevention of violence (e.g., his work with Oakland's Prevention Institute) stated, "We've come to understand that all these things add up to conflict and trauma which then helps to feed the cycle of violence. And then we blame the people. Then we say they're super predators. Then we say they're dysfunctional families." He continued, "The school system, the juvenile justice system, the foster system—all of which are taking children and young people who are traumatized and using approaches and systems that further the traumatizing." Why? He acknowledged, "They're trauma inducing systems rather than trauma informed systems."

Communities with high rates of violence are plagued with persistently high rates of trauma. Collective and community violence produce trauma, which prevents residents of a neighborhood from meeting their basic needs. Under these community-wide conditions, social networks, social relationships, and positive social norms deteriorate or disintegrate. Without viable networks, relationships, community partnerships, and positive social norms, violence in these neighborhoods and communities spirals out of control. Stakeholders across local, state, and federal levels of government, and in the private and nonprofit sectors, must recognize that existing frameworks are insufficient for understanding, addressing, and preventing trauma at a community or population level. Trauma-related factors to consider for a more comprehensive framework to address collective and community violence include the social-cultural environment, the physical/built environment, and the economic environment (Pinderhughes et al., 2015). The social-cultural environment focuses on the economic and social processes in a neighborhood or community, which contributes to decline, decay, disaffection, depopulation, and poverty. The physical/built environment examines the concrete and tangible infrastructure of a neighborhood or community to ascertain the effects of dilapidated buildings, deteriorating roads, and poor transportation services. The economic environment addresses inadequate access to economic and educational opportunities. Lack of access exacerbates crime and delinquency, truancy, psychological distress, and various health problems (Pinderhughes et al., 2015). Collectively, these environments for communities consumed by violence provide stakeholders a kaleidoscope of dystopia.

Injuries occur in violent communities from both acts of violence that are self-inflicted and violence targeting victims, witnesses, and bystanders. Perpetrators and victims of violence are injured and reinjured because their environments stay the same. Rich and Grey (2005) completed a narrative analysis which demonstrated that young men feel unsafe after violence-related injuries, and the study addresses the pathways young men take after enduring collective or community violence that result in recurrent injury. Emergent from the narrative analysis was a model to explain recurrent injury, which identifies these men's basic need for physical and psychological safety from the "code of the street" (see Figure 6).

The "code of the street" does not end when youth go to school. Fear of victimization and recurrent injury follows them from home to school and back again. A study by McGill et al. (2014) explained that these youth demonstrate post-traumatic stress (PTS) symptoms, and these young men and women are at significantly higher risk for developing school problems, including lower grade average, decreased standardized test scores in reading and math, and poor school attendance.

Researcher speculation about the role of neighborhood or community demographic makeup provided stakeholders with insights into why residents move and revealed antecedents to escalating violence, such as the background of newer residents. Competition models explaining how diversity increases or lessens collective or community violence run the gamut. "In contrast to models emphasizing that segregation of ethnic and racial populations causes ethnic conflict, competition arguments hold that desegregation causes ethnic conflict. A core hypothesis ... is that desegregation of labor markets intensifies ethnic competition, which in turn

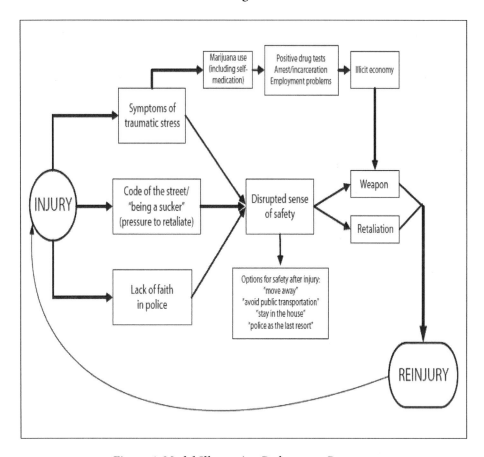

Figure 6: Model Illustrating Pathways to Recurrence

Reproduced from Rich, J.A., & Grey, C.M. (2005). Pathways to Recurrent Trauma Among Young Black Men: Traumatic Stress, Substance Use, and the "Code of the Street." *American Journal of Public Health*, *95*(5), 816–824. https://doi.org/10.2105/AJPH.2004.044560

raises the rate of ethnic collective action" (Olzak, 1992, p. 3). Olzak et al. (1996) asserts that a dominant residential ethnic group seeking to exclude resources, influence, and power from "in-migrants" is a tenet of the competition process. Many of the earlier competition models had binary choices where predominately white neighborhoods confronted "in-migrants" who were Black or African American. "In-migrants" were hypothesized as intruders whom dominant ethnic groups repel from their neighborhoods and communities with exclusionary violence. However, Bergesen and Herman (1998) contended that competition models may be mis-specified when Black or African Americans were considered the only minority population. In many urban communities throughout the U.S., a minority population may be the largest population in the area (Berube, 2003; Camarillo, 2007), yet some researchers assert that Olzak's (1992, 1996) and colleagues' models do not foresee this outcome or its implications.

White Americans may not be in competition in these communities—they may have moved away years ago, and in the intervening years, the neighborhood composition may have come to consist of multiple minority populations. These minority populations are in competition for resources, influence, and power, but there is little evidence of competition among America's racial and ethnic minorities producing exclusionary violence of the magnitude experienced within the Black-white binary competition models (Bergesen & Herman, 1998, p. 40). In response to demographic changes at the community level in the U.S., Bergesen and Herman (1998) introduced a reformulated competition model (p. 41):

> We propose an ethnic competition model similar to Olzak's. Our formulation differs from Olzak's version, however, by acknowledging African Americans as the majority population when the neighborhood is the relevant level of analysis. We also propose that the key element is not so much labor market competition, but the arrival of new racial/ethnic immigrants into residential areas within a different racial/ethnic majority already established. In Los Angeles, this means the rapid in-migration of Latinos and Asians in the 1980s into neighborhoods that were predominately African American. In such a situation, we hypothesize defensive backlash violence from African Americans in those neighborhoods in which the rate of in-migration by nonblack minorities is increasing.
>
> What could be called hyper-ethnic succession, then, represents demographic situations in which a rapid in-migration of new ethnic groups alters the ethnic composition and produces resentment that fuels defensive backlash violence by a residential area's dominant racial/ethnic group.

Both Olzak's (1992, 1996) and colleagues' model and the model of Bergesen and Herman (1998) may account for some of the community violence in major urban areas such as L.A. and Chicago. Other models shift the focus from desegregation triggering collective or community violence to segregation being a root cause for violence. Some cities with higher levels of segregation have higher rates of violence (Massey, 2001; Ousey, 1999; Shihadeh & Flynn, 1996), regardless of the racial/ethnic composition of residents in the neighborhood or community (Krivo et al., 2009). Peterson and Krivo (1993) found that Black people were more likely to be victims of homicide in segregated neighborhoods and communities, and Bisciglia (2014) found Hispanics/Latinx people were more likely to be victims of homicide in segregated residential areas. Black spatial segregation is entrenched and highly resistant to change (Shihadeh & Flynn, 1996). To induce change, some competition models focus on segregation contributing to more community violence, and integration lessening that violence. More integrated cities have smaller differences in homicide rates for white and Black Americans (LaFree et al., 2010). These competition models provide perspectives for why community violence occurs and endures, even as neighborhoods or communities change demographically and economically.

As neighborhoods and communities change in residential areas in urban, suburban, and rural settings, music has provided a safe space for residents, especially youth, to express their angst about the collective or community violence where they reside. Musical genres that emerged from this landscape were hip-hop music and gangster rap. In the 1980s and 1990s, hip-hop and rap narrated the lived experiences of neighborhood kids who wrote, produced, and performed music about the code of the streets, as well as collective and community violence. Their anthems became a part of popular culture and resonated with youth in and outside of their communities, and their audiences were no longer local but national and eventually global. Kids in the "hood" and the "burbs" now had something in common: their varied understandings of pop culture references about South Central L.A., Compton, New York City, Brooklyn, and Chicago, among others. Hip-hop and rap were explored in the 2015 Hollywood blockbuster *Straight Outta Compton*. The musicians whose lives were shown in the movie have shared their experiences about growing up in Compton, as have many of their peers. The artistry of hip-hop and rap is contested in the media by parents, government officials, media watchdogs, and regulators, who perceive it as glorifying violence and misogynistic behavior (Herd, 2009). Musicians believe that critics would rather ignore them and their stories or eliminate them altogether. Denise Herd (2009) considers the musicians' perspective: "At the most basic level, preventing media violence requires changing social conditions—poverty, poor access to education, and discrimination—that promote violence in the lives of rappers and the communities from which they emerge" (p. 404). Regina Bradley (2017) maintained that focus on hip-hop as a mainstream phenomenon, focus on "its musicality and its associated aesthetics," should not hide in plain sight how "It served as a context for complicating and recognizing a transition into a post–civil rights movement era" (p. 141).

Amanda Nell Edgar (2016) agreed that hip-hop and rap provide a useful context for social commentary regarding the plight of urban American when she stated, "Marked by tension and conflict, 'Fuck tha Police' became an icon in public discussions of racial violence exemplifying discourses both resisting and justifying police violence in poor Black neighborhoods" (p. 223). In the twenty-first century, musicians, fans, and media critics debate "Fuck tha Police," a song that is decades old, on a new platform, YouTube. Edgar (2016) is among media users who employ social media as a performative and spatial place to reestablish public community discourses about the roles hip-hop and rap play in examining the systemic context of community violence. Edgar (2016) stated: "Social media commentary offers a record of contemporary listeners' interpretations of the song's meaning and motivations for its use through the track's YouTube comment sections" (p. 224). As the commentaries proliferate online and offline, it is imperative that media users understand "...the processes that are at work and to acknowledge that there are different messages being communicated to listeners who occupy different spaces and places and who identify with space or place according to different values of scale" (Forman, 2000, p. 88). Rap emerged as a voice for Black and Latinx youth, many of whom lived among a socially disenfranchised population in turbulent neighborhoods or communities. These "locals" define space as a physical place or locality, and they too perceive space as a metaphorical "hood" that transcends a physical place. They are fans of hip-hop culture and rap music, and while they are a part of a fandom that transcends physical boundaries and demarcations on a map, their experiences are unique, and their relationships with the lyricist and the lyrics involve additional cultural meanings. This chapter explores the role of hip-hop and rap as a conduit for residents of turbulent neighborhoods and communities. These tools of pop culture enable residents and media users to comprehend and express their shared experiences and to challenge the status quo.

Celebrity Narratives Addressing Collective and Community Violence

To understand collective and community violence in South Central L.A., including Compton, and in South Side and West Side Chicago, a historical understanding is necessary to fully comprehend the effects of community and neighborhood evolution regarding changing demographics, income stratification, property devaluation, and declining trust in government, which when taken together act as an accelerant for communities that are a tinderbox. South Central L.A. during World War II prospered as its munitions industries attracted labor, but when the war was over, the prosperity ended (The Observer, 2000). Compton is an urban yet suburban area adjacent to South Central L.A. that bills itself as "the Hub City" because of its location on the main rail artery between L.A. and the San Pedro docks. Compton's location along a main route for industry and goods brought prosperity, which attracted African Americans. In the 1960s, Compton became the first city in California to have an African American political majority. As the demographic composition of Compton changed, its economic prosperity dissipated. In the 1970s and 1980s, the emergence of gang warfare between the Bloods and Crips (The Observer, 2000) and the 1981 debut of crack cocaine resulted in economic despair, addiction, and an explosion in collective and community violence (Graves, 2017). Gangs sold crack to residents of Compton to make money, and the money and illegal nature of the business attracted guns, which exacerbated the violence.

This process unfolded in communities and neighborhoods from the West Coast in L.A. to the midwest in Chicago to cities throughout the southern and eastern regions of the U.S. Politicians lambasted the situation, and their policies further isolated urban areas like Compton. "Meanwhile, in the span of a few years, poor neighborhoods were transformed by the guns and gangs into warring kingdoms, with plenty of civilian casualties scattered among the fallen soldiers. For every million crack users, there were several million more people who felt the impact even though they didn't use themselves" (Graves, 2017). Compton went into decline.

Violence Begets Violence on the Streets of South Central L.A. and Compton

The rap group N.W.A immortalized the grim reality many residents of Compton, South Central L.A., and similar communities and neighborhoods in the U.S. faced in the 1980s and 1990s. The group's members Ice Cube, Dr. Dre, Eazy-E, MC Ren, and DJ Yella (and formerly Arabian Prince) used their lyrics and the commercialization of rap music to refocus the country's attention on the "code of the street" and its adverse effects, including a high murder rate and the protracted combat between gangs and law enforcement with residents caught in the middle (Tse, 2015). Individual and community drug addiction and juvenile and young adult hyper-sexualization were also addressed in N.W.A songs, which are part of a genre of music known as "gangsta rap." The homicide rate would peak in L.A. County in 1992, the year the Rodney King riots occurred. Interviewer Alex Gale (2015) asked Ice Cube about this time period and its depiction in the movie *Straight Outta Compton*:

Why did the movie use the Rodney King verdict and the L.A. riots as such a prominent backdrop?
We wanted to show, why did we make this kind of music? That was the first thing: What made us N.W.A? That's what we wanted to show. We wanted to show the neighborhood affecting us, but then we had an effect right back on the neighborhood. We wanted to show that when we did a song like "Fuck Tha Police" that it wasn't just about us, it wasn't just about what happened to us. It was more of an anthem for people to be able to fight back and to have a song they can all rally around that feels the same way they feel. We wanted to show that our music had an impact on the community as a whole.

How did seeing the riots affect your music and what you wanted to do?

You can hear on *The Predator,* you can hear on *Death Certificate*: I was trying to really warn people what was coming and what was the feeling of the community. As an artist, I first tried to be even-handed. I didn't want to just be the grim reaper with all the bad news. I wanted to do all kinds of different records. I just wanted to show my versatility as an MC. But I felt like I had to speak on the riots in songs like "We Have to Tear This Muthafucka Up." I was working on my records when the riots happened, so I kind of switched reels a little bit.

What significance do you think "Fuck Tha Police" has today?

I think it just shows the problem at hand. The problem is, first of all the police are trained to win no matter what. Win an argument, win a situation—that's how they're taught. You add racism to that and it's just an evil combination, and people are starting to recognize that. The camera phones, social media, everybody's more in tune with each other. Things are shown instantly, so it's really up to the prosecutors and the judge and the politicians to start holding these officers more accountable. Even captains, lieutenants and chiefs have to hold their own officers more accountable for what they do and not always [have] just tons of excuses.

Do you think things are getting better or worse when it comes to police brutality?

I think it's the same. What we got to do is hold these dudes more accountable. We need body cameras on all these cops and we need it to be a federal offense if they tamper with those cameras, manipulate those cameras in any kind of way or obstruct those cameras. And we need these good cops to start snitching on these bad cops. They talk shit about our neighborhoods for having a no-snitch policy, but they have a no-snitch policy in their department, and that's the problem. The good cops need to point out these bad cops, get them out of here and get your dignity and respect back from the community.

Fortunately, after the Rodney King riots, things settled down. Tse (2015) underscored that crime waned, the crack epidemic ended, and more effective policing emerged. Sadly, tennis superstars Venus and Serena Williams were reminded that years after N.W.A. became famous, community violence persisted in Compton. Their sister Yetunde Price was murdered by a gang member in their hometown of Compton in a drive-by shooting in 2003 (Carlson & Hewitt, 2018). She was not the intended target. Police maintained that the murderer was a member of the Southside Crips (Carlson & Hewitt, 2018). In 2017, a panel discussion called "A Family Affair, Presented by Oath" took place in Compton. The discussion included Venus and Serena Williams and was moderated by American media personality, sportswriter, and journalist Jemele Hill (MAKERS via YouTube, 2017). The panel discussed community and collective violence in urban communities and neighborhoods and the role the Williams non-profit organization The Yetunde Price Resource Center (YPRC) is playing in disrupting the narrative that people of color are less than or at a deficit. The center endeavors to shift the narrative—it wants people of color to perceive themselves as important and as an asset, to empower people who are victimized to prevent and recover from trauma. As the Williams sisters championed the work of YPRC, they became emotional during the panel discussion, especially when they discussed their slain sister. Their public grieving was a reminder that family relations of victims are themselves victims. The man who murdered Yetunde Price was released in 2018 after serving 12 years of a 15-year sentence because of "good behavior" (Carlson & Hewitt, 2018). When he was released back into South Central L.A. and Compton communities and neighborhoods, he should have noticed that differences exist: "Compton also experienced a major demographic shift as a result of black flight in the Riots' wake. According to the 2010 Census, it is now two-thirds Hispanic or Latino" (Tse, 2015). Compton is an example of how some things change while other things stay the same.

The tensions that existed in Compton when it shifted from majority white to majority Black continued as the community's neighborhoods became increasingly more Latinx. The hostility African Americans felt in Compton in the 1950s dissipated as whites moved out of the community (Sides, 2004). In the 1970s, 80s, and 90s, Compton, a predominantly African American dystopia associated with blight, economic hardships, gang violence, high crime rates, and police brutality popularized in N.W.A.'s music, would later haunt the Compton of the 2000s. The Compton of the 2000s desperately sought to turn the page on the caricature Compton had become in the media (Jennings, 2015). Oftentimes, the popular representations and perceptions of Compton left out Latinx people, who became a majority in 2000 (Sides, 2004). As the Latinx residents of Compton sought resources from local schools to address the needs of their children, they came to realize that they were perceived as a threat to the longtime bastion of Black political empowerment in the community (Straus, 2009). Political Scientist Wilbur Rich (1996) observed: "The school pies feed many families, and slicing it is a major event in the local economy" (p. 5). Straus (2009) reiterated this point when she stated, "In schools, residents of the same neighborhood converged for the most personal of reasons: the welfare and education of their children. But schooling also affected the welfare of adults in the community, as the school system served other functions such as employment and empowerment" (p. 508). In Compton, Latinx parents wanted more funds for bilingual education, and since they were a demographic majority in the community, they used protests and activism to put pressure on Compton stakeholders to get it. African Americans who built their power in opposition to white control and domination were willing to use their broad networks of educators, organizations, ministers, and politicians to take an oversized share of resources from a group they now "Othered" (Henig et al., 1999). Compton's tensions along racial, ethnic, and language lines have evolved over the decades, but they persist, as does Compton's gang violence.

Homicides in Compton had lessened over the years. Demographics of the community changed, but the conditions that nourish gang participation and violence remained the same. Eventually, homicides increased, and they tripled from 2015 to 2016, with much of the community violence associated with gang feuds (Cruz, 2016). In February 2016, a one-year-old girl was killed as she stood by her crib, with police in pursuit of perpetrators believed to be gang members targeting her father. The death toll increased in May 2016 as seven more people were fatally shot (Cruz, 2016). In response to the increased homicide rate, Captain Matthew Burson of the Operations Safe Streets Bureau, the gang unit for the Compton police department, stated, "We're looking at an entrenched network of violence dating back to the mid–1970s." Community leaders came together to promote and encourage civic unity among African American, Latinx, and other racial and ethnic communities. "New groups continue to form, such as the Compton Community Partners, a group of African American and Latino grass-roots activists committed to launching a biracial organization to advance the educational welfare of black and Latino youth in the city" (Camarillo, 2007, p. 26). Community partnerships offer a way forward so that the community can heal itself, which is why Venus and Serena William's YPRC (2020) is based in Compton. The center collaborates with other organizations to offer trauma-informed programs that promote individual and community-wide healing and resiliency. The YPRC ensures that victims of direct or indirect violence have access to resources. Where there are no resources, the center works with community stakeholders to create them.

Chicago's Violence Is No Easy Fix

NBA star Dwayne Wade can empathize with the Williams sisters. Wade's cousin was pushing her infant child in a stroller when she was shot in the head and killed in Chicago. Both men, Darwin Sorrells, Jr., and Derren Sorrells, were charged with first-degree murder and first-degree attempted murder and were gang members on parole for gun convictions

(Ellis & Kuo, 2016). Chicago has been dealing with some of the worst collective violence of any major city in the country. In response to the situation, elected officials and law enforcement have been under increasing pressure to reduce violent crime. Some civilians, including celebrities such as Chicago native and entertainer Chance the Rapper, complain that the response has been ineffective, while others complain that celebrities such as rap sensation Chief Keef only contribute to the problem. Both these men have lost a family member or friend to the violence, yet their reaction to the collective and community violence has been different. In the midst of this upheaval, the "U.S. Justice Department recently told us that Chicago police have long been quick to turn to excessive force or deadly force against African-American and Latino residents, often without facing consequences" (Glanton, 2017). As violence spirals out of control, outsiders who think they can come in, quickly diagnose the problem, introduce a quick-fix, and leave, are not taken seriously by stakeholders genuinely looking for a viable course of action to end the bloodshed.

One of the men to visit and stay long enough to gain an understanding of the problem was the Rev. Al Sharpton. His visits to Chicago in 2013 "opened his eyes to the reality of Chicago's violence" (Glanton, 2017). Sharpton said, "You need a major overhaul to stop this violence." He continued, "You can't address the problem without addressing underlying factors like jobs, after-school programs and the proliferation of guns." Because there was no organized gang structure, there were no leaders for Sharpton to meet with to broker a peace accord or reconciliation. Sharpton said, "The more I stayed and walked around at night, the more I realized that these guys didn't even know each other. They were spontaneous and organic." Basically, there was no one to sit down and talk to (Glanton, 2017). The violence involved youth who answered to the "code of the street" more than to a leader of their gang or crew. These youth dealt with violence throughout their day. They had no sanctuary from violence. Julia Burdick-Will (2013) addressed the lack of safety for youth contending with collective and community violence in Chicago (p. 343):

> However, many underperforming schools, especially in Chicago, also deal with high levels of violence on a daily basis. Of the approximately 100 high schools in Chicago, two-thirds called police to intervene in at least one violent incident on school grounds during the first seven months of the 2009-2010 school year, and one-quarter of schools called the police more than 17 times during that period. Five percent of schools reported at least 51 violent crimes in one year. This means that police are involved in violent conflicts at these schools on average close to twice a week.

Something needs to be done to mitigate the violence. An unlikely solution could be rappers and their artistry, which are a means of expression that appeals to residents, especially Black and Latinx youth and young adults living in Chicago's South Side and West Side neighborhoods. The narratives and values of Chicago rappers like Chief Keef and Chance the Rapper, which are distilled into their music, distributed globally, and covered in the media, are among the most relatable forms of communication to instigate or mitigate the violence experienced by Black and brown youth. According to William Lee (2017), since both rappers emerged as teenage rap prodigies in the early 2010s, each has carved out his own identity and fan base. "Beyond their divergent musical styles, the artists exemplify the dueling personalities within black communities on the South and West sides fighting for the souls of men and boys" (Lee, 2017).

Andrew Barber, whose *Fake Shore Drive* hip-hop blog took notice of the rappers early in their musical trajectory, explained, these men "… come from totally different backgrounds. Telling two different stories. They're seeing things a different way. That's why they're both so important." Chief Keef's message resonates with young Black and brown males who identify with the struggles he explores in his music, as well as the fight to survive the "code of the street." Chief Keef, born Keith Cozart, is known as much for his problems with law enforcement as for his music: "the Black Disciples-linked youth who was mostly raised by his grandmother, was busted for selling heroin at 15 and pointing a gun at a Chicago police officer at 16, according to court records" (Lee, 2017). Despite his troubling adolescence, when fellow South Side native rap superstar Kanye West reworked Keef's local hit "I Don't Like," Keef gained industry-wide exposure, and his song became an international platinum-selling hit (Lee, 2017). With superstardom comes increased media scrutiny, and in a 2012 ABC *Nightline* special, "Hidden America: Don't Shoot, I Want to Grow Up," host Diane Sawyer addressed the violence in Chicago and Keef's role in it, "simultaneously scrutinizing the detrimental elements of his music and persona, in regards to the alarming gang violence in Chicago" (Alexis, 2012a).

MTV News's coverage of the *Nightline* special focused on two crucial takeaways: (1) Chicago's inner-city gang wars contributed to 419 people being killed across a dozen neighborhoods in the city in 2012, which outnumbered the number of U.S. troops who were killed in Afghanistan in the previous year, and (2) CeaseFire volunteer and "violence interrupter" Lamont Evans exclaimed, "…with all the technology, you can beef with a guy in a whole other state," adding that gang wars have turned into "beef over rap" (Alexi, 2012a). In response to the media coverage, Chicago rapper MC Lupe Fiasco found the circumstances untenable and commented during an interview with Baltimore's 92Q that the culture Chief Keef represents scares him (Alexis, 2012b). Lupe said:

Not him specifically but just the culture that he represents. The murder rate in Chicago is skyrocketing, and you see who's doing it and perpetrating it—they all look like Chief Keef. When it comes to the point that, you know, that kids who are doing the killings, and they're kids 13 to 19 years old, and you can replicate that in New Orleans, you can replicate that in Oakland. All the kids look the same.

A few days after the interview, Keef took to Twitter to relay his displeasure with Lupe: "Lupe fiasco a hoe ass n---a And wen I see him I'ma smack him like da lil bitch he is #300." Lupe tried to make peace in a tweet, stating, "I cant go 4 that @ChiefKeef & I cant let the people I love, including you my ni—a, go 4 that either. We kings not f---ing savages and goons, I love u lil bruh @ ChiefKeef ... i really do from the bottom of my f---ing heart. I know that street sh—like the back of my hand." The two rappers engaged in a Twitter exchange which elicited reactions from concerned fans. The encounter left Lupe feeling defeated, as he tweeted: "My father I have spoken the truth to them yet it has only made my life in this world more troubled." He continued, "I can bear this no longer ... i have spoken peace only 2 receive vitriol and malice in return. My brother seeks destruction my sister seeks attention paths to nothingness. i'd die for them ... but they'd probably spit on my grave ... i still will die for them ... just bury me in a place far from their reach.... Amin." Afterward, Keef claimed tweets attributed to him were from hackers. Yet he knows how to use social media to generate buzz for his music, and young listeners pay attention to him in part because of his gang ties and the symbolism of those ties as a sign of authenticity for teens in turbulent neighborhoods. "Even in neighborhoods where teens are recruited as gang assassins, Chief Keef gave hope to gangsters that their rhymes could be a means for escape as it had been for Chief Keef himself" (Lee, 2017).

Chance the Rapper, whose full name is Chancelor Bennett, is no stranger to Chicago's violence. Chance's close friend was stabbed to death in 2011 (Porter, 2016). Chance used music as an outlet to express himself and address the hardships of his hometown. Chance became famous yet avoided the notoriety associated with Chief Keef. He won over parents and teachers, who commended him for the millions of dollars he donated and helped raise for Chicago Public Schools (Lee, 2017). Chance is also recognized for his activism following disagreements with former Illinois Governor Bruce Rauner and former Mayor Rahm Emanuel (Lee, 2017). Chance was born on the South Side of Chicago. His father Ken Williams-Bennett worked as an aide to Chicago's former mayor Harold Washington and during Mayor Emanuel's term served as the deputy chief of staff (Porter, 2016). Chance and his father did volunteer work for then Senator Obama prior to his history-making presidential election in 2008 (Porter, 2016). Chance uses his platform to address anti-violence in Chicago.

In 2014, Chance and his brother, Taylor, started an anti-violence media campaign that used the hashtags #SaveChicago, #FaithInAction, and #Put-TheGunsDown to draw attention to safe places in Chicago neighborhoods for people to come together peacefully (Porter, 2016). Here are Chance's tweets related to the anti-violence media campaign (Chandler, 2014):

> He had talked to Churches, Schools, Outreach Prog's and Business's, trying to get them to commit to saving every life possible yesterday. The plan was to get these mass numbers of people out on street corners Friday night with posters and banners with the plea #SAVECHICAGO.
>
> His plan was to get radio stations like @WGCI and @Power92Chicago to say "PUT YOUR GUNS DOWN CHICAGO" every hour on the hour the wk before. all he asked of me was to say something on social media. and so i did ambiguously through tweets that hinted at an album, or a song #MAY23rd.
>
> And even though i was outta town i checked in constantly. come to FIND OUT WE WENT 42 HOURS FROM THURSDAY TO SATURDAY NIGHT W/O ONE SHOOTING.

The anti-violence media campaign was considered a success, because there were no shootings during a a 42-hour time period over Memorial Day weekend in Chicago, in 2014 (Porter, 2016). Chance is passionate about Chicago, and he will defend the city against anyone, including President Donald Trump.

During an interview on ESPN's *The Undefeated*, he responded to Trump's tweet that he would "send in the Feds" over Chicago's homicide rate, and his frustration with city stakeholders regarding his perception that the problem had gotten out of hand (Williams, 2017). Chance responded to the tweet: "I hope he's coming in to do some type of federal overturn of our state and city budgets in terms of schooling and housing." He continued, "I'm tired of n***as talkin' about Chicago like it's a Third World country. Like, that it's not a place of booming business with a very successful downtown and all types of new development." In the August 20, 2016, issue of *Billboard* magazine, he addressed the city's crime rate (Williams, 2016): "My dad is getting the call every morning, updates on how many kids got shot the day before. In a time of crisis he tried to be strategic, and he should have been more compassionate." There was also recognition that law enforcement plays a role in Chicago's collective and community violence, which Chance recognized, stating, "There's a larger conversation we need to have about the role of police officers, their relationship to the people as enemy or executioner, when they're not supposed to be either." Chance focuses on the role of residents and law enforcement in the perpetuation of violence in Chicago's neighborhoods, and he does not want bystanders to get caught in the crossfire. His comments to *Billboard* magazine were a continuation of his shared remarks from an October 2015 radio interview with Hot 97 (Williams, 2016), where he addressed the role of the Black Lives Matter movement in holding communities, their stakeholders, and law enforcement accountable: "I think the only thing that's really going to make a change in terms of how we feel as citizens in terms of safety and our relationship with the police, is if we start seeing more federal indictments, arrests, and convictions of police officers."

Chance realizes that one of the most challenging factors in mitigating violence in Chicago is firearms and access to guns. He understands that gun violence is contributing to the loss of lives in Chicago, especially among young perpetrators and victims on the South Side and West Side. In 2018, Chance joined a Chicago rally that was a part of Parkland students' Road to Change tour, which pushed for gun control (Hinton, 2018). Before the event, youth chalked on the sidewalks surrounding the event phrases such as "enough" and "stop killing us," while people turned in assault rifles for a "metro gun share program" sponsored by the Brady Center to Prevent Gun Violence. This happened as the names of 147 young people who had been killed from June 15, 2017, to June 15, 2018, were read off (Hinton, 2018). Chance and fellow Chicago native Jennifer Hudson, as well as former U.S. Representative Gabby Giffords (who was shot in the head in 2011), spoke at the rally. Chance energized the crowd and fostered togetherness, insisting, "It's so important for us to link up and talk about stuff that's going on here. Everyone on this stage is anti-gun violence—from people in our community to people policing our community."

Chance and other celebrities from the Chicago and South Central L.A. metropolitan areas use their experiences and their platforms in the media to express their concerns for these turbulent communities and neighborhoods. They are coalescing around efforts to mobilize stakeholders in their cities, states, and the country, to do a better job of combatting collective and community violence.

Public Health in Turbulent Communities Must Address the Violence

Comedian and host of CNN's *United Shades of America*, W. Kamau Bell tackled violence in Chicago during an episode of his show, and his diagnosis and treatment for the problem is something stakeholders can agree upon (Penrice, 2017). Bell explained, "I graduated high school in Chicago." He continued, "Chicago was always in the news as being America's most violent city or gang-ridden, and I lived in Chicago for a long time, and yes, there are areas that are like that, but that's not true for the whole city. And even what you're saying about those areas [that are], you're misrepresenting. And then Donald Trump went out of his way [to target] Chicago and then even targeted Dwayne Wade's cousin, who was killed, and I was like, 'We have to do Chicago.'" Bell spoke with current gang members, and he responded that the solution to Chicago's violence is no secret: "They all know what the solutions are to gang violence. They all know what the solutions are to crime," he observed. "We need jobs. We need better schools. When you look at Chicago, they closed a bunch of the public schools and the schools are underfunded. [When] you walk on the South and West sides of Chicago, there's miles and miles of undeveloped land that's just sitting there," he continued. "There's not many tall buildings. There's not a lot of businesses. There's not a lot of places for people to go. There's not a big population density. And when that happens, there's no jobs." Bell recognized that stakeholders must acknowledge the importance of economic development in the creation of jobs and prosperity and the need for an effective and well-funded education system to mitigate collective and community violence. Still, at their epicenter, collective and community violence are diseases.

Collective and community violence are public health issues, and public health can only be addressed by looking at the whole patient. Violence in these communities will not be solved if stakeholders deny the multifaceted nature of the problem, and public health experts need to be on the frontlines addressing the whole patient. Healthcare professionals observe the violence in various care settings, including hospital emergency rooms, in inner-city clinics, in schools, and in public spaces (Valenti et al., 2007). A goal of healthcare professionals in turbulent communities should be violence prevention and mitigation, to introduce adaptive messages and behaviors as a means of intervention to course-correct the violence. Otherwise, violence acts as a contagion, with patterns of collective and community violence plaguing communities and neighborhoods through society (Parker, 2015). "Many hospitals engage in community-building activities that address the housing, economic, environmental, workforce, and other needs of vulnerable populations" (Bos et al., 2017, p. 6). These activities may not be interventions, yet many of them directly or indirectly reduce some of the causes of violence.

A multifaceted intervention that has been effective with public health approaches at the epicenter of efforts to combat collective and community violence include the Cure Violence Health Model, developed by Gary Slutkin of the University of Illinois at Chicago (Ranford et al., 2013). The model consists of three major components (*Community Violence as a Population Health Issue: Proceedings of a Workshop*, 2017, p. 32–33):

> The first component aims to interrupt transmission to stop violent events before they happen, primarily by interrupting conflict to prevent retaliation. The

second component involves identifying and changing the thinking of the highest potential transmitters of violence, largely those involved in the gang lifestyle, to reduce the number of violent individuals in the community. The third component works to change community norms to create social pressure to stop violence, which … requires engaging community leaders, residents, business owners, and faith leaders to bring awareness to the devastation gun violence has on communities and to change attitudes so that community members reject violence in the community. Too often … community members become desensitized to violence and accept it as the way things are. Overcoming that acceptance is an important step to changing community norms.

Successful interventions address the social-cultural or physical/built environments of turbulent communities and neighborhoods. Social-cultural environment involves using community assets, especially community members, to build out violence prevention and health promotion programs to combat community trauma and engender healing and connection between residents (Pinderhughes et al., 2015). Strategies within the physical/built environment entail improving the physical environment, reducing blight, creating spaces for positive interaction—helping community members locate places that instill community culture, pride, and a sense of community (Pinderhughes et al., 2015). Some of these interventions address social-cultural or physical/built environments but do not have a public health emphasis like Oakland Promise, the city of Oakland's $23 million dollar initiative to give babies born into poverty a $500 college savings account, or Oakland's partnership with Kiva Zip, a non-profit organization that provides zero-interest loans for inner-city entrepreneurs who otherwise would not secure funding (Stock et al., 2016). Many community interventions to address community violence are akin to Oakland's initiatives and address underlying factors that contribute to a toxic environment that foments violence. Other interventions involve community institutions and partnerships to combat violence (Hammond & Arias, 2011). A snapshot of these interventions entails gun buy-back programs, antibullying programs at schools, escort services for children in dangerous neighborhoods, after-school programs, safe zones, and anger management and emotion regulation programs. Some interventions, such as CeaseFire, incorporate content and outreach that use a public health approach and address the social-cultural environment of inner cities.

CeaseFire is a public health program designed to prevent shootings by changing attitudes, behaviors, and social norms about gun violence (Whitehill et al., 2012). The most prominent component of CeaseFire is the use of specialized outreach workers, also referred to as OWs (Skogan, 2008). "The OWs, sometimes called violence interrupters, are recruited for their credibility and influence among high-risk youth in the target communities. They are often former gang members or were previously involved in the drug trade" (Whitehill et al., 2012, p. 204). Another strategy to stop violence is a literal ceasefire in turbulent neighborhoods between law enforcement and the communities they serve and protect. Law enforcement must stop tactics that diminish police-community relations and harm public safety. Law enforcement must build trust between officers and residents. To achieve a more cooperative police-community relationship, the Urban Institute (2016) recommended the following steps to improve relations between police and communities of color (p. VII):

1. Hire, train, and assess police to mitigate implicit biases and to promote procedurally just interactions with citizens.

2. Hold police accountable through community satisfaction surveys, civilian review boards, body-worn cameras, and the collection of key data (e.g., use-of-force data, racial data on police stops and arrests).

3. Create more positive police-community interactions through accountable foot patrols, police training in de-escalation tactics, and events that allow officers to engage with citizens outside of an enforcement context.

4. Prioritize policing and prosecution of violent crimes and firearms trafficking, rather than broader, indiscriminate strategies (e.g., stop and frisk) that alienate community members.

Law enforcement and other community stakeholders should seek funding from the COPS Office, which provides training and technical assistance, and provides access to compiled information resources about specific crime and operational issues. COPS outreach focuses on programming, interventions, and funding to reduce crime, repair disorder, reduce recidivism, improve public trust in government, produce and disseminate research, and improve victim safety.

REFERENCES

Alexis, N. (2012, October 23). *Chief Keef's music scrutinized in Chicago gang violence special.* MTV News. http://www.mtv.com/news/2499556/chief-keef-nightline-special-chicago-gang-violence/.

Alexis, N. (2012, September 6). *Lupe Fiasco considers retirement after Chief Keef spat.* TV News. http://www.mtv.com/news/1693272/lupe-fiasco-chief-keef-considers-retirement/#:~:text.

Anderson, E. (1999). *Code of the street: Decency, violence and the moral life of the inner city.* W.W. Norton.

Bell, C.C., & Jenkins, E.J. (1993). Community violence and children on Chicago's southside. *Psychiatry, 56(1),* 46–54. https://doi.org/10.1080/00332747.1993.11024620.

Bergesen, A., & Herman, M. (1998). Immigration, race, and riot: The 1992 Los Angeles uprising. *American Sociological Review, 63(1),* 39–54. https://doi.org/10.2307/2657476.

Berube, A. (2003). Racial and ethnic change in the nation's largest cities. In B. Katz & R.E. Lang

(Eds.), *Redefining urban & suburban America: Evidence from Census 2000, Volume I* (pp. 139–140). Brookings Institution Press.

Bieler, S., Kijakazi, K., La Vigne, N., Vinik, N., & Overtom, S. (2016). *Engaging communities in reducing gun violence: A road map for safer communities*. Justice Policy Center. https://www.urban.org/sites/default/files/publication/80061/2000760-engaging-communities-in-reducing-gun-violence-a-road-map-for-safer-communities.pdf.

Bisciglia, M.G. (2014). Segregation and Hispanic homicide: An examination of two measures of segregation on rates of Hispanic homicide in major metropolitan areas. *SAGE Open, 4(1)*, 1–10. https://doi.org/10.1177/2158244013517242.

Bjerregaard, B., & Lizotte, A.J. (1995). Gun ownership and gang membership. *Journal Criminal Law and Criminology, 86(1)*, 37–58. https://doi.org/10.2307/1143999.

Blumstein, A. (1995). Youth violence, guns, and the illicit-drug industry. *Journal Criminal Law and Criminology, 86(1)*, 10–36. https://doi.org/10.2307/1143998.

Bos, J.V. D., Creten, N., Davenport, S., & Roberts, M. (2017). Cost of community violence to hospitals and health systems: Report for the American hospital association. Milliman. https://www.aha.org/system/files/2018-01/community-violence-report.pdf.

Bradley, R. (2017). Introduction: Hip-hop cinema as a lens of contemporary Black realities. *Black Camera, 8(2)*, 141–145. https://doi.org/10.2979/BLACKCAMERA.8.2.08.

Brady, S.S., & Donenberg, G.R. (2006). Mechanisms linking violence exposure to health risk behavior in adolescence: Motivation to cope and sensation seeking. *Journal of the American Academy of Child and Adolescent Psychiatry, 45(6)*, 673–680. https://doi.org/10.1097/01.chi.0000215328.35928.a9.

Brookmeyer, K.A., Henrich, C.C., & Schwab-Stone, M. (2005). Adolescents who witness community violence: Can parent support and prosocial cognitions protect them from committing violence? *Child Development, 76(4)*, 917–929. https://doi.org/10.1111/j.1467-8624.2005.00886.x.

Burdick-Will, J. (2013). School violent crime and academic achievement in Chicago. *Sociology of Education, 86(4)*, 1–24. https://doi.org/10.1177/0038040713494225.

Buss, T.F., & Abdu, R. (1995). Repeat victims of violence in an urban trauma center. *Violence and Victims, 10(3)*, 183–194.

Camarillo, A.M. (2007). Cities of color: The new racial frontier in California's minority-majority cities. *Pacific Historical Review, 76(1)*, 1–28. https://doi.org/10.1525/phr.2007.76.1.1.

Carlson, A., & Hewitt, B. (2018, August 2). The story of the tragic killing of Venus & Serena Williams' big sister: "There was blood everywhere." *People Magazine*. https://www.yahoo.com/entertainment/story-tragic-killing-venus-serena-194430844.html.

Centers for Disease Control and Prevention. (2002). Nonfatal Physical Assault-Related Injuries Treated in Hospital Emergency Departments—United States, 2000. *Morbidity and Mortality Weekly Report, 51(21)*, 460–463. https://www.jstor.org/stable/23313148?seq=1.

Centers for Disease Control and Prevention. (2011). *The national intimate partner and sexual violence survey*. National Center for Injury Prevention and Control https://ncvc.dspacedirect.org/handle/20.500.11990/1550.

Chandler, D.L. (2014, May 27). *Chicago's Chance the Rapper helps stop gun violence in city for 42 hours*. News One. https://newsone.com/3011373/chicagos-chance-the-rapper-chicago-violence/.

Cook, P.J., Lawrence, B.A., Ludwig, J., & Miller, T.R. (1999). The medical costs of gunshot injuries in the United States. *JAMA, 282(5)*, 447–454. https://doi.org/10.1001/jama.282.5.447.

Cruz, N.S. (2016, June 2). Gang feuds to blame for recent Compton violence, officials say. *Los Angeles Times*. https://www.latimes.com/local/crime/la-me-compton-homicides-20160602-snap-story.html.

Dahlberg, L.L., & Krug, E.G. (2002). Violence: A global public health problem. In E.G. Krug, L.L. Dahlberg, J.A. Mercy, A.B. Zwi, & R. Lozano (Eds.), *World report on violence and health* (pp. 1–21). WHO. https://www.who.int/violence_injury_prevention/violence/world_report/en/full_en. pdf?ua=1.

Dahlberg, L.L., & Mercy, J.A. (2009). History of violence as a public health problem. *Virtual Mentor (VM), 11(2)*, 167–172. https://doi.org/10.1001/virtualmentor.2009.11.2.mhst1-0902.

Edgar, A. (2016). Commenting straight from the underground: N.W.A., police brutality, and

YouTube as a space for neoliberal resistance. *Southern Communication Journal, 81(4)*, 223–236. https://doi.org/10.1080/1041794X.2016.1200123.

Fagan, J., and Wilkinson, D. (1998). Guns, Youth Violence, and Social Identity in Inner Cities. In M. Tonry & M. Moore (Eds.), *Youth Violence, Vol. 24. Crime and Justice: A Review of Research* (pp. 105–188). University of Chicago Press.

Farr, V. (2004). The new war zone: The ubiquitous presence of guns and light weapons has changed the definitions of "war," "victim," and "perpetrator." *The Women's Review of Books, 21(5)*, 16–16. https://doi.org/10.2307/4024331.

Farrell, A.D., & Bruce, S.E. (1997). Impact of exposure to community violence on violent behavior and emotional distress among urban adolescents. *Journal of Clinical Child Psychology, 26(1)*, 2–14. https://doi.org/10.1207/s15374424jccp2601_1.

Fitzpatrick, K.M., & Boldizar, J.P. (1993). The prevalence and consequences of exposure to violence among African-American youth. *Journal of the American Academy of Child & Adolescent Psychiatry, 32(2)*, 424–430. https://doi.org/10.1097/00004583-199303000-00026.

Forman, M. (2000). "Represent": Race, space and place in rap music. *Popular Music, 19(1)*, 65–90. https://doi.org/10.1017/S0261143000000015.

Gale, A. (2015, August 13). Ice Cube: "Police have become our worst bullies." *Billboard Magazine.* https://www.billboard.com/articles/columns/the-juice/6663762/ice-cube-police-brutality-nwa-straight-outta-compton-interview.

Glanton, D. (2017, February 5). Think Chicago's violence is an easy fix. Ask the Rev. Al Sharpton. *Chicago Tribune.* https://www.chicagotribune.com/columns/dahleen-glanton/ct-trump-scott-violence-glanton-20170202-column.html.

Gorman-Smith, D., Henry, D.B., & Tolan, P.H. (2004). Exposure to community violence and violence perpetration: The protective effects of family functioning. *Journal of Clinical Child and Adolescent Psychology, 33(3)*, 439–449. https://doi.org/10.1207/s15374424jccp3303_2.

Graves, W. (2017, August 5). *How N.W.A.'s Straight Outta Compton made gangsta rap the new reality: Nearly 30 years ago, six Compton youth got real and changed hip-hop forever.* ConsequenceofSound.net. https://consequenceofsound.net/2017/08/how-n-w-as-straight-outta-compton-made-gangsta-rap-the-new-reality/.

Hammond, W.R., & Arias, I. (2011). Broadening the approach to youth violence prevention through public health. *Journal of Prevention & Intervention in the Community, 39(2)*, 167–175. https://doi.org/10.1080/10852352.2011.556574.

Hening, J.R., Hula, R.C., Orr, M., & Pedescleaux, D.S. (1999). *Color of school reform: Race, politics, and the challenge of urban education.* Princeton University Press.

Herd, D. (2009). Changing images of violence in rap music lyrics: 1979–1997. *Journal of Public Health Policy, 30(4)*, 395–406. https://doi.org/10.1057/jphp.2009.36.

Hinton, R. (2018, June 16). Parkland students, Chance the Rapper headline anti-violence rally, "Scary times." *Chicago Sun Times.* https://chicago.suntimes.com/2018/6/16/18418401/parkland-students-chance-the-rapper-headline-anti-violence-rally-scary-times.

Jennings, A. (2015, August 14). Compton worries *Straight Outta Compton* could give people the wrong idea. *Los Angeles Times.* https://www.latimes.com/local/lanow/la-me-ln-violent-straight-outta-compton-isn-t-the-real-compton-mayor-says-20150813-story.html.

Kliewer, W., & Sullivan, T.N. (2008). Community violence exposure, threat appraisal, and adjustment in adolescents. *Journal of Clinical Child and Adolescent Psychology, 37(4)*, 860–873. https://doi.org/10.1080/15374410802359718.

Krivo, L.J., Peterson, R.D., & Kuhl, D.C. (2009). Segregation, racial structure, and neighborhood violent crime. *American Journal of Sociology, 114(6)*, 1765–1802. https://doi.org/10.1086/597285.

Krug, E., Dahlberg, L., Mercy, J., Zwi, A., & Lozano, R. (2002). *World report on violence and health.* WHO. https://www.who.int/violence_injury_prevention/violence/world_report/en/full_en.pdf?ua=1.

LaFree, G., Baumer, E.P., & O'Brien, R. (2010). Still separate and unequal? A city-level analysis of the Black-White gap in homicide arrests since 1960. *American Sociological Review, 75(1)*, 75–100. https://doi.org/10.1177/0003122409357045.

Lee, W. (2017, July 28). Chance and Chief Keef: A tale of two rappers. *Chicago Tribune.* https://www.chicagotribune.com/entertainment/music/ct-ae-chance-the-rapper-and-chief-keef-comparison-0730-20170729-story.html.

MAKERS [Oath, Inc]. (2017, December 3). *A family affair, presented by Oath* [Video]. YouTube. https://www.youtube.com/watch?v=8BtDMwy2NSk.

Massey, D. (2001). Segregation and violent crime in urban America. In E. Anderson & D.S. Massey (Eds.), *Problem of the century* (pp. 314–344). Russell Sage.

McGill, T.M., Self-Brown, S.R., Lai, B.S., Cowart-Osborne, M., Tiwari, A., Leblanc, M., & Kelley, M.L. (2014). Effects of exposure to community violence and family violence on school functioning problems among urban youth: The potential mediating role of posttraumatic stress symptoms. *Frontiers in Public Health, 2(8)*, 1–8. https://doi.org/10.3389/fpubh.2014.00008.

Miller, L.S., Wasserman, G.A., Neugebauer, R., Gorman-Smith, D., & Kamboukos, D. (1999). Witnessed community violence and antisocial behavior in high-risk, urban boys. *Journal of Clinical Child Psychology, 28(1)*, 2–11. https://doi.org/10.1207/s15374424jccp2801_1.

Miller, T.R., Cohen, M.A., & Rossman, S.B. (1993). Victim costs of violent crime and resulting injuries. *Health Affairs, 12(4)*, 186–197. https://doi.org/10.1377/hlthaff.12.4.186.

Mondragon, D. (1992). Hospital costs of societal violence. *Medical Care, 30(5)*, 453–460. https://www.jstor.org/stable/3766175?seq=1.

Moore, M., & Tonry, M. (1998). Youth violence in America. In M. Tonry & M. Moore (Eds.), *Youth Violence, Vol. 24. Crime and Justice: A Review of Research* (pp. 1–26). University of Chicago Press.

National Academies of Sciences, Engineering, and Medicine, Health and Medicine Division, Board on Population Health and Public Health Practice, & Roundtable on Population Health Improvement. (2017). *Community Violence as a Population Health Issue: Proceedings of a Workshop.* National Academies Press (U.S.).

National Center for Injury Prevention and Control, Division of Violence Prevention. (2020). *Firearm violence prevention fast facts.* Centers for Disease Control and Prevention. https://www.cdc.gov/violenceprevention/firearms/fastfact.html.

The National Child Traumatic Stress Network. (2021). *Community violence.* https://www.nctsn.org/what-is-child-trauma/trauma-types/community-violence#:~:text.

The Observer. (2000, January 8). Life and death in South Central LA. *The Guardian.* https://www.theguardian.com/theobserver/2000/jan/09/life1.lifemagazine4.

Olzak, S. (1992). *The dynamics of ethnic competition and conflict.* Stanford University Press.

Olzak, S., & Shanahan, S. (1996). Deprivation and race riots: An extension of Spilerman's analysis. *Social Forces, 74(3)*, 931–961. https://doi.org/10.2307/2580387.

Olzak, S., & Shanahan, S., & McEneaney, E.H. (1996). Poverty, segregation, and race riots, 1960–1993. *American Sociological Review, 61(4)*, 590–613. https://doi.org/10.2307/2096395.

Osofsky, J.D., Wewers, S., Hann, D.M., & Fick, A.C. (1993). Chronic community violence: What is happening to our children? *Psychiatry, 56(1)*, 36–45. https://doi.org/10.1080/00332747.1993.11024619.

Ousey, G.C. (1999). Homicide, structural factors, and the racial invariance assumption. *Criminology 37(2)*, 405–426. https://doi.org/10.1111/j.1745-9125.1999.tb00491.x.

Parker, N. (2015, November 5). Anti-gang programs approach violence as a disease. *Ebony.* https://www.ebony.com/news/anti-gang-programs-approach-violence-as-a-disease/.

Penrice, R.R. (2017, May 21). *W. Kamau Bell on how to solve Chicago's violence and why Black celebrities host shows about race.* The Root. https://www.theroot.com/w-kamau-bell-on-how-to-solve-chicago-s-violence-and-wh-1795195067.

Peterson, R.D., & Krivo, L.J. (1993). Racial segregation and urban Black homicide. *Social Forces, 71(4)*, 1001–1026. https://doi.org/10.1093/sf/71.4.1001.

Pinderhughes, H., Davis, R., & Williams, M. (2015). *Adverse community experiences and resilience: A framework for addressing and preventing community trauma.* Prevention Institute. https://www.preventioninstitute.org/sites/default/files/publications/Adverse%20Community%20Experiences%20and%20Resilience.pdf.

Porter, L. (2016, August 12). 10 reasons Chance the Rapper is more than just a rapper. *Essence.* https://www.essence.com/news/reasons-chance-rapper-more-just-rapper/.

Ransford, C.L., Kane, C., & Slutkin, G. (2013). Cure violence: A disease control approach to reduce violence and change behavior. In T. Akers & E. Waltermauer (Eds.), *Epidemiological Criminology: Theory to Practice* (pp. 232–242). Routledge.

Rich, J.A., & Grey, C.M. (2005). Pathways to recurrent trauma among young Black men:

Traumatic stress, substance use, and the "code of the street." *American Journal of Public Health, 95(5)*, 816–824. https://doi.org/10.2105/AJPH.2004.044560.

Richters, J.E., & Martinez, P. (1993). The NIMH community violence project: I. Children as victims of and witnesses to violence. *Psychiatry, 56(1)*, 7–21. https://doi.org/10.1080/00332747.1993.11024617.

Rosenthal, B.S. (2000). Exposure to community violence in adolescence: Trauma symptoms. *Adolescence, 35(138)*, 271–284.

Schwab-Stone, M., Ayers, T.S., Kasprow, W., Voyce, C., Barone, C., Shriver, T., & Weissberg, R.P. (1995). No safe haven: A study of violence exposure in an urban community. *Journal of the American Academy of Child and Adolescent Psychiatry, 34(10)*, 1343–1352. https://doi.org/10.1097/00004583-199510000-00020.

Schwab-Stone, M., Chen, C., Greenberger, E., Silver, D., Lichtman, J., & Voyce, C. (1999). No safe haven. II: The effects of violence exposure on urban youth. *Journal of the American Academy of Child and Adolescent Psychiatry, 38(4)*, 359–367. https://doi.org/10.1097/00004583-199904000-00007.

Schweig, S. (2014). Healthy communities may make safe communities: Public health approaches to violence prevention. *National Institute of Justice Journal, July 2014(273)*, 1–7. https://www.ojp.gov/pdffiles1/nij/244150.pdf.

Shihadeh, E.S., & Flynn, N. (1996). Segregation and crime: The effect of Black social isolation on the rates of Black urban violence. *Social Forces, 74(4)*, 1325–1352. https://doi.org/10.1093/sf/74.4.1325.

Sides, J. (2004). Straight into Compton: American dreams, urban nightmares, and the metamorphosis of a Black suburb. *American Quarterly, 56(3)*, 583–605. https://doi.org/10.1353/aq.2004.0044.

Sims, D.W., Bivins, B.A., Obeid, F.N., Horst, H.M., Sorensen, V.J., & Fath, J.J. (1989). Urban trauma: A chronic recurrent disease. *The Journal of Trauma, 29(7)*, 940–947.

Skogan, W.G., Hartnett, S.M., Bump, N., & Dubois, N. (2008). Evaluation of CeaseFire-Chicago. Northwestern University. https://www.ojp.gov/pdffiles1/nij/grants/227181.pdf.

Stock, S., Bott, M., & Carroll, J. (2016, June 3). *Economy tied to gun violence in Oakland*. NBC Bay Area. https://www.nbcbayarea.com/news/local/economic-disparity-tied-to-gun-violence-in-oakland/2077357/.

Straus, E.E. (2009). Unequal pieces of a shrinking pie: The struggle between African Americans and Latinos over education, employment, and empowerment in Compton, California. *History of Education Quarterly, 49(4)*, 507–529. https://doi.org/10.1111/J.1748-5959.2009.00227.X.

Tellez, M.G., Mackersie, R.C., Morabito, D., Shagoury, C., & Heye, C. (1995). Risks, costs, and the expected complication of re-injury. *American Journal of Surgery, 170(6)*, 660–664. https://doi.org/10.1016/s0002-9610(99)80037-3.

Tse, C. (2015, August 14). *How Compton become the violent city of "Straight Outta Compton."* LAist. https://laist.com/2015/08/14/city_of_compton.php.

Valenti, M., Ormhaug, C.M., Mtonga, R.E., & Loretz, J. (2007). Armed violence: A health problem, a public health approach. *Journal of Public Health Policy, 28(4)*, 389–400. https://doi.org/10.1057/palgrave.jphp.3200150.

Voisin, D.R., Hotton, A.L., & Neilands, T.B. (2014). Testing pathways linking exposure to community violence and sexual behaviors among African American youth. *Journal of Youth and Adolescence, 43(9)*, 1513–1526. https://doi.org/10.1007/s10964-013-0068-5.

Voisin, D.R., Neilands, T.B., Salazar, L.F., Crosby, R., & Diclemente, R.J. (2008). Pathways to drug and sexual risk behaviors among detained adolescents. *Social Work Research, 32(3)*, 147–157. https://doi.org/10.1093/swr/32.3.147.

Voisin, D., Takahashi, L., Berringer, K., Burr, S., & Kuhnen, J. (2016). "Sex is violence": African-American parents' perceptions of the link between exposure to community violence and youth sexual behaviors. *Child & Family Social Work, 21(4)*, 464–472. https://doi.org/10.1111/cfs.12162.

Voisin, D.R., Tan, K., Tack, A.C., Wade, D., & DiClemente, R. (2012). Examining parental monitoring as a pathway from community violence exposure to drug use, risky sex, and recidivism among detained youth. *Journal of Social Service Research, 38(5)*, 699–711. https://doi.org/10.1080/01488376.2012.716020.

Whitehill, J.M., Webster, D.W., & Vernick, J.S. (2013). Street conflict mediation to prevent youth violence: Conflict characteristics and outcomes. *Injury Prevention, 19(3),* 204–209. https://doi.org/10.1136/injuryprev-2012-040429.

Widom, C.S. (1989). Mechanisms in the cycle of violence. *Science, 244(4901),* 160–166. https://doi.org/10.1126/science.2704995.

Wilkinson, D., & Fagan, J. (1996). The role of firearms in violence "scripts": The dynamics of gun events among adolescent males. *Law and Contemporary Problems, 59,* 55–90. https://scholarship.law.columbia.edu/cgi/viewcontent.cgi?article=3262&context=faculty_scholarship.

Williams, B. (2016, August 12). *Chance the Rapper addresses Chicago's gun violence, police brutality.* Huff Post. https://www.huffpost.com/entry/chance-the-rapper-police-brutality_n_57ae2fe3e4b007c36e4ed3b1.

Williams, B. (2017, February 16). *Chance the Rapper: I'm "tired" of Chicago being seen as a "third world country."* Huff Post. https://www.huffpost.com/entry/chance-the-rapper-chicago-third-world-country_n_58a5e3c7e4b037d17d25b76d.

Wolf, R.V. (2012). *Law enforcement and public health: Sharing resources and strategies to make communities safer.* Center for Court Innovation. https://www.courtinnovation.org/sites/default/files/documents/LawEnfPubHealth.pdf.

Yetunde Price Resource Center (YPRC). (2021). *About: Who was Yetunde Price?* https://www.yprcla.org/#about.

Index

262   **Index**